LIBRARY OF NEW TESTAMENT STUDIES

410

formerly the Journal for the Study of the New Testament Supplement series

Editor
Mark Goodacre

A FORMER JEW

Paul and the Dialectics of Race

LOVE L. SECHREST

t&t clark

Copyright © Love L. Sechrest, 2009

Published by T&T Clark International
A Continuum imprint
The Tower Building, 11 York Road, London SE1 7NX
80 Maiden Lane, Suite 704, New York, NY 10038

www.continuumbooks.com

British Library Cataloguing-in-Publication Data
A catalogue record for this book is available from the British Library

ISBN: 978-0-567-46274-9 (hardback)

Typeset by Data Standards Ltd, Frome, Somerset, UK
Printed in Great Britain by the MPG Books Group, Bodmin and King's Lynn

To Edward A. Sechrest Jr.

CONTENTS

ACKNOWLEDGMENTS

This monograph represents a revision of my dissertation completed at Duke University in the program in religion, under the supervision of Professor Joel Marcus. I will never forget his warmth, generosity, and wit, and the way that he unstintingly gave equal measures of encouragement and criticism. His high standards and profound graciousness made him a model mentor, and he helped to make seamless my transition from junior colleague, to colleague, to friend. My other friend and mentor at Duke, Dr Willie Jennings, was no less encouraging and influential on my thinking and development. I owe them both a deep debt of gratitude.

Several colleagues and friends helped refine this work over its development. Many thanks to Richard Hays, Marianne Meye Thompson, Mitzi Smith, Grant Parker, E.P. Sanders, J.D.R. Kirk, Kim Connor, and Susan Carlson Wood who all read drafts or portions of this work at varying points; I am also grateful for comments and suggestions from anonymous reviewers. While I am solely responsible for the errors that remain, I have avoided many others through their help.

Finally, I want to thank my family for their love and the thousand tangible expressions of confidence and support as I wrote: my daughters, Paige and Audrey, my mother, J. Rachel Lazarus, and my sisters, Rosalind Williams and Deb Colwill. My love and gratitude know no bounds for my husband, Ed, who has made my life richer in every way, full of laughter and music and joy. He makes every dark day brighter and every bright day brilliant; this book could not have been written without him.

LIST OF FIGURES

ABBREVIATIONS

AB	Anchor Bible
Abraham	Philo, *On the Life of Abraham*
adj.	adjective
Adul. amic.	Plutarch, *Quomodo adulator ab amico internoscatur*
Ag. Ap.	Josephus, *Against Apion*
Alex. fort.	Plutarch, *De Alexandri magni fortuna aut virtute*
Amat. narr.	Plutarch, *Amatoriae narrationes* [spurious]
Ant.	Plutarch, *Antonius*
Ant. rom.	Dionysius, *Antiquitates romanae*
ASV	Authorized Standard Version
BDAG	W. Bauer, F.W. Danker, W.F. Arndt, and F.W. Gingrich, *A Greek-English Lexicon of the New Testament and Other Early Christian Literature* (Chicago: University of Chicago Press, 3rd edn, 1999)
BDB	F. Brown, S.R. Driver, and C.A. Briggs, *A Hebrew and English Lexicon of the Old Textament* (Oxford: Oxford University Press, 1907)
Bibl. hist.	Diodorus Siculus, *Bibliotheca historica*
CBQ	*Catholic Biblical Quarterly*
Cher.	Philo, *On the Cherubim*
Comp. Thes. Rom.	Plutarch, *Comparatio Thesei et Romuli*
Cons. Apoll.	Plutarch, *Consolatio ad Apollonium* [spurious]
CPJ	*Corpus Papyrorum Judaicarum*
Diogn.	*Epistle to Diognetus*
Dreams	Philo, *On Dreams*
Embassy	Philo, *On the Embassy to Gaius*
Flight	Philo, *On Flight and Finding*
Gen. Socr.	Plutarch, *De genio Socratis*
Geogr.	Strabo, *Geography*
God	Philo, *On God*
Her. mal.	Plutarch, *De Herodoi malignitate*
HeyJ	*Heythrop Journal*
Hist.	Herodotus, *History*

HTR	*Harvard Theological Review*
ICC	International Critical Commentary
Il.	Homer, *Iliad*
J.A.	Josephus, *Jewish Antiquities*
JBL	*Journal of Biblical Literature*
JSNT	*Journal for the Study of the New Testament*
JSNTSS	Journal for the Study of the New Testament Supplement Series
J.W.	Josephus, *Jewish War*
LCL	Loeb Classical Library
Lib. ed.	Plutarch, *De liberis educandis* [spurious]
LLS	author's translation
LS	Charlton T. Lew and Charles Short, *A Latin Dictionary* (Oxford: Clarendon Press, 1969)
LSJ	H.G. Liddell, R. Scott, and H.S. Jones, *A Greek–English Lexicon* (Oxford: Oxford University Press, 9th edn, 1996)
LXX	Septuagint
Marc.	Plutarch, *Marcellus*
Mart. Pol.	*Martyrdom of Polycarp*
Moses	Philo, *On the Life of Moses*
MT	Masoretic Text
NA[27]	Erwin Nestle and Kurt Aland (eds), *Novum Testamentum Graece*, 27th edn
NAU	New American Standard Bible, Update
NET	New English Translation
NIB	New Interpreter's Bible
NICNT	New International Commentary on the New Testament
NIV	New International Version – US
NIVB	New International Version – UK
NJB	New Jerusalem Bible
NLT	New Living Translation
NovT	*Novum Testamentum*
NovTSup	Novum Testamentum Supplements
NRSV	New Revised Standard Version
NTS	*New Testament Studies*
Od.	Homer, *Odyssey*
pf.	perfect
Planting	Philo, *On Planting*
Praec. ger. rei publ.	Plutarch, *Praecepta gerendae rei publicae*
ptc.	participle
Quaest. nat.	Plutarch, *Quaestiones naturales*
Quaest. rom.	Plutarch, *Quaestiones romanae et graecae*

Reg. imp. apoph.	Plutarch, *Regum et imperatorum apophthegmata*
Rewards	Philo, *On Rewards and Punishments*
Rom. ant.	Dionysius Halicarnassus, *Roman Antiquities*
RSV	Revised Standard Version
Sera.	Plutarch, *De sera numinis vindicta*
Soll. an.	Plutarch, *De sollertia animalium*
Spec. Laws	Philo, *On the Special Laws*
Sull.	Plutarch, *Sulla*
TDNT	G. Kittel and G. Friedrich (eds), *Theological Dictionary of the New Testament* (trans. Hans G.W. Bromiley; 10 vols; Grand Rapids: Eerdmans, 1964–76)
TLG	*Thesaurus linguae graecae*
WBC	*Word Biblical Commentary*

INTRODUCTION

Chapter 1

THE 'THIRD RACE' AND PAULINE STUDIES

Ethnicity and race are among the primary organizing principles of human history.[1] These principles structure societies both large and small, from nations and political parties to classrooms and congregations. The legacy of historic ethnic attachments runs through much modern domestic and international conflict; hence, the study of race and ethnicity as socio-historical phenomena can only produce a richer understanding of the contemporary scene. While present-day theorists would tend to agree with the idea that constructions of ethnicity and race vary over time, most begin their study of them at the dawn of modernity, despite the fact that identity discourse appears in ancient civilizations. All of this indicates that thoughtful attention to identity formation in the ancient world and the study of the historical roots of current social dynamics will produce a better understanding of race relations in our times.

However, increased attention to the question of identity formation in the ancient and modern world only serves to reveal the extraordinary complexities of the subject. The terminological debates within the social sciences about the very meaning of key terms (e.g., race, ethnicity, identity) create a need for extreme caution in importing these terms to studies of the ancient world. Sociologists increasingly refer to both race and ethnicity as concepts that are socially constructed, that is, wholly dependent on prevailing social dynamics for meaning and significance.[2]

---

1   Drawn from Paul Spickard and W. Jeffrey Burroughs, 'We Are a People', in Paul Spickard and W. Jeffrey Burroughs (eds), *We Are a People: Narrative and Multiplicity in Constructing Ethnic Identity* (Philadelphia: Temple University Press, 2000), pp. 1–19 (1). Spickard and Burroughs are speaking specifically about ethnicity, but this same statement applies equally to the broader category of ethnic and racial identity.

2   E.g., Martin Bulmer and John Solomos, 'Introduction: Rethinking Ethnic and Racial Studies', *Ethnic and Racial Studies* 21.5 (1998): 822–25 (822). Fredrick Barth was among the first to articulate this perspective in his seminal introduction to *Ethnic Groups and Boundaries: The Social Organization of Culture Difference* (London: Allen and Unwin, 1969). Howard Winant's additional focus on the historical dimension is important for this study and nuances the now commonplace understanding of the social construction of race ('Introduction' to *The New Politics of Race: Globalism, Difference, Justice* [Minneapolis: University of Minnesota Press, 2004]).

However, popular use of the terms in research on ancient peoples and ancient texts communicates that these terms are signs of ontological or 'essential' realities – terms that refer to physical descent and other biological phenomena.[3] The fact that ideas about race and ethnicity change across epochs and social contexts not only goes unacknowledged but also is routinely unexamined.

The introduction of other factors into discussions about identity, such as the effects of culture and religion, muddy the waters even further. While some theorists see such factors as additional non-negotiable 'essences' in the social construction of ethnic and racial identity, many see religion as optional and peripheral to defining the identity of a people.[4] Yet, as we here consider the ancient context in which Christianity emerged, we will need to remind ourselves that secularization is a modern phenomenon, even if secularization and the privatization of religious belief may have caused some recent theorists to marginalize the importance of religion in identity constructions. Thoroughly saturated with religious sentiment, ancient Jews and Christians transparently understood their identity and their place in the cosmos via a religious meta-narrative. Further, the ambiguities involved in the coincidence of race, ethnicity, and religion, and the resulting questions about core identity arise not only in contemporary discussions about Jewish identity in Israel and elsewhere in the West, but also in discussions about the historical roots of modern identity conflict. For example, Shaye Cohen hopes that his examination of Jewishness in the ancient world can contribute to the modern dialogue about Jewish identity.[5] In the United States, race and religion are pertinent to historical investigations about the way in which Christian

---

3   Jonathon Hall, for instance, insists that putative common descent is the *sine qua non* of ethnicity in any epoch (*Hellenicity* [Cambridge: Cambridge University Press, 2002], pp. 36–37). See Denise Kimber Buell's nuanced critique of Hall's limited use of ethnicity in *Why This New Race? Ethnic Reasoning in Early Christianity* (New York: Columbia University Press, 2005), p. 40.

4   'Religion' is a term often complicated by political or ideological definitions of what counts as 'religious' in the first place. Because the word 'religion' often refers to a voluntary affiliation with a group having a bounded set of beliefs and doctrines in modern Western discourse, herein I rely on Wilfred Cantwell Smith's observations about 'faith' and 'cumulative traditions' when discussing religion and religious phenomena. For Smith, 'faith' and 'cumulative traditions' refer to separate realities; the former encompasses a relationship with the transcendent while the latter deals with the cultural expressions of that relationship (*The Meaning and End of Religion* [Minneapolis: Fortress, 1991]). For purposes of comparing the role of religion in identity formation across epochs, I will use the word 'religion' to refer to Smith's cumulative traditions as cultural expressions of a relationship with deity. In other words, religious phenomena are embedded in cumulative cultural traditions, practices, and discourse that evolve over time.

5   Shaye Cohen, *The Beginning of Jewishness* (Berkeley: University of California Press, 1999), p. 347.

identity merged with 'whiteness' and American national identity to form a foundation for the institution of slavery, contributing to the formation of identity structures that continue to influence civil society.[6] In truth, I hope that this exploration of ethnicity and race among ancient Christians will illuminate present-day race relations, and especially the intersection between race and Christian identity.

Hence, given an increasing awareness of the way that historical formulations affect modern society, students of ancient religious texts are becoming more and more interested in questions about ethnicity and identity formation. Indeed, there is perhaps no more engaging site for this kind of inquiry than those earliest New Testament documents written by Paul of Tarsus. What conceptions of race and ethnicity girds the intergroup dynamics figured in these epistles? What might these documents say about race relations then and now? In the early Christian period, Paul was perhaps among the first to articulate the boundaries between two of the world's most enduring religious traditions, and his legacy may have significantly affected the ability and desire of members of these traditions to conceive of themselves in racial or ethnic terms. By developing models for ancient constructions of race and ethnicity and using them as a framework for examining Pauline thought on Christian identity, we will be able to describe Pauline Christianity as a nascent but distinctive ancient racial group that draws on a Jewish understanding of race in Second Temple Judaism. I believe that distortions in modern popular notions of race and ethnicity and lack of information about ancient notions of race obscure the fact that for Paul, adoption of Christian belief amounted to a change in racial identity.

Thus, this investigation of race and Christian identity in Paul begins where several lines of inquiry converge. The issues addressed herein must be situated within the framework of at least three kinds of questions in New Testament scholarship and related fields. First, this research is similar to a growing body of literature that investigates the phenomena of race and ethnic identity in antiquity. Some of these studies examine ancient peoples with a view to understanding whether phenomena we now associate with ethnic or racial identity also existed in antiquity; others examine the relationship between Christian thought and contemporary constructions of identity, asking how our understanding of the biblical text influences modern discussions about group membership. Second, as

---

6 Jessie Daniels, *White Lies: Race, Class, Gender, and Sexuality in White Supremacist Discourse* (New York: Routledge, 1997), p. 41; Winthrop Jordan, *The White Man's Burden: The Historical Origins of Racism in the United States* (New York: Oxford University Press, 1974); Vincent L. Wimbush, 'Introduction' to Vincent Wimbush (ed.), *African Americans and the Bible: Sacred Texts and Social Textures* (New York and London: Continuum, 2000), p. 19.

an investigation of group identity in the Pauline corpus, this study also relates to the voluminous body of scholarship on Paul's relationship to the Jewish people. Finally, a third, much smaller line of inquiry examines whether the fledgling Χριστιάνοι group conceived of itself as a separate 'race' – that is, as a group that no longer regarded itself as a sect or offshoot of Judaism. Since the questions in this investigation touch on these several lines of inquiry, this chapter will conduct a brief review of the scholarship in these areas before ending with an overview of the book and a final word about methodology.

1. *Race, Ethnicity, and New Testament Scholarship*

a. *Race and Ethnicity in Antiquity*
At least two classes of scholarly works juxtapose the study of race and ethnicity with studies of the ancient world, with two broad but opposing goals in mind. One body of work probes the way that modern understandings about race and ethnicity interact with interpretations of ancient texts and ancient culture, while a second group explores how ideas from ancient texts affect contemporary opinions about identity. Studies in the first category that use the concepts of race and ethnicity to better understand ancient culture are most often found in Late Ancient studies and Classical studies. Jonathon Hall's exploration of Greek ethnic identity in *Ethnic Identity in Greek Antiquity* and *Hellenicity* provides examples of book-length treatments of this kind, while Cornell and Lomas's edited collection *Gender and Ethnicity in Ancient Italy* demonstrates the breadth of studies in this category.[7] Frank M. Snowden's *Before Color Prejudice* also contributes to a body of scholarship on ethnic and racial identity in antiquity by analyzing images and portrayals of dark-skinned peoples in the ancient world.[8] According to Snowden, images and portrayals of blacks in classical antiquity bear none of the pejorative and negative associations of Enlightenment-era color prejudice against dark skin. Within the context of Christian scholarship, Gay Byron's more recent *Symbolic Blackness and Ethnic Difference in Early Christian Literature* provides a balanced analysis of images of blacks in early Christian literature inside and outside of the canon.[9]

7 Jonathon Hall, *Ethnic Identity in Greek Antiquity* (Cambridge: Cambridge University Press, 1997); id., *Hellenicity* (Cambridge: Cambridge University Press, 2002); Tim Cornell and Kathryn Lomas (eds), *Gender and Ethnicity in Ancient Italy* (London: Accordia Research Institute, University of London, 1997).

8 Frank M. Snowden, *Before Color Prejudice: The Ancient View of Blacks* (Cambridge, MA: Harvard University Press, 1983).

9 Gay Byron, *Symbolic Blackness and Ethnic Difference in Early Christian Literature* (London: Routledge, 2002).

While these studies and others like them take the concepts of race and ethnicity for granted by implicitly using modern definitions of race and ethnicity, Benjamin Isaac's *The Invention of Racism in Classical Antiquity* boldly attempts to understand whether phenomena we now associate with racist ideology also existed in antiquity.[10] The book identifies what Isaac describes as 'proto-racist' attitudes from the Classical and Greco-Roman eras and examines their influence on thinkers in the Enlightenment: this work thus displays a dual interest in the ancient and early modern contexts. Similar to Isaac's examination of the influence of ancient ideas on modern thought, the second body of work in this research trajectory uses the concepts of race and ethnicity to understand how ancient texts affect modern culture.

If studies of ancient ethnic groups in the first category are more common in Classics and Late Ancient studies, projects in this second category are especially prominent in Biblical studies, and investigate how the biblical texts shape modern identity politics. Cain Hope Felder looks at the portrayal of black peoples in the Bible and explores the nexus of race, ethnicity, ideology, and biblical interpretation. His *Troubling Biblical Waters* is in some ways a transitional work in that it considers both the presence of blacks in antiquity and the ideological consequences that emerge from the appreciation of those facts in the modern world, especially with reference to Christian constructions of race, class, and kinship.[11] Musa Dube's *Postcolonial Feminist Biblical Interpretation* maintains that the Bible's status as a normative text makes it impossible to extricate the biblical narrative from the oppressive effects of the narrative.[12] Especially sensitive to areas where biblical authors appeal to Conquest or Exodus images, Dube's work advocates a scholarship that is

---

10   Benjamin Isaac, *The Invention of Racism in Classical Antiquity* (Princeton and Oxford: Princeton University Press, 2004).

11   Cain Hope Felder, *Troubling Biblical Waters: Race, Class and Family* (Maryknoll, NY: Orbis Books, 1989). Felder's work is one of the earliest works in the now growing area of African American biblical hermeneutics. For an introduction to this body of work, see Abraham Smith, ' "I Saw the Book Talk": A Cultural Studies Approach to the Ethics of an African American Biblical Hermeneutics', *Semeia* 77 (1997): 115–38; Vincent L. Wimbush, 'Historical/Cultural Criticism as Liberation: A Proposal for an African American Biblical Hermeneutic', *Semeia* 47 (1989): 43–55; cf. id., 'Introduction' to *African Americans and the Bible*. Other book-length treatments and examples of African American biblical hermeneutics include Randall Bailey (ed.), *Yet with a Steady Beat: Contemporary U.S. Afrocentric Biblical Interpretation* (Atlanta: Society of Biblical Literature, 2003); Cain Hope Felder (ed.), *Stony the Road We Trod: African American Biblical Interpretation* (Minneapolis: Fortress, 1991); Wimbush (ed.), *African Americans and the Bible*; Michael Joseph Brown, *Blackening of the Bible: The Aims of African American Biblical Scholarship* (Harrisburg, PA, London, and New York: Trinity Press International, 2004).

12   Musa Dube, *Postcolonial Feminist Biblical Interpretation* (St. Louis, MO: Chalice Press, 2000).

sensitive to the effects of imperialism in the biblical narrative and on the
readers of this narrative.

Especially important for this investigation are three works that explore
the implications of Pauline thought for race relations and identity politics.
Daniel Boyarin locates the genesis of aspects of modern Christian identity
politics in the Pauline corpus in *A Radical Jew: Paul and the Politics of
Identity*.[13] Boyarin maintains that Pauline theology is supersessionist,
obliterating the legitimacy of racial and ethnic difference and especially
Jewish difference and that it normalizes a single identity that is white,
male, and European. This work identifies Paul as the theological center of
Christian thought on ethnic difference and interrogates the implications of
Paul's theology for modern identity discourse. While Boyarin thinks that
Pauline theology flattens difference, Brad Braxton comes to the opposite
conclusion, maintaining that Paul's argument in Galatians preserves
ethnic particularities among Christians. In *No Longer Slaves: Galatians
and African-American Experience*, Braxton seeks insight into modern race
relations through African American biblical hermeneutics.[14] Far from
seeing Paul as the 'Jewish cultural critic' of Boyarin's reading, Braxton's
Paul is sympathetic to Jewish culture aside from specific boundary-marker
practices, but passionately resists efforts to force Gentiles to adopt a
Jewish ethnic identity as a condition of entering the people of God.

Caroline Johnson Hodge presents yet a third reading of Paul that has
implications for interethnic conflict in *If Sons Then Heirs: A Study of
Kinship and Ethnicity in the Letters of Paul*. This work is an exploration of
ethnic constructs in Paul's arguments about Christian identity, and it
forcefully challenges the view that Christianity is a religion that transcends
ethnicity and eschews markers of culture and human practice. Hodge
argues that in Paul kinship and ethnicity are not metaphorical, but that
the concepts of lineage, paternity, and peoplehood are central to his
arguments; according to Hodge, they are the pre-eminent categories for
understanding status before God.[15] Like this present work, Hodge
seriously examines kinship themes in Paul and thus advances Biblical
studies, but like Boyarin's and Braxton's efforts, her work continues to
take the concepts of race and ethnicity for granted by using modern
definitions for them, particularly focusing on the idea of physical descent
as determinative of ethnoracial identity.[16] She concludes that for Paul,

13   Daniel Boyarin, *A Radical Jew: Paul and the Politics of Identity* (Berkeley: University
of California Press, 1994).

14   Brad Braxton, *No Longer Slaves: Galatians and African American Experience*
(Collegeville, MN: Liturgical Press, 2002).

15   Caroline Johnson Hodge, *If Sons Then Heirs: A Study of Kinship and Ethnicity in the
Letters of Paul* (New York: Oxford University Press, 2007), pp. 4–5.

16   Following Denise Kimber Buell, I am using the term 'ethnoracial' as an indicator of
the blend of continuity and discontinuity between ancient and modern constructs of race and

Gentiles in Christ form an Abrahamic lineage that is subordinate to the Jewish lineage. Hodge's work – which seems particularly animated by a desire to avoid what she sees as the anti-Judaism of much Pauline scholarship – repudiates the more widely accepted idea that the church is composed of both Jews and Gentiles who receive redemption through faith in Christ.

Daniel Boyarin, Caroline Johnson Hodge, and Brad Braxton draw portraits of Paul and his relationship to Judaism that have intriguing implications for contemporary race relations and ethnic conflict, yet each is limited by their implicit assumptions about the nature of race and ethnicity. By failing to interrogate the forces that shape race and ethnicity in Paul's ancient context, each work assumes continuity between ancient and modern ideology on this point. Consequently, these authors' assumptions about the nature of ethnic identity handicap their conclusions about the significance of their findings. Nevertheless, these works are key dialog partners, both with respect to the way that Pauline theology has shaped and continues to shape modern identity politics, but also with reference to how Paul related to the constructs of Judaism inside and outside of the fledgling Christian movement. Thus, each of us explores Paul's relationship to the Jewish people and participates in the broader stream of scholarship on this question.

b. *Paul and Judaism*

The opening section of Gerd Lüdemann's *Paulus und das Judentum* develops a framework that clearly lays out the discussion in New Testament scholarship about Paul's relationship to the Jews.[17] Given the sheer volume of this scholarship, Lüdemann's identification of the three major moves in the literature on this topic and the scholars who have been most closely associated with these shifts is elegant, even if its simplicity now understates the current state of scholarship. According to Lüdemann, major thinkers have variously understood Paul as anti-Jewish, Jewish, and un-Jewish. His association of the anti-Jewish Paul with G. Klein and R. Bultmann, the Jewish Paul with W.D. Davies, and the un-Jewish Paul with Davies's student E.P. Sanders accurately captures the history of scholarship in this area, though other contemporary scholars could be added to each of these lines of thought, especially the latter two.

Scholars now recognize that the composition of many of the early New Testament documents took place in an atmosphere of boundary testing and identity formation. Charged invective in these early documents once

---

ethnicity described above (see 'Rethinking the Relevance of Race for Early Christian Self-Definition', *HTR* 94.4 [2001]: 449–76 [450 n. 3]; ead., 'The Politics of Interpretation: The Rhetoric of Race and Ethnicity in Paul', *JBL* 123.2 [2004]: 235–51 [236]).

17   Gerd Lüdemann, *Paulus und das Judentum* (Munich: Chr. Kaiser Verlag, 1983).

mistaken for a historical description of the Judaism contemporary with early Christianity is now routinely interpreted as the polemic of sibling rivalry. Prior to World War II, New Testament scholars interpreted God's work in Christ as addressing the problem of primitive Jewish religion, that is, God in Christ corrects the failures of the Jewish religion. These older readings understood that over the centuries Jews had misconstrued and corrupted God's original provision of the law as a means of dealing with sin, so that Judaism in the time of Christ had become legalistic and mechanistic, with a distorted perspective about God that completely ignored the idea of grace. This description is similar to Lüdemann's summary of Klein's anti-Jewish Paul. Klein notes that Paul interacts with Israel's history only insofar as he reinterprets this history as Christian, as for example in Romans 4 and Galatians 3. The Jews have misunderstood the law, putting their confidence in works of law instead of in the righteousness of faith. Paul understands that the new covenant in Christ is not a renewal of the old covenant, but its abolition – the church is the new Israel that takes the place of the old.[18] According to Lüdemann, Klein and Bultmann both fail to take adequate account of Paul's convictions about Israel's ultimate salvation in Rom. 11.11-36.[19]

In the wake of the anti-Jewish theology and anti-Semitic politics that gave rise to the Shoah, W.D. Davies published his conception of Paul's relationship to Judaism in the now-famous *Paul and Rabbinic Judaism* in 1948. In Davies's portrait of Paul, Paul's self-understanding remained commensurate with the thought-world of early rabbinic Judaism. For Davies, Paul does not conceive of Christianity and Judaism as distinct entities, and it is therefore inappropriate to refer to Paul's 'conversion', as his student E.P. Sanders would later.[20] Davies's 'Jewish Paul', in opposition to Klein and Bultmann, recognized continuity between Israel and the church such that the church was an extension of the Jewish community.[21] Davies's Paul saw Jesus as the new Torah, the very embodiment of Torah, and the common Exodus language in Paul and Judaism led Davies to describe Pauline Christianity as the new Exodus (e.g., redemption, liberty, adoption, new creation). Lüdemann aligns M. Barth and F. Mussner with this 'Jewish Paul' trajectory and associates this conception of Paul's relationship to Judaism with the *Sonderweg* thesis, in which scholars describe Judaism and Christianity as frameworks for salvation that stand side-by-side.[22] In addition, another group of scholars

18   Ibid., p. 13.
19   Ibid., pp. 13–14.
20   W.D. Davies, *Paul and Rabbinic Judaism: Some Rabbinic Elements in Pauline Theology*, with a Foreword by E.P. Sanders and a Biographical Overview by Dale C. Allison Jr. (Mifflintown, PA: Sigler Press, 1998), p. lii.
21   Lüdemann, *Paulus und das Judentum*, p. 15.
22   Ibid., pp. 15–16.

in this 'Jewish Paul' category nuances Lüdemann's description by emphasizing Paul's attempts to reshape Judaism.[23]

Dissatisfied with the way that Davies overlooked differences between Pauline theology and rabbinic theology, Sanders described his understanding of the relationship between Paul and Judaism over thirty years ago in the landmark *Paul and Palestinian Judaism*.[24] This book described the 'pattern' of Second Temple Jewish religion based on first-hand investigations of primary Jewish texts for the period, in contrast to the portrait of Judaism that had been constructed by mirror-reading New Testament polemic. Instead of the legalistic, mechanistic religion of works righteousness assumed in the Bultmannian trajectory, Sanders described the pattern of Jewish religion using the construct 'covenantal nomism'. Covenantal nomism was a system of religion that had at its center the idea that God had elected Israel as a people to stand in a special relationship with him. In grateful response to this gracious act of election, Israel accepts the commandments of God, signaling her intention to remain within the covenant relationship via obedience to the commandments. Pauline Epistles and Gospel polemics notwithstanding, Sanders's study of the relevant texts convincingly maintained that the idea of covenantal nomism was nearly ubiquitous in the Palestinian Jewish literature of the period. In the final section of this work, Sanders re-examined the relationship of Paul to Judaism in view of his description of Jewish religion, concluding that Paul's beliefs follow a different pattern of religion, particularly in the area of soteriology. With the publication of *Paul, the Law, and the Jewish People* in 1983, Sanders continued his work on Paul's soteriology with a sustained examination of key passages and concluded with a description of Pauline Christianity as pointing toward a 'third race', where race refers to a separate sociological entity.[25]

With Krister Stendhal's previous work along a similar trajectory, Sanders's work represented a critical turning point in NT studies, virtually introducing another category of Pauline scholarship that scrambles the elegant simplicity of Ludemann's non-Jewish, Jewish, and un-Jewish framework.[26] Later dubbed the 'new perspective on Paul' by J.D.G. Dunn, Sanders's portrait of the Judaism of Paul's day has elicited a

---

23   See for example J.D.G. Dunn, 'Who Did Paul Think He Was? A Study of Jewish–Christian Identity', *NTS* 45 (1999): 174–93.

25   E.P. Sanders, *Paul and Palestinian Judaism: A Comparison of Patterns of Religion* (Minneapolis: Fortress, 1977).

25   E.P. Sanders, *Paul, the Law, and the Jewish People* (Minneapolis: Fortress, 1983), pp. 171–79.

26   See Stendhal's seminal essay 'The Apostle Paul and the Introspective Conscience of the West', *HTR* 56.3 (1963): 199–215, and the fuller statement of his thinking in *Paul among Jews and Gentiles* (Philadelphia: Fortress, 1976).

variety of reactions.[27] While some scholars reject Sanders's covenantal nomism, many have come to accept Sanders's general description of Jewish soteriology, though not all of them agree that Paul's own theology differed from this portrait.[28] Other 'new perspective' interpreters wrestle with questions about whether Paul's descriptions of Jewish 'works righteousness' misconstrued the prevailing posture of Jews vis-à-vis the law.[29] For example, Lloyd Gaston sees the new perspective as the starting point for his version of a two-covenant approach to justification, in which his Paul never calls Jews to faith righteousness in Christ: Torah is for Jews, and Christ is for Gentiles.[30]

In truth, Sanders's concluding perspective in *Paul, the Law, and the Jewish People* on Pauline Christianity as a 'third race' opens up a host of new questions. For example, what concepts best describe the sociological character of Jewishness in the Second Temple period? Was Jewishness primarily a matter of race, ethnicity, religion, lineage, or politics? What was Paul's relationship to his Jewish heritage, and how did it differ from that of Jews who were contemporary with Paul inside and outside of the Christian movement? What was Paul's attitude toward Judaism, and how did he envision his relationship to non-Christian Jews? More to the point, was Sanders correct in his description of Pauline theology as pointing toward a third race? Ultimately, this characterization reintroduces the

27   James D.G. Dunn, 'The New Perspective on Paul', *Bulletin of the John Rylands University Library of Manchester* 65.2 (1983): 95–122.

28   Critiques of covenantal nomism include D.A. Carson, Peter T. O'Brien, and Mark A. Seifrid (eds), *Justification and Variegated Nomism: A Fresh Appraisal of Paul and Second Temple Judaism* (Tübingen: Mohr Siebeck; Grand Rapids: Baker Academic, 2001); and Seyoon Kim, *Paul and the New Perspective: Second Thoughts on the Origin of Paul's Gospel* (Tübingen: Mohr Siebeck, 2002). Dunn's interpretation of Paul is indebted to the general idea of covenantal nomism, but disputes Sanders's contention that Paul's soteriology is categorically different (Dunn, 'New Perspective', pp. 100–101).

29   See for example Stephen Westerholm's *Perspectives Old and New: The 'Lutheran' Paul and his Critics* (Grand Rapids: Eerdmans, 2004).

30   Lloyd Gaston, *Paul and the Torah* (Vancouver: University of British Columbia Press, 1987). See also John G. Gager's development of this thesis in *The Origins of Anti-Semitism* (New York: Oxford University Press, 1983) and Stanley Stowers' *A Rereading of Romans* (New Haven: Yale University Press, 1994). The Gaston/Gager hypothesis does not seem to have proven persuasive to a majority of NT scholars. Gaston's work founders on (1) his interpretation of 'works of law' as a phrase unique to Paul and his discussion of Gentiles – but the phrase was later found at Qumran; and (2) his strained interpretation that Paul used ἄνθρωπος and 'under the law' to refer exclusively to Gentiles and their situation outside of Christ (Gal. 2.16; Rom. 2.12; 3.19, etc.). For detailed critiques of this approach see James D. G. Dunn, *Jesus, Paul and the Law: Studies in Mark and Galatians* (Louisville: Westminster John Knox, 1990), pp. 233, 262; Westerholm, *Perspectives Old and New on Paul*, pp. 313, 319; and Boyarin, *A Radical Jew*, pp. 33, 42–45, esp. 272–73 n. 9; contra Hodge (*If Sons then Heirs*, pp. 9–11, 110–11, 153, 157 n. 38) who depends on the Gaston/Gager hypothesis and Stowers' development of it.

question of race in antiquity, this time in the guise of the definition of the word 'race' for Jews of the period.

c. *Christians as the 'Third Race'*

The word γένος ('race, family, kind') appears in the New Testament 20 times, in Matthew, Mark, Acts, 1 and 2 Corinthians, Galatians, Philippians, 1 Peter, and Revelation. In 14 of the 20 occurrences the word is used as a reference to people-groups.[31] In Paul's three uses that are of interest here, he explicitly refers to Judaism as a race in Gal. 1.14, and he implies that non-Christian Jews are a race in 2 Cor. 11.26. In context, Paul's reference to the 'race of Israel' in Phil. 3.5 probably refers to non-Christian Jews. To be sure, the observation that Paul considers Israel a race is especially interesting in light of his use of the phrase 'the Israel of God' in Gal. 6.16, a phrase that most scholars interpret as a title for the church of Jews and Gentiles. Beyond the Pauline corpus, γένος appears as a direct reference to Christians only in 1 Pet. 2.9, although the exalted Christ of the Apocalypse intriguingly identifies himself as 'the race of David' in Rev. 22.16 (ἐγώ εἰμι ... τὸ γένος Δαυίδ).

More important, however, is the fact that the number of implicit and explicit references to Christians as a race increases in the works of the Apostolic Fathers and beyond, becoming a common way to refer to Christian worship in the third century – so much so that the phrase was picked up by Christian opponents and used to deride them.[32] A fragment of the now-lost early second-century apocryphal *Preaching of Peter* contains perhaps the earliest known use of this motif.[33] Clement of Alexandria quotes the *Preaching of Peter* where the author warns his readers against the worship of Greeks and Jews (μὴ κατὰ τοὺς Ἕλληνας σέβεσθε τὸν θεόν ... μηδὲ κατὰ Ἰουδαίους σέβεσθε, *Stromata* 6.5.41), and calls his Christian addressees 'ye who worship him anew in the third manner' (ὑμεῖς δὲ οἱ καινῶς αὐτὸν τρίτῳ γένει σεβόμενοι Χριστιανοί).[34] David Wright describes another early appearance of this motif in Aristides' *Apology* (c.125 CE), where the Greek text refers to three classes of worshippers, Greek, Jews, and Christians, though the better Syriac text of this apology divides humanity into four classes: barbarians, Greeks,

31 Γένος refers to people-groups in Mk 7.26; Acts 4.6, 36; 7.13, 19; 13.26; 17.28, 29; 18.2, 24; 2 Cor. 11.26; Gal. 1.14; Phil. 3.5; 1 Pet. 2.9; Rev. 22.16. For other usages see Mt. 13.47; Mk 9.29; 1 Cor. 12.10, 28; 14.10.

32 Adolph Harnack, *The Mission and Expansion of Christianity in the First Three Centuries* (trans. and ed. James Moffat; New York: G.P. Putnam's Sons; London: Williams & Norgate, 1908), 1.273–78.

33 See David F. Wright, 'A Race Apart?' Jews, Gentiles, Christians', *Bibliotheca Sacra* 160 (April–June 2003): 131–41. Translations in this section come from the Loeb edition of the texts cited except where otherwise noted.

34 Harnack's translation; *Mission*, p. 247.

Jews, and Christians.[35] The *Epistle to Diognetus*, written early in the latter half of the second century, also refers to Christians as a race (*Diogn.* 1.1; καινὸν τοῦτο γένος), again in the context of describing 'the religion of the Christians, ... which God they obey and how they worship him' (*Diogn.*, 1.1). According to *Diognetus*, Christianity is a religion that is proclaimed to the Gentiles (*Diogn.*, 11.1, 3) but is attacked by Jews for its foreignness (*Diogn.*, 5.17). Likely contemporary with *Diognetus* is the *Martyrdom of Polycarp* (c.155–156), which while not identifying Christians as the *third* race nonetheless identifies them as a race.[36] The work first speaks of the 'great nobility of the godly and reverent race of the Christians' (*Mart. Pol.* 3.2; τὴν γενναιότητα τοῦ θεοφιλοῦς καὶ θεοσεβοῦς γένους τῶν Χριστιανῶν), later calling those who know God through Christ 'the race of the upright' (τοῦ γένους τῶν δικαίων; *Mart. Pol.* 14.1; also 17.1). Harnack and Wright particularly note the 'blunt expression' in Pseudo-Cyprian's *De Pascha* written in 242–243 CE – 'We Christians are the third race' – in a context that may suggest that the phrase was a well-known expression.[37] In fact, Harnack cites several instances from other texts of this 'racial' reference to Christians apart from a specific identification as the 'third-race': *Martyrdom of Ignatius of Antioch*, 2; Eusebius, *Hist. eccl.*, 4.26.5; pseudo-Josephus, *Testimonium de Christo*; *Sibylline Oracles* 4.136.[38]

The body of literature that analyzes this evidence is considerably smaller than in the research described in the sections above. Harnack's *The Mission and Expansion of Christianity in the First Three Centuries* involves a sustained look at the third-race motif, where Harnack describes the 'triad' of Gentiles, Jews, and Christians as the 'church's basal conception of history' in the early period.[39] Peter Richardson's *Israel in the Apostolic Church* revisits Harnack's analysis and tries to nuance Harnack's synthesis of the data.[40] Richardson explores the third-race motif in pursuit of his thesis that Christians did not begin to call themselves 'Israel' until relatively late. According to Richardson, the first application of the title 'Israel' to the church is in Justin Martyr's *Dialogue with Trypho* (c.160 CE). Contrary to Harnack, Richardson maintains that

35 Wright, 'A Race Apart?', p. 134, citing Aristides, *Apology* 2 (Greek), 15 (Syriac); see also Harnack, *Mission*, pp. 246–47; Peter Richardson, *Israel in the Apostolic Church* (Cambridge: Cambridge University Press, 1969), pp. 22–23.

36 For a brief discussion of the dating of these works, see Bart Ehrman (ed.), *Apostolic Fathers* (2 vols; LCL; Cambridge, MA, and London: Harvard University Press, 2003), 2.127 (*Diogn.*); 1.361–62 (*Mart. Pol.*).

37 Harnack, *Mission*, p. 250; Wright, 'A Race Apart?', p. 136.

38 Harnack, *Mission*, p. 245.

39 Ibid., p. 250. Also see Wright, 'A Race Apart?' for an examination of the third-race motif in early Christian literature.

40 Richardson, *Israel*, p. 14 n. 1, p. 22.

there was no normative view of the relationship between Jews and Christians in the 'sub-apostolic' period. With respect to Paul, Richardson specifically denies that Paul applies the phrase the 'Israel of God' to the church.[41]

Of a different opinion are Denise Kimber Buell and Caroline Johnson Hodge, who explore the meaning of 'race' in the early Christian period and connect it with themes in Paul.[42] Buell begins to interrogate ancient views of race and ethnicity, noting two important differences between modern and ancient conceptualizations of race: first that 'race was often deemed to be produced and indicated by religious practices' and second that 'ethnicity was ... seen to be mutable' despite a frequent connection between ethnicity and physical descent. The findings in this book relative to ancient concepts of race and ethnicity are congruent with these insights and my development of Pauline theology is a more consistent application of them. According to Buell and Hodge, Paul substitutes spirit for shared blood as the basis for Gentile–Christian kinship with Jews, enabling them to *become* Jews.[43] In contrast, this book describes Christian identity in Paul as one in which those who had been born Gentiles or Jews receive in Christ a new and separate ethno-racial identity. Although Buell's monograph is an excellent investigation of the religious construction of race in post-canonical early Christian literature, with reference to Paul, the article she co-wrote with Hodge, and Hodge's monograph on the subject, fundamentally privilege kinship as constitutive of ethno-racial identity as is typical of modern assumptions about race. Buell and I agree that religion often produces race in antiquity, yet Buell's and Hodge's treatments of Paul subordinate that observation to the notion of fictive kinship, so that Paul reckons Gentiles as Jews inasmuch as they are members of Abraham's lineage. My conclusion, that Pauline theology constructs a change in religious belief and practice as a change in ethno-racial identity, is more in keeping with the religion-as-race paradigm shift that Buell and I both share.

Indeed, it is important to comment on the way that Harnack, Richardson, and Wright, for all their disagreements, use common assumptions about what the ancients meant when they applied the Greek word γένος to Christians. Each of them notes that all of the extant uses of the phrase appear in contexts that describe Christians as having a separate or distinctive way of worship, and each implies that the religious

---

41 Ibid., p. 25.

42 Buell, *New Race*; ead., 'Rethinking the Relevance of Race'; ead., 'Race and Universalism in Early Christianity', *Journal of Early Christian Studies* 10.4 (2002): 429–68; Denise Kimber Buell and Caroline Johnson Hodge, 'The Politics of Interpretation: The Rhetoric of Race and Ethnicity in Paul', *JBL* 123.2 (2004): 235–51; Hodge, *If Sons then Heirs.*

43 Buell and Hodge, 'The Politics of Interpretation'; Hodge, *If Sons then Heirs.*

contexts in which the phrases appear mean that γένος 'does not *really* refer to a "race"'. Harnack's comment on the fragment from the *Preaching of Peter* described above represents the attitudes of these three scholars:

> This writer ... distinguishes Greeks, Jews, and Christians ... by the degree of their knowledge and worship of God. But the remarkable thing is his explicit assumption that there are *three* classes ... and his deliberate description of Christianity as the new or *third* genus of worship ... It is to be remarked that Christians do not yet call themselves 'the third race'; it is their worship which is put in the scale. The writer classifies humanity, not into three peoples, but into three groups of worshippers.[44]

Notwithstanding Harnack's translation of the phrase τρίτῳ γένει as 'in the third manner' and his assertion that Christians 'did not yet call themselves the third race', it does seem as if the Greek sentence ὑμεῖς δὲ οἱ καινῶς αὐτὸν τρίτῳ γένει σεβόμενοι χριστιανοί can be translated, 'But you who worship him anew in the third race are Christians'. Indeed, the only thing standing in the way of such an understanding is Harnack's assumption, held by both Wright and Richardson, that *the word 'race' cannot refer to people-groups classified by religion*.

2. *Studying Race and Ethnicity*

With this work situated at the intersection of these three different lines of thought, I can now clarify the questions that drive this analysis. Beginning with the observation that some early Christians identified the movement as a 'race', I examine what ancient Jewish and Christian writers would have meant by such terminology. I am interested in identifying the assumptions that contemporary scholars bring to the consideration of race in antiquity, especially through a consideration of the continuities and discontinuities between modern ideas about ethnicity and race on the one hand, and ancient perspectives on these ideas on the other. As I take up questions about Jewish and Christian identity in Paul, I endeavor to understand whether, how, and where popular and/or theoretical discussions about nation, race, ethnicity, and identity formation affect the analysis. That each of these ideas has its own history is rather well understood; what is less well understood are the details about the ways in which the concepts have shifted in the past and are still in flux in the present.

Investigation of the early motif of 'racial' Christianity reveals two perspectives that relate to Christian self-understanding in the apostolic

---

44   Harnack, *Mission*, p. 247; Wright, 'A Race Apart?', p. 135; Richardson, *Israel*, p. 23.

period. With Harnack, we could view the early Christian period as one in which the 'triad' of Jews, Gentiles, and Christians formed the 'basal concept of history', or with Richardson we could see this period as one in which there is a varied but growing sense of discontinuity between the church and Israel/the Jewish people. On either reading, we eventually come to the question about where and whether either of these views on continuity and discontinuity has points of contact with the New Testament. In different ways, both Richardson and Buell investigate Pauline continuity and discontinuity with the racial Christianity motif that becomes explicit in non-canonical early Christian writings. Though these authors take different approaches to the question of whether the Pauline corpus exhibits the racial Christianity motif, the fact that they interrogate the Pauline corpus at all means that questions about the early Christian race motif intersect with New Testament research on Paul's relationship to Judaism.

Although most contemporary New Testament scholars would probably distance themselves from Bultmann's anti-Jewish Paul, there is as yet no clear consensus in New Testament scholarship as to whether Davies's Jewish Paul or Sanders's un-Jewish Paul best captures all of the nuances of the relationship between Israel and the church in Pauline theology. Davies's Jewish Paul underscores the elements of continuity between Israel and the church, while Sanders's un-Jewish Paul focuses on the discontinuity. Yet it seems clear that in Paul's thought there is both continuity (Rom. 4; 11.25-32) *and* discontinuity (1 Cor. 9.19-23; 10.32; Gal. 6.16) between the church and Israel. Given that I describe Pauline Christianity as a nascent but distinctive ancient racial group that draws on a Jewish understanding of race in Second Temple Judaism, it will be no surprise to learn that this work lies closer to Sanders's un-Jewish Paul than to either of the other two portraits. This exploration of the racial character of Paul's thought will help account for the presence of both continuity and discontinuity as impulses in Paul. Paul's use of the more fluid racial constructions of Jewish thought allowed him to express his apocalyptic convictions about the new creation in Christ while simultaneously affirming his eschatological hope about the salvation of Israel.

Thus, I investigate the nature of ethnic and racial identity and intergroup relations in Jewish and Christian thought around the turn of the era generally and in Pauline texts specifically. The investigation proceeds in two parts, and each contains two chapters described in more detail below. Part I identifies and develops models that clarify and contrast ancient and modern conceptualizations of ethnicity and race, while Part II uses these models as resources for examining Paul's self-identity, his ideas about Christian identity, and the relationships between the groups in his social world. However, before proceeding with an overview of these chapters and the concluding chapter, a final characterization of this work is in order. I do not intend to make a claim about the socio-historical understanding of identity that actually prevailed in Paul's house churches, the sociological dynamics that operated between his house churches and other Christian or non-Christian groups in his milieu, or the timing of the 'parting of the ways', that is, the separation of Christianity and Judaism. Though I use social-science theory and data to help describe the nature of race as an idea and the way the idea has changed in history, I use this data only to clarify the nature of race and race relations in Paul's era. I maintain that race, as those saturated in the thought-forms of ancient Judaism understood the idea, illuminates the radical and apocalyptic character of the consequences of faith in Christ in Paul's thought. In other words, I use the idea of race as a window into Paul's theology of Christian identity, making no claims about whether his churches embodied this thinking.

a. *Part I – Models of Racial and Ethnic Identity*

Part I, comprised of Chapters 2 and 3, contains a description of the evolution of race and ethnicity as concepts in both the modern and ancient contexts, thus allowing us to discern differences between contemporary thought and use of these terms in the ancient world between 100 BCE and 100 CE. This goal requires the construction of a language about ethnicity and group identity that mediates between the ancient and modern horizons, so that we are able to define and use the concepts in a way that allows meaningful comparisons between the separate contexts.

Chapter 2, 'Race and Ethnicity in Modernity', uses data from sociology and cultural anthropology to describe contemporary thought about ethnicity and race, focused mainly on US society.[45] This chapter describes the evolution of the understanding of race through the earliest 'biological' constructions of race as lineage through the conception of race as an imagined anthropological 'type' or Darwinian subspecies in the eighteenth and nineteenth centuries. The chapter describes the development of the twentieth-century notion that race is 'socially constructed' and other trends in postmodern theory. A final section describes several models of

---

45   Although I occasionally refer to studies on race and ethnicity that emerge from outside of the USA, my particular interest in race relations in this context emerges from my conviction that Anglo-American dysfunction in this area spread much like a global virus during the colonial expansion of the eighteenth and nineteenth centuries. This influence arguably extends into the postcolonial twentieth and twenty-first centuries through embedded messages about race in the popular cultural artifacts exported by the US entertainment industry. For more on this topic, see the introduction to Howard Winant's *The New Politics of Race* and Paul Gilroy's *Against Race: Imagining Political Culture beyond the Color Line* (Cambridge, MA: Harvard University Press, 2000).

ethnicity and race from sociology, cultural anthropology, and studies of nations and nationalism for later use in examining Paul's thought.

While it might have seemed more natural to discuss the ancient conception of race and ethnicity before discussing the modern context, I discuss the modern era first because of the way that outdated connotations of race and ethnicity are retained in common use long after theorists in these areas have discarded the older notions. After clarifying in Chapter 2 the several ways that the concepts have operated on the modern scene, Chapter 3, 'Race (γένος) and Ethnicity (ἔθνος) in Antiquity', describes the understanding of race and ethnicity in the ancient world. Using Classical studies and other historical descriptions, this chapter presents a literary analysis and synthesis of nearly five thousand Greek passages about identity from Jewish and non-Jewish authors from around the turn of the era, using the data to develop models of ancient non-Jewish and Jewish ethnic and racial identity. Analyzing these models and the differences between the Greco-Roman and Jewish models of ethnicity and race, the chapter concludes with a discussion of the lines of continuity and discontinuity between antiquity and modernity. This analysis produces a definition of race and ethnicity that bridges modernity and antiquity, as well as a description of the Jewish understanding of race as a threefold dialectic involving social identity, religious identity, and physical identity (e.g., kinship).

b. *Part II – The Racial Character of Pauline Christianity*

Part II investigates the character of Christian identity in the Pauline corpus with particular attention to the nature of relationships between the groups in Paul's context. Both of the two chapters in this section consider Pauline texts against the backdrop of the identity structures discussed in Part I, but pursue the analysis of Christian identity in slightly different ways. The first, 'Paul's Self-Identity and Relational Matrix', approaches the question of Paul's relationship to Judaism through an examination of his self-identity and group affiliation, in effect learning about the nature of Christian group identity by finding out what Paul said about himself and the group or groups to which he belonged. This chapter, Chapter 4, examines the Pauline corpus in light of the threefold identity dialectic revealed in Part I. For example, the first section of the chapter contains a survey of Paul's use of kinship themes, paying closest attention to passages where ideas about kinship or physical descent play a significant role in his arguments about Christian identity. The bulk of the chapter, however, considers those statements where Paul speaks about his identity as an Israelite or member of the Jewish people, and those passages in which he speaks of himself as the apostle to the Gentiles. Together these sections of Chapter 4 show how Paul's particular understanding of his mission illuminates his conception of Jewish identity and its relationship to the Christian community.

Chapter 5, 'The Dialectics of Race Relations in Christ', builds a portrait of Christian identity and intergroup relations based on a close reading of passages in Galatians. The chapter begins with an exploration of Christian identity and Jewish identity in terms of key identity parameters introduced in Chapter 2: membership criteria, membership indicia, and group name. Next, the chapter investigates Paul's understanding of the relationship between the Jewish and Christian communities, comparing the evidence from Chapter 4 that Paul saw the gathering of Israel as part of his mission and self-identity, with additional evidence in Galatians about Paul's mission. This section examines the intergroup relationships depicted in Galatians 2–4, and gives insight about race relations in Paul's social setting. This chapter continues to explore the dialectics of race in Paul's thought, though here we focus on intragroup dynamics in terms of group indicia and boundaries, and intergroup dynamics in terms of group assimilation and differentiation processes.

c. *Conclusion*

Finally, Chapter 6, 'Racial Christianity and Identity Politics', describes the way that my portrait of Christian identity attends to concerns raised by three other scholars who have considered identity issues in Paul, engaging Daniel Boyarin, Brad Braxton, and Caroline Johnson Hodge. This final chapter describes the points at which each of these portraits forms a contrast with the description of Pauline Christianity developed herein. The chapter concludes with a final reflection on the way that this portrait presents an opportunity to reimagine Christian dialogue with Jews and the nature of race-relations within the Christian confession.

Part I

Models of Racial and Ethnic Identity

I deliberately use the terms 'race' and 'ethnicity' interchangeably
... This decision is intended to signal my views that neither term
has a one-to-one counterpart in antiquity and that neither can be
neatly distinguished from the other even in modern parlance. I
also want to keep modern readers alert to the contemporary
stakes of historical work. By excluding the category of race from
work on classical antiquity we risk conveying the implications
that our modern legacy of racial thinking can be shut off when
we turn to examine ancient texts, and that our versions of
ancient history are either irrelevant or alien to the ways that we
tackle questions of human sameness and difference in the
present.

Denise Kimber Buell, 'Rethinking the Relevance of Race',
p. 450 n. 3

Chapter 2

RACE AND ETHNICITY IN MODERNITY

Race and ethnicity are sociohistorical concepts, yet we question whether the concepts refer to the same kinds of social dynamics in the modern and ancient contexts, a concern that prompts an investigation into the ways that the concepts have evolved over time. However, a straightforward investigation of race and ethnicity quickly becomes complicated by modern debates about the nature of race and ethnicity. Scholars working in the field freely admit that 'no one seems to understand very well how ethnicity works' and that there is neither a common definition of it nor a unifying theory that engages its relationship to similar concepts such as 'race' and 'nation'.[1] For example, some believe that race is wholly different from ethnicity, while others maintain that race is a special case of ethnic identification, which is a natural and primordial characteristic of human society existing from antiquity. While some theorists question the collapse of race into ethnicity as analytical concepts and the associated move of eliminating race as a category of modern American life, others explore the relationship of race and ethnicity to class.[2] With this in mind, my investigation will need to clarify the utilization of racial and ethnic categories in the modern context before investigating how these categories functioned in the ancient world.

The confusion about race and ethnicity in the popular imagination is even greater. Even though everyone participates in at least one ethnicity, since about the 1950s many whites have not seen themselves as having ethnicity, labeling blacks and others as 'ethnic'.[3] The idea that white is 'normal' and that ethnicity is a characteristic of peoples who deviate from

---

1 Spickard and Burroughs, 'We Are a People', p. 1.

2 T.K. Oommen, 'Race, Ethnicity and Class: An Analysis of Interrelationships', *International Social Sciences Journal* 46.1 (1994): 83–93 (84); Lee D. Baker, 'The Color Blind Bind', in Ida Susser and Thomas C. Patterson (eds), *Cultural Diversity in the United States* (Malden, MA: Blackwell, 2001), pp. 103–19; Ronald Takaki, 'Reflections on Racial Patterns in America', in Ronald Takaki (ed.), *From Different Shores: Perspectives on Race and Ethnicity in America* (New York and Oxford: Oxford University Press, 3rd edn, 2002), pp. 23–36.

3 Richard Jenkins, *Rethinking Ethnicity: Arguments and Explorations* (London: Sage Publications, 1997), p. 14.

this norm is still pervasive in some quarters, as is the more current tendency to equate ethnic peoples with minority status subgroups.[4] One scholar describes the increasingly elected nature of ethnicity in popular culture, that is, the tendency within the majority culture in the USA to view ethnicity as optional and celebrated during ad hoc cultural occasions, but otherwise tucked away and subsumed by the category of whiteness.[5]

Relying on data from biological and medical science, today most contemporary social science literature about race tries to dismantle the outdated but persistent notions that race concerns observable physical differences between groups (i.e., phenotype) and that racial differences are signs of inborn intellectual and behavioral qualities. Study of human genetic variation suggests that racial groupings by skin color or facial features are arbitrary and misleading. Scientists estimate that there is as much or more intragroup genetic variation as there is variation between races, and that while geographic concentrations of genetic patterns do exist, there are no discrete or abrupt boundaries corresponding to dramatically distinct races.[6] Accordingly, social scientists describe race and ethnicity as 'socially constructed', referring to the fact that these concepts do not represent natural, primordial, or essential properties of human differentiation. Instead, races and ethnic groups are, like nations, 'imagined communities' with elastic boundaries that shift and flex with the vagaries of ideological and political struggle. People become members of a

4   Michael Banton describes this phenomenon as 'minus one ethnicity' (*Racial and Ethnic Competition* [Cambridge: Cambridge University Press, 1983], p. 65), though Tonkin, McDonald, and Chapman point out that the concept of 'ethnicity' has had this 'us' vs. 'them' duality throughout much of recorded history (Elizabeth Tonkin, Mary McDonald, and Malcolm Chapman, 'Introduction' to *History and Ethnicity* [ASA Monographs; London and New York: Routledge, 1989], pp. 15–16).

5   Herbert Gans, 'Symbolic Ethnicity and Symbolic Religiosity: Towards a Comparison of Ethnic and Religious Acculturation', *Ethnic and Racial Studies* 17.4 (October 1994): 577–92.

6   Colin Kidd, *The Forging of Races: Race and Scripture in the Protestant Atlantic World, 1600–2000* (Cambridge: Cambridge University Press, 2006), pp. 5–7. Compare this discussion with that of Armand Marie Leroi, who challenges the prevalent idea among contemporary scientists that race is genetically meaningless due to great intrarace genetic variation (Armand Marie Leroi, 'A Family Tree in Every Gene', *New York Times*, 14 March 2005). Leroi argues for the return of race as a meaningful physical category because physical variation does occur in predictable patterns that correlate to race if one considers groups of genes by the hundreds. However, even if his arguments about genetic variation stand, we will see that the problem with race does not concern the validity of patterns of physical variation as though 'race' as a category merely conveyed physical information about a group. The problem with race has to do with the socially defined *meanings* assigned to physical variation, which link negative assumptions about social and intellectual characteristics to physical aspects of race. For a discussion of the slippery and often unsatisfying relationship between genetic race and identity see Amy Harmon, 'Love Ya K2a2a, Whoever You Are', *New York Times*, 22 January 2006.

group based on criteria that the group selects or that powerful outsiders impose on group members.[7] Yet even though scholars now routinely describe the worthlessness of race as a signifier of intellect and behavior, these factors continue to exert powerful influences on the daily lives of millions of people in the USA and elsewhere. Thus, the oft-acknowledged constructed, or imagined, nature of race and ethnicity is in tension with the tangible social effects of racial and ethnic identity in many societies. In other words, race is real, even if it is also imagined.

1. *The Modern Concept of Race*

While the word 'race' is common in antiquity, the ancients do not generally tether the concept to observations about skin color or physical traits as is done in the modern context.[8] Social scientists often refer to 'folk concepts' about race, that is, popular concepts in which race refers to the grouping of human communities by means of inheritable patterns of skin color, hair textures, facial features, and personality traits. If such folk concepts about race as an essential property of human physiology and psychology have all but disappeared from social-science literature, social scientists have failed to conceptualize a new terminology for race that differentiates these folk ideas from the theoretical idea that race is a phenomenon that assigns social meaning to physical characteristics.[9] In other words, race as a meaningful physical property has not disappeared from the popular imagination. Modern society sees racial differences as real and physical, as opposed to imaginary and constructed, and this is nowhere more apparent than in race discourse about American athletics.[10]

While many scholars locate the onset of the modern conception of race in the sixteenth or seventeenth century, Jesse Daniels describes Christian anti-Semitism in the medieval period as the pre-modern antecedent to modern racism. Christian beliefs about Jews combined with negative images of the Jewish body – body odor, inferior physical characteristics, association with peculiar blood, diseases, and so on – and aligned these offensive body images with negative moral and intellectual characteristics, seeing both the former and the latter as transmitted by 'Jewish blood'.[11]

---

7 Bulmer and Solomos, 'Rethinking Ethnic and Racial Studies', p. 822.

8 In other words, images of black people in antiquity were seen in both positive and negative contexts and were not inextricably linked to a pejorative ideological discourse. For opposing perspectives on this question see Frank M. Snowden's study *Before Color Prejudice*, and Gay Byron's more recent study *Symbolic Blackness*.

9 Michael Banton, *Racial Theories* (Cambridge: Cambridge University Press, 1987); Baker, 'Color Blind', p. 1.

10 See John Hoberman, *Darwin's Athletes: How Sports Has Damaged Black America and Preserved the Myth of Race* (Boston: Houghton Mifflin, 1997), pp. 28–51.

11 Daniels, *White Lies*, p. 12.

More frequently, modern social scientists date the rise of modern racism, that is, that ideology which in turn produces race as a meaningful category, from the beginning of European colonialism and the 'first contact' of the world's most light-skinned peoples of Europe with the world's most dark-skinned peoples of Africa.[12]

The age of European colonialism in the sixteenth through eighteenth centuries produced a discourse about race that focused on the simple 'fact' of distinct races, a discourse arising from reflection on the differences between Europeans and the Asians and Africans encountered in the so-called Age of Discovery. Winthrop Jordan discusses the way that European aesthetics and negative connotations of 'blackness' combined with the Europeans' opinions about the inferiority of the African peoples' religion and society, such that the combination of aesthetics and perceived inferiority would later become the touchstones of racist discourse.[13] However, those initial sixteenth-century concepts of race focused on the idea of race as lineage, as opposed to the idea of race as a construct for grouping people by phenotype. Thus, Europeans answered questions about why Africans differed from them by proffering explanations about descent from different primordial ancestors. In addition, this earliest phase of the race discourse in modernity proceeded explicitly in terms of the biblical narrative, so that Europeans sought to identify the ancestors of modern races analogously to the way that Jews were identified as members of Abraham's race.[14] While negative associations about the color of Africans stood side-by-side with this concept of lineage, color associations in the earliest period were not yet determinative for

12 Oommen, 'Race, Ethnicity and Class', p. 84; Jordan, *The White Man's Burden*, p. 5.

13 Jordan (*The White Man's Burden*, pp. 5–25) carefully documents the absence of the word 'race' per se as a construct for articulating the British and French fascination with the nature of differences between themselves and the Africans they encountered in the sixteenth century. He contrasts this preoccupation with the more muted responses of the Spanish and Portuguese, for whom the contact with darker peoples had been of much longer duration. According to Jordan, the negative connotation of blackness was incipient racism and a precursor of later race discourse. On the other hand, by emphasizing the absence of 'race' terminology in this period, Michael Banton seems to suggest that racism – that ideology that is inextricably linked with and productive of the modern construct of race – appears far later in the modern scene, in the eighteenth and nineteenth centuries. Banton's error lies in too woodenly associating a concept with occurrence of a particular word.

14 See Jordan, *The White Man's Burden*, pp. 9–10 for a discussion about the idea of Africans' descent from Ham, and the so-called curse of Ham. For a book-length treatment of the curse of Ham, see David M. Goldenberg, *The Curse of Ham: Race and Slavery in Early Judaism, Christianity, and Islam* (Princeton: Princeton University Press, 2003). See also Kidd, *Forging of Races*, pp. 121–67, for a description of the way that Christian thinkers struggled to reconcile apparently different races with the biblical account of monogenesis in Genesis (i.e., human descent from a single set of primordial parents), a problem which created what Kidd dubs a 'crisis of faith' for Christian orthodoxy.

membership in a particular race. For instance, many would have considered the offspring of Moses and his Ethiopian wife as racially Jewish, even though these children would have been different in skin color from most other Levantine Jews.[15]

In addition, the earliest English uses of the word 'race' occur in contexts in which it is synonymous with the sixteenth- to eighteenth-century ideas of 'nation'. These uses are particularly notable in the discourses about English and French national identity, where French national feeling drew on the ebb and flow of tensions between Franks and Gauls, while English dialogue marshaled appeals to the 'most noble' Saxons of Germanic descent in contention against Stuart monarchs.[16] In this way, the early modern context adds the idea that cultural differences are biological and natural. For example, in this period some English people spoke of the Irish as savage, wild, wicked, and uncivil, and later began to speak of blacks and Native Americans in much the same way.[17] Thus, discourse about 'national character' began to mimic race and economic-class discourse as peoples related themselves to others in ways that included beliefs about the ingrained psychological characteristics of groups.[18] In other words, the early modern period is a time in which the notions of race and nation emphasize religion and common ancestry, even as race and nation also become increasingly associated with character and behavioral qualities.[19]

North American perspectives on race are closely bound up with the history and economics of the eighteenth- and nineteenth-century European North Atlantic slave trade of African peoples. Scholars divide, however, on the question of whether slavery spawned racism as an ideology that protected the economic interests of whites via the exploitation of black labor, or whether racist white and black status distinctions were nothing more than exaggerated versions of status distinctions already at work within European society. In the first case, racist ideology provides a powerful new *rationalization* for slavery, which acts as an *ex*

15 Banton, *Racial Theories*, pp. xi, 7.

16 Banton, *Racial and Ethnic Competition*, p. 33. 'Race' also figured in discourse concerning the American Revolution (Banton, *Racial Theories*, pp. 12–13). We will see that this use of race as equivalent to nation occurs in the ancient context as well.

17 Lee D. Baker, *From Savage to Negro: Anthropology and the Construction of Race, 1896–1954* (Berkeley and Los Angeles: University of California Press, 1998), pp. 11–14; Matthew Frye Jacobson, *Whiteness of a Different Color: European Immigrants and the Alchemy of Race* (Cambridge, MA: Harvard University Press, 1998), pp. 39–90; Audrey Smedley, *Race in North America: Origin and Evolution of a Worldview* (Boulder, CO: Westview, 1993), pp. 27, 34.

18 Banton, *Racial and Ethnic Competition*, p. 33.

19 See Colin Kidd's *Forging of Races* for a broader discussion about the way that interpretations of Scripture participated in the social construction of race in the Anglo-American context.

post facto justification of an institution initiated on economic grounds. In the second case, however, racism provides an ideological *explanation* of the enormous difference in technological advancement, prestige, power, and economic status between European colonists and Asian and African peoples in European colonies.[20] Rationalizations associated with these latter explanations could proceed in at least two different directions. First, consistent with the prevailing Christian ethos, slavery was sometimes viewed in terms of the 'white man's burden', a burden that assumed the 'responsibility to educate and civilize brown and black peoples'.[21] Alternately, pro-slave rhetoric that relied on environmental explanations for the differences in races rationalized slavery as stimulating blacks to productive labor, reasoning that peoples in such enervating climates would labor only under the threat of punishment. When it came time to fill the vast labor shortages needed to make the 'New World' productive, this kind of logic soon broke down, as happened when the idea that blacks were uniquely capable of working in the heat was juxtaposed with the idea that the hot environment left blacks incapable of developing the resources for civilization.[22]

By the nineteenth century, there were several competing ideas about race in the popular imagination, the most important of which was the notion of race as anthropological type. We can see anthropological type as a conceptual descendant of Platonic forms and the conceptual ancestor of Weberian ideal types, later used in the analysis of religious forms. When 'scientific racism' offered scientific 'proofs' of racial typology, typological constructs of race represented the most pernicious error about race in the modern period. Typological thinking in this context suggests that outward differences of phenotype that were due to acclimatization to

20   Audrey Smedley (*Race*, pp. 13–36) postulates the development of American racist ideology as a rationalization for the extreme deprivations of African slavery. In favor of the idea that racism builds upon prior European status distinctions, see Banton, *Racial and Ethnic Competition*, pp. 37–38. The question is a difficult one and amounts to a choice between maintaining that blacks were disparaged because they were slaves and thus even lower in status than the lower classes in European society, or whether they were enslaved because they were black. Jordan's descriptions (*The White Man's Burden*, pp. 1–25) of the way that 'black' functioned in the European aesthetics of the sixteenth century could tilt the balance toward the latter, though Gay Byron's study might favor the former, in that similar aesthetics in antiquity did not result in a wholesale disparagement of black peoples per se (Byron, *Symbolic Blackness*). The question may be moot, for as Jacobson points out, even if the status of American blacks mimicked disparagement of non-Anglo Saxon Europeans early in the colonial period, it was the possibility of defining themselves as non-black that enabled the construction of the notion of a 'white race' as a polar opposite of a 'black race' and set the terms of race relations for US history to date (*Whiteness*, pp. 274–80).

21   Charles Hirschman, 'The Rise and Fall of the Concept of Race' (unpublished paper, 26 August 2003), pp. 1–2.

22   Banton, *Racial Theories*, p. 8.

particular geographic regions actually reflect permanent differences in human moral and cultural capacity, mental ability, and other psycho-social characteristics.[23] The concept of type attempts to explain human phenotypic diversity by surmising the primordial existence of a representative human specimen that possesses all of the characteristic qualities of a given type or class of organisms, and which gives rise to presently observed phenotypes, though perhaps in a less pure form than the original representative. More importantly, the idea that typological inferiority was *permanent* became the unique and lasting contribution of typological thinking. Throughout this period, the concept of type depicted biological, social, and psychological differences between Europeans and Africans as derived from inherited capacities based on superior or inferior stock. While the precepts of Darwinian evolution are fundamentally at odds with these theories in that Darwinian evolution is by definition based on the impermanence of types in nature, typological ideas about race persist, and may even dominate, popular conceptions of race today.[24]

The twentieth century produced an emphasis on two ideas, ethnicity and culture, that have in some ways overwhelmed discussion of race per se. Social-scientific focus on ethnicity and culture works to highlight the sociological dimensions of race and race relations, and indeed, in many quarters these concepts have sometimes functioned as substitutes for the idea of race.[25] Franz Boas, regarded by many as the father of modern anthropology, almost single-handedly changed the early twentieth-century discourse about race by introducing the concept of culture. He and his intellectual heirs defined culture as the collective heritage of a group embedded in the practices, norms, and ideas that shape the lives and thoughts of group members.[26] Boas refuted the common association between culture and race, and maintained the equality of races and the diversity of cultures with equal fervor.[27] According to Boas, environment is determinative of cultural difference. Peoples of color are not inferior,

23 Banton, *Racial and Ethnic Competition*, p. 34; Richard Jenkins, 'Social Anthropological Models of Inter-Ethnic Relations', in John Rex and David Mason (eds), *Theories of Race and Ethnic Relations* (Cambridge: Cambridge University Press, 1986), pp. 170–86. See also Oommen, 'Race, Ethnicity and Class', p. 83.

24 Banton, *Racial and Ethnic Competition*, pp. 43–45; Sandra Wallman, 'Ethnicity and the Boundary Process in Context', in John Rex and David Mason (eds), *Theories of Race and Ethnic Relations* (Cambridge: Cambridge University Press, 1986), pp. 226–45 (229).

25 Virginia R. Dominguez, 'Invoking Culture: The Messy Side of Cultural Politics', in Marianna Torgovnick (ed.), *Eloquent Obsessions: Writing Cultural Difference* (Durham: Duke University Press, 1994), pp. 237–57; Banton, *Racial Theories*, p. xii; Gerd Baumann, *The Multicultural Riddle: Rethinking National, Ethnic, and Religious Identities* (New York and London: Routledge, 1999), p. 87.

26 Baumann, *Multicultural Riddle*, pp. 24–25.

27 Just as Boas refuted the common elision of race with culture that was popular in the late nineteenth- and early twentieth-century Social Darwinist movement, the modern

but have particular cultures and particular historical locations. In terms of the early twentieth-century American context in which he lived, he defined the ideology of racism as the reason for black inferiority, as opposed to seeing black inferiority as derived from inherited features from a so-called inferior stock. Since then, social scientists approach Boas's theorizing of culture with even greater nuance by noting the frequently performative and evolving nature of culture.[28]

Another major emphasis in the twentieth century examines race as class, and focuses on race relations vis-à-vis the position of different races relative to the economic means of production. Marxist approaches to race and ethnicity see material economic conditions as the basic explanation for the emergence and maintenance of racism.[29] Marxist theories would hold that as European capitalism expanded into territories with abundant natural resources, the constraining factor in the expansion was access to and control of a source of cheap labor. As there were obvious advantages in securing a servile labor pool, beliefs that justified the inferiority of Africans and Native Americans became incorporated into the structure of capitalist societies. Thus, racial categories exist to serve the interests of ruling classes, and workers in such societies have not yet realized that their best interests lie in aligning themselves along the lines of class interests rather than race interests.[30]

A frequently heard critique of Marxist analysis of race and ethnicity focuses on the Marxists' alleged reductionistic elision of the category of race to that of class. If, as Marxists claim, one cannot abstract race from class since race has a concrete impact on class-consciousness and class has a reciprocal relationship with race, then one would expect to see the validation of the Marxist prediction that race relations will begin to disappear into class interactions.[31] On the contrary, modern experience reveals that race boundaries remain stubbornly impervious to class-based political action.[32]

Thus, the West has devoted an ever-increasing amount of attention to

---

preoccupation with culture as an explanation for racial differences begins to mimic the logic of race as an essential human characteristic (Kenan Malik, *The Meaning of Race* [New York: New York University Press, 1996], pp. 149–77).

28   Baumann, *Multicultural Riddle*, pp. 81–96.

29   John Solomos, 'Varieties of Marxist Conceptions of "Race", Class and the State: A Critical Analysis', in John Rex and David Mason (eds), *Theories of Race and Ethnic Relations* (Cambridge: Cambridge University Press, 1986), pp. 84–109 (86).

30   Banton, *Racial and Ethnic Competition*, p. 87.

31   Donald Horowitz, *Ethnic Groups and Conflict* (Berkeley: University of California Press, 1985), p. 13.

32   Solomos, 'Marxist Conceptions', p. 92. Though Marxist positions assume that social bonding will arise among members occupying the same class position, Rex notes that ethnic and cultural bonds actually pre-empt the formation of class bonds (John Rex, 'The Role of

the concept of race, beginning with an early, horrified fascination with the idea of race in the wake of Nazi atrocities in the 1940s, to the more recent sustained and deliberate deconstructions of the idea. Yet in recent years, modern scholarship displays a decided preference for ethnicity as an analytic category over the former emphasis on race. With this in mind, the next section will examine some of the reasons for and results of this shift in emphasis.

2. *Ethnicity in Late Twentieth-Century Scholarship*

As with race, the concept of ethnicity exists from antiquity through to the present, yet never before have there been as many models of ethnicity that are being offered by an ever-widening group of disciplines. In the late 1960s, Fredrik Barth's introduction to *Ethnic Groups and Boundaries* initiated something of a sea change in ethnic studies by proposing that ethnic groups are not strictly defined through shared culture as is most often assumed, but by means of variable and socially defined ethnic boundaries.[33] From that period, ethnographers began to analyze ethnic phenomena from the point of view of group members, becoming increasingly sensitive to the historical particularities of social context and exploring the manner in which ethnic groups persisted, changed, or assimilated with respect to other groups and with respect to the larger society in which they participated. The ensuing decades saw an emphasis on the analysis of the construction and maintenance of ethnic boundaries, as scholars began to understand how forces both external and internal to an ethnic group influence the shape, durability, and permeability of ethnic boundaries. Theorists noted the evolving and elastic nature of ethnic boundaries, in addition to conflicts and relationships between majority and minority groups.

By the 1980s, an assimilationist model of ethnicity, which expected minority and marginal subgroups to assimilate into the majority culture, began to give way to models which emphasized cultural diversity and multiculturalism; nevertheless the boundary-focused 'ethnicity model' inspired by Barth continued to exert considerable influence in the

---

Class Analysis in the Study of Race Relations – A Weberian Perspective', in John Rex and David Mason [eds], *Theories of Race and Ethnic Relations* [Cambridge: Cambridge University Press, 1986], pp. 64–83 [66–69]).

33 Frederick Barth, 'Introduction' to *Ethnic Groups and Boundaries*, pp. 10–11, 14–16; Jenkins, 'Social Anthropological Models', p. 174; Talcott Parsons, 'Some Theoretical Considerations on the Nature and Trends of Change of Ethnicity', in N. Glazer and D. Moynihan (eds), *Ethnicity: Theory and Experience* (Cambridge: Cambridge University Press, 1975), pp. 53–83 (56–57, 60–61).

literature.[34] Despite several other emerging themes in the research, the basic perspective about the socially constructed nature of ethnicity remained uncontested, even though the emphasis on social dynamics tended to reify culture.[35] Throughout the period, some sociologists and anthropologists debated the degree to which the essence or core of ethnicity concerns the notion of common descent or common history. On the other hand, other studies reflected the belief that common language and religion were the most frequent and stable resources for the construction of ethnic identification, and scholars debated the extent to which each of these parameters resulted in bonds which were more or less intense than class or social status.

a. *Conceptual Overlaps: Ethnicity, Race, and Religion*

Perhaps the most frustrating ambiguity in the study of ethnicity involves the overlap between the ideas of race and ethnicity, and the tendency of some to differentiate the categories even as others insist that race is only a special instance of ethnicity. Much of the problem stems from the fact that in the pre-modern period and stretching into the eighteenth and nineteenth centuries, 'race', 'nation', and 'ethnic group' were synonyms that referred to people-groups having a commonly held belief in a common origin and/or heritage.[36] If some theorists now emphasize the territorial components of common origin while others stress kinship and common ancestry, the emphasis on common descent constitutes the most persistent definition of ethnicity in the most recent discussions.[37]

Our more narrow concern at present, however, is the debate about the distinctions between race and ethnicity. Both sets of theorists, that is, those who insist on differentiating race from ethnicity and those who see race as a subset of ethnicity, agree that the most important component of race is the permanent nature of phenotype as a marker of race. They disagree, however, on the significance of skin color as a marker of identity

---

34   Pierre Van den Berghe, *Ethnic Phenomenon* (New York: Praeger Publishers, 1987), pp. 4–5; Jenkins, 'Social Anthropological Models', pp. 176–77.

35   Jenkins ('Social Anthropological Models', pp. 176–77) notes that the emphasis on 'cultural differences' can 'appear to be blaming the victims for their own disadvantage. There is a paradox here, insofar as the very stance [that emphasizes culture] which can be a powerful counterbalance to ethnocentrism may, at the same time, let prejudice in by the back door'.

36   Banton, *Racial and Ethnic Competition*, p. 64. Two elements of this formulation are important to distinguish: first, the belief in a common origin could be derived from a memory of migration or colonization, a common phenotype, or a common culture; second, the shared *belief* in a common descent operates independently of the actual *reality* of that common descent.

37   Common language is perhaps the next most commonly cited 'central' component of ethnic identity (Horowitz, *Ethnic Groups and Conflict*, pp. 14–16).

and factor in intergroup relations. Some theorists who distinguish race from ethnicity maintain that the permanent nature of racial affiliation as constituted by skin color produces profound and qualitative differences between 'race relations' and 'ethnic relations', that is, between groups that differ in terms of skin color, and those differing by language, religion, or national origin. While it is possible for persons to 'change ethnicity' when ethnicity is computed in terms of differences in language, religion, or even national origin (perhaps through intermarriage or concealment), such change is impossible when skin color is the marker of group membership, and tragic when membership mediates access to key social and economic resources. The fact that ethnic associations are sometimes voluntary, gated (i.e., restricted to those bearing some proof of identity), and often indicative of status and class provides additional evidence of the fundamental difference between race and ethnicity.[38] Moreover, these theorists maintain that it is not too difficult to discern the basically negative associations of race as regards status. If ethnicity is a political resource, race on the other hand generally serves as a political liability to the pursuit of desirable social status. An approach that confuses race and ethnicity is an approach that fails to take account of the fact that racial groups have had their identity imposed on them in a negative and oppressive way, and have been denied access to key social and economic resources.[39]

A number of scholars, however, maintain that the differences between race relations and ethnic relations are differences of degree rather than differences of kind. According to these scholars, race involves the more general problem of group relations and stigmatized identities, which are complicated by the unusually rigid group membership boundaries that derive from the use of observed physical characteristics as markers.[40] Others maintain that the idea that race is wholly imposed overlooks the important observation that whenever black intellectuals and popular icons engage in political or cultural resistance movements or self-identification projects, they themselves are actively participating in the construction of race, albeit by bending and co-opting formerly negative images into resources for engaging the broader culture.[41] In addition, the

---

38   P.J. Sunderland, '"You May Not Know It But I'm Black": White Women's Self Identification As Black', *Ethnos* 62.1–2 (1997): 32–58; Jenkins, 'Social Anthropological Models', pp. 177–78.

39   Rex, 'The Role of Class Analysis', pp. 71–72.

40   Banton, *Racial and Ethnic Competition*, pp. 72–73; similarly Van den Berghe, *Ethnic Phenomenon*, pp. 240–41.

41   Bulmer and Solomos, 'Rethinking Ethnic and Racial Studies', pp. 822–25; cf. Joel Marcus, who thinks a similar dynamic may have been at work among ancient Jews who rehabilitate negative labels by embracing them ('The Circumcision and the Uncircumcision in Rome', *NTS* 35 [1989]: 67–81). However, despite the sympathetic motives that prompt the

dynamics between groups differentiated by color are essentially similar to those of groups differentiated by culture, language, or religion, even though each of these ethnic markers introduces its own set of complicating factors. The exclusive group dynamics in modern race relations that assigns group membership involuntarily can also be at work in intraracial or intra-ethnic relations, which normally involve only inclusive, voluntary processes of group membership. Rex, for example, would maintain that the 'interethnic' religious conflict in Northern Ireland has more in common with the racial conflict in the USA than with the much milder 'interracial' conflict between black and white Parisian bourgeoisies.[42] One might add that the same is true of the Nazi party pogrom against Jews in World War II Germany, despite the fact that many would now class it as ethnic conflict.

The question about whether race is a special case of the more general category of ethnicity has points of contact with the problem of distinguishing an ethnic group from a religious group, and can be illustrated by the particularly difficult question regarding the character-ization of modern Jews. As with the discussion above about the overlap between race and ethnicity, the overlap between ethnicity and religion involves the different kinds of boundaries that are involved in the constructions of ethnic versus religious identity, as well as the difference between ascribed and involuntary constructions on the one hand, and assumed and voluntary constructions of identity on the other. These factors, as has been mentioned, also appear in conjunction with racialized constructions of identity.

One possible approach to identifying members of the Jewish commu-nity contains an ascriptive element and thus shares a dynamic typical of US constructions of race. The practice of identifying a child as a member of the Jewish community based on matrilineal descent tends to operate somewhat like the old 'one drop rule' in US black–white relations, in that

---

promotion of this viewpoint, quite a number of black intellectuals would perhaps prefer to be described as being engaged in resistance through the *deconstruction* of race. See for example bell hooks, *Outlaw Culture: Resisting Representation* (New York and London: Routledge, 1994), pp. 173–82; Gilroy, *Against Race*.

42   Rex, 'The Role of Class Analysis', pp. 72–78. It is important to mention, however, that while the collapse of race into ethnicity as an analytical category is often motivated by an anti-racist desire to eviscerate race of its power as an idea in modern society, the related idea of the color-blind society has had the (unintended?) consequence of supporting an anti-affirmative action political agenda. Failure to track the participation of minority groups in key areas of society such as government, education, health care, and labor sectors results in failing to document the persistence of institutional racism (see Lee Baker's 'Color Blind').

both constructions function to eliminate hybrid identities.[43] Just as a person in the USA was historically considered black if the person possessed even one drop of Negro blood, so too does this approach to membership in the Jewish community erase the 'partial' status of children born of mixed marriages, incorporating the child born of a Jewish mother and non-Jewish father, while excluding the child of a Jewish father and non-Jewish mother. In this particular dimension both cases ascribe group identity based on a permanent boundary marker and consign 'mixed' offspring to a less privileged status. Yet the religious aspects of Jewish identity complicates the Jewish case, involving an aspect highlighted by some and diminished by others, but potentially adding a voluntary component to Jewish identity that is wholly missing in folk constructions of race.[44] While Brodkin, a white secular American Jew, describes the US context as one in which Jews have slowly evolved into ordinary garden-variety 'white folk', Azoulay, a black religious Israeli immigrant to the United States, strongly contests this description. Azoulay's *Black, Jewish, and Interracial* insists on the non-racial and essentially religious nature of Jewish identity, and explores the ambiguities faced by Black Jews with

43   The old 'one-drop' rule of black identity has become a de facto folk concept about race, even though the rule itself has faded from US political discourse. Since there has never been objective means of establishing the presence of 'one drop of Negro blood', the rule amounts to the assignment of everyone known to have evidence of African ancestry to the black category, whether that knowledge came from physical or genealogical evidence (Smedley, *Race*, pp. 8–9). According to F. James Davis, estimates of the number of African Americans with mixed African, European, and Native American heritage range from 75% to 90% ('Defining Race: Comparative Perspectives', in David L. Brunsma [ed.], *Mixed Messages: Multiracial Identities in the 'Color-Blind' Era* [Boulder, CO, and London: Lynn Rienner, 2006], pp. 15–31 [16]). Notwithstanding the advent of the mixed race category in tracking ethnic and racial information, only 2.4% of Americans assign themselves to this category, despite the fact that the idea of a 'pure race' is an embarrassing relic of a discredited scientific past (Hirschman, 'Rise and Fall of the Concept of Race', pp. 21–29). In other words, in the USA most of us are technically 'mixed race' though only a few of us have identities constructed around this particular circumstance. See Kerry Ann Rockquemore, 'Deconstructing Tiger Woods: The Promise and Pitfalls of Multiracial Identity', in Heather M. Dalmage (ed.), *The Politics of Multiracialism* (Albany: State University of New York, 2004), pp. 125–41 (126–28).

44   The debate about whether modern Jewishness represents an ethnic or religious identity is a fascinating problem, as it not only highlights the questions about the role of religious identity in the secularized West, but also includes complications arising from discourses about national identity, given the modern state of Israel and its internal dialogue about religion vis-à-vis Israeli citizenship. In addition, complications about the construction of Jewish identity also rise out of discourses about national identity emerging from the European and American Jewish Diaspora, where Jewish 'ethnic' identity becomes secondary to allegiance to the 'national' identity of the Diaspora host country. See Jonathon Webber, 'Jews and Judaism in Contemporary Europe: Religion or Ethnic Group?' *Ethnic and Racial Studies* 20.2 (April 1997): 257–79; Karen Brodkin, *How Jews Became White Folks and What That Says about Race in America* (New Brunswick: Rutgers University Press, 2000).

reference to their hybrid 'interracial' identity in the context of the racially charged atmosphere in the United States.[45] Azoulay's book raises the question about the *racial* character of religious Jewish identity in much the same way that secular Jewish identity raises questions about the *ethnic* character of Jewishness.[46]

On the other hand, Webber argues for the ethnic nature of identity in the European Jewish Diaspora against the earlier essentialist views of Jewish identity that stressed the indissoluble mystical bonds of the worldwide Diaspora community. He finds that the importance of the memory of the Shoah, the 'symbolic religiosity' of highly attenuated versions of traditional Jewish practices, and the high rates of exogamous marriage and low rates of synagogue affiliation, serve to fix the concern of the Jewish community more on the question of group survival than on the preservation and propagation of Jewish religious culture.[47] As with the US Jewish community described by Brodkin, Webber finds that European Jews have stronger attachments to their respective national communities than to traditional Jewish culture, leading Webber to conclude that this group is better compared to modern ethnic groups united by a shared sense of destiny than to modern religious groups.[48]

Webber's study utilizes 'symbolic religiosity' and 'symbolic ethnicity', concepts that were developed in a pair of articles by Herbert Gans. 'Symbolic ethnicity' is a possibly lengthy intergenerational process by which Americans adopt an ethnic posture that minimizes interference with the processes of assimilation and acculturation through the occasional use of highly attenuated ethnic symbols such as food, rites of passage, and minor holidays that have been abstracted from the original cultural context. Gans states that such abstracted cultural practices become in the end actual stand-ins for that culture, and thus diminish the need to participate fully in the culture.[49] Similarly, 'symbolic religiosity' is the consumption of religious symbols that have been abstracted, apart from regular participation in a religious culture, in order to express feelings of

---

45   Katya Gibel Azoulay, *Black, Jewish, and Interracial: It's Not the Color of Your Skin, But the Race of Your Kin, and Other Myths of Identity* (Durham: Duke University Press, 1997).

46   The idea of Jewishness as a racial category has perhaps disappeared from the modern American scene given the prevailing folk concept of race as signified by skin color and the way that nineteenth-century European immigrants were absorbed into the white race. See Jacobson's *Whiteness* for a book-length treatment of this topic.

47   Webber, 'Jews and Judaism in Contemporary Europe', p. 270.

48   Ibid., p. 259. Gans comes to a somewhat different conclusion when he describes US Jews as a religio-ethnic group, but with ethnic secular characteristics (Gans, 'Symbolic Ethnicity and Symbolic Religiosity', p. 580).

49   Herbert Gans, 'Symbolic Ethnicity: The Future of Ethnic Groups and Cultures in America', *Ethnic and Racial Studies* 2 (1979), pp. 1–20 (9).

religious identification in a way that avoids direct conflict with dominant secular lifestyles.[50] Thus, both ethnicity and religion become symbolic and elected forms of identity, modes of identity that are different from the involuntary and permanent aspects of racial identity.

This brief survey has provided some insight into the complexities and ambiguities in modern discussions of race and ethnicity, complexities that result in an overall lack of precision in the literature in distinguishing ethnicity from race, and in understanding the contribution of such elements as physical characteristics, religion, language, and national origin to the construction of identity as a whole. However, rather than seeking to identify the essential or core elements constitutive of ethnicity, or trying to separate the concept of race from ethnicity and confronting the political fallout of doing so or failing to do so, recent discussion has shifted from debating the content of ethnicity to examining the context of identity construction. As will become apparent in subsequent sections, this shift has resulted in a de-emphasis on studying the discrete identity markers and group boundaries that have for so long been the staple of ethnic studies in the West.

b. *Ethnicity in Postmodern Studies*
Dissatisfaction with the legacy of overly simplistic racialized identities that are the products of oppressive colonial and national regimes has led to a more recent emphasis on the idea of difference as opposed to prior emphases on ethnic, racial, and religious identity.[51] One scholar maintains that the very eagerness to talk about identity at all is symptomatic of the postmodern condition, a condition perhaps mainly characterized by the fluidity and uncertainties of rapid change.[52] The rapidly changing nature of postcolonial Western society includes a proliferation of 'new' voices in the dialogue about the construction of identity, voices long silenced in modernity. Ethnic, racial, and tribal groups are no longer just spoken about; they now speak for themselves.

Leaning on a variety of scholars from a broad array of disciplines, New Testament scholar Abraham Smith describes postmodernism as resistance to foundationalism, totalizing discourse, and a mechanistic rationalism:

> Postmodernism questions any theory which posits an absolute, unquestionable *foundation* for the grounding of truth ... also ... *totalizing* schemes for explaining any or all of reality, whether these totalizing schemes include metanarratives about the essence of the

---

50 Gans, 'Symbolic Ethnicity and Symbolic Religiosity', pp. 577, 585.
51 Ann Phoenix, 'Dealing with Difference: The Recursive and the New', *Ethnic and Racial Studies* 21.5 (1998): 859–80 (861).
52 Bulmer and Solomos, 'Rethinking Ethnic and Racial Studies', pp. 825–26.

universe or humanity or the self ... [It] *demystifies* any belief that appears natural and universal. It exposes such a belief as a 'modern' power play and the 'reason' behind it as a temporal, situated rationality.[53]

If we leave to other authors a detailed description of the onset and character of the shift from modernity to postmodernity and the characteristics of postmodernity proper, we can here be content with a brief summary of the emphases in postmodern analyses of identity.[54] Generally, three major trends in ethnic and racial studies research distinguish the postmodern approach, though these trends are hard to isolate from each other. Postmodern identity studies (1) reject constructions of identities based on some 'essential' group characteristic, (2) embrace fluid and hybrid constructions of identity, and (3) emphasize perspectives from previously marginalized groups.

The most distinctive characteristic of postmodern identity studies concerns the rejection of essentialized subjects and social contexts. Indeed, rejection of essentialism almost serves as a given in recent studies, whether the studies are self-consciously postmodern or not. Pnina Werbner defines essentialism as the act of *violently* imputing a fundamental, basic, and necessary constitutive quality to a person, social category, ethnic group, religious community, or nation. In rejecting essentialism, most postmodern identity studies move away from the reification of race, culture, and religion, and reject the simple enumeration of racial or cultural characteristics that are assumed to define the 'essence', boundaries, or nature of the group in question. Werbner, however, is careful to differentiate violent essentialism from simple objectification, recognizing the political difference between an internal 'objective' enumeration of characteristics by a minority group, and the violent imposition of group characteristics and boundaries by powerful outsiders who want to maintain the status quo.[55]

53   Abraham Smith, '"I Saw the Book Talk"', pp. 118–19.

54   For a general description of postmodernity and implications for the study of identity see Phoenix, 'Dealing with Difference'; Ali Rattansi, 'Just Framing: Ethnicities and Racisms in a "Postmodern" Framework', in Linda Nicholson and Steven Seidman (eds), *Social Postmodernism: Beyond Identity Politics* (Cambridge: Cambridge University Press, 1995), pp. 250–86; Anthony Smith, *Nationalism and Modernity* (London and New York: Routledge, 1998), pp. 199–220; Pnina Werbner and Tariq Modood (eds), *Debating Cultural Hybridity: Multi-Cultural Identities and the Politics of Anti-Racism* (Los Angeles and London: University of California Press, 1985).

55   Pnina Werbner, 'Essentialising Essentialism, Essentialising Silence: Ambivalence and Multiplicity in the Construction of Racism and Ethnicity', in Werbner and Modood (eds), *Debating Cultural Hybridity*, pp. 228–30; Rattansi, 'Just Framing'; Ali Rattansi, 'Western Racisms, Ethnicities, and Identities in a "Postmodern" Frame', in A. Rattansi and S. Westwood Rattansi (eds), *Racism, Modernity, and Identity* (Cambridge: Polity Press, 1994), pp. 15–86; Malik, *Meaning of Race*, pp. 149–77.

This distinction is of a piece with the observation that it is well-nigh impossible to eschew essentialism completely in discussions of the politics of race or group identity.[56]

Postmodern studies also note that individual identity involves a tension between several possible subject positions, as for example when black men or white women stand as either oppressed subject or oppressing subject depending on context. These theorists reject essentialized perspectives on social contexts inasmuch as culture no longer refers to the compendium of a group's traditions, beliefs, and rituals. The idea of culture, rather, refers to the context within which meaning about identity, values, location, and so on is negotiated. As a result, these scholars view identity as an amalgamation of multiple possible subject positions, an amalgamation that may sometimes vary by situation and that produces a construction of identity that is chosen and not imposed. Since identity is resolved in response to forces that vary from location to location, identity is ambiguous and not fixed, and shifts dependent on context. The concept of identity itself becomes fragmented as different contexts represent different possibilities under which gender, class, ethnic, religious, common history, and other kinds of affiliations can all vie for pre-eminence. The plethora of possible identity constructions could produce a situation in which identity vanishes and ceases to become an important social element at all, either for the group or for the individual. In reality, however, theorists recognize that people do not hold all subject positions with the same level of passion or commitment, and one's choices about selected lines of identification are more constrained than theory might suggest, especially once other complicating elements from the environment are factored in. Nevertheless, if identity is even partially selected and situational, then identity becomes in many regards a political statement, even and perhaps especially if identity emerges from a context in which a number of social forces struggle for dominance.

The second characteristic of postmodern studies of identity is hostility to rigid categorizations of identity or other scientific classification schemes. An important consequence of this theme is the fact that postmodern identity discourse is especially suspicious of biologically based notions of shared origin or common descent. This rejection of rigid categories of group identity produces an emphasis on fluidity and complexity in group identification. Deconstruction of rigid categorizations of identity additionally highlights the power dynamics of modern constructions of identity.[57] New studies emphasize hybridity and multi-

---

56   Chetan Bhatt, 'Contemporary Geopolitics and "Alterity" Research', in Martin Bulmer and John Solomos (eds), *Researching Race and Racism* (London and New York: Routledge, 2004), pp. 16–36 (32, 34).

57   Bhatt, 'Contemporary Geopolitics'; Rattansi, 'Just Framing', p. 275.

racial or multi-ethnic identities and the possibilities such identities offer in resisting the lingering and powerful forces of oppression that feed on rigid categorizations of groups.[58] Theoretically, hybrid identities offer resistance through implicit and explicit boundary crossings that transgress sacrosanct borders. For example, consider the way that the multiracial community politically contests ethnic categories in the US census and elsewhere. While supporters see in the 'multiracial' category a deconstruction of invented but nonetheless rigid and oppressive racial categories, cynics see a new institutionalized essentialism that reifies existing racial schemas, since the new 'non-black' categories do nothing to destabilize the notion of a 'pure' whiteness at the top of the racial hierarchy.[59] As a theoretical construct, the notion of hybridity challenges the status quo only to the degree that it problematizes any notion of purity – be it racial, ethnic, or national.

This new emphasis on fluidity, complexity, and hybridity challenges older thinking about ethnicity and race and contains a potent appeal to the ideal of a common humanity.[60] Theorists view hybridity as powerfully disruptive of existing hierarchies, failing to conform to the imposed limits and categories that have been deliberately structured to maintain the status quo. However, the emphasis on common humanity that either sustains or accompanies an emphasis on hybridity often fails to interrogate the social structures that continue to operate to maintain inequalities. This emphasis ironically presses common humanity to the point where difference disappears and ends up sustaining the status quo.[61] Theorists who appeal to hybridity as a resistance strategy must recognize that culture, ethnicity, and race continue to be utilized as political resources.[62]

A third emphasis in postmodern theorization seeks to reverse one of the most tragic results of the modern era – the silencing of categorized and

---

58   Werbner and Modood, *Debating Cultural Hybridity*, p. 1.

59   Maria P.P. Root, 'Rethinking Racial Identity Development', in Spickard and Burroughs (eds), *We Are a People*, pp. 205–20 (211–12); David L. Brunsma, 'Mixed Messages: Doing Race in the Color-Blind Era', in Brunsma (ed.), *Mixed Messages*, pp. 1–11 (2–3); Kim M. Williams, 'Linking the Civil Rights and Multiracial Movements', in Heather M. Dalmage (ed.), *The Politics of Multiracialism: Challenging Racial Thinking* (Albany: State University of New York, 2004), pp. 77–97. Rainier Spencer criticizes advocates of the multiracial movement who insist that the offspring of black and white parents are multiracial. Spencer notes that such advocates reify blackness and ignore the history of African Americans by naming them black, given estimates that 75% to 90% of all African Americans have a mixed-race heritage ('New Racial Identities, Old Arguments: Continuing Biological Reification', in Brunsma [ed.], *Mixed Messages*, pp. 83–102 [87–94]).

60   Paul Gilroy, *Against Race*, pp. 327–56.

61   Claire Alexander, 'Beyond Black: Rethinking the Colour/Culture Divide', *Ethnic and Racial Studies* 25.4 (2002): 552–71 (561).

62   Werbner and Modood, *Debating Cultural Hybridity*, pp. 1–25.

stigmatized people-groups who previously stood as objects to be assimilated, possessing differences that must be overcome. Postmodern identity studies retrieve and embrace those previously muted voices from the margins. Just as the stylized and stereotyped 'Other' has been integral to identity formation in the colonial West as that which national identity was established over and against, so now postmodern and postcolonial studies deliberately seek to privilege and reclaim the stories and concerns of the powerless and to challenge the construction of national narratives to include these pluriform voices.[63]

Political concerns, never absent in identity studies, are now increasingly and explicitly articulated as central elements in various analyses, and the determined focus of the scholarship on previously marginalized groups produces what critics term the 'tyranny of identity politics' and the 'radical chic of the margins'.[64] Indeed, the tyranny of identity politics may silence individuals who articulate a perspective about their own identity that is in tension with their group's claims about identity; such tensions are especially sharp in multiethnic personal identification.[65] Yet critics aside, even sympathizers note that the focus on so many sets of marginalized concerns and possible subject locations inevitably results in a fragmented perspective on identity and group relations, and an inability to articulate common themes and common political concerns, a fragmentation that thus dilutes the gains explicitly sought by postmodern theorists.[66] As a result, some analysts in effect resist the new complexities introduced by postmodern theorization and mourn the loss of simpler identity formulations that facilitate political action.[67] Consequently, the increasing complexity of identity can yield ambiguous results in terms of politics. Greater emphasis on hybrid identity lends itself to the resistance of the kind of categorization of the 'Other' that has served as a foil for self-identification in the colonial imagination. However, hybrid identities and emphasis on reclaiming marginal voices and perspectives also leads to greater political fragmentation, and thus creates intrinsic obstacles to the forging of anti-racist and anti-colonial political alliances.

63   Homi Bhabha's work has been particularly influential in this area. See especially *The Location of Culture* (New York: Routledge, 1994).

64   Phoenix, 'Dealing with Difference', p. 859; Alexander, 'Beyond Black', pp. 560–61.

65   Stephan Cornell, 'That's the Story of Our Life', in Spickard and Burroughs (eds), *We Are a People*, pp. 41–53 (50–51); Nira Yuval-Davis, 'Ethnicity, Gender Relations and Multi-Culturalism', in Werbner and Modood (eds), *Debating Cultural Hybridity*, pp. 193–208 (200–201).

66   Bulmer and Solomos, 'Rethinking Ethnic and Racial Studies', p. 826.

67   Phoenix, 'Dealing with Difference', p. 879; Alexander, 'Beyond Black', pp. 553, 559; Smith, '"I Saw the Book Talk"', pp. 127–28.

c. *Models of Race, Ethnicity and Nation*

In current discourse, models of ethnicity that attempt to describe internal
and external group dynamics reflect, to greater or lesser degrees, some of
these hallmarks of postmodern ethnic and racial studies. Below I consider
four models that will be useful in our study of Paul's theology in Part II.

1. *The Narrative Basis of Identity: Stephen Cornell*

As described above, one important trend in ethnic and racial studies is the
tendency to move away from analysis that emphasizes difference to move
towards an emphasis on hybridity. Stephen Cornell's work on narrative as
an organizing principle for identity construction integrates these two
approaches and provides a framework for evaluating Paul's identity
discourse. Cornell maintains that identity takes a narrative form particularly during periods of rupture when events shatter often-unarticulated
assumptions about identity or cause them to come under scrutiny. In
addition, Cornell suggests that identity narratives expose intergroup
power relations.[68]

Moving beyond the bare assertion of the socially constructed nature of
ethnic and racial identity, Cornell insists that groups are constantly
negotiating identity in the midst of changing circumstances and challenges
in the environment. Identity emerges as a narrative that captures the
group's understanding of its experiences and central beliefs, as well as the
values attached to group membership. According to Cornell, group
narratives have subjects, verbs, and objects: the narrative subject is the
group; verbs convey the group's story in terms of past and anticipated
events; and the object of the narrative is an internalized value judgment
about the group, promoting group pride, guilt, superiority, determination,
and so on. Cornell describes a three-step narrative process: *selection* of
events that comprise the episodes in the narrative; narrative *plotting* that
tell how events are linked to each other and to the group; and, most
importantly, *interpretation* that describes the significance of the narrative
for group identity. Such narratives are ethnic to the degree that the
selection, plotting, and interpretation of events uses group identity or an
ethnic boundary as an organizing principle, producing a story about 'us
versus them' that communicates the meaning of membership for group
members and outsiders.

An important element of Cornell's work is its sensitivity to variation
over time. Group narratives may become thin or attenuated by distance
from the key events in the narrative. For most groups, identity narratives
will be hidden or taken for granted during times of stability but
forefronted during times of turmoil, prompting a new iteration of the
narrative process as group members struggle to make sense of new events

---

68   The following discussion summarizes Cornell, 'That's the Story of Our Life'.

or circumstances. The purpose of the narrative process is not only to make sense of the events causing the rupture in the taken-for-granted nature of the group's identity, but it may also serve to situate the group vis-à-vis new allies or enemies. As we will see in Chapter 5, this is precisely the process that Paul uses to articulate the relationships between the groups in his social world in the aftermath of Christ.

Power relations stand at the heart of the narrative process. When some subgroups have differing interpretations of the same events, power relations will dictate the terms of the story. Power relations will privilege some narrators over others within the group and may even determine the version of the narrative that gains public currency, as when a majority group's story about a subordinated group prevails over the minority group's version of its own history. Richard Jenkins elaborates on this point by describing the dialectic between intrinsic and extrinsic definitions of identity.[69] Jenkins reserves the term 'group' for the case of identity that emerges from within a collective where the collective is self-aware and names itself (e.g., 'Jewish'), while the term 'category' is assigned to the case of collectives which have been defined and named by outsiders (e.g., 'Hispanic'). Jenkins notes that since ethnic groups and ethnic categories assume the presence of an audience, each process is implicated in the other, and thus the process of identification is revealed as a dialectic around these two impulses. Cornell defines *hegemonic narratives* as those that undergird moral or legal claims to power and substantiate existing power arrangements. In contrast, *subversive narratives*, written from below, seek to undermine existing power alignments.[70] In other words, power is latent in the narrative itself, depending upon whether and how the group in question utilizes resources to promote its version of events, naming itself and defining others.

Finally, Cornell's narrative approach also takes up the postmodern emphasis on hybridity. *Narratives of multiplicity* emphasize integration over separation; such narratives subvert rigid racial categories that pressure mixed-race individuals to adopt one parental heritage over the other. Narratives of multiplicity focus on connection and describe intertwined lines of descent that blur boundaries and shade differences. These narratives challenge the status quo through stories that deny implicit or hidden assumptions in many prevailing narratives. We will see that Cornell's distinctions between hegemonic and subversive narratives as well as his emphasis on the connective nature of integrating narratives will be fruitful for analyzing the relationship between the Christian race and the Jewish race in Paul, helping us to imagine ways of appropriating Paul's narratives today.

69 Jenkins, *Rethinking Ethnicity*, pp. 53–73, 80.
70 Cornell, 'That's the Story of Our Life', pp. 48–49.

2. *Racial Formation Theory: Howard Winant*

Are Paul's narratives hegemonic or subversive? Howard Winant's racial formation theory will facilitate analysis of Paul's identity narrative as a 'racial project'. Racial formation is the mechanism by which political, economic, and social forces combine to determine the meaning of racial categories.[71] For Winant, race relations emerge in the context of 'projects' that combine the representational elements of race with the institutional and structural elements of race. Racial projects concretize race relations by interpreting racial dynamics in terms of the effort to organize or distribute resources in keeping with a particular construal of race.[72] Thus, we can identify a project or narrative as racist if it creates or perpetuates essentialism and buttresses existing hierarchies among racial groups. According to Winant, the statement 'Today, many Asian Americans are highly entrepreneurial' is not racist because it does not essentialize – the statement refers to a given context ('today') and does not overgeneralize ('many'). The statement 'Asian Americans are naturally entrepreneurial', on the other hand, is a racist project by this definition. Similarly, a support group for black contractors is not a racist project in and of itself, unless, for instance, its organizers were determined to steal clients from non-black contractors, thus creating or reinforcing hierarchical relations between racial groups.[73]

The power of this proposal lies in its ability to understand race and racism in shifting contexts by examining the results of certain racial projects and discourses. Developed to examine racial dynamics in the context of color-blind policy prescriptions – which, according to Winant, can perpetuate existing racial hierarchies – we will be able to use this theory to evaluate the effects of Paul's third-race formulation in its ancient context, as well as its meaning in a modern context.

3. *Criteria and Indicia of Identity: Donald Horowitz*

Known primarily for his work on ethnic conflict, Donald Horowitz wrote some shorter articles about the dynamics of ethnic identity.[74] Horowitz begins with the observation that people can change ethnic identity, for example through intermarriage or conversion. Even though theorists often distinguish ethnicity from voluntary affiliation by virtue of the fact that ethnicity is an ascribed identity acquired at birth, Horowitz maintains

---

71 Michael Omi and Howard Winant, *Racial Formation in the United States: From the 1960s to the 1990s* (New York and London: Routledge, 2nd edn, 1994), pp. 61–62.

72 Ibid., p. 56.

73 Winant, *The New Politics of Race*, p. 46.

74 The following discussion of Horowitz's work on ethnic identity is drawn from Donald L. Horowitz, 'Ethnic Identity', in Glazer and Moynihan (eds), *Ethnicity*, pp. 111–40. Horowitz's major works on ethnic conflict include *Ethnic Groups in Conflict* and *The Deadly Ethnic Riot* (Los Angeles: University of California Press, 2001).

that ascription and voluntary affiliation are two ends of a continuum and that *both* may be associated with ethnicity.[75] Most people, in fact, have multiple ascribed identities that they invoke or select depending on the situation.

For our purposes, Horowitz's most helpful contribution involves his identification of the relationship between *membership criteria* and *membership indicia* of identity. Criteria of identity are those cultural elements upon which the group as a collective determines itself to be alike or unlike some other group. Examples of identity criteria include African ancestry as the traditional criterion of membership in the black race, and worship of the God of Abraham, Isaac, and Jacob as an ancient criterion for membership in τὸ γένος τῶν Ἰουδαίων.[76] Indicia of identity, on the other hand, are those indicators that people use in assessing identity, and which individually may vary in terms of the degree of accuracy by which they correctly assess identity. Some indicia may be physical, as for instance with skin color and hair texture in the case of modern African Americans and circumcision for Second Temple Jews, while others may be material or cultural, for example, clothing, surname, or language.

> Indicia are evidence of identity; unlike criteria, they do not define it. They are shorthand; they develop after criteria have been adopted (however tacitly). As surrogates, indicia of identity are probabilistic and subject to contradiction, much as the wearing of a uniform or the insignia of an organization can be contradicted by reference to an authoritative roster of members. The confusion between the two arises in part because *long usage of an indicium may result in its being treated increasingly as [a criterion].*[77]

Thus, indicia do not exhaustively determine the question of ancestry or ethnic identity, even if many use them this way. Further, as these ideas are rarely explicitly articulated in a particular culture, criteria and indicia may easily become confused in common understanding. In Chapter 5, we will see that Horowitz's contention that identities tend to crystallize around symbolic or real indicia perfectly captures the way that circumcision functions in Paul's arguments about identity.[78]

With his emphasis on enumerating the criteria and markers of identity, Horowitz's model is inherently essentialist. Nevertheless, because Horowitz's work focuses on criteria and indicia that emerge from within groups, it is an illustration of Werbner's distinction between a violent,

---

75   Horowitz, 'Ethnic Identity', pp. 113–14.
76   See Est. 3.13; *3 Macc.* 7.10. On the broad contours of membership in the Jewish community see E.P. Sanders, *Judaism: Practice and Belief, 63 BCE–66 CE* (Philadelphia: Trinity Press International, 1992), pp. 241–78.
77   Horowitz, 'Ethnic Identity', p. 120 (emphasis added).
78   Horowitz, 'Ethnic Identity', p. 120.

outwardly imposed essentialism and an insider's enumeration of membership criteria; thus his observations remain useful for our discussion about Jewish and Christian identity in Paul.

4. *A Sociohistorical Perspective: Anthony D. Smith*

Although Anthony Smith's work is open to the postmodern criticism of involving inordinately firm categorical distinctions with respect to the constituent parts of ethnicity, his framework easily facilitates transhistorical comparisons of the most commonly discussed components of ethnicity. Of the theorists who discuss race, ethnicity, or nationalism, Smith's work is both sustained by and indebted to a historical perspective, and he has done more than any other author in the field to explicitly establish ethnicity as a meaningful category for antiquity.[79] Since his work comes closest to providing the kind of framework within which we may compare ancient and modern constructions of ethnicity, we will discuss it in more detail than that devoted to the other models.

For Smith, the question that energized a series of books and articles spanning the eighties and nineties concerns the relationship between ethnic identities and nations, and the possibility of a causal link between the two.[80] While most studies of nationalism generally focused on developments from the late eighteenth century, Smith constructed his framework from evidence of national ties and sentiments far earlier in the historical record, as far back as the second millennium BCE. The framework is historical in that it draws on data from different epochs, and sociological in that it constructs a coherent developmental sequence that is explanatory and comparative.[81] Most importantly, Smith asks substantive questions about the meaning of national identity and sentiments, and interrogates the way that meaning is associated with

---

79   Omi and Winant do affirm the socio-historical nature of race and racism (Winant, *The New Politics of Race*, pp. xviii, 162; Omi and Winant, *Racial Formation*, p. 55), but undermine this key observation by insisting that it is a phenomenon that dates from the sixteenth century (Winant, *The New Politics of Race*, pp. ix, 153–54). With reference to scholarship that studies aspects of ethnicity in the ancient world, most simply assume ethnicity as a valid category in antiquity and import modern ideas about ethnicity to their studies. See for example Hodge, *If Sons then Heirs*; Byron, *Symbolic Blackness*; Hall, *Ethnic Identity in Greek Antiquity*; id., *Hellenicity*; Ray Laurence and Joanne Berry (eds), *Cultural Identity in the Roman Empire* (New York: Routledge, 1998); Irad Malkin (ed.), *Ancient Perceptions of Greek Ethnicity* (Cambridge, MA: Harvard University Press, 2001); Richard Miles, *Constructing Identities in Late Antiquity* (London: Routledge, 1999).

80   Anthony Smith, *The Ethnic Origins of Nations* (Oxford: Blackwell, 1986), pp. 1–3.

81   Ibid., pp. 6–7.

cultural expressions of identity and varies depending on circumstances in the particular historical context.[82]

Smith's historical and sociological framework for the examination of the origin of nations also contributes to the debates about modernism and instrumentalism in national and ethnic studies.[83] By the late twentieth century, the modernist perspective held that the nation was not a natural or standard element in human society, but that it was a thoroughly modern phenomenon and a product of capitalism, industrialism, urbanism, bureaucracy, secularism, and so on. Many modernists held that nations and nationalisms are necessary only in modernity; others saw nationalism as a product of the intelligentsia's manipulation of the media for the political mobilization of the masses.[84] Many modernists are also *instrumentalists*, regarding ethnicity as a malleable instrument, as opposed to *primordialists* who regard ethnic sentiment as a naturally occurring part of the human condition. Smith concedes that nationalism as an ideology does date from the late eighteenth century and that it was not until the late seventeenth century that Europeans began to speak of 'national character' and a common national identity, but he also rightly maintains that there are parallels in the ancient world for nationalistic movements and the idea of 'national character'.[85] One can concede political manipulation of national sentiment by elite intelligentsia in modernity without reducing the idea of a nation to an imaginary construct, since such manipulation requires antecedent cultural ties and sentiments if they are to strike a popular chord among the masses and prove durable enough to sustain concerted political action.[86] People do not die for constructs born from the imaginations of the elite unless these constructs resonate in the hearts of the masses.

These last two statements represent the kind of remark that leaves Smith open to the postmodern charge of essentialist thinking. In effect, Smith is struggling with a problem we broached earlier in our discussion about race: the problem that constructs of the human imagination wield

82 As will become evident in the critique of Smith's work, this examination of the *meaning* of expressions of identity and the transformation of such meaning through different periods is the characteristic that most serves to rescue this body of work from essentialism.

83 See Smith, *The Ethnic Origins of Nations*, pp. 7–13; and Anthony Smith, 'The Problem of National Identity: Ancient, Medieval, and Modern?' *Ethnic and Racial Studies* 17.3 (1994): 375–99 (376–78).

84 Smith, 'The Problem of National Identity', p. 377.

85 Nationalistic movements in the ancient world occurred especially in the context of territories liberated from outsiders. Two noteworthy examples of these kinds of movements are the mid-second-century-BCE Hasmonean Revolt of the Jews, and the turn-of-the-era Gallic resistance to Caesar's campaigns (Smith, *The Ethnic Origins of Nations*, p. 11).

86 Smith, 'The Problem of National Identity', p. 377; also Umut Özkirimli, *Theories of Nationalism* (New York: St. Martin's Press, 2000), pp. 121–27.

great power over human social life, for all their 'imaginary' nature.
Nations and races are not unreal by virtue of being constructed, despite
the fact that they are intangible and malleable both in the present and over
time. The watershed observation of the postmodern era – that identity is
constructed and responsive to authentic social forces in the environment –
seems to stand in tension with an acknowledgment of the reality and
power of the effects that issue from particular constructions of identity.
We will encounter something of a similar tension when we examine
interpretations of Paul's use of familial language to describe relationships
in the church.

For Smith, ethnicity is transmitted through history via particular forms
that shape the experience of a people, forms that reside in myths,
memories, values, and symbols. According to Smith these myths,
memories, values, and symbols structure the *mythomoteur* myth, the
constitutive or central myth in the myth-symbol complex of a people.
These myths are contained in historically conditioned forms (i.e., sacred
texts, rites, etc.) that transmit the sometimes-changing meanings and
expressions associated with the symbols across time.[87] Accordingly, Smith
defines pre-modern ethnic groups as 'named human populations with
shared ancestry, myths, histories, and cultures, having an association with
a specific territory and a sense of solidarity'. He goes on to identify six
features associated with *ethnie*:[88]

1　Collective name: When *ethnie* become aware of themselves as a
group, they typically identify themselves with a name that begins to
summarize the distinctive history of the group, as well as communicating something about group characteristics and achievements.
Ethnie that were unnamed in antiquity may have been in the process
of ethnic formation.[89]

2　Common myth of descent: According to Smith, this element is the
sine qua non of ethnicity, as it serves to articulate the group's
understanding of its origins and destiny. Myths of common descent

---

87　Smith, 'The Problem of National Identity', p. 15.

88　Smith, *The Ethnic Origins of Nations*, pp. 22–32. Here Smith uses the French term
ethnie, which is equivalent to the Greek ἔθνος, a definition that is of limited help since it
erroneously assumes a well-understood and widespread knowledge of the ancient Greek
word ('The Origins of Nations', *Ethnic and Racial Studies* 12.3 [July 1989]: 340–67 [340]). The
French terminology is very widely used in ethnic studies literature and is probably an attempt
to escape accretions from folk concepts about ethnicity in contemporary use.

89　Smith explicitly rules out the case of a community that has been named by others,
since the important element with reference to ethnicity is the group's awareness of itself as a
group, communicated in the name that they choose for themselves (*The Ethnic Origins of
Nations*, pp. 22–24). We might add that in antiquity, a name was associated with the potency
or essence of the thing named, so that the choice of a collective name begins to convey
something important about how a group sees itself.

answer the question 'why are we one community?' by saying, 'because we came from the same ancestor at a certain time period, and thus necessarily belong together and share the same tastes'.[90] Myths of common descent act as cognitive maps for the community, providing a framework by which the community makes sense of its experiences. The Homeric canon, the Bible, and Iranian Book of Kings provide ancient examples of shared myths of common descent in antiquity.[91]

3 Shared history: The intergenerational glue of an ethnic group is its shared history, including especially myths of origins and group liberation. The more striking and well known that these myths of group formation and group deliverance are, the greater the chances for the ethnic group to survive and endure: 'That which, in the end, defines an ethnic group is its unique history *and its unique response to that history*, and from these flow its other cultural marks of individuality and its sense of collective uniqueness.'[92] Thus, a shared history provides the forms or containers for the interpretation and preservation of later experiences. Not surprisingly, the keeping of history can also result in conflict between two or more ethnic traditions within a group as factions struggle for monopoly over the interpretation of history, a struggle that in turn heightens the ethnic consciousness throughout the population and deepens its sense of shared identity and shared destiny.

4 Distinctive shared culture: Most commonly, language and religion are viewed as the most important signs of cultural distinctiveness, but customs, practices, institutions, laws, architecture, dress, food, and music are often just as marked.[93] The greater the number of cultural markers or the more distinctive the marker, the greater is the intensity of the ethnic sentiment. The fact that ancient Jewish religion addressed itself to all these parameters perhaps provides insight into its extraordinary longevity.

5 Association with a specific territory: *Ethnie* either reside in a specific

---

90 Smith, *The Ethnic Origins of Nations*, pp. 24–25.

91 Ibid., p. 24. See also Hodge's excellent discussion of kinship and common descent in ancient literature (*If Sons then Heirs*, pp. 19–42). Discussing the often constructed and invented nature of kinship alliances in the ancient world, Hodge notes that Paul engages in the construction of what she calls 'intellectual kinships' (pp. 38–41).

92 Smith, *The Ethnic Origins of Nations*, pp. 65–66 (emphasis added). The italicized phrase in this quotation moves toward salvaging Smith's overall framework from a violent, outwardly imposed essentialism as discussed above. Specifically, here Smith describes cultural distinctiveness in terms of the group's response to its own history.

93 Ibid., pp. 26–28. Smith maintains that the common practice of using language as the differentiator *par excellence* is an oversimplification, since there are many examples where the opposite holds. Serbo-Croat, for example, is a single language for all intents and purposes, but this common language does not prevent the religiously based ethnic divisions between Orthodox Serbs and Catholic Croats.

territory or can identify a place for which there is a symbolic or
historical attachment.

6   Sense of solidarity: The community's sense of identity or belonging
    to the group is crucial to the formation of an ethnic community.
    Ethnic solidarity may wane or be mixed or perhaps even over-
    powered, but in times of stress – especially during wartime – this
    solidarity will reemerge, perhaps even stronger than before.[94] Smith
    emphasizes war as the most important factor in creating and
    stimulating latent ethnic feeling.[95] War fosters a sense of unity
    through the mobilization and training of armies, and wars fought
    over territorial boundaries solidify a community's attachment to
    and identification with a particular land.[96] In addition, war
    stimulates ethnic attachment through propaganda that portrays
    the enemy in unfavorable terms.

Smith does not woodenly insist that all six characteristics are present and
easily identifiable in all *ethnie*. Groups in the process of ethnic formation
will be engaged in shoring up those elements of group identity that are
weak insofar as they are able, while ethnic categories are groups that are
deficient in several of these key areas.[97] Nor does Smith insist that
ethnicity was the main mode of social organization in the premodern
period; instead, he maintains that ethnicity was an important mode of
human organization and socialization from the early third millennium BCE
to today.[98] *Ethnie* emerge and re-emerge at different periods, and are able
to adapt and change as a mode of organization in response to changes in
their environment. Ancient *ethnie* are persistent yet malleable, and the
formation and durability of *ethnie* are assisted by (1) religious forms, (2)
movement towards sedentary lifestyles, and (3) warfare, as discussed
above. After examining the ancient data, Smith concludes that ancient
Egyptians, Israelites, Greeks, and possibly Sassanid Persians were ethnic
communities that can be classified as ethnic states (as opposed to modern
nations), and that many others shared similar characteristics but cannot
be definitely classified as ethnic states due to gaps in the surviving data.

Özkirimli helpfully identifies an important criticism of Smith's

---

94   Ibid., pp. 29–30. While Smith insists that shared myths of common descent form the
sine qua non of ethnic identity, W. Connor insists that this sense of group solidarity is central
to ethnic grouping (*Ethnonationalism: The Quest for Understanding* [Princeton: Princeton
University Press, 1994], p. 197).

95   Anthony Smith, *The Ethnic Revival* (Cambridge: Cambridge University Press, 1981),
pp. 74–75.

96   Ibid., pp. 74–79; also see Smith, *The Ethnic Origins of Nations*, pp. 37–41.

97   Smith, *The Ethnic Origins of Nations*, p. 31. Hispanics are perhaps the best-known
modern example of an ethnic category, as this category contains peoples from widely
different geographical areas, having significantly different cultural markers.

98   Ibid., p. 32.

ethno-symbolism that concerns us here, that Smith confuses ancient *ethnie* and modern nations by erroneously attributing a fully developed group consciousness and sense of history to ancient *ethnie*. Most ancient peoples were largely unaware of their cultural distinctiveness, or at best, the acknowledgment of cultural idiosyncrasies only extended as far as the elite class.[99] This objection rightly points to the general dearth of evidence about the thoughts and opinions of the masses in antiquity. Nevertheless, as far as Second Temple Jews are concerned, military conflict around the turn of the era points toward a greater awareness of and participation in a sense of cultural distinctiveness on the part of common Jewish people of the era. If war acts as both a stimulant and sustenance for ethnic sentiment, the Hasmonean revolt in the second century BCE and the wars with Rome in 66 and 132 CE bracket our period of interest, marking times in which ethnic self-awareness was high among Jews.[100] In addition, evidence for the regular collection of the temple tax from the Jewish Diaspora throughout the first century suggests that this kind of sentiment persisted even during times of peace. Thus, even if the intensity of Jewish ethnic sentiment waxed and waned, we have evidence in the historical record for a strong sense of group solidarity that likely transcended social and class divisions in Jewish society from the middle of the second century BCE to the beginning of the second century CE.

3. *Summary*

This chapter reveals that an awareness of and attention to the dialectical relationship between internal, external, and individual forces that operate in identity formation yield the best hope of understanding the complexities of identity. As we attempt to compare identity concepts across epochs, we will need to keep in mind four important observations from modern scholarship regarding the nature of race and ethnicity. *First, modern popular (or 'folk') concepts about race focus on biological characteristics and especially skin color.* Modern society first thought of race as a universal human characteristic centered in kinship and lineage, and now thinks of race as primarily associated with skin color and minority-group status. Recent moves in the scholarly literature to focus on social context and other group characteristics in understanding group identity (i.e., to 'de-essentialize' identity) have not yet taken hold of the popular imagination, and they elude many scholars outside of racial and

---

99 Özkirimli, *Theories of Nationalism*, p. 184. Also see Aletta Norval, 'Thinking Identities: Against a Theory of Ethnicity', in Edwin N. Wilmsen and Patrick McAllister (eds), *The Politics of Difference* (Chicago and London: University of Chicago, 1996), pp. 59–70.

100 Fergus Millar, *The Roman Near East: 31 BC – AD 337* (Cambridge, MA, and London: Harvard University Press, 1993), p. 337.

ethnic studies. This chapter noted the ways that some privilege common experience over common descent in defining identity. For example, some Jews focus on the experience and memory of the Shoah as the defining criterion of Jewish ethnicity, while others have focused on matrilineal descent. While not discussed here, some people are similarly debating the core criterion of membership in the black race, defining 'blackness' through a focus on a shared history of slavery and experience of segregation, as opposed to a focus on African descent.[101] However, such subtleties do not yet dominate the racial discourse in the USA, as society largely views race as a matter of skin color and physical descent. This common construction of race presents the biggest obstacle to a trans-historical comparison of the concepts of race and ethnicity and a fresh consideration of the ethnic contours of Paul's identity and language for the Christian community.

Second, there is disagreement in modern scholarship about (1) whether race and ethnicity are synonymous terms and (2) whether race and ethnicity are always based on common descent. Up through the nineteenth century, most people regarded races, ethnic groups, and nations as synonymous entities based on common ancestry and/or a common homeland. Today, there is a tendency to elide the terms or to posit that race is a subset or special case of ethnic social dynamics. While most students of nations and nationalism emphasize common ancestry and kinship as the basis of ethnic groups, races, and nations, much postmodern identity scholarship rejects any one characteristic as 'essential' to ethnicity or race, especially biologically based characteristics such as kinship. The tension between these two viewpoints is that between historical reconstructions and postmodern theorizing. Despite postmodern preferences about the nature of group identity, modern scholars must not deny a preference for kinship as the basis of group identity in history where these tendencies can be documented by material or literary artifacts. Conversely, students of ancient *ethnie* must not elevate kinship as the *sine qua non* of ethnicity because of the dominance of this idea in modern scholarship.

Third, identity emerges in narratives that are articulated in the context of intergroup and intragroup power relations. The narratives that make identity meaningful in a given context are often implicit, surfacing particularly during times of conflict or rupture in a way that may either substantiate or subvert power relationships and connections between groups. In addition, group-defined social boundaries that constitute an insider's perspective are often in tension with outsider definitions of the group that emerge from power imbalances between the groups. These power imbalances not only serve to suppress a weaker group's expression

101   Rachel L. Swarns, 'African American Becomes a Term for Debate', *New York Times*, 29 August 2004.

of its identity, but may also mute an individual's articulation of self-identity. Racial formation theory provides a means by which we can evaluate disparities in intergroup relations by assessing the degree to which racial projects and discourses preserve hierarchical racial arrangements. This theory will prove useful in evaluating the nature of intergroup relations among the groups in Paul's social and interpersonal matrix.

Finally, race and ethnicity are fluid and malleable; they are socially defined via narratives that vary across context and history. Theorists recognize that group-identity narratives of race and ethnicity vary over time and change from culture to culture. Thus, with reference to *group identity*, an understanding of identity for a particular historical and geographic context should identify (1) the criterion or criteria around which group identity is organized and (2) the indices or distinguishing features associated with group membership. Criteria of identity are those cultural elements upon which the group as a collective determines itself to be like or unlike some other group, while indicia of identity are those indicators that people use in assessing identity (e.g., religion, language, dress, surname, physical appearance) and which individually may vary in the degree of accuracy. For example, if a membership badge serves as an easily recognized but fallible indicium of identity, a roster of members in good standing would serve as an authoritative criterion in the event of disputes about membership. Moreover, *personal identity* is often in flux in that individuals do not cling to all elements of identity with the same level of passion or commitment. Identity is often ambiguous; it is both selected and situationally dependent on contextual forces that vary from location to location.

Chapter 3

RACE (γένος) AND ETHNICITY (ἔθνος) IN ANTIQUITY

The last chapter's review of the evolution of race and ethnicity in the modern period was an important preliminary to the analysis of ethnic and racial identity in antiquity and a discussion about the lines of continuity between antiquity and modernity with respect to these concepts. There seem to be, however, at least four possible methodological objections to this kind of inquiry. First, one might maintain that the concepts of ethnicity and race did not exist in antiquity, that the ancients did not have a word that corresponds to the modern concept of ethnicity since the English word only approximates the Greek ἔθνος. However, just as few would deny that 'gender', 'class', and 'culture' exist in antiquity although these concepts lack equivalent Greek lexemes, ancient texts reflect a confluence of ideas similar to those associated with the modern idea of ethnicity.[1] For example, some modern classicists speak of a Greek ethnic consciousness as revealed in a passage from the fifth-century-BCE historian Herodotus (b. 484 BCE). In the voice of the Athenians, Herodotus gives the following description of the Athenians' reasons for refusing to defect to the Persians in the Persian War of 480–479 BCE:

> There are many important reasons that would prevent us from doing this even if we wanted. First and foremost, there are the statues and temples of gods that have been sacked and destroyed; it is necessary for us to avenge these with all our might rather than come to an agreement with the man who did this. In addition, there is the matter of the Greek nature (τὸ Ἑλληνικόν) – that is, our common blood (ὅμαιμόν), common tongue (ὁμόγλοσσον), common shrines and altars (θεῶν ἱδρύματά τε κοινὰ καὶ θυσίαι) and similar customs and habits (ἤθεα τε ὁμότροπα); it would not be good for the Athenians to betray these things.[2]

---

1 Hall, *Hellenicity*, pp. 17–18.
2 Herodotus, *Hist.* 8.144, my translation; also see Dionysius, *Ant. rom.* 1.29–30, who mentions group name, group founder, and territory as elements of identity in addition to those discussed by Herodotus. The Herodotus passage is cited by many scholars interested in the phenomenon of ancient ethnicity: Hall, *Hellenicity*, p. 189; id., *Ethnic Identity in Greek Antiquity*, p. 7; Isaac, *The Invention of Racism*, p. 112 and those authors cited there; and Ray

Although the word ἔθνος does not appear in this selection, the passage exhibits many of the features that we have come to associate with ethnicity: common descent, language, religion, customs, and ways of life.

Secondly, with respect to the question of race, a related objection observes that even though translators commonly render the Greek word γένος with the English 'race', the concept was vastly different in antiquity. Scholars almost unanimously reject the idea that γένος had anything to do with skin color or physical appearance among the ancients. Yet this way of posing the objection confuses membership criteria with membership indicia, two concepts that we have distinguished from each other in Chapter 2. In the modern era, for example, dark skin color is an *indicium* of membership in the Black race. The *criterion* of membership in the Black race has to do with descent from native Africans, or more simply, with biological kinship. In order to maintain that race in antiquity is wholly different from race in the modern world, we would have to dissociate the element of real or constructed kinship totally from the ancient idea. Since many social scientists assert the centrality of kinship with reference to ethnic identity, as we saw in the previous chapter, this would be a difficult conclusion to maintain.

A third objection insists that racism is the key component of the modern idea of race and denies that antiquity knew anything of modern racism. However, we find that precision in defining racism facilitates a cross-historical comparison of this phenomenon as well, a task that classicist Benjamin Isaac explores thoroughly in *The Invention of Racism in Classical Antiquity*. Isaac defines a racial group as a group of people who are believed to share imagined physical, mental, or moral characteristics that are wholly determined by unchangeable factors such as hereditary characteristics, climate, or geography. With this definition in hand, Isaac argues for the existence in antiquity of 'proto-racism', a set of ideas that are the precursors of the 'scientific' racism of the seventeenth and eighteenth centuries.[3] Isaac convincingly demonstrates his thesis through an analysis of a wide array of ancient, late ancient, and Enlightenment texts.[4] Ultimately, however, his success rests on his methodological precision in defining race and racism in a way that facilitates examination of the phenomena in different contexts.

Laurence, 'Territory, Ethnonyms, and Geography: The Construction of Identity in Roman Italy', in Ray Laurence and Joanne Berry (eds), *Cultural Identity in the Roman Empire* (New York: Routledge, 1998), pp. 95–110 (99).

3 Isaac, *The Invention of Racism*, pp. 34–35.

4 Ibid., pp. 15–23. I should note here that although Isaac sometimes considers Christian (and Jewish) sources in his survey of primary sources, he deliberately avoids a systematic analysis of Christian attitudes and ideals with reference to racism in antiquity. Citing Gal. 3.28, he notes that 'Christian attitudes were from the beginning partly similar and partly different' from those of the Greeks and Romans who are his main objects of study (p. 14).

Specifically, his understanding of race accommodates not only the idea in Nazi Germany of the 'Jewish race', but also the situation of the 'Black and White races' in contemporary American society. In fact, his definition suits any group that has been the object of imagined attributed characteristics derived from factors beyond human control. Likewise, Isaac defines racism via the key element of determinism, a move that allows us to view the geographic and climatologic determinism of antiquity as a not-too-distant ideological cousin of the biological determinism of the present epoch.

Finally, one might object that given the difficulties in defining ethnicity and race in the modern period, we cannot expect to be able to provide a definitive description of these slippery concepts in antiquity. Yet, while it is true that no study could offer a definitive portrait of race or ethnicity for any epoch, we can note the kind of language that appears in the discourse in the ancient context, much like the way that theorists detected shifts in how moderns invoke the ideas. In other words, this analysis will not yield certainties about the nature of identity in antiquity, but in comparison to the innumerable studies that simply assume that prevailing ideas also apply in antiquity, it will significantly advance our understanding of ἔθνος and γένος in antiquity and improve our ability to detect shifts in the ideas over time. Thus, these first two chapters seek a single methodological goal by pursuing a framework for race and ethnicity that will facilitate the trans-historical recognition and analysis of these modes of group identity, particularly as these phenomena are present during the early Christian era. Where the previous chapter described the modern understanding of ethnicity and race, this chapter theorizes the contours of ethnicity at the turn of the era by examining Jewish, Christian, and non-Jewish Greek literature.

We begin by recognizing that the Greek words ἔθνος ('people', 'nation') and γένος ('race', 'kind') are the words that have the closest relationship to the modern concepts of ethnicity and race, respectively, in that they are etymologically and conceptually related to the terms used in modern discourse. Although there are several synonyms for these Greek words that could have been reviewed, ἔθνος and γένος represent the points at which there are the surest connections between the ancient and modern concepts and thus represent the best opportunities to detect continuities and discontinuities in the two contexts. Hence, this chapter describes the contours of ethnicity at the turn of the era via an analysis of the discourses in which ἔθνος and γένος appear in Jewish and non-Jewish Greek texts from 100 BCE to 100 CE. The discourse analysis in this chapter not only reveals how ancient authors used the words in the period, but also describes the set of ideas that writers routinely associated with group identity at the time, together producing an approximation of the contours of identity in antiquity.

1. *The Etymology of Race and Ethnicity*

The English noun 'ethnicity', which expresses the property that exists when something is said to be ethnic, was a new word in the early 1940s. 'Ethnic', in turn, is that which pertains to nations or races, as described in the following excerpt from a popular modern English dictionary:

> Ethnic, or ethnical, *adj.* concerning nations or races; pertaining to gentiles or heathen; pertaining to the customs, dress, food, etc. of a particular racial group or cult; belonging or pertaining to a particular racial group; foreign; exotic; between or involving different racial groups ... [Greek *ethnos* a nation].[5]

Both the noun 'ethnicity' and the adjective 'ethnic' loosely derive from the Greek ἔθνος, while the phrase 'ethnic group' serves for the noun that would precisely correspond to the Greek but is missing in English. Modern French, on the other hand, uses the common noun *ethnie* to parallel ἔθνος, though the French noun *ethnicité*, which is parallel to the similar English word, is rarer.[6]

In antiquity, however, ἔθνος appeared in a broad range of contexts, some going well beyond what we mean by 'ethnicity', 'ethnic', or '*ethnie*'.[7] For example, in the eighth century BCE, Homer uses the word to describe swarms of bees and flies and flocks of birds (bees: *Il.* 2.87; flies: 2.469; birds: 2.459). Elsewhere, ἔθνος applies to warriors, the dead, and groups of young men (warriors: *Il.* 2.92; young men: 3.33; 'tribes of the dead': *Od.* 10.526).[8] Even when using the word to refer to people-groups in a way that seems more familiar to moderns, later writers still employ it with a great deal of elasticity. For example, Herodotus uses ἔθνος to describe the inhabitants of a Greek city and for groups spread over several cities, while Plato uses the word to describe the Penestai, the serf class in Thessaly.[9] Occasionally, Aristotle uses ἔθνος as virtually equivalent to the word

---

5 *Chambers Dictionary* (1993 edn) s.v. 'ethnic'.

6 Tonkin, McDonald, and Chapman, *History and Ethnicity*, p. 11; Smith, *The Ethnic Origins of Nations*, p. 21. Tonkin, McDonald, and Chapman point out that the word 'ethnicity' entered English usage late, and only after German racist ideology created sensitivity to the word 'race' (*History and Ethnicity*, p. 14). In other words, the English noun which would ordinarily have corresponded more closely to the Greek ἔθνος was not needed, since the English word 'race' already performed the needed function. For example, ethnology was understood as 'the study of races'.

7 Hall, *Ethnic Identity in Greek Antiquity*, p. 34.

8 LSJ, s.v. γένος; see also Hall, *Ethnic Identity in Greek Antiquity*, p. 34 and Tonkin, McDonald, and Chapman, *History and Ethnicity*, p. 12.

9 πόλις: 'oldest lineage', Herodotus, *Hist.* 7.161 (trans. Godley); groups of Libyans in various cities: Herodotus, *Hist.* 4.171-72; 4.197; 4.183; groups of Scythians in various cities: Herodotus, *Hist.* 4.5, 17. Plato: *Leg.* 776d; *Rep.* 420b, cf. 421c. See also Hall, *Ethnic Identity in Greek Antiquity*, pp. 34–35.

βάρβαρος in a manner reminiscent of the way later Jewish and Christian writers denigrate non-Jews, and similar to the way some moderns employ 'tribe' to identify primitive peoples who are deficient in civilization.[10] Later, Romans in the empire would use the word to refer to the provinces outside Italy in general (Appian, *Bella Civilia* 2.13).

Many Greek and Latin words are synonyms of ἔθνος, and these words form the language of ethnicity in antiquity and into the modern era. In Latin, the key synonyms are *populus* ('people'), *tribus* ('a division of the people, a tribe'), and the important word *natio* ('birth, breed, kind, race'), in addition to *civis* ('citizen'), *civitas* ('citizenship, the state'), and *barbarus* ('foreign, strange', as a substantive, 'barbarian').[11] In Greek, key synonyms are λάος ('people'), φύλη and φῦλον ('tribe'), πόλις ('city, government'), and βάρβαρος ('barbarian'). None, however, is as important as the word γένος ('race'; Latin *gens, genus*), which with ἔθνος is one of the principal objects of this analysis.

According to Jonathon Hall, γένος is related to γίγνομαι (γίνομαι after Aristotle) meaning 'to come into being, to become' and is thereby either 'the mechanism through which one's identity is ascribed (i.e., birth) or the collective group in which membership is thought to be ascribed through birth'. For Hall, the idea of 'putative common descent' is the quintessence of ethnicity in antiquity, or indeed in any epoch. Hall's methodology for analyzing ancient Greek ethnicity via mythical genealogies hinges on his conviction about the centrality of common descent, and seems to dovetail with his suggestion about the etymology of γένος.[12] However, even though I will presently accept the notion that kinship is an important idea associated with γένος, there is something to be said for the idea that the notion of 'kind' connects the varied uses of γένος, perhaps even better than the idea of 'birth' or 'origin'. As a preliminary example, we might consider the headings under γένος in a standard dictionary of ancient Greek summarized as follows:

I. Race, stock, kin; direct descent as opposed to a collateral relationship.

10 Aristotle, *Politica* 1324.b.10: Rackham translates ἐν τοῖς ἔθνεσιν with 'among ... the non-Hellenic nations'. Tonkin, McDonald, and Chapman, *History and Ethnicity*, pp. 12–13 give background on the development of the word βάρβαρος and note that Aristotle only applies the word ἔθνος to non-Greeks. *Third Maccabees* 6.9 and Gal. 2.15 provide examples of derogatory references to 'Gentiles'.

11 Tonkin, McDonald, and Chapman, *History and Ethnicity*, p. 13. LS, s.v. *populus, tribus, natio, civis, civitas, barbarus*.

12 Hall, *Hellenicity*, pp. 25, 35–36. According to Hall, ethnic consciousness comes from putative common descent and cohabitation in a given homeland and communicates ideas of kinship with shared ancestors (ibid., pp. 36–37). Isaac likewise sees kinship at the heart of most definitions of race, a situation that he thinks is likely the product of overlapping or synonymous use of 'ethnicity' and 'race' (Isaac, *The Invention of Racism*, p. 25).

II.   Offspring, even of a single descendant; collectively, offspring, posterity.
III. Generally, race of beings; clan, house, family; tribe as a subdivision of ἔθνος; caste; breed, with respect to animals.
IV.   Sex, gender.
V.   Class, sort, kind. In logic, as opposed to species (εἶδος); in the animal kingdom equivalent to the taxonomic idea of 'class'; genus, a species of plant, and so later, γένη meaning 'crops'; ἐν γένει, as concerning all, generally.[13]

The idea of 'kind' is explicit in group V, and is just under the surface in IV in the sense of 'kind of gender' and used, for example, in the fairly common phrase 'woman-kind' (τὸ θῆλυ γένος).[14] Further, the idea of 'kind' is not so hard to infer in groups II or III; this emerges especially in group III in the sense of animal breeds, while group II describes people-groups in terms of those who are descended from a particular ancestor. Group I, communicating 'race' in the sense of a large descent group, is the most common use of the word, but as we shall see, often occurs in contexts that tell something about the kind of large people-group under discussion, in terms of characteristics, geographic origin, or inhabited territory.[15]

---

13   Summary paraphrased from LSJ, s.v. γένος. For purposes of comparison, a summary of the entry for ἔθνος follows:

I. Number of people living together, company, band of comrades; particular tribes; of animals, swarms, flocks. After Homer, nation, people (γένη being a subdivision of ἔθνος).
   a. later, foreign, barbarous nations as opposed to Greeks; cf. Gentiles vs. Jews
   b. at Rome = *provinciae*
   c. class of men, caste, tribe
   d. sex
   e. part, member
II. Of a single person, a relation

14   Translations of passages from the selected authors follow the Loeb (LCL) edition unless otherwise noted. Similarly, passages from the New Testament follow the NRSV and those from the Septuagint are taken from Brenton's translation. Throughout, 'LLS' identifies a translation as the author's own. For the passages that use γένος in expressions about gender, see Dionysius, *Ant. rom.* 4.11.9 '... our wives, our daughters, and women-folk (τὸ θῆλυ γένος) [treated] like slaves ...' (LLS); also in Dionysius, *Ant. rom.* 4.11.4; 4.15.4.7; Diodorus, *Bibl. hist.* 3.53.4; 32.12.3; Plutarch, *Quaest. rom.* 286C; Josephus, *J.A.* 4.219; Philo, *Embassy* 320; *That God Is Unchangeable* 121.

15   *Specific kind* of kinship group (II): Plutarch, *Sera.* 559D ('If a city is a single and continuous whole, surely a family [γένος] is so too, attached as it is to a single origin which reproduces in the members a certain force and common quality pervading them all' [LLS]).
   General kind of kinship group (III): Josephus, *J.A.* 9.124 ('... to bury her, out of respect for her lineage, for she came of a line of kings' [LLS]).
   Kind of large, 'racial' group (I): Strabo, *Geogr.* 15.1.8 ('... and that the Sibae were descendants of those who shared with Heracles in the expedition, and that they retained

As with the overlapping modern terms discussed in Chapter 2, the ancient words γένος and ἔθνος often appear as synonyms. For example, Herodotus describes Greeks as both a γένος (1.143) and an ἔθνος (1.56), while Diodorus Siculus and Josephus refer to named groups as both γένος and ἔθνος in the same sentence.[16] According to most scholars, where both γένος and ἔθνος refer to the same people-group, γένος emphasizes kinship; Anthony Smith goes on to suggest that ἔθνος emphasizes cultural attributes.[17] As for the large number of synonyms for these words, there is generally little to distinguish 'tribe', 'nation', or 'race'. This is possibly because these boundaries were more fluid in antiquity than they are today,[18] more probably because kinship was commonly attributed to large and small collectives that inhabited the same territory. However, given numerous references to kinship in antiquity, we should bear in mind that the ancients were as capable of inventing kinship ties for political gain as moderns are (see for example 1 Macc. 12.5-23).[19]

I end this overview of the etymology of ἔθνος and γένος with a final comment about the way in which the nuances of the ancient words survive in the modern English usage. The modern use of the word 'ethnicity' began to mimic the Jewish-Christian use of ἔθνος as the idea of 'race' became increasingly problematic. Whereas in early modern discourse everyone had 'race', by the latter half of the twentieth century, language about 'ethnicity' was increasingly assigned to outsiders, taking on an us-versus-them duality that characterized the related terms across recorded history.[20] Strongly communicating otherness and difference, 'ethnicity' and 'ethnic group' became clandestine synonyms for 'race', as that term lost favor in many arenas. Thus, by referring to 'ethnicity' rather than 'race', theorists hoped to utilize an analytic concept that described a

---

badges of their descent [σύμβολα τοῦ γένους σώζοντας], in that they wore skins like Heracles, carried clubs, and branded their cattle and mules with the mark of a club' [LLS]). Isaac (*The Invention of Racism*, p. 135) describes the way that ancients derived group characteristics from properties associated with the climate or terrain that the group inhabited.

16 Diodorus, *Bibl. hist.* 2.46.4: '... waged continuous wars against the nation (ἔθνος) to such a degree that they left in existence not even the name of the race (τοῦ γένους) of the Amazons'; Josephus, *J.A.* 15.384: '... and I think I have, by the will of God, brought the Jewish nation (ἔθνος) to ... a state of prosperity ... We have erected in our country ... and embellished our nation (γένος)'.

17 Smith, *The Ethnic Origins of Nations*, p. 21; Tonkin, McDonald, and Chapman, *History and Ethnicity*, p. 12; Hall, *Ethnic Identity in Greek Antiquity*, pp. 35, 38.

18 Steven Grosby, 'Religion and Nationality in Antiquity', *European Journal of Sociology* 32 (1991): 229–65 (236).

19 See the excellent discussion of this topic in Hodge, *If Sons then Heirs*, pp. 19–42.

20 Tonkin, McDonald, and Chapman, *History and Ethnicity*, pp. 15–16.

universal human phenomenon but only succeeded in developing a vocabulary that marked strangeness and otherness.[21]

2. Race (γένος) and Ethnicity (ἔθνος) in Non-Jewish, Jewish, and Christian Authors

a. Methodology

In this section I examine occurrences of ἔθνος and γένος in the works of the nine Jewish, Christian, and non-Jewish collections that contain the heaviest use of these words between 100 BCE and 100 CE: the OT, the Jewish Apocrypha, Diodorus Siculus, Dionysius Halicarnassus, Philo, Josephus, the NT, Strabo, and Plutarch. Including attestations in the Septuagint, the data include 2,689 occurrences of ἔθνος and 2,228 occurrences of γένος.[22] Thus, not including the Septuagint, this examination includes roughly 70 to 75 percent of the known attestations of ἔθνος and γένος in the period.

Of the collections selected for analysis, the Septuagint technically stands outside of the period of interest. The exact dating of the Greek versions of the Hebrew Bible and Apocrypha cannot be dated closer than the broad range of third to first century BCE, though the Greek translations of the Pentateuch likely occurred earlier in the period, with the Apocrypha in the mid to late portion of the period. Nevertheless, I included these documents because these texts were very important in the early Christian thought-world and they are critical for a study of Paul's self-identity and that of Second Temple Jews and other early Christians.

Before proceeding, we should pause for a note about the non-Jewish Greek-speaking authors contained in this study. In comparison with Hellenistic cultural influence on Rome, Rome had a relatively mild impact on the cultural attitudes of Greek-speakers in the eastern empire.[23] Thus, even when they write about Romans and Roman history, Diodorus Siculus, Dionysius Halicarnassus, Strabo, and Plutarch write as outsiders. While they are all sympathetic to Rome to greater or lesser degrees, they

---

21   Ibid.

22   Herein the word 'Septuagint' (LXX) refers to the Greek translations of the Hebrew Scriptures and the Jewish Apocrypha, though charts and graphs in the appendix show these works separately. Both ἔθνος and γένος are very commonly used between 100 BCE and 100 CE. There are nearly 2,800 occurrences of forms of γένος in 62 of the TLG database's 127 authors of the period, and over 2,400 occurrences of ἔθνος in 32 turn-of-the-era authors in the database. TLG is a searchable digital database of ancient Greek works.

23   Fergus Millar notes that the Roman legions represented practically the whole of the Roman presence in the east (*Roman Near East*, p. 32). See also Greg Woolf on how Greeks and Romans differed in their respective understandings of identity in 'Becoming Roman, Staying Greek: Culture, Identity and the Civilizing Process in the Roman East', *Proceedings of the Cambridge Philological Society* 40 (1994): 116–43.

are all non-Jewish Greek-speaking authors who write about Romans and others for non-Jewish Greek-speaking audiences in the East.[24] In other words, their accounts of various groups, customs, conflicts, and beliefs do not describe what such circumstances actually were, merely the way in which the Greek-speaking outsiders who wrote about them perceived these peoples. The perspectives of these authors on the lifestyles of the people they describe were colored not only by their own literary purposes and social locations, but also by their perspectives on group identity, using, for example, typical caricatures of the barbarian 'Other'.[25] With this in mind, we could refer to these authors as 'Greeks' who exhibit attitudes about identity consistent with 'Greek ethnicity'. However, the matter of a Greek ethnic identity may be problematic in and of itself, as some might maintain that it is difficult to differentiate attitudes reflecting a 'Greek' ethnic identity from attitudes reflecting a more generalized 'Hellenistic culture' or 'Hellenism' that would have been shared with Romans and Jews.[26] With this in mind, herein I will refer to Diodorus Siculus, Dionysius Halicarnassus, Strabo, and Plutarch as non-Jewish

---

24   Laurence, 'Territory, Ethnonyms, and Geography', p. 102.

25   While space does not permit a full-blown description of the literary and rhetorical purposes of the authors considered in this study, information of this kind is readily available. *The Oxford Classical Dictionary* gives succinct descriptions of the dates and major works of all of the authors discussed: Simon Hornblower and Antony Spawforth (eds), *Oxford Classical Dictionary* (Oxford: Oxford University Press, 3rd rev. edn, 2003). Balsdon provides a succinct description of the background and literary purposes of the Greco-Roman authors reviewed here in J.P.V.D. Balsdon, *Romans and Aliens* (Chapel Hill: University of North Carolina Press, 1979), pp. 193–206. Similar information for the Jewish Apocrypha and Pseudepigrapha is available in David A. De Silva, *Introducing the Apocrypha: Message, Context, and Significance* (Grand Rapids: Baker Academic, 2002); James Charlesworth (ed.), *The Old Testament Pseudepigrapha* (2 vols; New York: Doubleday, 1983). Those interested in Philo should not miss Goodenough's introduction (Erwin Ramsdell Goodenough, *An Introduction to Philo Judaeus* [Oxford: Blackwell, 2nd edn, 1962]), in addition to the more general information in Emil Schürer's classic *The History of the Jewish People in the Age of Jesus Christ* [ed. Geza Vermes and Fergus Millar; trans. T.A. Burkill; 3 vols; Edinburgh: T&T Clark, 1973]). Shaye Cohen has a detailed analysis of Josephus's audience and apologetic purposes in his book on Josephus as a historian (*Josephus in Galilee and Rome: His Vitae and Development as a Historian* [Columbia Studies in the Classical Tradition, 8; Leiden: Brill, 1979], pp. 91–100, 169–79); and Steve Mason has a more recent short summary in *Understanding Josephus* (Journal for the Study of the Pseudepigrapha Supplement Series, 32; Sheffield: Sheffield Academic Press, 1998, pp. 64–104). See Balsdon, *Romans and Aliens*, p. 30 for a description of the way that images of barbarians operated in the Greco-Roman world. Additional information on the Greco-Roman literature analyzed here is available in Tim Cornell, 'Ethnicity as a Factor in Early Roman History', in Tim Cornell and Kathryn Lomas (eds), *Gender and Ethnicity in Ancient Italy* (London: Accordia Research Institute, University of London, 1997), pp. 9–22. In the same volume, Kathryn Lomas discusses the Greek–barbarian dichotomy mentioned in the text above in 'Introduction', pp. 1–8 (3).

26   Hall maintains that an earlier Greek ethnic identity dissipated into a general cultural Hellenism by the fifth century BCE (Hall, *Hellenicity*, p. 7).

authors, though we shall presently revisit the question of the degree to which they shared concepts about racial and ethnic identity.[27]

Although there are a number of studies that investigate the identity and characteristics of various ethnic groups in antiquity, few analyze the nature of ethnicity or race in antiquity, or the relationship of the ancient concepts to the modern ones.[28] Here, two goals drive the study of the Greek words ἔθνος and γένος and the concepts of 'ethnic group' and 'race' associated with them. The first goal is to confirm that standard lexica document usages and semantic ranges of the words consistent with the period of interest. The second and more important goal is to assess the contours and features of identity in antiquity by identifying the network of ideas that are most often associated with these words.[29] Thus, below I catalogue passages where ἔθνος and γένος appear in twelve categories, though there is some overlap between categories that I will discuss forthwith:[30]

(1) People-Groups and Classes	(7) Religion
(2) Group Description	(8) Language
(3) War or Conflict	(9) Group Name
(4) Land and Territory	(10) Kinship
(5) Government	(11) Humanity
(6) Customs, Lifestyle and Laws	(12) Group Founder

27 For the balance of this chapter, I will refer to Dionysius Halicarnassus as 'Dionysius' and Diodorus Siculus as 'Diodorus'.

28 Benjamin Isaac's study of racism (*The Invention of Racism*) and Denise Kimber Buell's study of post-canonical early Christian literature (*Why This New Race?*) are noteworthy exceptions to this general observation.

29 An exhaustive approach to the study of ancient ethnicity and race would seek not only identity passages containing the Greek words from which the modern concepts are derived but also passages that contain similar ideas, even where the words ἔθνος and γένος do not appear, as in the Herodotus passage discussed earlier (*Hist.* 8.144). This more exhaustive study would first have to discover the set of ideas that are associated with identity in the period, perhaps as here through the analysis of ἔθνος and γένος passages, before analyzing non-ἔθνος/γένος identity passages, or risk imposing a modern understanding of ethnicity and race onto the ancient data. In other words, the analysis undertaken in this work forms a necessary first step towards a more definitive or ideal analysis of ancient identity. However, we should not underestimate the gains represented by the approach taken here. As stated earlier, an investigation of the continuities and discontinuities between ancient and modern perspectives of identity that centers on ἔθνος and γένος begins at the point at which there is the surest connection between the ancient concepts and the modern concepts, given the history and etymology of the English words.

30 Two additional analytical categories are omitted from this discussion: 'Non-People-Groups' in ἔθνος data and the 'Genus, Type, or Heading' group in γένος data. These categories routinely appear in the passages of interest as shown in Figures A.1 through A.4 in the appendix, but because they represent inanimate objects, they are not pertinent to our analysis of ethnicity and race.

Since the local contexts around a usage of ἔθνος and γένος routinely
contain ideas that fall into multiple categories, I noted every applicable
category; thus the total number of occurrences across all categories
exceeds the 4,917 ἔθνος and γένος passages reviewed.[31] Analysis of the
frequency with which certain topics recur provides insight into the relative
importance of the components of identity during the period. For example,
if we find that the kinship idea occurs far more frequently in contexts
containing a reference to γένος than in ἔθνος contexts, we will have
verified that in antiquity, race involves kinship more often than an ethnic
group or *ethnie* involves kinship, as suggested earlier. Likewise, if we find
that ideas about customs occur with a far higher frequency in the vicinity
of ἔθνος than in the vicinity of γένος, we will have found support for
Smith's assertion that ἔθνος connotes similarity of cultural traits. An
additional goal of the study is to determine whether the Jewish and non-
Jewish authors differ with respect to the most salient or important features
of group identity. In other words, we will determine, for example, if
kinship and customs were as important for non-Jews as they were for
Jews.

The following sections describe the twelve categories listed above in
more detail, and provide examples of the kinds of passages assigned to
each category. The first section describes the analysis of ἔθνος passages
across seven categories, and the second section, beginning on page 81,
describes the analysis of γένος passages in the remaining five categories.
Given the fact that the categories overlap considerably, I describe each
category only once either in the ἔθνος section or in the γένος section,
usually depending on where the category exhibits the greatest frequency.
Footnotes give summary information about overlapping data. Figures
A.1 through A.4 in the appendix depict the frequency of ἔθνος and γένος
passages respectively by author or body of literature.

b. Ἔθνος *in Non-Jewish and Jewish Authors*
1. *Group Description*[32]

In ἔθνος passages, the Group Description category indicates that for the
ancients ethnicity often communicates something about 'kind' when
applied to people-groups. This category tracks texts in which authors
convey information about groups through simple, one-word adjectives, or
occasionally through longer, more detailed narratives. In order to avoid
excessive doubling of category assignments, I use two conventions in

---

31 The 4,917 occurrences is the sum of the 2,689 occurrences of ἔθνος and the 2,228
occurrences of γένος mentioned above.

32 The Group Description category in γένος passages: see Philo, *Dreams* 1.68: τὸ
αὐτομαθὲς γένος; *Flight* 147; *Dreams* 2.15: τῆς ἀθανάτου κακίας γένος; *Cher.* 8, 106: τὸ
εὐδαιμονίας γένος.

assigning potentially overlapping categories. First, simple militaristic characterizations such as 'warlike' are allocated to the War or Conflict category, and second, adjectives derived from the names of regions, like 'Italian' or 'Syrian', are catalogued with the Land and Territory category. With reference to a potential overlap between the Group Description category and the People-Groups and Classes category, the Group Description category contains *characterizations* of groups while the People-Groups and Classes category points to group *distinctiveness, function, or identity*.[33] For example, I assign a reference to a small or unfriendly group to the Description category, while assigning the New Testament reference to a people 'producing fruits of the kingdom' (Mt. 21.43) to the People-Group category. The latter category either identifies the function of the group or defines the constitution of the group in terms of membership criteria.[34]

The simple descriptive passages in this category are relatively infrequent but occur in many of the authors in the study.[35] The Group Description category appears frequently in Strabo, who describes various peoples as brigandish, savage, and barbarian (*Geogr.* 3.4.27; 8.1.1; Book 7 fragments, no. 48).[36] This category contains passages with references to 'great and populous' nations, phrases which commonly describe successful people-groups or successful migrations in Plutarch (*Sull.* 4.1) and often in Philo (*God* 178; *Moses* 1.222, 240; *Rewards* 95). For example, Dionysius' description of Greek colonization under Oenotrus illustrates this motif:

> This then was the time when the Greeks sent the colony into Italy. Oenotrus left Greece because he was dissatisfied with his portion of his father's land ... They were accompanied by many of their own people – for this **nation** is said to have been very populous (πολυάνθρωπον) in early times – and by as many other Greeks as had less land than was sufficient for them.[37] (Dionysius, *Ant. rom.* 1.11.2)

---

33   The γένος section below describes the 'People-Groups and Classes' category in more detail.

34   For example, a Jewish reference to 'abominable and lawless Gentiles' (*3 Macc.* 6.9) gets allocated both to the Description and to the People-Group categories, since 'abominable and lawless' fits the simple characterization parameter, but the reference to 'Gentiles' denotes a large group that, from the Jewish perspective, is distinctive for being composed of non-Jewish people.

35   See Figures A.1 and A.2 in the appendix.

36   'Barbarian' is used commonly in antiquity, functioning as an identifier of non-Greek peoples for Greeks (and Romans), as well as a characterization of a type of culture, similar to the way that ἔθνος or 'Gentile' functions in the Jewish world. In addition to the references in Strabo, see also Philo, *Planting* 67; *Cher.* 91; *Abraham* 181; and Dionysius, *Ant. rom.* 7.70.4.

37   For the remainder of this chapter, the English words translating ἔθνος (and γένος in the next section) are shown in bold. With reference to the passage above, the context of an example from Plutarch illuminates the implied praise in πολυάνθρωπος: 'For instance, as

Other descriptions seem to convey something about the military prowess of a people, even though unaccompanied by narration of battles or other conflicts. For example Diodorus tells us that Ethiopians feel neither pain, fear, nor any other emotion (*Bibl. hist.* 3.18), that they, along with the Trogodytes, are 'beastlike' (*Bibl. hist.* 3.31), and elsewhere describes nations as 'brutish and unfriendly' (*Bibl. hist.* 17.105). These 'outsider' descriptions of others from Dionysius stand in stark contrast to Jewish insider self-characterizations:

> For this is your wisdom and understanding before all nations, as many as shall hear all these ordinances; and they shall say, Behold, this great **nation** is a wise and understanding people. For what manner of nation is so great, which has God so near to them as the Lord our God is in all things in whatsoever we may call upon him? And what manner of nation is so great, which has righteous ordinances and judgments according to all this law, which I set before you this day? (Deut. 4.6; see also Exod. 19.6)

2. War or Conflict[38]

The War or Conflict category is important in both Greek and Jewish sources, which suggests the precedence of conflict for ancient concepts of ethnicity. It is the most prominent category for Diodorus, Dionysius, and Plutarch, and the second most prominent category for the Jewish Scriptures (OT), Josephus, Strabo, and Philo. This category includes Plutarch's descriptions of multi-nation armies (*Marc.* 12.3; *Ant.* 37.3), as well as military strategy:

> For the Auruncans were a warlike **nation** and by the stature, strength, and forcefulness of appearance in which they had brutality, they were exceedingly formidable. (Dionysius, *Ant. rom.* 6.32.3)

> Later, the **race** (γένος) of the Romans from Latinus never engaged in a war against a **nation** (ἔθνος) unannounced, but first sent a spear into the country of the opposing nation as a sign. (Diodorus, *Bibl. hist.* 8.26.1; see also 1.3.2)

Narratives of conquests, battles, and so on form the bulk of this category in both non-Jewish and Jewish literature:

> And coming together to the same place, both armies pitched their camps

---

legate, Sulla captured Copullus, chieftain of the Tectosages; and as tribune, he persuaded the great and populous **nation** of the Marsi to become friends and allies of Rome' (Plutarch, *Sull.* 4.1).

38   The War or Conflict category in γένος passages: overall, there are more than ten times as many ἔθνος passages as γένος passages: 88 total γένος war passages, as compared to 970 ἔθνος passages. See examples in Dionysius, *Ant. rom.* 4.25.3; Josephus, *J.W.* 5.461; Diodorus, *Bibl. hist.* 2.46.4; Josh. 4.13-14; Judg. 6.2; and *Pss. Sol.* 17.7.

a little distance apart from each other at the city of Eretum, which belongs to the Sabine **nation**. (Dionysius, *Ant. rom.* 5.45.4, LLS)

And all said to their neighbors: 'If we all do as our kindred have done and refuse to fight with the **Gentiles** for our lives and for our ordinances, they will quickly destroy us from the earth. (1 Macc. 2.40)

He decided to obliterate the whole **nation**, for he hated the Jews by nature because he was of the race of the Amelikites. (Josephus, *J.A.* 11.211, LLS; see also 3.301)

In the Septuagint, this category includes war imagery in the context of God-talk. God's action of scattering Israel through the agency of conquering nations was a recurring motif; by contrast, such imagery is much rarer in the New Testament:

And you have seen all that the Lord our God has done to all these **nations** before us; for it is the Lord our God who has fought for you. (Josh. 23.3)

And I will scatter to every wind all his assistants round about him, and all that help him; and I will draw out a sword after him; and they shall know that I am the Lord, when I have scattered them among the **nations**; and I will disperse them in the countries. (Ezek. 12.14-15; see also Ps. 67.31; Rev. 11.18; 13.7)

For **nation** will rise against **nation**, and kingdom against kingdom, and there will be famines and earthquakes in various places. (Mt. 24.7//Mk 13.8//Lk. 21.10)

3. *Land and Territory*[39]

The Land and Territory category is another very important element in group identity in our period and includes ἔθνος passages that distinguish people-groups by their country, that is, by reference to the territory they inhabit or a group's territory of origin in the case of migration. Although the territory category is the most prominent category in Strabo, this category is probably still underestimated, since our methodology focuses on the local context and may well have missed instances in which a concern for geography is implicit. Arguably, all of Strabo is concerned with territory, as the work is nothing less than Strabo's philosophy of geography.[40]

---

39 The Territory category in γένος passages: in Greco-Roman literature γένος frequently appears in passages in which land defines the territory of origin or territorial boundaries: Strabo, *Geogr.* 9.2.25; Dionysius, *Ant. rom.* 1.27.1; Diodorus, *Bibl. hist.* 3.8.1; 3.20.2-3; 4.25.2; 4.29.2; 2 Macc. 8.9; cf. Mk 7.26; Acts 18.2; cf. 18.24.

40 Strabo, *Geogr.* 1.1.16, LLS: 'Therefore the greater part of geography is according to the needs of the body politic; for the place of activity is the land and sea, which is where we

Strabo's use of ἔθνος often appears with a proper noun qualifier, as in the phrase 'the Egyptian peoples', which Jones usually translates as 'the Egyptian tribes' in the LCL edition. This proper noun qualifier could designate the lineage or descent of a people or tribe, or alternately, could designate a group's geographic origin – as, for example, in the two ways of understanding the phrase 'the tribe of Judah'. In almost all cases, these kinds of phrases are interpreted here as territorial references, and this for two reasons. First, it is nearly always possible to identify a matching geographic region in the maps supplied in the LCL edition of Strabo's *Geography*. Second, these local contexts almost never give other indications of an interest in the lineage or descent of the group in question. In the following examples, only the last citation is a case in which the context indicates a dual interest in lineage and territory:

> The Aetolians Homer always speaks of under one name, classing cities not **tribes** under them. (Strabo, *Geogr.* 9.4.18)

> Now the Greeks used to suppose that the Getae were Thracians; and the Getae lived on either side of the Ister, as did also the Mysi, these also being Thracians and identical with the people who are now called the Moesi ... And the Phrygians themselves are Brigans, a Thracian **tribe**, as are also the Mygdonians, the Bebricians. (Strabo, *Geogr.* 7.3.2; see also 8.3.17; 9.4.18)

> Now as for the Epeirotes, there are 14 **tribes** of them, according to Theopompos, but of these the Chaones and the Molossi are the most famous, because of the fact that they once ruled over the whole of the Epeirote country – the Chaones earlier and later the Molossi; and the

---

live ... And the greatest generals are those able to rule land and sea and to unite nations and cities under one authority and political administration. It is clear, therefore, that all geography is derived from the actions of commanders'. In γένος passages, this same geographic emphasis also appears in Josephus: '[Lysimacus] says "The people of the Judeans (Ἰουδαίων)." What kind of people? Foreigners or a race native to a country (τὸ γένος ἐγχώριος)? Why does he call them Judeans (Ἰουδαῖος) if they are Egyptians (Αἰγυπτίους)?' (*Ag. Ap.* 1.314). Similarly, Cohen argues for a geographic interpretation of Ἰουδαῖος in the use of the phrase τὸ γένος Ἰουδαῖος in Josephus, but calls this terminology 'antiquated' as if the usage were uncommon in the era, whereas this study reveals a widespread use of this geographic emphasis in the period (Shaye Cohen, ' " Ἰουδαῖος τὸ γένος" and Related Expressions in Josephus', in Fausto Parente and Joseph Sievers (eds), *Josephus and the History of the Greco-Roman Period: Essays in Memory of Morton Smith* [Leiden and New York: E.J. Brill, 1994], pp. 23–38 [37–38]). Nevertheless, there are important considerations in translating Ἰουδαῖος. Caroline Johnson Hodge (*If Sons then Heirs*, pp. 11–15) notes that (1) the translation should preserve the continuity between the ancient and modern Jewish people; (2) the translation should not 'reinforce the assumption that religious commitments are separate from particularities of identity such as homeland' (p. 12); and (3) the translation should be multivalent, incorporating ancestral, cultural, religious, and/or territorial notions. Hodge finally opts to leave the word untranslated, while herein Ἰουδαῖος are 'Jews' who define themselves in terms of religious, ancestral, social, and territorial particularities.

Molossi grew to still greater power, partly because of the kinship of their kings, who belonged to the family of the Aecidae [offspring of Zeus and Aegina, judge of Hades], and partly because of the fact that the oracle at Dodona was in their country, an oracle both ancient and renowned. (Strabo, *Geogr*. 7.7.5)

The following passages reveal two other common motifs: the tendency to associate the character of a people with the kind of territory inhabited by it and the importance of autochthony, that is, native territorial origin. Both of these motifs point to the salience of land and territory in ancient group identity:

The Romans, too, took over many **nations** (ἔθνη) that were naturally savage owing to the regions they inhabited, because those regions were either rocky or without harbours or cold or for some other reason ill-suited to habitation by many, and thus not only brought into communication with each other peoples who had been isolated, but also taught the more savage how to live under forms of government. But all of Europe that is level and has a temperate climate has nature to cooperate with her toward these results; for while in a country that is blessed by nature everything tends to peace, in a disagreeable country everything tends to make men warlike and courageous; and so both kinds (γένη) of country receive benefits from each other, for the latter helps with arms, the former with products of soil. (Strabo, *Geogr*. 2.5.26)

And it is said that many **peoples** (ἔθνη) of all kinds dwell in the whole of India, which is immensely large, and none of these have an original foreign creation, but all seem to be autochthonous. (Diodorus, *Bibl. hist*. 2.38.1, LLS; see also 3.2.1)[41]

Land and territory are also important components of identity in Jewish literature. The OT has, after Strabo, the second highest incidence of territorial associations with ἔθνος. The Zechariah passage below demonstrates that the land sometimes stands for the people of Israel by metonymy:

From these [ancestors], [the inhabitants of] the islands of the **Gentiles** were divided by their land, each according to his tongue, by their tribes and by their **nations**. (Gen. 10.5, LLS)

And I said, What are these coming to do? And he said, These are the horns that scattered Judah, and they broke Israel in pieces, and none of them lifted up his head: and these are come forth to sharpen them for their hands, *even* the four horns, the **nations** that lifted up the horn against the land of the Lord to scatter it. (Zech. 1.21, NRSV)

---

41   For additional insight into these motifs, see Isaac, *The Invention of Racism*, p. 135.

The following passage from Philo may point to self-consciousness in Jewish Diaspora communities with reference to their distance from the traditional Jewish homeland. Here Philo denies the culpability of Diaspora Jews who are unable to attend the Passover celebration in Judea:

> For settlers abroad and those dwelling in other regions are not wrong-doers like they were lacking equal honor, even as there is no room for these people because the **nation** is so populous that one region cannot contain it, but it has sent out colonies in all directions. (Philo, *Moses* 2.232)

4. *Government*[42]

As illustrated by the passages below, this category captures ἔθνος occurrences in proximity to references to organized polities, political philosophies (democracy or monarchy), and the civic functions of government (e.g., paying/receiving of tribute, administration of provinces). The last passage in the group below begins to hint at the close relationship between military conflict, polity, and ethnic identity that has been suggested by Smith:[43]

> For all the **nations** around us are governed by aristocracies and in no state do the plebeians lay claim to an equal share in the government. (Dionysius, *Ant. rom.* 6.62.4, LLS)

> And so it comes to pass, as I have said before, that the boundaries and the political organizations of **nations** and places are always undergoing changes (Strabo, *Geogr.* 9.5.8).[44]

> For what is more fraught with confusion than want of government? ... Do not countries and **nations** and regions of the earth lose their old abundant happiness when their governments are dissolved? (Philo, *Dreams* 2.286-87)

> Now Paulus, who captured Perseus, annexed the Epeirotic **tribes** to Macedonia, divided the country into 4 parts for purposes of administration, and apportioned one part to Amphipolis, another to Thessaloniceia, another to Pella, another to the Pelagonians. (Strabo, *Geogr.* Book 7 fragments no. 48)

---

42   The Government category in γένος passages: the kinds of government references in γένος passages are essentially the same as in ἔθνος passages: 1 Macc. 3.32; Josephus, *J.A.* 13.212; Philo, *Spec. Laws* 2.95. Dionysius exemplifies the ancient preference for pure, unmixed races: *Ant. rom.* 3.10.4; see also Philo, *Names* 117.

43   Smith, *The Ethnic Revival*, pp. 74–75.

44   See Strabo, *Geogr.* 9.5.8, Jones (LCL), p. 411 n. 1. See also 9.5.4; cf. 3.4.19; 4.1.1; 8.3.10.

In addition, this category includes references to treaties made with other groups, conciliar decisions/activities, citizenship, and so on. As such, these kinds of contexts can suggest something about the power dynamics that operate between different social groups as in Mk 10.33//Mt. 20.18//Lk. 18.32 and Jn 18.35. This category also refers to contexts in which leadership or ideas of authority or rule are prominent. Passages of this type can reveal evidence of social conflict and power imbalances between groups as a feature of ethnicity:

> Consequently, for much of the time of what is remembered of the reign of the kings, they kept an orderly government and continued to have a most happy life, as long as the aforementioned system of laws remained. And with reference to this, they conquered more **nations** (ἐθνῶν ... πλείστων ἐπεκράτησαν) and had greater wealth than anyone else and adorned their lands with monuments and buildings. (Diodorus, *Bibl. hist.* 1.71.5, LLS)

> The poet [Homer] ... intimates a fact which is common to and true of all **countries**, that whole regions and their several parts undergo changes in proportion to the power of those who hold sway. (Strabo, *Geogr.* 9.5.4; see also 7.3.11)

5. *Customs, Lifestyle, and Laws*[45]

The Customs, Lifestyle, and Laws category appears in only 11 percent of the ἔθνος texts and includes passages in which manner of life or culture of the people distinguishes one group from another. Although this category occurs with a relatively low level of frequency, customs and laws do help differentiate groups. In the first passage below, Philo's claim about the wide appeal of the Jewish law is a familiar theme in his writings and in other Jewish apologetic literature.[46] However, his comment about the near-universal distaste for the laws of others suggests that laws and customs were common points by which groups distinguished themselves. The passage from Diodorus below reports a custom that he, and presumably his audience, found strange; such reports were common

---

45 The Customs, Lifestyle, and Laws category in γένος passages: Customs, etc. are even more infrequent in γένος passages than in ἔθνος passages and are thus an unimportant feature of race as defined by the ancients: Dionysius, *Ant. rom.* 1.30.1–2; Josephus, *J.A.* 12.261; *J.W.* 5.461. Sometimes seen in connection with ancestral traditions and marriage: Gal. 1.14; *3 Macc.* 1.3; Diodorus, *Bibl. hist.* 17.110.4; 5.21.5; Strabo, *Geogr.* 15.1.49; Gen. 34.15-16; Lev. 20.18.

46 In Josephus, this motif about the appeal of Jewish law surfaces in comments about the nobility of a willingness to die for the law (*Ag. Ap.* 1.209-212). Philo boasts that 'everyone' was 'afraid' of the Jews, of harming them or their institutions, because of the wide protection of their rights (*Embassy* 159). See also Philo, *Hypothetica* 6.9; and Wis. 6.17-21.

themes in the 'outsider' perspectives of the non-Jewish Greek literature of Strabo, Plutarch, and Dionysius.[47]

> We may fairly say that mankind from east to west, every country and **nation** and state (χώρα καὶ ἔθνος καὶ πόλις), show aversion to foreign institutions, and think that they will enhance the respect of their own by showing disrespect for those of other countries. It is not so of ours. They attract and win the attention of all, of barbarians, of Greeks, of dwellers on the mainland and islands, of **nations** of the east and the west, of Europe and Asia, of the whole inhabited world from end to end. (Philo, *Moses* 2.19-20; see also 2.17)

> It is a peculiarity of the whole Scythian and Sarmatian **race** (ἔθνους) that they castrate their horses to make them easy to manage; for although the horses are small, they are exceedingly quick and hard to manage. (Diodorus, *Bibl. hist.* 7.4.8; see also 2.45.1-5; 34/35.1.3)

In the next passage, Strabo comes close to the idea that identity is socially constructed in that this passage seems to reject the logic of environmental determinism, logic that would play a key role in the US slave debates of the eighteenth and nineteenth centuries. The passage is particularly interesting in that it indirectly suggests the currency of the ideas that Strabo disputes, namely, that environmental climate determines a people's characteristics:

> For such a distribution of animals, plants, and climates as exists is not the result of design – just as the differences of **race** (ἔθνη), or of language, are not, either – but rather of accident and chance. And again, as regards the various arts and faculties and institutions of mankind, most of them, when once men have made a beginning, flourish in any latitude whatsoever and in certain instances even in spite of the latitude; so that some local characteristics of a people come by nature, others by training and habit. For instance, it was not by nature that the Athenians were fond of letters, whereas the Lacedaemonians ... were not so; but rather by habit. So also the Babylonians and the Egyptians are philosophers, not by nature, but by training and habit. And further, the excellent qualities of horses, cattle, and other animals, are the result, not merely of locality, but of training also. But Poseidonius confounds all this. And when he approves of such a division into three continents as is now accepted, he uses as an illustration the fact that the Indians differ from the Ethiopians of Libya, for the Indians are better developed physically and less parched by the dryness of the atmosphere.[48] (Strabo, *Geogr.* 2.3.7)

---

47   Josephus' lopsided description of the Essenes in *Jewish War* also displays tendencies in this direction (cf. *J.A.* 18.18-22; *J.W.* 2.119-161).

48   It is interesting to note that Jones translates ἔθνη as 'race' instead of 'nation' in the LCL edition of the Strabo passage above. Is it possible that Jones made this choice because

Marriage customs form a common theme in this category, as illustrated by the following texts. The passage from Dionysius about a senatorial decree resolves difficulties arising from 'mixed marriages' in a concern related to the ancient preference for ethnic purity.[49] On this point, we should also note that the ethnic identifiers of the parties persist after the marriage.

> They ratified an equitable decree of the senate, that if any woman of the Roman **nation** (ἔθνους; translated as 'race' by Cary in LCL) lived in wedlock with a Latin man or a Latin woman with a Roman man, they would decide for themselves whether they wanted to remain with their husbands or to return to their homeland. (Dionysius, *Ant. rom.* 6.1.2, LLS)

> [He was] mad with passion for women and the intemperance of sexual intercourse, not satisfied with those from the countryside but with many wives from foreign **nations**, transgressing the law of Moses ... (Josephus, *J.A.* 8.191, LLS)

The passage from Josephus above not only illustrates the linkage of ἔθνος with marriage customs, but also the difficulty in distinguishing customs and laws from religious practices, particularly in the case of literature by Jews or about Jewish customs. Thus, the Customs, Lifestyle, and Laws category often overlaps with the Religion grouping, especially in Jewish literature, but remains a separate classification since this kind of overlap is rare in non-Jewish literature.

> 'Do not live according the customs of the **nations** which I drive out from before you; for they have done all these things, and I have abhorred them'. And I said to you, 'You shall inherit their land, and I will give it to you as a possession, a land flowing with milk and honey. I am the Lord your God, who have separated you from all the **nations**'. (Lev. 20.23-24, LLS)

It is also clear from the passage above that the difference between Israel and other peoples with reference to customs occurs in conjunction with religious ideas. Jewish religious customs and laws were distinctive among ancient peoples in that they extended to every aspect of life, including sex, birth and death rites, clothes, food, farming, labor, military, crime and punishment, social welfare, foreign policy, government, finance, and trade. In context, the following ἔθνος passages show the extent of these laws, as well as their basis in religious ideals:

---

he too heard echoes of modern racial polemic in this ancient text? On another note, Isaac points out that Strabo is unusual in his opposition to the idea that environment determines character, in this passage and elsewhere, e.g., *Geogr.* 14.2.16, where Strabo objects to the idea that drinking from a certain fountain can make a male 'effeminate' (μαλακίζουσα τοὺς πιόντας ἀπ᾽ αὐτῆς; *The Invention of Racism*, pp. 91, 135).

49   See Isaac, *The Invention of Racism*, pp. 109–14.

Six years you will sow your land, and gather its harvest; but in the seventh year, you will let it rest, and leave it, and the poor of your **nation** will eat it ... Six days you will work, and on the seventh day there is rest, so that your ox and your donkey may rest, and that the son of your maidservant and the proselyte may be refreshed. Keep all the things whatsoever I have commanded you; and make no remembrance of other gods ... For when I drive out the **nations** from your presence and widen your territory, you will not offer the blood of my sacrifice with leaven. (Exod. 23.10-18, LLS)

You will not walk deceitfully among your **people** (ἐν τῷ ἔθνει σου); you will not rise up against the blood of your neighbor: I am the Lord your God. (Lev. 19.16, LLS)

Whoever has sex with his relative has revealed the shame of the nakedness of a relative; they will die childless ... In addition, do not walk in the customs of the **nations** that I drive out from before you, for they have done all these things, and I have abhorred them ... Make a distinction between clean and unclean birds and do not defile your souls with cattle, or with birds, or with any creeping things of the earth ... because I the Lord your God am holy, who separated you from all **nations** to be mine. (Lev. 20.20-26, LLS)

The Lord spoke to Moses, saying, 'speak to the priests the sons of Aaron, and thou shalt tell them that they shall not defile themselves in their **nation** for the dead.' (Lev. 21.1)

And I said to them, We of our free-will have redeemed our Jewish brothers who were sold to the **Gentiles**; and did you sell your brothers? ... What you are doing is not good: Do not in this way walk in the fear of our God because of the reproach of the **Gentiles** our enemies. Both my brethren, and my acquaintances, and I, have lent them money and corn: let us now leave off this exaction. (Neh. 5.8-10)

Not surprisingly, the Customs, Lifestyle, and Laws category also appears in texts alongside the Government classification. Religious overtones accompany customs and laws even where these occur in conjunction with the more 'secular' context of government, as shown in these two texts:

And there would arise from their number a certain king who would make war on the Jewish **nation** and their laws, deprive them of the form of government based on these laws, spoil the temple and prevent the sacrifices from being offered for three years. (Josephus, *J.A.* 10.275)

Jason changed the **nation's** way of life and altered its form of government in complete violation of the law so that not only was a gymnasium constructed at the very citadel of our native land, but also the temple service was abolished. (*4 Macc.* 4.19-20)

6. *Religion*[50]

The word 'religion' has had as tortured a history in the West as the words 'ethnicity' and 'race'.[51] A survey of modern dictionaries of religion provides much information on problems in theorizing religion but little in the way of an actual definition.[52] Indeed, one prominent scholar in the field abandons the attempt at definition in light of this variety and all but embraces the chaos: 'Religion ... is a term created by scholars for their intellectual purposes and therefore is theirs to define'.[53] With this in mind, herein I pursue an 'operational' framework for religion by focusing on its phenomenology, an approach that suits my interest in historical comparisons.[54] Building on Wilfred Cantwell Smith's category of 'cumulative traditions' for purposes of examining the discourse in Greek documents in our period of interest in this section, I use the word 'religion' as a category for the cultural expression of human piety.[55] Thus, this

---

50   The Religion category in γένος passages: among the non-Jewish authors: Dionysius, *Ant. rom.* 2.65.2; Diodorus, *Bibl. hist.* 5.5.1; Plutarch, *Sera* 58A. For Jews, religion is as important for race as it is for ethnicity: Judg. 8.20; Jer. 38.1; 1 Pet. 2.9; Philo, *Migration* 63; idem, *Embassy* 3; Josephus, *J.A.* 3.313.

51   See Wilfred Cantwell Smith's description of the historical evolution of the word 'religion', from early ancient references to rites, practices, and piety through to the reified Enlightenment association with bodies of doctrine and bounded communities (*The Meaning and End of Religion*, pp. 19–79). Also see James Thrower, who proceeds in terms of what he sees as a fundamental division between those who discuss religion as a response to the transcendent Other and those who explain religion as a human construct (*Religion: The Classical Theories* [Washington, DC: Georgetown University Press, 1999]). One very interesting attempt to bridge this divide appears in the critically acclaimed work of Roy Rappaport, *Ritual and Religion in the Making of Humanity* (Cambridge: Cambridge University Press, 1999). Rappaport sees in the phenomenon of ritual the center of religion and the means by which humans establish and convey social meaning and convention.

52   The *Continuum Dictionary of Religion* (ed. Michael Pye [New York: Continuum, 1994], s.v. 'religion') eschews essentialist conceptions, defining religion as a system of belief and ritual with 'subjective depth and social extension', noting that adherents will prefer definitions that reflect their faith experience but will inevitably do so in terms that will conflict with the truth claims from other religions. *The New Dictionary of Religions* (ed. John R. Hinnells [Oxford: Blackwell, rev. edn, 1995], s.v. 'Religion') says that religion encompasses everything concerning beliefs in gods and goddesses or other transcendent 'ultimate concerns', but the *HarperCollins Dictionary of Religion* (ed. Jonathon Z. Smith [New York: HarperCollins, 1995]) adds that definitions of religion in terms of 'ultimate concern' or 'worldview' are too broad and admit too much to the category.

53   Jonathon Z. Smith, 'Religion, Religions, Religious', in Mark C. Taylor (ed.), *Critical Terms for Religious Studies* (Chicago and London: University of Chicago Press, 1998), p. 281.

54   Jan Platvoet discusses how 'operational' definitions of religion can act as provisional frameworks for scholars interested in investigating the historical particularities of given manifestations of religion ('The Definers Defined', *Method and Theory in the Study of Religion* 2 [Fall 1990]: 180–212).

55   For more on Smith's 'cumulative traditions' see p. 4 n. 4 above.

category includes passages that contain references to a deity, or to artifacts, practices, language, states of consciousness, or persons associated with religious cults (e.g., priests, temples, sacrifices, prayers, worship, faith, etc.).

This category is the most prominent one in both the New Testament and Jewish literature and practically vanishes as a classification in non-Jewish literature.[56] Below, Dionysius speaks of Rome's tolerance for religious plurality – a limited tolerance that endured as long as the Roman people themselves remained untainted by foreign practices. We should also notice that Dionysius assumes that devotion to one's ancestral religion is normative. The second passage from Strabo reflects the Greco-Roman fascination with 'strange' religious practices that often appears in texts in this category.

> But alike in all [the Romans'] words and actions with reference to the gods a reverence is shown such as is seen among neither Greeks nor barbarians. And ... notwithstanding the influx into Rome of innumerable **nations** which are under every necessity of worshipping their ancestral gods according to the customs of their respective countries, yet the city has never officially adopted any of those foreign practices. (Dionysius, *Ant. rom.* 2.19.2)

> So then the suspicion that the wifeless men of the Getae are in a special way reverential (εὐσεβεῖς) towards the gods is clearly contrary to reason, whereas the interpretation that zeal for religion is strong in this **tribe** (ἔθνει), and that because of their reverence for the gods the people abstain from eating any living thing, is one which, both from what Poseidonius and from what the histories in general tell us, should not be disbelieved. (Strabo, *Geogr.* 7.3.4; see also 4.3.2)

Seventy percent of the total ἔθνος passages in this category occur in Jewish literature and the New Testament. These occurrences mainly fall into the well-known translation of ἔθνος to name 'Gentiles', that is, non-Jewish peoples, or 'pagan', to name non-Christian peoples. Because we now classify Christianity as a religious group, the word 'pagan' comes to identify those defined by means of their religious associations. Our observation that ἔθνος overwhelmingly appears in religious contexts suggests that the 'Gentile' terminology also represents identification by means of religious association. In other words, 'Gentile' is a religiously loaded term in Jewish and Christian literature.

In fact, religion may be even more conspicuous in Jewish literature than is explicitly revealed in this analysis. Although religion is the most prominent category in the Jewish and Christian literature, I probably undercount the passages in this grouping, since the method used here

---

56 See Figures A.1 and A.2 in the appendix.

assigns category tags to passages only where there was an explicit reference to a material or cultural expression of religious piety.[57] Indeed, given the overall religious tone of these works, one might argue that the religious category is implicit in almost all of the ἔθνος and γένος passages in these works. In other words, the category in Jewish and Christian literature presents a situation similar to that seen in the Land and Territory category in Strabo. In both cases, one could maintain that the applicable categories saturate the works in question to the point that nearly all of the passages in these works implicitly reflect a concern with the applicable issue. Yet, here, as was true of the Land and Territory classification in Strabo, we find that even when using a more conservative methodology that likely undercounts religious references, religion emerges as a key component in Jewish ethnic identity (see Appendix, Figures A.1 and A.2). The following passage from Philo relates kinship to ἔθνος, but it is not too difficult to see that religion is the true criterion of membership given Philo's reference to the 'highest kinship' based on God's law:

> For he assumed with good reason that one who was their fellow-tribesman and fellow-kinsman, related to them by the tie which brings the highest kinship, the kinship of having one citizenship, and the same law, and one God who has taken all members of the **nation** for His portion, would never sin in the way just mentioned [that is by greed and injustice to the poor]. (Philo, *Spec. Laws* 4.59)

Similarly, in Book 15 of the *Jewish Antiquities*, Josephus describes the centrality of Jewish religion by observing that whoever controls the Jerusalem temple has 'the whole nation in his power', inasmuch as control of the temple cult means control of Jewish worship (Josephus, *J.A.* 15.248). Elsewhere, as shown below, he preserves an edict from Claudius that sets Jewish ancestral culture (τὰ πάτρια ἔθη) roughly parallel to religious beliefs (τὰς ... δεισιδαιμονίας; see also *J.A.* 19.280-285; and cf. Gal. 2.14-16). Since a similar earlier edict from Claudius in *J.A.* 19.280-285 echoes portions of Claudius' *Letter to the Alexandrians*, we have evidence that suggests that Josephus has captured the edict reliably.[58] With this in mind, it is possible that Josephus' version of the edict represents either Claudius' own views on the religious nature of a people's ancestral customs, or widespread opinion about the basis of Jewish customs. On either interpretation, however, Josephus' inclusion of these decrees without further comment attests a basic level of assent with the ideas they present.

---

57   This underestimation of religious passages applies equally to the γένος analysis.
58   *CPJ* 2.36-55; Mary Smallwood, *The Jews under Roman Rule* (Leiden: Brill, 1981), pp. 246 nn. 101, 102; cf. p. 229 n. 38.

It is right therefore, that the Jews throughout the whole world under our
sway should also observe the customs (τὰ πάτρια ἔθη) of their fathers
... I enjoin upon them also by these presents to avail themselves of this
kindness in a more reasonable spirit, and not to set at naught the beliefs
about the gods held by other **peoples** (τὰς τῶν ἄλλων ἐθνῶν
δεισιδαιμονίας). (Josephus, *J.A.* 19.290)

The religion category also includes passages containing religious speech,
such as praise, judgment, or blessing. The 1 Timothy passage below
contains part of an early Christian doxology, while the Galatians passage
represents an exposition of a religious principle:

Without any doubt, the mystery of our religion is great: He was revealed
in flesh, vindicated in spirit, seen by angels, proclaimed among **Gentiles**,
believed in throughout the world, taken up in glory. (1 Tim. 3.16)

But when I saw that they were not acting consistently with the truth of
the gospel, I said to Cephas before them all, 'If you, though a Jew, live
like a **Gentile** and not like a Jew, how can you compel the **Gentiles** to
live like Jews?' We ourselves are Jews by birth and not **Gentile** sinners;
yet we know that a person is justified not by the works of the law but
through faith in Jesus Christ. And we have come to believe in Christ
Jesus, so that we might be justified by faith in Christ, and not by doing
the works of the law, because no one will be justified by the works of the
law. (Gal. 2.14-16)

Religious language often appears in combination with military language
in Jewish literature, as shown in the following passages. God vents his
wrath on a given people via their military defeat by a nation that acts as
his agent.

O God ... your hand utterly destroyed the nations, and you buried them;
you afflicted the **nations**, and cast them out. For they did not inherit the
land by their sword, and their own arm did not deliver them, but your
right hand, and your arm, and the light of your countenance delivered
them, because you were well pleased by them. (Ps. 43.2-3, LLS)

Therefore I delivered him into the hands of the prince of the **nations**,
and he wrought his destruction. (Ezek. 31.11)

A voice of many **nations** on the mountains, like many **nations**; a voice of
kings and **nations** gathered together: the Lord of hosts has given
command to a war-like **nation** ... to come from a land from afar, from
the utmost foundation of heaven; the Lord and his warriors are coming
to destroy the whole world. (Isa. 13.3-5, LLS)

'I will bring upon you a **nation** from far, O house of Israel', says the
Lord, 'a **nation** the sound of whose language you shall not understand
... and they shall devour your harvest, and your bread and your sons,
and your daughters; and they shall devour your vineyards, and your fig-

plantations, and your olive yards; and they shall utterly destroy with the sword your strong cities, in which you trusted'. (Jer. 5.15-17, LLS)

The last set of passages included in this survey of the religious associations with ἔθνος comes from Philo's portrait of the Jewish nation as priests and mediators for all humanity. According to Philo, Jews offer sacrifices and the worship that is due to God on behalf of those who fail to recognize God:

> [God gave Moses a] kingship of a nation more populous and mightier (πολυανθρωποτέρου καὶ κρείττονος ἔθνους), a **nation** destined to be consecrated above all others to offer prayers for ever on behalf of the human race (τοῦ γένους τῶν ἀνθρώπων) that it may be delivered from evil and participate in what is good. (Philo, *Moses* 1.149)

> The reason of this is that the Jewish **nation** is to the whole inhabited world what the priest is to the state. For the holy office in very truth belongs to the nation because it carries out all the rites of purification and both in body and soul obeys the injunctions of the divine laws ... Now if He exists whom all Greeks and barbarians unanimously acknowledge, the supreme Father of gods and men and the Maker of the whole universe ... then it was the duty of all men to cleave to Him and not introduce new gods staged as by machinery to receive the same honors ... And therefore it astonishes me to see that some people venture to accuse of inhumanity the **nation** which has shown so profound a sense of fellowship and goodwill to all men everywhere, by using its prayers and festivals and first-fruit offerings as a means of supplication for the human race in general and of making its homage to the truly existent God in the name of those who have evaded the service which it was their duty to give, as well as of itself. (Philo, *Spec. Laws* 2.163, 165, 166-67; see also *Rewards*, 114)

7. Group Name[59]

This investigation did not confirm Anthony Smith's comments that a group name is an important expression of an ethnic group's self-awareness. Instead, I found that concern for a group name was generally rare in both ἔθνος and γένος passages across almost all of the authors examined, though it was most concentrated in Strabo. Passages in this category include cases in which the author is concerned to name correctly the people-group under discussion. The prevalence in Strabo flows from the nature of Strabo's work, since a primary concern in his *Geography* is the correct association of peoples with territory:

---

59   The Name category in γένος passages: the association of group name with γένος is infinitesimally small, nowhere among the Jewish and Christian writers and only occasionally in the non-Jewish sources as in Strabo (*Geogr.* 5.1.10).

These writers, however, on account of the continual migrations, changes of political administrations, and intermixtures of **tribes** seem to have confused both the names and the **tribes**, so that they sometimes present difficult questions for the writers of today. (*Geogr.* 9.5.21)

He does not say with reference to the Lydians or the Meïones whether they are two peoples or are the same, and whether they live by themselves or are included in another race (γένος). For thus would a distinctive **nation** (ἔθνος) be able to be hidden.[60] (*Geogr.* 14.5.24, LLS)

They say, 'Come, let us wipe them out as a **nation**; let the name of Israel be remembered no more'. (Ps. 82.5 LXX; also Gen. 25.16)

Very often, I also classify passages in this category as Founder category texts, since authors frequently assert that the name of a people-group comes from the founder of the group:

But Porcius Cato says that the Sabine **race** (Σαβίνων ἔθνει) received its name from Sabus, the son of Sancus, a divinity of that country, and that this Sancus was by some called Jupiter Fidius. (Dionysius, *Ant. rom.* 2.49.2)

But [Xanthus of Lydia] says that Lydus and Torebus were the sons of Atys; that they, having divided the kingdom they inherited from their father, both remained in Asia, and from them the **nations** over which they reigned received their names. His words are these: 'From Lydus are sprung the Lydians, and from Torebus the Torebians. There is little difference in their language and even now each **nation** scoffs at many words used by the other, even as do the Ionians and Dorians. (Dionysius, *Ant. rom.* 1.28.2)

The New Testament also shows a tendency towards deriving a name for followers of Jesus Christ from Jesus as the founder of the movement. In the first three passages below, the 'name' discussed in the passage is that of Jesus, and the text describes distinctive actions that the group performs to spread knowledge about Jesus and his legacy. The context of the first passage describes what disciples do or suffer because they identify with Jesus and what he represented, while the second passage describes actions that seek to create additional disciples who will identify with Jesus and what he represented. The last passage is not a γένος or ἔθνος passage but is included to contrast with the preceding Romans passage on the issue of 'name'. With other English versions, the NRSV in Rom. 1.6 suggests that the Gentiles (or nations) are 'called to belong to Jesus Christ' (κλητοὶ Ἰησοῦ Χριστοῦ), interpreting the genitive Ἰησοῦ Χριστοῦ as a genitive of possession. When interpreted this way, we can see that the Romans passage may be an early movement towards naming the group after the

---

60 See also *Geogr.* 1.2.34; 6.3.8; 7.3.12; Diodorus, *Bibl. hist.* 2.43.5.

possessor or founder of the group, a tendency that culminates in the naming narrated in Acts 11.26.

> Then they will hand you over to be tortured and will put you to death, and you will be hated by all **nations** because of my name. (Mt. 24.9 and parallels)

> Through whom we have received grace and apostleship to bring about the obedience of faith among all the **Gentiles** for the sake of his name, including yourselves who are called to belong to Jesus Christ; to all God's beloved in Rome, who are called to be saints: Grace to you and peace from God our Father and the Lord Jesus Christ. (Rom. 1.5-7)

> [Acts 11.26: So it was that for an entire year they met with the church and taught a great many people, and it was in Antioch that the disciples were first called 'Christians'.]

b. Γένος *in non-Jewish and Jewish Authors*
1. *People-Groups and Classes*[61]

The People-Groups and Classes category involves γένος phrases that designate people-groups of varying sizes who share one or more attributes. Examples of these groups include smaller sets such as plebeians, artisans, senators, and slaves, and larger sets such as races or nations. These usages are unified by the idea that γένος identifies groups organized around a common set of characteristics. We can begin by citing examples of γένος passages that refer to economic classes:

> ... four **classes** of men live in the region, one from which kings were appointed. (Strabo, *Geogr.* 11.3.6, LLS)

> For there would have been no middle way, mark you, either the whole multitude of commoners would have perished, or even the patrician **class** (τῶν πατρικίων ... γένος) would not have survived. (Dionysius, *Ant. rom.* 7.44.4; cf. 'commoners' in Plutarch, *Sera* 558C)

> Such in general terms, are the groups into which the body politic of the Indians is divided. Further, it is not lawful to marry someone from another **class** or to follow another calling or trade, for example that a soldier should become a farmer, or an artisan a philosopher. (Diodorus, *Bibl. hist.* 2.41.5, LLS)

As mentioned, the word is often used to describe types of artisans or professionals, as when Strabo refers to 'several kinds of Chaldean

---

61 The People-Groups and Classes category in ἔθνος passages: ἔθνος designates named and unnamed groups (e.g., Mt. 21.43; Dionysius, *Ant. rom.* 10.60.5) and non-Jewish 'Gentiles' (Josephus, *J.A.* 19.328; 3 *Macc.* 6.9). Less frequently, Jews use ἔθνος when referring to themselves: Josephus, *Ag. Ap.* 1.168; Philo, *Abraham* 98; see also Lk. 7.5.

A Former Jew

astronomers' (Strabo, *Geogr.* 16.11.6), Josephus describes a 'kind of ventriloquist' (Josephus, *J.A.* 6.330) and Diodorus describes historians as certain kinds of writers (Diodorus, *Bibl. hist.* 1.9.2). This class of usages also applies to religious sects, as when Josephus describes the Essenes and Zealots:

> The **sect** of the Essenes, however, declares that Fate is mistress of all things, and that nothing befalls men unless it be in accordance with her decree. (Josephus, *J.A.* 13.172; see also *J.W.* 1.63)

> ... in which the **sect** who were called the zealots flourished, who substantiate their name by their works. (Josephus, *J.W.* 7.268, LLS)

When γένος refers to large people-groups, the usage is virtually equivalent to a similar and common use of ἔθνος. Strabo uses γένος in conjunction with pastoral and nomadic peoples (Strabo, *Geogr.* 11.4.3), and Josephus frequently refers to the Jewish people as a γένος, most often as Judeans (Josephus, *J.A.* 9.211), but also as the race of Hebrews (Josephus, *J.A.* 2.216; 4.127, 201; 9.211; 10.183) and as Israelites (Josephus, *J.A.* 2.202). On occasion, translators render γένος as 'nation' and therefore assume its synonymity with ἔθνος. In some cases, one could wonder whether such translations emerge from a modern avoidance of a now problematic term, as especially in the case of a post-World War II avoidance of the phrase 'the Jewish race':

> On receiving this letter the Jews did not immediately hurry to make their departure, but they requested of the king that at their own hands those of the Jewish **nation** (τοὺς ἐκ τοῦ γένους τῶν Ἰουδαίων) who had willfully transgressed against the holy God and the law of God should receive the punishment they deserved. (*3 Macc.* 7.10)

> [Costobarus] thought that if Herod were deprived of the greater part of his power, it would be a simple matter for him to become ruler of the Idumaean **nation** (Ἰουδαίων γένους). (Josephus, *J.A.* 15.257)

> Indeed there are many races (φῦλα) of mankind among which the mother-cities do not rule over their colonies but are subject to them. The greatest and most conspicuous instance of this is the Spartan state, which claims the right not only to rule over the other Greeks, but even over the Doric **nation** (Δωρικοῦ γένους) of which she is a colony. (Dionysius, *Ant. rom.* 3.11.2; 1.28.1; Philo, *Names* 189)

As mentioned earlier, in cases where the words appear in proximity to each other, some scholars try to distinguish ἔθνος from γένος by maintaining that γένος connotes an emphasis on kinship while ἔθνος connotes an emphasis on culture or society. In other cases, however, it is difficult to discern the distinction in meaning between the two words when they appear in close proximity and parallel to each other. The following two passages illustrate this kind of difficulty:

> And I think I have, by the will of God, brought the Jewish nation (ἔθνος) to such a state of prosperity as it has never known before. Now as for the various buildings which we have erected in our country ... with which, as the most beautiful adornment, we have embellished our **nation** (γένος), it seems to me quite needless to speak of them to you. (Josephus, *J.A.* 15.384)

> But you are a chosen **race** (γένος ἐκλεκτόν), a royal priesthood, a holy nation (ἔθνος ἅγιον), God's own people, in order that you may proclaim the mighty acts of him who called you out of darkness into his marvelous light. (1 Pet. 2.9)

In the fragment from Josephus, Herod discusses his accomplishments on behalf of the people and describes the prosperity of the nation in terms of architectural and other material embellishments made on behalf of the 'race'. Given Herod's own Idumean descent, we cannot *definitively* conclude that the phrase 'our race' emphasizes a shared kinship with the audience.[62] The supposed distinction between ἔθνος and γένος is even more difficult to maintain in the second passage from 1 Peter, given the lack of kinship within the Christian community, as kinship is normally understood.

2. *Language*[63]

This classification captures those passages in which language defines groups or contributes to group distinctiveness. Analysis shows that language appears infrequently in discourses containing either γένος or ἔθνος, which implies that this feature does not figure prominently in ancient conceptions of identity. Nevertheless, one passage from Dionysius shows the similarity between ancient and modern identity concepts on this point (cf. the discussion of Herodotus, *Hist.* 8.144 above, pages 54–55). Dionysius sees language, customs, kinship, and territory as mutually defining group identity:

> I am persuaded, therefore, that these nations changed their name along with their lifestyle (βίων), but cannot believe that they both partake of a common **race** (κοινοῦ δὲ ἄμφω μετειληφέναι γένους), for this reason, among many others – because their languages are different and preserve not the least resemblance to each other ... For if kinship (τὸ συγγενὲς)

---

62 Cf. Josephus' reference to Herod as a 'half-Jew' (ἡμιιουδαῖος) in *J.A.* 14.403.

63 The Language category in ἔθνος passages: references to the ways that languages distinguish nations appear in ἔθνος passages with the same relatively low frequency level as in γένος passages: Dionysius, *Ant. rom.* 1.84.4; Dan. 3.4. See also Philo, *Tongues* 12; Diodorus, *Bibl. hist.* 11.17.2; cf. Josephus, *J.A.* 20.64.

is to be regarded as the reason why two nations speak the same language, the contrary must, of course, be the reason for their speaking a different one, since surely it is not possible to believe that both these conditions arise from the same cause. For, although it might conceivably happen, on the one hand, that men of the same nation (ὁμοεθνεῖς) who have settled at a distance from one another would, as a result of associating with their neighbors, no longer preserve the same fashion of speech (τὸν αὐτὸν τῆς διαλέκτου χαρακτῆρα), yet it is not at all reasonable that men sprung from the same **race** (ἐκ ταυτοῦ φύντας γένους) and living in the same country should not in the least have even one word of agreement with one another in their language. (Dionysius, *Ant. rom.* 1.29.2-4; Cary's translation in the LCL edition altered; cf. Dan. 3.7; Philo, *Confusion* 150)

On the other hand, the next example suggests that ancients were as cognizant as modern scholars are of the unreliability of language as an indicator of ethnicity:[64]

Then the fourth **race** in Crete ... commingled with mixed barbarians who, after a time, adopted the language of the Greeks of the countryside. (Diodorus, *Bibl. hist.* 5.80.2, LLS)

3. Kinship[65]

As maintained by several writers reviewed in Chapter 2, kinship is an extremely important category for defining race in the ancient world. The relative importance of kinship compared with other elements of race, however, varies by group context. Kinship is much more important among the non-Jewish Greek-speakers than among Jews, though Josephus seems to be a bridge figure between non-Jews and Jews, as we will see below.

There are three relatively distinct subcategories within the idea of kinship. Moving from the loosest kinship bond to the tightest, I call these three connections 'relationship', 'lineage', and 'family'. The relationship idea includes references to a looser degree of kinship among group members, that is, involving relationships outside of the immediate family

---

64 Fergus Millar's excellent social history of the Roman East represents an exception to the general reluctance of modern scholars to put much credence in language as an ethnic identifier. Language distinctions form an important part of Millar's partitioning of the geographic and political boundaries of peoples, though he is careful to avoid overinterpreting linguistic variation, especially among multilingual peoples. See Millar, *Roman Near East*, pp. 233–35, and especially the role of language in the discussion of Judea/Syria Palestine on pp. 337–86.

65 The Kinship category in ἔθνος passages: far less frequently than in association with γένος, a few ἔθνος passages communicate kinship as a characteristic of nations: Philo, *Spec. Laws* 3.131; Deut. 10.15; Dionysius, *Ant. rom.* 3.10.3; see also Josephus, *J.A.* 17.330.

or line of descent. In *Ant. rom.* 10.49.3, Dionysius uses γένος in the
context of 'filial devotion' (τὸ γένος εὐσεβές, lit. 'the piety with reference
to race'), and elsewhere he uses συγγενής and γένος synonymously when
contrasting the way in which the Curiatii and the Horatii esteem honor
and kinship (Dionysius, *Ant. rom.* 3.17.5; Plutarch, *Quaest. rom.* 289D;
Amat. narr. 772A; Tob. 2.3). Along these lines, γένος often appears in
phrases that mean 'next of kin':

> And let the damsel's defense be undertaken by her father or brother or
> whosoever, failing these, be considered her next of **kin** (τοῦ γένους).
> (Josephus, *J.A.* 4.247)

> The Derbices worship Mother Earth; and they do not sacrifice, or eat,
> anything that is female; and when men become over seventy years of age
> they are slaughtered, and their flesh is consumed by their nearest of **kin**
> (οἱ ἄγχιστα γένους). (Strabo, *Geogr.* 11.11.8)

The Lineage subcategory includes those occurrences of γένος that refer to
a particular physical line of descent or ancestry. By and large, lineage
refers to kinship groups that are larger than the family subcategory.

> Once among the Argives the **line** of Heracleidae (τὸ Ἡρακλειδῶν γένος)
> became extinct, from which it was their ancestral custom to select the
> Argive king. (Plutarch, *Alex. fort.* 340C, LLS)

> My brothers, you descendants of Abraham's **family** (υἱοὶ γένους
> Ἀβραάμ), and others who fear God, to us the message of this salvation
> has been sent. (Acts 13.26, NRSV)

> I will speak for her in order to give her to you as a wife, for her
> inheritance can come to you and you alone if you are from her **people** (ἐκ
> τοῦ γένους αὐτῆς) and you find the girl beautiful and sensible. (Tob.
> 6.12, LLS)

Passages in this subcategory sometimes refer implicitly or explicitly to the
idea of inheritance:

> A figurative reference, I think, to the virtue ... [that is by] **descent** –
> which permeates their natures. (Plutarch, *Praec. ger. rei publ.* 820 A,
> LLS)

> The kingly office ... ought to descend to the **natural heirs** (τοὺς κατὰ
> γένος) or the testamentary heirs (κατὰ διαθήκας; Dionysius, *Ant. rom.*
> 4.34.4).

In addition, folk ideas about race often appear in standard translations of
this class of usages. Note the way that translators use 'blood' for γένος in
the following passages:

> The brothers, though reckoned as half brothers **by blood** (τοῦ γένους),
> did not think it enough to give a half affection to each other, but

showed a twofold increase of tenderness. (Philo, *Virtues* 225, Colson
and Whitaker)

The spirits of those having a counterfeit and base nature have
engendered a **blood**, overthrown and humbled. (*Lib. ed.* 1C, Babbitt)[66]

The last subgroup, the Family subcategory, refers mostly to immediate
and extended families. Although the boundaries between this subgroup
and the other subgroups are sometimes blurred (see for example the
fourth text in the group below), the first three passages of the following set
make clear references to a concept similar to the modern notion of
'nuclear family'.

The **offspring** of Alexander (τὸ μὲν ᾿Αλεξάνρου γένος) abandoned the
service of the Judeans after they grew up in the country, ranging
themselves with the Greek tradition. (Josephus, *J.A.* 18.141, LLS)

But also told of her **family** (τὸ γένος), saying 'I am called Rebecca, and
my father was Bathuel ... and our brother Laban'. (Josephus, *J.A.*
1.248, LLS)

... children of adultery, not able to be assigned to either **family**...
(Philo, *Decalogue* 130, LLS)

He took refuge in Tarquinii, a Tyrrhenian city, from whence his **family**
on his mother's side had originally come. (Dionysius, *Ant. rom.* 5.3.2)

Other passages in this subgroup seem to have clans in view, which are
bigger family groups:

The ones who built the fortress and called it Baris were the kings and
high priests of the Hasmonean **family** (του ᾿Ασαμωναίων γένους) who
were before Herod. (Josephus, *J.A.* 15.403, LLS)

And all the conditions which would render it impossible to perpetuate
the **clan** combined together in the case of those 306 men – namely that
they left behind them no infant children, no wives with child, no
brothers still under age, no fathers in the prime of life. (Dionysius, *Ant.
rom.* 9.22.3, LLS)

They should sacrifice a maiden from the **house** of the Aepytide (ἐκ του
Αἰπυτιδῶν γένους), anyone at all; and if the one on whom the lot fell
could not be devoted to the gods, they should sacrifice whatever maiden
any father from the same **family** (ἐκ τοῦ αὐτοῦ γένους) might freely
offer. (Diodorus, *Bibl. hist.* 8.8.2)

The difference between family and lineage is one of scale; families are
smaller than groups demarcated by lineage. These three subcategories all

---

66   This work is erroneously attributed to Plutarch, but may have been written in the
same era as his authentic works.

potentially overlap, and the lineage and family subcategories are perhaps the hardest to distinguish from each other. For instance, the following passage from Strabo could be either in the lineage subcategory or in the family subgroup:

> The **descendants** (οἱ ἐκ τοῦ γένους) of the royal family not only reign as kings, but also hold other offices, in accordance with seniority of birth; and property is held in common by all kinsmen (τοῖς συγγενέσι), though the eldest is lord of all. One woman is also wife for all; and he who first enters the house before any other has intercourse with her. (Strabo, *Geogr.* 16.4.25; see also Diodorus, *Bibl. hist.* 2.46.3)

A final example from Plutarch shows how difficult is it to translate γένος once one has become sensitive to the evolution of the term 'race' in modernity:

> For as the warts, birthmarks, and moles of the fathers disappear in the children to reappear later in the children of sons and daughters ... and ... the **family** likeness (τὸ γένος ὁμοιότητος) reappearing and emerging after so many ages as if from the depths of the earth ... so too the first generations often conceal and submerge traits and passions of the soul, while later ... the family nature breaks out and restores the inherited bent for vice or virtue. (Plutarch, *Sera* 563B)

How should one translate τὸ γένος ὁμοιότητος? The sentiment here is that members of families share virtue and vice as inheritable characteristics that persist across many generations. The length of time implicit in the passage in combination with the idea of inheritable character would together suggest that a better translation for τὸ γένος ὁμοιότητος would be 'the racial likeness' in keeping with early modern connotations of race during the period of scientific racism. Although the mention of fathers, sons, and daughters supports the translation 'family likeness', the reference to generations makes it difficult to avoid the conclusion that this sentiment represents an ancient precursor to the racial typology and scientific racism of the seventeenth through nineteenth centuries.[67]

---

67 Plutarch does not express idiosyncratic ideas in the text above since other authors express similar sentiments (e.g., Strabo, *Geogr.* 1.1.34: 'From the kinship [γένος] of the peoples and their common characteristics ... the Armenians and that of the Syrians and Arabians betray a close affinity, not only in their language, but in their mode of life and in their bodily build [τὴν διάλεκτον καὶ τοὺς βίους καὶ τοὺς τῶν σωμάτων ξαρακτῆας].') In *The Invention of Racism*, Isaac cogently defends the proposition that ideas such as those contained in the Plutarch and Strabo passages mentioned here are ancient precursors of modern racism, ideas that are absorbed uncritically by the Enlightenment heirs of the classical tradition.

4. Humanity[68]

Texts in this sparse category include the use of γένος in phrases that refer to the human race: 'race of men', 'human race', 'mortal race', and so on. These phrases often appear in religious contexts, in contrasts between humanity and deity, or in passages that describe the relationship between humanity and deity:

> For who knows that but God, having a fatherly cure for the human **race** and foreseeing future events, removes some persons from life prematurely? (Plutarch, *Cons. Apoll.* 117 D, LLS)

> The universe is mixed, and that between the **race** of gods and that of mortals (τοῦ θείου καὶ θνητοῦ γένους) some third order of being exists which is that of demons. (Dionysius, *Ant. rom.* 1.77.3, LLS)

These kinds of phrases form an especially important category in Philo, and references to humanity are significant in the New Testament as well given the size of the corpus (see Appendix, Figures A.3 and A.4). With regard to Philo, scholars debate the extent of his universalism and the degree to which he directs his writings to Jewish insiders. As Philo's universalism bears on the question of how he understood Jewish identity, we note that γένος passages in Philo commend to all peoples the life of virtue lived in accordance with nature:

> It must needs be that mortal man (θνητόν) shall be oppressed by the nation of the passions and receive the calamities which are proper to created being, but it is God's will to lighten the evils which are inherent in our **race** (τοῦ γένος ἡμῶν). (Philo, *Who Is the Heir?* 272)

> And if, therefore, one gives thanksgiving for men (ἀνθρώπον), do so not only for the human **race** (γένους), but also give thanks for the species and most essential parts: for men, women, Greeks and barbarians, mainland dwellers and those on the islands. (Philo, *Spec. Laws* 1.211)

Yet, as the following passage indicates, Philo may not have thought that all humanity really would or could attain this kind of life:

> All who practice wisdom, either in Grecian or barbarian lands, and live a blameless and irreproachable life ... avoid the gathering of busybodies and abjure the scenes which they haunt ... They are the closest observers of nature and all it contains ... These are indeed but a small number left in their cities like an ember of wisdom to smolder that virtue may not be altogether extinguished from our **race**. (Philo, *Spec. Laws* 2.44-48)

---

68 The Humanity category in ἔθνος passages: all 40 New Testament references to humanity occur in ἔθνος passages (e.g., Mt. 24.14; 25.32-40). In contrast there are 13 passages in which ἔθνος refers to Jews (mainly in Luke-Acts as in Lk. 7.4-5) and 95 uses of the 'non-Jewish peoples' meaning, as in Mt. 6.32 (see also 1 Cor. 5.1; Rom. 3.24-30).

In other words, Philo's universalistic language could camouflage Jewish particularism or ethnocentrism if, in Philo's mind, the rare men in the various cities of this text are actually observant Jews. This conclusion finds support elsewhere in Philo when he maintains that the life of virtue is one that is lived in conformity with Nature, which for Philo is a life of conformity to the Jewish law:

> This is the aim extolled by the best philosophers, to live agreeably to nature; and it is attained whenever the mind, having entered on virtue's path, walks in the track of right reason and follows God, mindful of His injunctions, and always and in all places recognizing them all as valid both in action and in speech. (Philo, *Migration* 128; see also *Abraham*, 4–6)

Thus, the humanity category in Philo may be nothing more than an indicator of the kind of group solidarity that Anthony Smith identified as a hallmark of *ethnie*.

5. *Founder*[69]

Founder passages are those instances that contain some reference to the founder of the race or *ethnie*, whether referring to the founder of the human race (Philo, *Spec. Laws* 4.123) or to the founder of a division of humanity. The latter is by far the most frequent type of founder reference:

> Rhodians honor Helius as the founder of the **race** (ἀρχηγὸν τοῦ γένους). (Diodorus, *Bibl. hist.* 5.56.4, LLS)

> They tell a myth that the original founder of the **race** (γένους) was a certain hero who changed from a snake. (Strabo, *Geogr.* 13.1.14, LLS; cf. *Geogr.* 5.2.4)

> [God] commanded them to circumcise their foreskins, desiring that the **race** (γένος) sprung from him would remain with others not mixed together. (Josephus, *J.A.* 1.192, LLS)

This category does not constitute a significant association in the ideas surrounding ethnicity or race in the period.[70] It is interesting to note,

---

69   The Founder category in ἔθνος passages: references to the founder of the Jews are, counter-intuitively, much more common in association with ἔθνος than with γένος: Gen. 17.5; Sir. 44.19; Philo, *Moses* 1.242. In the New Testament the number of occurrences in ἔθνος passages could be as high as 41 as shown in Figure A.1 in the Appendix, or as low as 4 (i.e., Gal. 3.7, 8, 14; Rom. 4.17-18). The high number begs the question posed herein, in that Jesus may be construed as the founder of this newly formed people: Rom. 1.3-6; Gal. 2.15-16; Eph. 2.10-14; 3.6; Acts 9.15-17; 11.17-18. At this point in the discussion, I say that 'founder' texts support an ethno-racial construal of Christianity only if it is possible to see Christianity as a nascent race or ethnic group on other grounds.

70   Figures A.3 and A.4 in the Appendix depict the relative dearth of passages in this category.

however, that of all the categories described above, this category perhaps bears the closest relation to the idea of shared history, an element that is very important in Smith's model of ancient *ethnie* as described in Chapter 2, though it is of very low importance here. The low incidence of this motif possibly suggests that Smith has overemphasized the importance of shared history in his model.

3. *Non-Jewish and Jewish Perspectives on Race and Ethnicity*

There are two findings that help confirm that the usages and semantic ranges of ἔθνος and γένος that are documented in standard lexica apply for the period of interest. First, we find that authors used the words in two ways: either to refer to, describe, or classify groups, or to refer to humanity as a whole. Second, we find that ἔθνος and γένος have much in common and that the words often functioned as synonyms in antiquity.[71] Synonymous use of γένος and ἔθνος appears in Christian, Jewish, and non-Jewish sources, as the following passages illustrate.

> But you are a chosen **race** (γένος ἐκλεκτόν), a royal priesthood, a holy **nation** (ἔθνος ἅγιον), God's own people, in order that you may proclaim the mighty acts of him who called you out of darkness into his marvelous light. (1 Pet. 2.9)

> 'Though the sky should be lifted up to a greater height', says the Lord, 'and though the ground of the earth should be lowered beneath, yet I will not cast off the **race** of Israel', says the Lord, 'for all that they have done ... [but] if these laws cease from before me', says the Lord, 'then shall the **race** of Israel cease to be a **nation** before me forever'. (Jer. 38.35-37, LLS)

> Consequently, the neighboring barbarians, despising their weakness and remembering past injuries against them, waged continuous wars against this **nation** to such a degree that not even the name of the **race** of the Amazons was left. (Diodorus, *Bibl. hist.* 2.46.4)

Figure 3.1 depicts the most salient elements of ethnicity and race in relation to each other and consequently gives insight into the more important goal in this chapter, namely, determining the features

---

71 Similarities in the usages of ἔθνος and γένος emerge from a comparison of the categories depicted in Figures A.1 through A.4 in the appendix. Even though the graphs depict different curves, they share ten of the categories shown on the x-axis; only with reference to the 'Genus, Type, Summary' usage is there a category that appears on one chart but not in the other.

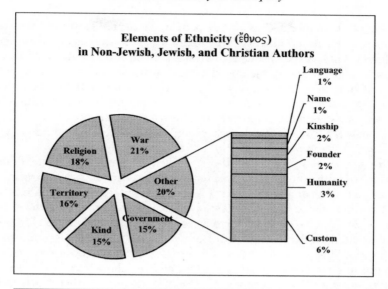

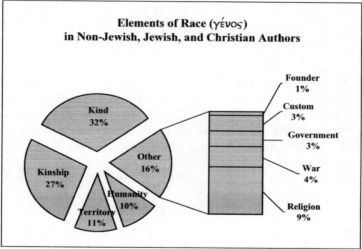

Figure 3.1 – Elements of Ethnicity and Race at the Turn of the Era

associated with ethnic and racial identity in the early Christian period.[72] Here the 'kind' group represents a consolidation of the people-groups and description categories, while the 'humanity' category represents occasions on which the words refer to all people, viewing humanity as either a collection of people-groups, as in the phrase 'all nations', or as members

---

72 For Figures 3.1 through 3.6, I omit frequencies of less than one percent from the diagrams (i.e., frequencies for name, language, and founder categories).

of the class of mortals, as in 'all people'. Interpreting these two usage groups in terms of identity, we might say that they each represent a different kind of consciousness at work in a text, in the first case a consciousness of group membership, and in the second case a consciousness of humanity or mortality. The figure shows that the latter plays a relatively insignificant role in constructions of ethnicity (3%), but that this consciousness is more important in constructions of race (10%). Group awareness (i.e., 'kind'), on the other hand, is important in both cases (15% in ἔθνος, 32% in γένος).[73]

We see that across all authors studied, the most prominent ideas associated with ethnicity are war, territory, government, religion, and to a lesser degree, customs. Likewise, Figure 3.1 shows that territory, religion, and kinship tended to be the most prominent associations with the idea of race aside from the group consciousness factor described above.[74] In other words, ethnicity had to do with how and with whom the group was in opposition, the group's religion, the territory the group occupied, the way the group governed or organized itself, and the characteristic qualities of the group (e.g., 'kind' in terms of class, profession, or other description). With regard to γένος, Figure 3.1 shows that race was overwhelmingly concerned with kinship and the group's characteristic distinctiveness (i.e., 'kind'). Ideas about territory, human consciousness, and religion appear about a third as frequently as these two largest categories.

In fact, instead of differentiating ἔθνος and γένος by custom and kinship as suggested earlier, where ethnicity emphasizes customs and race emphasizes kinship, we would do better to differentiate ethnicity and race by conflict and kinship respectively. This refinement brings us to our first major finding – that customs are not the *sine qua non* of ethnicity in antiquity, as some maintain and many others assume. In line with the general conclusions about ethnicity presented above, the author of the following text sees differences in customs as symptomatic of a *prior*

---

73   The critical importance of group consciousness in constructions of identity is a major theme in Walker Connor's work on national identity (*Ethnonationalism*, p. 197).

74   We also see that the ideas of group name, group language, and group founder are relatively unimportant for both ethnicity and race. As mentioned earlier, the findings about name and founder are in tension with Anthony Smith's model of ancient *ethnie*, while the ancient data about group language concurs with modern skepticism about the importance of language in forming group identity. On the issue of 'name', Smith sees group naming as indicative of group awareness, while our findings suggest that group awareness can exist independently of group naming, particularly in Jewish literature. On the other hand, this study does confirm Smith's emphasis on religion, but finds that religion is far more important in ancient group identity than in modern constructions; again this is particularly true in Jewish literature. It may be that religion plays the role that Smith attributes to shared history, in addition to being the basis of cultural distinctiveness as described in Smith's model.

conflict between peoples, as opposed to a view of customs as the *source* of difference or conflict between peoples:

> But the local cities ... are unlimited in number and subject to diverse polities and laws (πολιτεία ... νόμοις) by no means identical, for different peoples have different customs (ἔθη) and regulations which are extra inventions and additions. The cause of this is the reluctance to combine or have fellowship with each other, shown not only by Greeks to barbarians and barbarians to Greeks, but also within each of them separately in dealing with their own **kin** (τὸ ἑκατέρου γένους ἰδία πρὸς τὸ ὁμόφυλον). And then we find them alleging causes for this which are no real causes, such as unfavorable seasons, want of fertility (ἀγονίαν καρπῶν or 'sterile offspring'), poverty of soil or how the state is situated, whether it is maritime or inland or whether it is on an island or on the mainland and the like. The true cause they never mention, and that is their covetousness and mutual mistrusts, which keep them from being satisfied with the ordinances of nature, and lead them to give the name of laws to whatever approves itself as advantageous to the communities which hold the same views.[75]

The low incidence of the association between customs and ethnicity or customs and race suggests that the ancients did not see customs and laws as reliable indicators of group membership. Given the skepticism about customs reflected in the passage above, those who see customs as the heart of ancient Judaism may be surprised to learn that its author is Philo (*Joseph*, 29–31). Indeed, these and other concerns prompt separate analysis of the Jewish and non-Jewish data. As mentioned earlier, the non-Jewish authors were Greek-speakers writing about Romans and other peoples in order to inform non-Jewish Greek-speaking audiences in the Roman East, information required precisely because the eastern Greek-speakers had little or no contact with these outsiders. In contrast, identity passages from the Jewish literature are insider literature, written by Jews about Jewish concerns. This literature discusses outsiders only insofar as they are in relationship to the Jewish people, and provides an interpretation of outsider actions for the insiders who are in relationship with these outsiders.

a. *Non-Jewish Ethnic and Racial identity*

Figure 3.2 shows the relative frequencies of identity topics in γένος and ἔθνος passages from non-Jewish Greek-speaking authors only. The percentages shown in these figures do not represent hard and fast criteria

---

75 Note that this author reports that some groups refuse to intermarry with other peoples because the ensuing union would produce sterile offspring, another incidence of what Isaac calls ancient 'proto-racism', which was absorbed in later Enlightenment thought, with reference to black–white mixed-race offspring. See Banton, *Racial Theories*, pp. 56–58.

about the factors that constitute race and ethnicity; if identity functioned in antiquity in any way similar to modern dynamics, there will be some factors of identity that will be emphasized in certain situations and de-emphasized in other circumstances. Instead, this data is suggestive of the importance of the various components that influence identity in broad terms. Figure 3.2 shows that religion and customs fade in importance as an element of identity when we consider the Greek writers who are neither Jewish nor Christian. Instead, territory and conflict emerge as the weighty elements of ethnicity, and kinship becomes the overwhelming determiner of race, with territory and group consciousness more distant influences on ideas about race.[76] Intriguingly, the contours of ethnicity and race described in these figures closely approximate modern ideas of nation and race.[77] Ethnicity among these ancient non-Jewish Greek-speakers seems to have primarily involved conflict, territory, and matters of group structure in a way that anticipates the basic features of the modern nation. Similarly, the emphasis on kinship and territory in constructions of race would seem to lend itself to the kind of boundary rigidity and permanence that characterize popular racial understandings in the modern era. That these ancient concepts cohere so well with our Western concepts of identity says something about the triumph of the Greco-Roman legacy in identity formation today.

It is also interesting to note that with respect to both ethnicity and race, territory forms an important part of non-Jewish identity constructions. The salience of territory in the profiles of ethnicity and race suggests that territory may have been a criterion of identity for the non-Jewish authors, and that the other elements may have been peripheral to identity construction, possibly acting as indicia of identity. From one perspective, kinship may even be dependent on territory, given that it is possible to posit a relationship between territory and kinship. The realities of travel in the ancient world lent permanence to territorial constructions of identity that compounded the already 'fixed' kinship basis of race. Thus, normative endogamous marriage practices and geographic constraints on travel produced a high degree of kinship within confined territories.

---

76 Strabo's overarching concern with geography does not skew this conclusion regarding the weightiest influences on concepts of ethnicity. When Strabo is removed from the model, conflict and territory remain the two most prominent categories, though the relative contributions of conflict and territory are reversed. Removing Strabo causes the territory category to go from 33% to 23% and the war category to go from 31% to 40%. Other categories do not change significantly with the removal of Strabo from the model.

77 Most scholars agree that nations are based on the belief in common kinship, and this recognition prompted many nineteenth- and early twentieth-century writers to equate race with nation. On this point, Connor cites an old European joke that 'a nation is a group of people united by a common error about their ancestry and a common dislike of their neighbors' (*Ethnonationalism*, p. 114).

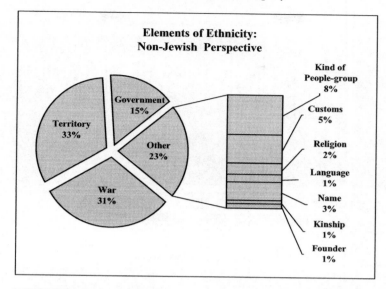

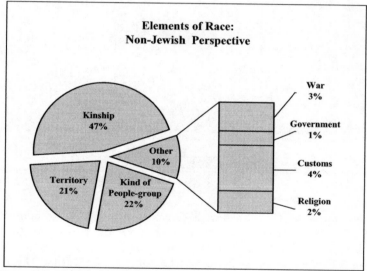

Figure 3.2 – Non-Jewish Elements of Ethnicity and Race at the Turn of the Era

Finally, we conclude this description of non-Jewish identity concepts with a brief consideration of the question about whether the non-Jewish authors investigated here represent a discrete ethnic identity or merely reflect more diffuse Hellenistic attitudes towards identity. Although the analysis of 'Greek' identity is not a major goal in this chapter, some of the results discussed above point towards the persistence of a common ethnic

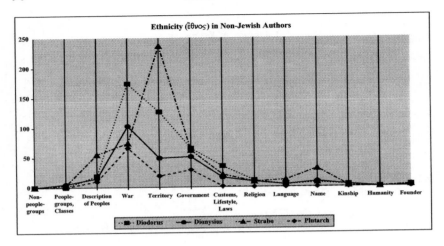

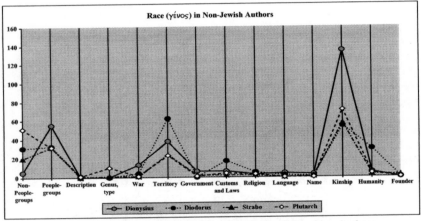

Figure 3.3 – Identity Profiles for Non-Jewish Greek-Speaking Authors

identity shared by the non-Jewish Greek-speaking authors considered, despite Jonathon Hall's contention that a Greek ethnic identity had dissipated long before the period considered here.[78] Far from demonstrating idiosyncratic tendencies on the subject of identity, Dionysius, Diodorus, Strabo, and Plutarch all exhibit a similar profile with respect to the prominence of ideas that were associated with race and ethnicity (Figure 3.3). So, although these findings alone cannot suffice to decide the matter, it is possible that the similarities among these turn-of-the-era non-Jewish Greek writers point to a persistence of Greek ethnic identity beyond the Hellenistic period. On the other hand, the observation that

78 Hall, *Hellenicity*, p. 189.

these writers lived in different locations points in the opposite direction, especially in view of the importance of territory in constructions of identity among the non-Jewish Greek-speakers. At the very least, we can say that the non-Jewish Greek-speakers shared common conceptions of and a common language about ethnic and racial identity.

b. *Jewish Ethnic and Racial Identity*

The data in Figure 3.4 does indeed show that there are clear differences between Jewish and non-Jewish data that the aggregating charts in Figure 3.1 masks.[79] An initial analysis of Jewish ethnic and racial identity among the authors studied shows some similarity with the corresponding charts for non-Jewish authors, with the significant difference that the Jewish charts in Figure 3.4 show the prominence of religion in the construction of identity. Thus, religion is the added major influence in Jewish ethnicity here, even though Jewish ethnicity exhibits many of the same major features as are prominent among non-Jewish authors. In addition, territory is not as important as conflict as an influence on Jewish ethnicity in this literature. The race construct reflects this same diminution of the importance of territory, and these observations probably reflect the effects of the Jewish Diaspora. In other words, social and religious identification across the Jewish Diaspora continued despite the lack of a territorial homeland.

The non-Jewish and Jewish concepts of race, however, may be less similar than these charts in Figures 3.2 and 3.4 suggest, because Josephus' work may skew the data in a way that is similar to the effect of Strabo's work on the non-Jewish profile. Specifically, Josephus fits the profile of the non-Jewish Greek-speaking authors on the question of race better than he matches the profile of other Jewish writers. Here 'profile' refers to tendencies to associate some ideas with the concept of race more regularly than others do. Figure 3.5(a) shows that the Josephus line fits the Jewish profile with reference to group consciousness, war, government, customs, and religion, but the data is off for territory and highly skewed for kinship. On the other hand, Figure 3.5(b) shows that the Josephus line fits all categories when compared with the non-Jewish authors examined, even kinship.

In terms of analysis, there are several possible reasons for Josephus' greater emphasis on kinship as compared to some other Jews. First, Josephus' use of Nicolaus and other Greco-Roman sources could alter the de facto profile of race towards conformance with non-Jewish perspectives. Differences in his audience and purpose as compared to other Jewish writers are more difficult to identify, but whatever his motivation

---

79 Christian authors are not included in Figure 3.4.

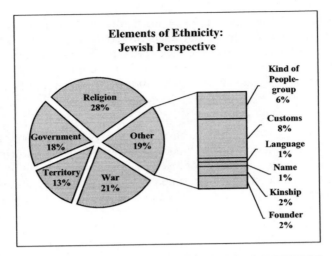

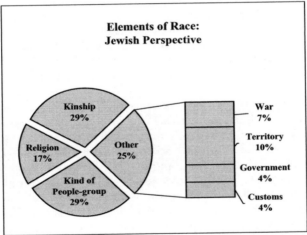

Figure 3.4 – Elements of Ethnicity and Race among Jews at the Turn of the Era

we do know that an emphasis on the more permanent aspects of Jewish culture (e.g., kinship) would be perceived as less threatening in view of the well-known Roman preference to keep 'foreign' religion at arm's length. This preference is obliquely evident in the following passage, in which Dionysius marvels at the Romans' ability to remain unaffected by the diversity of culture in the capital:

> And it may well seem a cause of wonder to many who reflect on the natural course of events that Rome did not become entirely barbarized on receiving the Opicans ... besides innumerable other nations ... [who] differed from one another both in their language and habits. ... For

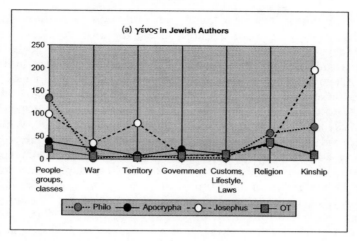

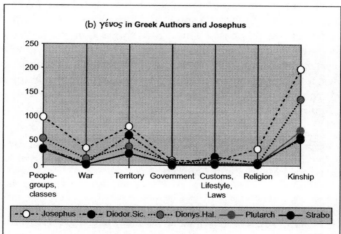

Figure 3.5 – Mismatch of Josephus and Other Jewish Authors

many others by living among barbarians have in a short time forgotten all their Greek heritage, so that they neither speak the Greek language nor observe the customs of the Greeks nor acknowledge the same gods nor have the same equitable laws (by which most of all the spirit of the Greeks differ from that of the barbarians). (Dionysius, *Ant. rom.* 1.89.3-4)[80]

80   Richard Alston points out that the Romans' relatively painless absorption of various ἔθνη indicates that the newly absorbed peoples did not perceive a clearly defined Roman ethnic identity. During the Roman empire, becoming Roman meant enjoying the benefits of Roman citizenship and did not involve a change in ethnic identity ('Changing Ethnicities:

Ancient sentiments held that 'pure', autochthonous races were superior, and that when peoples or cultures mixed, the more 'civilized' culture would degenerate from exposure to the more 'barbaric' one. Thus, Romans had great tolerance for religious and other diversity, until these other religions 'infected' Roman citizens. Benjamin Isaac discusses these themes in some detail, especially in the context of describing Roman hostility to Christianity, since from the Roman perspective Christianity necessarily involved betraying ancestral ties and religion.[81] With this background, Josephus' emphasis on Jewish lineage and antiquity, and his similar tendency to minimize the idea of 'conversion', may reflect an accommodation to Roman tastes that is unlike the emphasis on religion found in other Jewish literature.[82] In other words, kinship may be prominent in Josephus' profile of race because of his Roman social context.

When we consider the network of ideas associated with ἔθνος and γένος in the Jewish literature apart from Josephus, there is a much greater emphasis on religion. Figure 3.6 shows the models of Jewish ethnicity and race that reflect this emphasis. This figure shows that the dominant idea connected with γένος in these Jewish constructions of race is the sense of being a certain people, a sense apparently predicated on religious customs and values, and buttressed by kinship. The prominence of religion in these Jewish constructions of both ethnicity and race, however, is one of the most intriguing aspects of the models in Figures 3.4 and 3.6.[83]

'From the Egyptian to the Roman City', in Cornell and Lomas (eds), *Gender and Ethnicity*, pp. 85–86. For a nuanced approach to this issue, see Woolf, 'Becoming Roman, Staying Greek', and generally Millar, *Roman Near East*.

81 Isaac, *The Invention of Racism*, pp. 440–91. See also Mary Smallwood's discussion of an expulsion of Jews from Rome in 139 BCE because of proselytism (*The Jews under Roman Rule*, pp. 128–30, 202–10).

82 Shaye Cohen, 'Respect for Judaism by Gentiles According to Josephus', *HTR* 80 (1987): 425–29.

83 Other scholars come to very similar conclusions, although they are using different methodologies. For example, we have already noted that Buell's conclusions about the nature of race in the early Christian period is similar to the data presented here, although she does not consider Jewish literature (Buell, 'Rethinking the Relevance of Race'; see also Hodge, *If Sons then Heirs*, p. 43). In addition, Shaye Cohen characterizes Second Temple Judaism as 'ethno-religious', that is, as primarily ethnic in its earliest emphasis on shared kinship, while later acquiring a more religious orientation (Cohen, *The Beginnings of Jewishness*, pp. 109–39; see also John J. Collins, *Between Athens and Jerusalem: Jewish Identity in the Hellenistic Diaspora* [Grand Rapids: Eerdmans, 2nd edn, 2000], p. 152; and Millar, *Roman Near East*, pp. 337–38, 344–51, 357–62). Cohen, however, argues that proselytes were not accepted as equal members of Israel, and this argument tends to emphasize the importance of kinship in his description of Jewish identity (*The Beginnings of Jewishness*, pp. 160–62). His arguments on this point are not entirely convincing, however, at least for the period of interest to this study. The primary evidence supporting his conclusion comes from the much later rabbinic period. The only evidence that he cites from the first

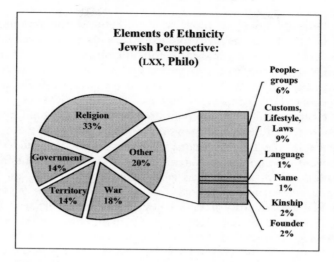

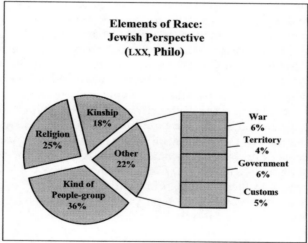

Figure 3.6 – Jewish Ethnicity and Race at the Turn of the Era

century is a negative comment about proselytes in Philo (*Moses* 1.147), which in context refers to the presence of Egyptians – former Jewish slave-owners – in the masses leaving Egypt in the Exodus. In comparison to Philo's other positive comments on proselytes which Cohen himself acknowledges (e.g., see below), there is weak evidence for his argument about the marginalized status of proselytes in the period (also see Buell, 'Rethinking the Relevance of Race', pp. 468–69 for a general critique of Cohen's use of 'ethnicity' as a category). For more information on proselytes and Jewish proselytism compare Scott McKnight's *A Light among the Gentiles* (Minneapolis: Fortress, 1991) with James Charles Paget's 'Jewish Proselytism at the Time of Christian Origins: Chimera or Reality?' *JSNT* 62 (1996): 65–103.

I have already noted that the contrast between the prominence of religion and the lower incidence of customs in both charts may surprise some students of ancient Judaism. Before attempting an interpretation of this finding, we should review the process used to associate passages with certain identity topics. With each ἔθνος and γένος passage, I noted every topic category that appeared in that passage. Thus, if a given passage refers to customs and religion, I registered occurrences in both categories, and likewise for any other combination of categories. The relatively low prominence in the customs category emerges not so much because customs were unimportant to these Greek-speaking Jews, but from two other factors. First, as discussed earlier, references to religion tend to accompany references to customs and laws. Second, in addition to passages that are primarily about religion, secondary or tertiary references to religion occur in many passages, accompanying many other categories (i.e., customs, kinship, war, land, government, etc.). In short, religion is likely a more prominent aspect of this Jewish identity construct than customs/laws because religion saturated most aspects of Jewish life in this literature and had a bearing on most of the elements relevant to identity.

The prominence of religion in this model of Jewish identity also results in the greater porousness of ethnic and racial bonds. This construction of identity is deeply at odds with modern folk constructions of race, with their permanent boundaries marked by skin color. When religion is pre-eminent in identity, acts of what we would call 'religious conversion' amount to a change in race or ethnicity. Philo especially provides insight on this process and on the standing of proselytes vis-à-vis native Jews, in a way that illuminates the concept of a change in identity. According to Philo, proselytes are warmly welcomed into Judaism as if they are fellow citizens (an ἔθνος-like idea) or native-born Jews (a γένος-like idea), and have reached an exalted state of being in the worship of God (*Embassy* 210–211; *Spec. Laws* 1.51-52).[84] God provides for proselytes and helps them because they have forsaken their false and vain ancestral customs,

---

84 Philo, *Embassy* 210–11: 'For all men guard their own customs, but this is especially true of the Jewish nation (ἔθνος). Holding that the laws are oracles vouchsafed by God ... they carry the likenesses of the commandments enshrined in their souls ... And those of other races (ἀλλοφύλους) who pay homage to them they welcome no less than their own countrymen (πολεμιωτάτοις).'

Philo, *Spec. Laws* 1.51-52: 'All of like sort to [Moses] ... whether they have been such from the first or through conversion ... have reached that higher state, obtain his approval. ... These last he calls "proselytes" ... because they have joined the new and godly commonwealth (φιλοθέῳ πολιτεία). Thus, while giving equal rank to all in-comers with all the privileges that he gives to the native-born (αὐτόχθοσι), he exhorts the old nobility to honor them not only with marks of respect but with special friendship and with more than ordinary goodwill. And surely there is good reason for this; they have left ... their country, their kinsfolk (συγγενεῖς), and their friends for the sake of virtue and religion.'

and have crossed over to serve God with a love of simplicity and truth (*Spec. Laws* 1.309). In Philo, there is even the sense that obedience to the law is more important than Jewish kinship (*Spec. Laws* 1.317-318; see also Josephus, *Ag. Ap.* 2.210).[85] Evidence for the favor with which proselytes were greeted in Judaism is much more than anecdotal.[86] The passage below, again from Philo, indicates that adoption of Jewish religion constituted a change in kinship and thus, on our model, a corresponding change in racial identity.

> He commands all members of the **nation** to love the incomers, not only as friends and kinsfolk (συγγενεῖς) but as themselves both in body and soul: in bodily matters, by acting as far as may be for their common interest; in mental by having the same griefs and joys, so that they may seem to be the separate parts of a single living being which is compacted and unified by their fellowship in it. I will not go on to speak of the food and drink and raiment and all the rights concerning daily life and necessary needs, which the law assigns to incomers as due from the native born (αὐτοχθόνων), for all these follow the statutes, which speak of the friendliness shown by him who loves the incomer even as himself. (Philo, *Virtues* 103–104)

While I do not mean to imply any literary relationship, Philo's description of the change in kinship not only echoes Paul's familial language for the church, but also evokes Paul's unity in Christ and body of Christ imagery. The similarity between the passage below and Paul's own use of horticultural metaphors and adoption language in Romans may instead suggest that Philo and Paul drew from a common tradition regarding the relationship between kinship, religious conversion, and racial identity.

---

85   Philo, *Spec. Laws* 1.317-18: 'But as for these kinships, as we call them, which have come down from our ancestors and are based on blood-relationship ... let them all be cast aside if they do not seek earnestly the same goal, namely the honor of God, which is the indissoluble bond of all the affection which makes us one. ... This promise of mine is confirmed by the law, where it says that they who do "what is pleasing" ... and what is "good" are sons of God'.

86   McKnight (*A Light among the Gentiles*, pp. 34–35) notes other indicators of an attitude that welcomes proselytes in the period (e.g., Josephus, *Ag. Ap.* 2.210, 2.261). The evidence about the level of *proselytizing* in Second Temple Judaism, on the other hand, is mixed. For a discussion of the data that supports a description of Judaism as a missionary religion see Paget, 'Jewish Proselytism', who refutes the arguments offered by S. McKnight, M. Goodman, and others who deny the prevalence of early Jewish missionary activity. Paget's criticism of the framework these scholars use to contest the idea that Second Temple Judaism was a missionary religion is valid, and his own analysis of the evidence supporting such a portrayal is nuanced. While I would concede from his arguments that there is fragmentary evidence that certain Jews engaged in aggressive mission, overall I do not think that hostility to idolatry, internal discussions of Jewish superiority, and a welcoming attitude to converts necessarily adds up to a missionary impulse (cf. Paget, 'Jewish Proselytism', p. 101).

> For a man is able even without knowledge to labor at the care of the soil, but a husbandman … will be anxious to bring under cultivation the trees that were before wild, to improve by careful treatment those already under cultivation, to check by pruning those that are over-luxuriant owing to excess of nourishment, to give more scope to those which have been curtailed and kept back, splicing on new growths to stem or branch; when trees of good kinds throw out abundant tendrils, he will like to train them under ground in shallow trenches; and to improve such as yield poor crops by inserting grafts into the stem near the roots and joining them with it so that they grow together as one. The same thing happens, I may remark, in the case of men, when adopted sons become by reason of their native good qualities congenial to those who by **birth** (γένεσιν, alt. 'by race') are aliens from them, and so become firmly fitted into the family. (Philo, *On Agriculture* 4–6)

On the other hand, other Jewish literature gives evidence that 'religious conversion' was a two-way street, in that there were border crossings from both sides of the boundary that separated Jews from others. The first three texts below shun apostasy from Judaism even as the earlier texts proclaimed conversion to Judaism and a welcome to proselytes. The Esther text suggests that, under certain circumstances, political motivations prompted participation in religious rites.

> You shall also say to the children of Israel, 'If any of the children of Israel, or of those who have become proselytes in Israel, will give of his seed to Moloch, let him be surely put to death; the **nation** upon the land will utterly stone him.' (Lev. 20.2, LLS)

> But having led him [i.e., Ptolemy] away, Dositheus, known as the son of Drimylus, a Jew by **birth** (τὸ γένος Ἰουδαῖος) who later changed his customs and apostasized and disguised his ancestral beliefs, arranged that a certain insignificant man should sleep in the tent; and so it turned out that this man incurred the vengeance meant for the king. (*3 Macc.* 1.3, LLS)

> For which reason destruction is just for all who being of the **race** of Abraham attempt new practices that pervert our normal ways. (Josephus, *J.A.* 5.113, LLS)

> Wherever the proclamation took place, the Jews had joy and gladness, feasting and mirth. Many of the **Gentiles** received circumcision and became Jews, because they feared the Jews. (Est. 8.17, LLS)

In summary, the clear difference between Jewish and non-Jewish identity among the authors studied has to do with the importance of religion in constructing ethnicity and race. While non-Jewish and Jewish ethnicity differed in that these Jews subordinated the major elements of ethnicity to religion, this model of Jewish racial identity differs markedly from the corresponding non-Jewish concepts. These versions of non-Jewish and Jewish constructions of race diverge in the way that kinship and territory so significantly dominate the idea of race among the non-Jewish Greek-speaking authors. In contrast, the Jewish concept of racial identity modeled here contains a strong sense of group consciousness that probably derived from the religious customs and laws that functioned as barriers to interactions with other groups. A focus on religion and kinship are second and third in prominence in the network of ideas that constitute race as exhibited in this Jewish literature. Unlike non-Jewish Greco-Roman constructions of identity surveyed here, territory is not at all important as an element of identity among Jews. Jewish racial identity among these authors consists of social identity (i.e., group consciousness), religious identity, and physical identity (kinship). Further, the fact that religion is important to both ethnicity and race in this model of ancient Jewish identity suggests that it is the criterion of identity and that other elements such as kinship, conflict, or even group consciousness are peripheral and act as indicia of identity. Here, religion is that element in the Jewish culture of the Second Temple period by which the group as a collective determined itself to be a group. Kinship, conflict, customs, and the like were indicia of identity, or indicators that insiders and outsiders used in assessing identity.[87] Further, since Torah was the embodiment of Jewish religion, we may state that the central criterion of Jewish identity for the Jews studied here was *the Torah-ordered worship of the God of Abraham, Isaac, and Jacob.*[88]

4. *Race and Ethnicity: Ancient and Modern Perspectives*

Ἔθνος and γένος are synonyms for each other in antiquity and we often use the modern terms similarly, but it is possible to distinguish ethnicity from race in both contexts. We have shown that in antiquity ἔθνος often, though not always, expresses something about social and territorial boundaries with other groups, while γένος often, though not always, communicates something about the distinctive characteristics of a kinship group. In antiquity, both words are associated with roughly the same

87 Jonathon Hall would dispute this analysis, regarding 'polythetic' definitions of ethnicity that see multiple factors influencing constructions of ethnicity as having limited heuristic value. Hall insists that kinship is a universal constant in definitions of ethnicity. According to him, modern scholars reject kinship as the basis of ethnicity only because the idea is 'alarmingly' too similar to 'biological' race (Hall, *Hellenicity*, pp. 11–13). In light of the data presented here, Hall's insistence on kinship as the basis of ethnic identity rejects data that represents an insider perspective, such as the Jewish data presented here, a perspective that he himself maintains is critical in the analysis of ethnicity.

88 For a description of the role of the law in 'common Judaism' see Sanders, *Judaism*, pp. 47–76, 190–212, 241–78.

identity elements, an observation that is consistent with the fact that they often operate as synonyms. Through separate analysis of the Jewish and non-Jewish data, I proposed that the *criterion* of identity was that element that was prominent in both the model of ethnicity and the model of race, and functioned as an element that unified the two models. Territory was the criterion of identity for ancient non-Jewish Greek-speaking authors studied and was likely the basis both for conflict and kinship claims. Religion was the criterion of identity for the ancient Jews studied and thus stood at the center of what made these people think of themselves as a separate group. Outsiders were 'nations' who did not worship the God of Abraham, Isaac, and Jacob, while outsiders who did worship the God of Abraham, Isaac, and Jacob could become members of the Jewish people. Thus, those who insist that it is inappropriate to identify 'Gentile' as an ethnic category in this literature are right only insofar as they have in mind modern definitions of ethnicity that privilege kinship and territory – and not the ancient Jewish notions like those that emerged here.[89]

Having considered some of the dynamics of ethnic and racial concepts in both antiquity and modernity, several points of contrast emerge. There is continuity between antiquity and modernity with regard to the Hellenistic idea of 'nation' (ἔθνος) reflected in the writings of these non-Jewish Greek speakers. Now as then, 'nation' conveys ideas about shared origin in terms of territory and putative kinship, and conjures images of governments and group structures and ethnic or international conflict. On

---

89 Charles H. Cosgrove, 'Did Paul Value Ethnicity?' *CBQ* 68 (2006): 268–90 (272–73) (cf. Hodge's excellent discussion in *If Sons then Heirs*, pp. 49–52). Relying partially on Esler's understanding of ethnicity in the ancient Mediterranean world (see Philip Esler, *Conflict and Identity in Romans* [Minneapolis: Augsburg Fortress, 2003], pp. 62–76), Cosgrove insists that ἔθνος, meaning 'people' or 'nation', is not a particular 'ethnicity or nationality' comparable to 'Jews', 'Greeks', 'Romans', etc. Both Cosgrove's and Esler's descriptions of ethnic identity differ from the analysis in this study on several fundamental points. First, Esler traces the modern concept of race and racist typology and concludes that since this kind of typology did not exist in antiquity, 'race' does not exist in antiquity (against him see the discussion of Isaac's thesis about ancient proto-racism above). Further, my analysis shows that γένος *does* have meanings in antiquity that have both similarities and differences with modern identity concepts (see below). Most importantly, both scholars fail to differentiate Greco-Roman and Jewish modes of understanding group identity. When describing differences between ancient and modern concepts Cosgrove describes ancient Mediterranean identity in terms of 'physical appearance, territory, customs, and character traits' ('Did Paul Value Ethnicity?', pp. 268–69), never explicitly describing the elements of Jewish ethnic identity, though his assumptions about Jewish ethnicity are regularly manifest (pp. 275–76). In fact, Cosgrove's analysis of Jewish ethnicity privileges kinship as the determinative factor in identity (pp. 280, 282–83 *et passim*). He neither reckons with Gal. 1.13 nor reconciles himself to the 'before' and 'after' flavor of Phil. 3.2-11 (cf. the readings of Gal. 2.13-15 and Phil. 3.2-11 offered below). In contrast, Esler's understanding of Jewish identity privileges territory, through its reliance on Greco-Roman concepts about ancient ethnic identity and modern ideas about the peripheral importance of religion (*Conflict and Identity*, pp. 62–76).

the other hand, Jewish group identity flowed from shared religion and family. Modern popular ideas about ethnic group identity focus on geo-political origin and thus mimic the non-Jewish emphasis on territory and kinship, while postmodern theorists in ethnic and racial studies are beginning to emphasize the importance of shared experience and culture in constructions of group identity, a methodology that mimics the dynamics of the ancient Jewish emphasis on shared religion. Thus, ancient non-Jewish or 'Greek' outsider perspectives triumph whenever modern scholars proclaim kinship as the *sine qua non* of ethnicity. Kinship as the essence of ethnicity is, after all, only a slight mutation of the tradition of territory as the criterion of identity, given that territory and kinship went hand-in-hand in antiquity. When members of the dominant culture assume that biology and permanence characterize race, they promote a construct of identity similar to that articulated by Greek outsiders about often-marginalized Others. However, scholars move towards something closer akin to the Jewish models discussed here wherever they discuss group identity in terms of a sense of belonging based on shared experience and values, putting less emphasis on biology or kinship.

In addition, there are similar tensions between insider and outsider perspectives in antiquity as in modernity, especially on the question of race. According to the ancient *non-Jewish* Greek-speaking outsiders surveyed here, kinship is determinative for race and thus race is permanent. On the other hand, less influential *Jewish* insider perspectives such as those analyzed here hold that another criterion – in this case religion – is more important in generating a strong group consciousness. Because these ancient Jewish authors held that religion was central to identity, they signaled that racial identity was not permanent. In other words, perspective and power shapes the role assigned to kinship in determining identity among both moderns and ancients. The insider perspectives of less powerful groups may see other aspects of identity as more important than kinship.

There is also a contrast between ancient and modern constructions of identity with reference to the way that the terms 'race' and γένος function in their respective historical settings. In antiquity, the term γένος did the work that most modern scholars want the word 'ethnicity' to connote. As with modern popular connotations of 'ethnicity', γένος connoted an awareness of a distinctive sense of group identity. Nevertheless, γένος was a term that peoples used of themselves and others, and it did not necessarily convey a sense of otherness, as 'race' does now. Ancient Jews and non-Jewish Greek-speakers used different terms to convey this sense of otherness. While non-Jews used the word βάρβαρος for the alien Other, Jews used ἔθνος to signal this otherness, a situation that has been completely inverted in the contemporary world where 'race' most often communicates deviance. Similarly, ancient use of the word γένος conveyed a sense of shared origin and present connectedness that the word 'ethnicity' often conveys in modern scholarship. Moderns are attempting to recover the ancient notion that race (or 'ethnicity' as a synonym) is a ubiquitous property of people-groups.

This analysis suggested that Torah ordered the religious relationship between the community and the God of Abraham, and that religion, via Torah, was the central criterion by which the Jewish community defined its identity as an ethno-racial entity. Going forward, we define a race as a group of people who within a given context believe they share any imagined or real combination of (a) kinship and (b) values or psychosocial characteristics,[90] and who transmit these values or physical, emotional, or mental characteristics within the self-defined boundaries of the racial group. This definition attempts to capture the significant, and perhaps even determinative, element of kinship that seems to accompany the idea of race across the ages. In addition, this definition skirts essentialism by its sensitivity to the social context in which the group defines itself, and it avoids issues of power by focusing exclusively on definitions about the group that emerge from within. Finally, this definition acknowledges that (imagined or real) values or personal/personality characteristics play a significant, sometimes determinative, role in constructions of race across history.

Finally, my analysis of ancient constructs of identity confirms the fluid and sociohistorical nature of ethnic and racial identity. Since the *meaning* of race and ethnicity change over time, we cannot discuss these phenomena in a given period without attention to the contextual parameters that shape the ideas in that period. As mentioned earlier, no study or dataset will ever be able to prove or define the nature of race or ethnicity for an era, and especially not in a case so far removed from our own. Nevertheless, just as there are factors in current discourse about identity that influence the prevailing ideas about race, so too were there features that contributed to the construction of race in antiquity. Our purpose here has been to nuance our understanding of ancient constructs of identity by identifying what those social factors might have been for the ancient Jews surveyed, before consulting modern identity theory with reference to the major forces shaping group membership.

What emerges is the idea that Jews understood the combination of kinship and values constituent of race as a dialectic involving *social identity* mediated by criteria and indicia of membership, *religious identity*

---

90 By psychosocial characteristics, I refer to individual or combined emotional, intellectual, or mental characteristics. Some common psychosocial stereotypes might include images of the 'cold' Briton, the 'violent' African American, or the 'clannish' Jew. For further information on how images from racist discourse correspond to more muted versions of these stereotypes in popular culture, see Daniels, *White Lies*.

ordered via Jewish law, and *physical identity* through biological kinship. Yet we will have learned nothing from our earlier survey of modern identity theory if we assume that all Jews held these views simply because the Jews in this study did.[91] It is one thing to acknowledge that the identity dialectics identified here flow from the stories and myths that comprise the central mythomoteur of the Jewish people in the Septuagint and Jewish Apocrypha, but it is also true that this trifold dialectic of social, religious, and physical identity emerges from certain tellings of these stories. Specifically, we cannot assume *a priori* that the apostle Paul shared these particular ideas about group identity, and it is to this question that we now turn.

91   Hodge, *If Sons then Heirs*, pp. 52–53. In addition, a failure to avoid this kind of totalitizing discourse would obscure the limits of this research. For example, this chapter examines the degree to which ancients and moderns shared ideas about 'race', a study which was facilitated by the presence of similar lexemes in English and Greek. Given that there is no word in Aramaic or Hebrew that corresponds to the Greek γένος, we are not able to establish a certain point of contact between the modern idea of race and group membership at Qumran.

Part II

The Racial Character of Pauline Christianity

Inasmuch as Paul was consistently repudiated as an 'apostate' by his contemporaries the label fits historical reality ... In this respect, it seems to me misleading to talk ... about Paul converting 'from one variety of Judaism to another', if the Jewishness of the new alternative was what most Jews denied. Nor is it adequate ... to regard Paul's interpretation of Judaism as 'a legitimate option for Jews ... within a wider range of options'. The fact is that the vast majority of Paul's contemporaries appear to have considered it illegitimate! ... To reinstate Paul in hindsight as a 'legitimate' Jew would be to impose a theological judgment over historical reality, and if this is practiced by Christians, it is in danger of becoming a form of Christian supersessionism. Christians now accept that they cannot force their definition of Judaism on Jews of today. It is easier, of course, to impose definitions of Jews of the past, but I doubt whether it is either historically or morally responsible to do so.

John Barclay, 'Paul among Diaspora Jews', pp. 118–19

Chapter 4

PAUL'S SELF-IDENTITY AND RELATIONAL MATRIX

Students of early Christianity will quickly intuit that if either of the
ancient Jewish models of identity shown previously operates as a
background for Paul's ideas about identity, the Jewish understanding of
race as a threefold dialectic involving social, religious, and physical
elements is the more likely candidate. Since it would be inappropriate to
maintain that all Jews everywhere shared the same notions about ethnicity
and race, what remains is a determination of whether Paul's concept of
Christian identity coheres with the dialectic that appeared in Greek-
speaking Jewish literature of the period. In addition, acknowledging that a
person's self-identity may vary from group assessments, this chapter
investigates Paul's understanding of Christian identity by analyzing his
self-concept as well as his group membership, in effect learning about the
nature of Christian group identity by examining what Paul says about
himself and the group or groups to which he belonged. We will see that
the Jewish dialectic does indeed form a framework for Paul's discussions
about identity, and that physical identity or kinship, that element of the
dialectic that might be most difficult to envision as a parameter of
Christian identity, figures prominently in Paul's concept of community.

1. *Community and Kinship in Paul*

a. *Kinship Language in the Septuagint and the New Testament*
Earlier, we saw that both ethnic and nationalistic discourse adopts the
language of family and kinship, and that this pattern holds in the ancient
world as well as the modern one. However, this kind of language is rare in
the context of religious groups in antiquity, so much so that according to
Wayne Meeks, the Christian practice in all likelihood derives from Jewish
usage.[1] Horsley, on the other hand, sees evidence of the communal burial
of slaves, freedman, family members, and members of civic associations

---

1 Wayne Meeks, *The First Urban Christians* (New Haven and London: Yale University
Press, 1983), pp. 86–87.

from Hellenistic and Roman Rhodes as potentially analogous to later
Christian intimacy.[2] In a similar vein, K.H. Schelkle suggests that the use
of 'brother' terminology in Greek religious societies evolved out of family-
oriented political and cultic communes, from about 150 BCE, that
eventually loosened their restrictive membership customs through adoption.[3] Though suggestive as a background for Christian practice, sparse
Hellenistic and Greco-Roman data cannot supplant the voluminous
kinship data in the Jewish context, which is much closer in history-of-
religion terms (e.g., Exod. 12.48-49; Lev. 18.26). Thus, we interpret the
Christian use of family imagery against a Jewish, rather than Greco-
Roman background. That Hellenistic household, civic, professional, and
religious associations exhibited intimacy beyond strict biological kinship
suggests that people-groups in a variety of settings experienced group
boundary extensions and boundary tension.

As we saw previously, it is difficult if not impossible to separate ethnic
or racial language from religious language in the case of the Jews of the
period, since religious concerns saturate the literature. Thus, Jewish usage
of terms such as father, brother, son, mother, sister, and daughter appear
in contexts that refer to deity and cult as well as in contexts that are more
secular. However, biblical literature exhibits differences in terms of the
frequency and intimacy of kinship language. For example, there are
differences between the OT and NT with respect to the use of the word
πατήρ in an explicitly religious sense. In the Pentateuch, πατήρ almost
exclusively refers to biological paternity. There are fewer than thirty
passages in the OT and the Jewish Apocrypha in the Septuagint that use
'father' with reference to God; by contrast, there are over fourteen
hundred uses of the word 'father' to communicate human kinship in these
texts.

In contrast, there is an increasing familiarity or intimacy in πατήρ
language with reference to God in the New Testament given the size of
that corpus. While πατήρ refers to God about 2 percent of the time in the
LXX, over 60 percent of the usages of the word in the NT refer to God.
This intimacy peaks in the Fourth Gospel where πατήρ primarily appears
on the lips of Jesus, and in the Johannine epistles the intimacy between
Jesus and God translates into a similar intimacy among the members of

    2 G.H.R. Horsley, *New Documents Illustrating Early Christianity* (Ancient History
Documentary Research Centre, Macquarie University; Alexandria, Australia: J. Bell and
Co., 1982), pp. 48–49.
    3 K.H. Schelkle, *Reallexikon für Antike und Christentum* (ed. Theodor Klauser; Stuttgart:
Hiersemann Verlag, 1954), 2.632–36 (632–33).

that community (e.g., 1 Jn 2.1, 9-14; 2 Jn 1.1-14).[4] In addition, the early church's references to Jesus as the 'son of God' in the singular contrasts with the rarity of such references in the OT and Jewish Apocrypha and their complete absence in Josephus' corpus.[5] Thus, one imagines that the greatly increased density of the use of 'father' to refer to God in the New Testament goes hand-in-hand with the routine reference to Jesus as the Son of God. Whatever one makes of the origin of these patterns (e.g., does the motif reflect Jesus' own practice?), the fact remains that both usages contribute to the heightened use of family language in the New Testament, a trend that is even more notable given the relative size of the NT corpus.

In addition, references to individuals as sons of God in the Septuagint are rare; in the NT, such references only occur with any discernible frequency in Paul, especially if we exclude references to Jesus as the 'son of God'.[6] As might be expected, familial language refers to physical kinship much less often in the New Testament than in the Septuagint. For example, Deut. 15.12 below exhibits the use of ἀδελφός in a context in which familial genetic consanguinity is not in view, communicating what we would today describe as an ethnic relationship.[7] Although these kinds of references are relatively infrequent in the OT and Apocrypha, such passages convey a sense of relatedness across the people of Israel, especially when used to refer to Jews in the Diaspora, as in Isa. 66.20 and 2 Macc. 1.1 below.

> And if your brother or sister, a Hebrew man or a Hebrew woman, is sold to you, he or she will serve you six years, and in the seventh year you will send them out free from you. (Deut. 15.12, LLS)

> And they shall bring your brothers out of all nations for a gift to the Lord with horses, and chariots. (Isa. 66.20, LLS)

> The Jews in Jerusalem and those in the land of Judea (οἱ ἀδελφοὶ οἱ ἐν Ἱεροσολύμοις Ἰουδαῖοι καὶ οἱ ἐν τῇ χώρᾳ τῆς Ἰουδαίας), To their

---

4   For more on this topic see Marianne Meye Thompson's study of paternal imagery vis-à-vis God in the New Testament, which includes a comparison with similar imagery in the OT and Second Temple Judaism, *The Promise of the Father: Jesus and God in the New Testament* (Louisville: Westminster John Knox, 2000), pp. 35–55.

5   There are 13 such references in the OT (Exod. 4.22; Deut. 14.1; 32.43; 1 Chron. 28.6; 2 Chron. 6.41; Ps. 2.7; 28.1; 81.6; Prov. 3.12; Hos. 2.1; Isa. 30.9; Jer. 3.22; Dan. 3.12) and four in the Apocrypha (*Odes* 2.43; 14.14; Wis. 2.18; 18.13) of which two are probably Christian interpolations.

6   E.g., Deut. 14.1; Hos. 2.1; Rom. 8.14, 19.

7   See Schelkle (*Reallexikon für Christentum*, 2.635–36), who documents several ways in which 'brother' terminology appears in the Old Testament: as a reference to a shared national community (e.g., Exod. 2.11; Lev. 10.4; Deut. 15.3, 12; Ps. 49.20), for more distant biological connections (Gen. 14.14; 24.48), for fellow clergy (2 Chron. 31.15; Ezra 3.8), and for friends (Job 19.13; 1 Kgs 9.13).

Jewish kindred in Egypt (τοῖς ἀδελφοῖς τοῖς κατ᾽ Αἴγυπτον
Ἰουδαίοις), Greetings and true peace. (2 Macc. 1.1)

Broadly speaking, the words πατήρ, υἱός, and ἀδελφός are used in similar
ways in the Septuagint. With the exception of the increased use of πατήρ
in references to God, the Gospels and Acts tend to follow the same
patterns of kinship language as appears in the Jewish literature, perhaps
reflecting Jesus' and the early church's Jewish *Sitz im Leben*. Although
Christian adaptation and broadening of kinship language appears in what
may be early material in the gospels (e.g., Mk 3.31, 35, 10.30; Mt. 25.40),
the use of ἀδελφός is especially striking in Paul.[8] The seven undisputed
letters account for about a third of all occurrences of the word in the New
Testament, and with the exception of Rom. 9.3, ἀδελφός refers exclusively
to religious as opposed to biological kinship in the Pauline and Deutero-
Pauline Epistles.[9] In addition, the Pauline and Deutero-Pauline Epistles
both exhibit the virtual replacement of biological kinship with a religious
use of kinship language. The fact that references to biological kinship
virtually disappear in Paul is not so remarkable on its own for several
reasons. First, Paul's activity took place within decades of Jesus' death
and resurrection, so his converts were among those in the earliest
generations of believers. In addition, Paul's itinerant ministry and clear
sense of mission to Gentiles meant that he preached to people who likely
had no familial connections with each other or with Jewish kinship
networks. Indeed, what is somewhat surprising is his emphasis on kinship
in view of this kind of a ministry.

Before we examine texts that feature Paul's particular kind of kinship
logic, it is necessary to say a word about the correlation between the
metaphors in Paul's symbolic universe and the way these symbols
functioned in his social universe. As a prelude to a study on the social
arrangements in the narrative context of Philemon, Norman Petersen
discusses the way that Paul metaphorically applies kinship language
drawn from the well-understood family context of the broader society to

---

8   See Schelkle, *Reallexikon für Christentum*, 2.636 for more on kinship language in the
gospels; see Meeks (*The First Urban Christians*, pp. 86–87); Lightfoot (*Notes on the Epistles of
St. Paul* [London: MacMillan, 1895], p. 151); Anthony Thistleton (*The First Epistle to the
Corinthians* [Grand Rapids and Cambridge: Eerdmans, 2000], pp. 114–15) on Paul's heavy
use of ἀδελφός.

9   E.E. Ellis argues that in the plural ἀδελφός is an early Christian technical term for
church leadership engaged in mission and preaching, possibly reflecting Jesus' own use of
kinship imagery for relationships among his disciples (*Prophecy and Hermeneutic* [Tübingen:
J.C.B. Mohr (Paul Siebeck), 1978], pp. 13–22). Ellis's description of the meaning of ἀδελφός
does not seem to hold in the Pauline corpus (see for example Rom. 8.12, 29; 1 Cor. 12.1; Gal.
5.13; Phil. 3.17; 1 Thess. 4.10), but his work highlights the widespread use of the terminology
across the New Testament tradition.

the church, among people who do not share 'real' biological kinship.[10] Yet even as Paul borrows family language from the broader society, he infuses the words with a transformed meaning to match the fact that the church operates with a different and more complex set of relational norms.[11]

Specifically, Pauline Christians cannot have the same kinds of relationships with God and Christ as indicated by the role names from the social universe, for example 'father', 'brother', 'Lord', because these relationships cannot be experienced in terms of the same kind of face-to-face social arrangements. Thus, these relationships are qualitatively different from biological familial associations, even when involving connections between believers.[12] Nevertheless, because Paul models relationships within the church and between God and the church on arrangements in the social universe, he and his associates think of the relationships in social terms, however metaphorical. According to Petersen, this means that we cannot comprehend family relationships within the church strictly with respect to the earthly world outside of the church. Instead, with reference to the church we have to cease speaking 'of the social categories of everyday life as symbolic, although they are such in a certain sense, and assign these categories to the realm of social arrangements. By doing this, we will be able to treat the symbolic forms in the context of Paul's symbolic universe, in which God and Christ are the principal actors.'[13]

Using the language of social anthropology, Petersen thus discusses an idea we have already encountered in our consideration of race as an 'imagined construct'. Earlier, I maintained that when we assign race to the category of 'imagined' or 'socially constructed' realities, we have not thereby emptied the idea of its power to shape behaviors and affect the quality of life for millions upon millions of people. When, for example, we translate an emphasis on the constructed nature of race into 'color-blind' social policies that fail to consider institutional racism, we may end by reifying the racism we hoped to eliminate through anti-racist programs. Similarly, in looking at Paul's use of kinship ideas, I will try to highlight places in which the labeling of Paul's usages as 'symbolic', 'metaphorical', or 'spiritual' threatens to underestimate the way in which Paul's family

---

10 Norman R. Petersen, *Rediscovering Paul: Philemon and the Sociology of Paul's Narrative World* (Philadelphia: Fortress, 1975), pp. 1–42. Here we should recall the idea of fictive kinship from Chapter 2 that so-called 'real' biological relationships are often based on a shared *belief* in a common ancestry that does not necessarily imply shared ancestry.

11 Petersen, *Rediscovering Paul*, pp. 23–25.

12 Paul's relationship with the congregation at Corinth illustrates this added complexity. Within this correspondence, Paul variously describes his relationship to them as one of slave, brother, and father (1 Cor. 4.15; 10.1; 2 Cor. 4.5).

13 Petersen, *Rediscovering Paul*, p. 28.

imagery shaped relationships and behavior between him and his brothers and sisters in Christ.[14]

b. *Kinship in Paul*

Below we consider three passages that illuminate Paul's understanding of Christian kinship: Rom. 4.1-25; 1 Cor. 10.1; and Phlm. 1.15-16. Of these three passages, we will consider Romans 4 in the most depth, since kinship is a dominant theme in that passage. I will discuss the other passages more briefly, since they shed light on Paul's concept of Christian kinship obliquely, in that those discourses reveal information about kinship even though Paul primarily pursues other rhetorical goals.

1. *Romans 4*

The Epistle to the Romans opens with a sustained argument that justification is by faith apart from works of law (Rom. 3.28). The first three chapters argue that both Jews and Gentiles are equally accountable to God, equally under the wrath of God for failure to meet the righteous requirements of the law, and thus equally in need of righteousness. In particular, the latter part of ch. 3 insists that justification and the righteousness of God come to Jew and Gentile alike on the basis of faith in Christ (3.20-22, 25-30).[15]

In ch. 4, Paul turns his hand to developing a proof for this concept from Scripture, insisting that his understanding of righteousness through faith is consonant with Abraham's story in Gen. 15.6 (cf. Rom. 4.3, 9). In conjunction with the closing verses of ch. 3, the opening verses of ch. 4 function as a statement of the main issues that Paul addresses in the balance of the chapter. First, he intends to prove that far from contradicting the law, the principle of justification through faith as opposed to works is in accordance with Torah (3.27-28, 31; cf. 4.1-8). Second, through the image of Abraham as the founding father of those who receive the promises of Israel, Paul establishes from Torah the universal application of the faith principle (3.29-4.1; cf. 4.9-17a). Third, Paul discusses the nature of Abraham's faith by drawing analogies

---

14 Daniel Boyarin's description of Paul's 'spiritual' hermeneutic is an especially troubling example of the kind of interpretation I am trying to resist. See Chapter 6 for my engagement with Boyarin's *A Radical Jew*.

15 Here I interpret the Greek phrase πίστις Χριστοῦ as an objective genitive. For the interpretation of πίστις Χριστοῦ as a subjective genitive, see M. Barth, 'The Faith of the Messiah', *HeyJ* 10 (1969): 363–70; L.T. Johnson, 'Romans 3.21-26 and the Faith of Jesus', *CBQ* 44 (1982): 77–90; Richard B. Hays, *The Faith of Jesus Christ: An Investigation of the Narrative Substructure of Gal. 3.1–4.11* (Grand Rapids and Cambridge: Eerdmans, 2nd edn, 2002). Certainty on this issue is difficult since not all of the evidence from the Pauline corpus points in the same direction (cf. Gal. 3.22; Gal. 2.16; see Hays, *Faith of Jesus Christ*, pp. 161–62).

between God's action on behalf of Abraham and God's action through Christ (4.17b-25). In the following discussion, I focus on the second step in the argument, with only brief glances at issues in the first and final sections.

In Paul, the phrase κατὰ σάρκα refers either to lineage and physical descent, as here in 4.1 (cf. Rom. 1.3; 9.5), or to a lifestyle, mode of being, or perspective, often appearing in explicit or implicit contrast to κατὰ πνεῦμα (cf. 1 Cor. 1.26; Rom. 8.4-5).[16] In these opening lines, Paul slides from a question about Abraham's physical kinship in 4.1 to a proposition about Abraham's justification by law in 4.2, a transition that prompts a closer inspection of Paul's use of the introductory εἰ γάρ phrase that connects the two verses:

> What will we say? Is Abraham found to be our ancestor by physical descent? Because if (εἰ γάρ) Abraham was justified by works, he has something to boast about, but not before God. (Rom 4.1-2, LLS)

In Paul, an introductory εἰ followed by an illustrative γάρ appears 24 times in the protasis of first- and second-class conditional statements. We also find that aside from Rom. 4.2, there are 22 cases in which the εἰ γάρ protasis introduces a restatement of all or part of a preceding statement, and the apodosis often, though not always, is an extension of the restated thought from the protasis. Aside from Rom. 4.1-2, the εἰ γάρ protasis clearly restates all or part of a preceding statement in the following cases: Rom. 4.14; 5.10, 15, 17; 6.5; 8.13; 11.15, 21, 24; 14.15; 15.27; 1 Cor. 2.8; 9.17; 11.6; 15.16; 2 Cor. 2.2; 3.9, 11; 8.12; Gal. 2.21; 3.18, 21; 6.3. Most often, the restatement is straightforward, as in the case of the εἰ γάρ clause in Rom. 8.11 and 8.12. In some cases, the εἰ γάρ clause restates something prior to the immediately preceding clause. For example, εἰ γάρ in Rom. 14.15a restates the clause in 14.13b, and Gal. 6.3a restates κενόδοξοι in 5.26a. All of the verses in the preceding list are first-class conditions, but the pattern also holds in the εἰ γάρ phrases in 1 Cor. 2.8 and Gal. 3.21, which occur in second-class conditions. First Thessalonians 4.14 is a case in which the pattern does not hold in a first-class condition, and Gal. 2.18 is a borderline case.

In Rom. 4.1-2, however, the εἰ γάρ restatement pattern is not as clear as it is in the cases listed above. Here the topic shifts from a consideration of

---

16   While it is possible to assign the occurrences of κατὰ σάρκα in Paul neatly to one of these two categories, it is interesting to note the number of times that the two categories of kinship and mode seem to converge. For example, consider the way in which Paul decides to boast κατὰ σάρκα in 2 Cor. 11.18 ('human standards' in NRSV and NET; 'world/worldly' in NIV, RSV) but ends up talking about lineage when he finally gets around to the actual boast three verses later in 11.21-22. There is a similar blurring of categories with reference to the phrase ἐν σαρκί in Phil. 3.3-4 (discussed below; see also the discussion on σάρξ in the section on Phlm. 16 below).

the means by which one sees Abraham as ancestor to a discussion of the grounds of Abraham's justification. Yet it is possible that the εἰ γάρ restatement pattern holds if Paul thinks of *physical descent* and *justification by law* as synonymous ideas, so that 4.1-2 means something along the lines of

> What will we say? Is Abraham found to be our ancestor by physical descent? Because if (εἰ γάρ) it was true that Abraham was justified by works [that is, if he established a line of descent], then it is also true that he had grounds for a boast, though not in God's eyes (Rom. 4.1-2, LLS).[17]

As Richard Hays notes, Paul equates justification by works of law, circumcision, and physical descent from Abraham throughout the discussion in 3.27–4.22.[18] These three ideas virtually coalesce into a unitary construct, which, intriguingly, also corresponds to the three elements in the Jewish dialectic of race: religious identity (justification), social identity (circumcision), and physical identity (descent from Abraham). In other words, Paul's discussion of justification by faith proceeds in terms of a racial framework.

In 4.9-12, Paul begins his interpretation of Gen. 15.6 with a question that deconstructs the traditional reckoning of circumcision as a sign of the covenant between God and Abraham's descendants. First, calling attention to Abraham's uncircumcised state during the time in which he received the gift of righteousness, Paul goes on to insist on that basis that Abraham's uncircumcised state has implications both for the circumcised and for the uncircumcised. By maintaining that Abraham's relationship with God precedes his receipt of circumcision, Paul positions faith as the defining element of identity vis-à-vis a relationship to God prior to the point at which circumcision is established as an indicium of identity. That is, Paul establishes faith as the *criterion* for membership in the community of Abraham's descendents, prior to the establishment of any membership *indicium*.

The thesis of 4.9-12 appears at the end of the paragraph in 4.11-12, in a

---

17 My translation of 4.1 follows the punctuation and the reasoning in Richard Hays's '"Have We Found Abraham to Be Our Forefather According to the Flesh?" A Reconsideration of Rom. 4.1', *NTS* 27.1 (1985): 76–98. Hays translates 4.1 with two questions: 'What then shall we say? Have we found Abraham (to be) our forefather according to the flesh?' (p. 81; cf. James D.G. Dunn, *Romans* [2 vols; WBC; Dallas: Word Books, 1988], 1.199). Based on analysis of similar sets of rhetorical questions elsewhere in Romans, he argues that the second question in the pair is (a) rhetorical, (b) a false proposition arising from the foregoing discussion, and (c) refuted in the subsequent discussion. In this case, Paul argues against the ethnic reasoning that insists that Abraham is the forefather of Jews only, an implication that arises from 3.29 (Hays, '"Have We Found Abraham?"', pp. 83–88).

18 Hays, '"Have We Found Abraham?"', p. 90.

two-verse sentence that makes claims about Abraham's relationship to two groups:

> He received circumcision as a seal of the righteousness that he had by faith while he was still uncircumcised, in order that he would be the ancestor of all who believe without being circumcised ... *and likewise the ancestor of those who are not only circumcised* (οὐκ ἐκ περιτομῆς μόνον) *but who also follow in the steps of the uncircumcised faith of our ancestor Abraham* (ἀλλὰ καὶ τοῖς στοιχοῦσιν τοῖς ἴχνεσιν ἐν ἀκροβυστίᾳ πίστεως πατρὸς ἡμῶν Ἀβραάμ). (Rom. 4.11-12, LLS, emphasis added)

In 4.11, Paul draws the conclusion that Abraham's uncircumcised state in Gen. 15.6 establishes the paternity of Abraham for uncircumcised believers, because like Abraham they receive righteousness through faith. The precise meaning of 4.12, however, is less clear. The ambiguity in that verse concerns whether Paul speaks of Abraham's paternity with respect to one group or two, a concern that raises questions in both this paragraph and the next (cf. 4.12, 4.16). At stake is whether Paul calls Abraham's paternity of *non-Christian* Jews into question. That is, is there one group in 4.12, a group of Jewish (e.g., circumcised) believers, or two groups, consisting of non-Christian and Christian Jews?

Figure 4.1 illustrates possible ways of interpreting the statements in 4.12 and 4.16 by displaying phrases in other literature that have syntax that is similar to these verses. We can see that when a definite noun precedes the 'not only x but also y' construction (οὐ μόνον ... ἀλλὰ καί), the construction modifies the single group or entity described by the noun, regardless of whether the words or phrases that make up the construction are anarthrous (Philo, *Spec. Laws* 1.307; cf. 2 Cor. 9.12) or articular (Philo, *Spec. Laws* 3.19). Further, when phrases within the construction are anarthrous, the 'not only x but also y' construction describes the group in terms of characteristics; articular phrases inside the construction divide the group in question into subgroups. For example, Figure 4.1 shows that the impious in *Spec. Laws* 3.19 are composed of two subgroups, and the group in *Moses* 1.34 has several characteristics.

In contrast, when not preceded by a definite substantive, the 'not only x but also y' construction defines two entities rather than one, as shown at the bottom of Figure 4.1, again, regardless of whether the phrases within the construction are articular (Philo, *Contemplative Life* 10; Josephus, *Ag. Ap.* 2.210) or anarthrous (Phil. 2.12; Josephus, *J.A.* 2.94). The phrases within the construction describe two groups when the clauses are articular and two ideas or qualities when the clauses are anarthrous. Analyses of additional 'not only x but also y' constructions in Paul, Philo, and Josephus confirm the interpretation described here. Our analysis suggests that Rom. 4.12, which has syntax similar to that of *Moses* 1.34, concerns a

	δούλους ἀπέφαινε **τοὺς οὐκ** ἐλευθέρους **μόνον**
	ἀλλὰ καὶ ξένους καὶ ἱκέτας καί μετοίκους
	He made slaves of men who were not only free but guests, suppliants and
	settlers (Philo, *Moses*, 1.34)
1 item,	**θεὸς** δὲ **οὐκ** ἀνθρώπων **μόνον, ἀλλὰ** καὶ θεῶν ἐστι
2 or more	θεόj
Characteristics	God is god not only of men but also of gods (Philo, *Spec. Laws*, 1.307)
(Preceding	
Definite	καὶ πατέρα περιτομῆς **τοῖς οὐκ** ἐκ περιτομῆς **μόνον**
Noun)	**ἀλλὰ** καὶ <u>τοῖς στοιχοῦσιν τοῖς ἴχνεσιν</u> τῆς ἐν ἀκρο
	βυστίᾳ πίστεως τοῦ πατρὸς ἡμῶν Ἀβραάμ (Rom. 4.12)
	And the father of the circumcision, for those who are not only
	circumcised but who follow in the footsteps of the uncircumcised faith of
	our father Abraham
	ἀσεβούοι δ᾽ **οὐκ** <u>οἱ δρῶντες</u> **μόνον, ἀλλὰ** καὶ ὅσοι <u>τοῖς δρῶσιν</u>
	To the impious, not only those doing the deeds but also whoever is
1 Group,	with those doing them (Philo, *Spec. Laws*, 3.19)
2 subgroups	
(Preceding	παντὶ **τῷ σπέρματι, οὐ** <u>τῷ ἐκ τοῦ νόμου</u> **μόνον ἀλλὰ** καὶ <u>τῷ ἐκ</u>
Definite	<u>πίστεως Ἀβραάμ</u>
Noun)	To all the seed, not only the seed having the law but also seed having the
	faith of Abraham (Rom. 4.16)
2 Groups	Οὗος μέν, . . . **οὐ** <u>τοὺς ὁμοφύλους</u> **μόνον, ἀλλὰ** καὶ <u>τοὺς</u>
(Preceding	<u>πλησιάζοντας ἀναπιμπλᾶσι</u>
Indefinite	This . . . infects not only their compatriots but also their neighbors
Noun)	(Philo, *Contemplative Life*, 10; cf. Josephus, *Ag. Ap.*, 2.210)
2 Ideas	μη. . . . ἐν <u>τῇ παρουσίᾳ</u> μου **μόνον, ἀλλὰ** νύν . . . ἐν <u>τῇ</u>
(Preceding	<u>ἀπουσίᾳ</u> μου, . . . ἑαυτῶν σωτηρίαν κατεργάζεσθε
Indefinite	Not only in my presence but now in my absence . . . work out your
Noun)	own salvation (Phil. 2.12; cf. Josephus, *J.A.*, 2.94)

Figure 4.1 – Groups in Romans 4.12

single group of people who are further described in terms of the additional
characteristics of circumcision and faithfulness.[19]

19   So many interpreters: e.g., Richard Hays, *The Conversion of the Imagination: Paul as
an Interpreter of Scripture* (Grand Rapids and Cambridge: Eerdmans, 2005), p. 76; Douglas
Moo, *The Epistle to the Romans* (NICNT; Grand Rapids and Cambridge: Eerdmans, 1996),
pp. 270–71; Neil Elliott, *The Rhetoric of Romans* (JSNTSS, 45; Sheffield: JSOT Press, 1990),
p. 161; Ernst Käsemann, *Commentary on Romans* (trans. Geoffrey Bromiley; Grand Rapids:
Eerdmans, 1980), p. 116; Dunn, *Romans*, 1.210-11. However, according to Dunn the
grammar identifies two groups, but the οὐ μόνον . . . ἀλλὰ καί syntax indicates that he has
only one group in mind (see also Brendan Byrne, *Romans* [Sacra Pagina, 6; Collegeville, MN:

Thus, when Paul calls Abraham the father of the single group 'who are not only circumcised but who also walk in the footsteps of . . . Abraham's faith', he answers the question posed in 4.1b with reference to the natural descendants of Abraham. To wit, a relationship with Abraham that is *merely* κατὰ σάρκα falls short of the relationship with the founding ancestor when considered from the perspective of faith. When 4.12 says that some of Abraham's seed 'walk in the uncircumcised faith of Abraham', Paul declares that these progeny of Abraham are those who have a faith commensurate with Abraham's faith; that is, they have a faith that comes apart from circumcision and the law (cf. 4.23-24).

So far, then, Paul's discussion of justification through faith in Romans 4 is predicated on kinship logic, but it uses a kinship logic that is completely at odds with a modern popular reckoning of descent. In this calculus of kinship, *faith* is the necessary and sufficient cause for *kinship*.[20] Paul establishes a new basis for the relationship between the believing, circumcised, 'biological' descendants and the founding patriarch. He emphasizes that their relationship to Abraham rests on faith notwithstanding the physical relationship acknowledged at the outset of this argument (cf. Gal. 2.15-16). Thus far, Paul has not denied that non-Christian Jews continue to have a unique relationship with the patriarch, but here he situates the locus of identity for believing Jews in the faith principle rather than in physical descent. Paul's argument completely reorders the calculus of ancestry via the principle of faith, by creating a shared history and kinship between uncircumcised Gentiles and circumcised Jews who had no shared history previously, thus anticipating a destiny whereby believing Gentiles participate in the blessings promised to Israel as children of Abraham.

But does this argument imply that Abraham's physical descendants are

---

Liturgical Press, 1996], pp. 150–51), while Sanday and Headlam point to the grammatical 'solecism' in this verse (W. Sanday and A.C. Headlam, *The Epistle to the Romans* [ICC; New York: Charles Scribner, 1911], p. 108). Moo also sees one group in 4.12 but is unable to account for the first article in 4.12, which precedes the οὐ μόνον . . . ἀλλὰ καί construction. My analysis does account for the first article, which puzzles Moo, though it is true that the articles in the last part of the construction do not strictly follow the patterns discussed above: it is anarthrous in the first part of the construction (οὐκ ἐκ περιτομῆς μόνον), but articular in the second part (ἀλλὰ καὶ τοῖς στοιχοῦσιν τοῖς ἴχνεσιν). Nevertheless, 4.12 belongs with the group shown in Figure 4.1, where the 'not only x but also y' grammar defines additional characteristics vs. subgroups. In this case the grammar augments the definite substantive (πατέρα περιτομῆς τοῖς) by restating a characteristic (ἐκ περιτομῆς) and giving a further description of the overall group (τοῖς στοιχοῦσιν τοῖς ἴχνεσιν . . . ἀκροβυστία πίστεως).

20 Given that we argued in the last chapter that religion was in a dialectical tension with kinship in formulating the boundaries of the Jewish community, the mere fact that Paul uses kinship logic is not in and of itself remarkable. The notion that a religious principle *supplants* kinship, however, would be surprising for some first-century Jews (see Hays, *The Conversion of the Imagination*, pp. 61–84, esp. 70–74).

excluded from God's promises to Israel when they do not participate in an Abraham-like faith that is apart from the law like the faith under discussion in 3.21-31? On the contrary, application of the same grammatical observations from the analysis of 4.12 above produces a reading of 4.16 that moves in the opposite direction. Similar to 4.12, a definite collective noun (τῷ σπέρματι) precedes the 'not only x but also y' construction in 4.16, but unlike 4.12, here there are articular substantives within the construction that further divide the superset consisting of Abraham's descendants into two subsets (cf. Philo, *Spec. Laws* 3.19 in Figure 4.1):[21]

> For this reason it is from faith, in order that the promise may rest on grace and be guaranteed to all his descendants (παντὶ τῷ σπέρματι) – not only to the one who is a descendant by the reckoning of the law (τῷ ἐκ τοῦ νόμου) but also to the one who is a descendant by reckoning from Abraham's faith (τῷ ἐκ πίστεως Ἀβραάμ) – for he is the ancestor of us all. (Rom. 4.16, LLS)

If it were not for the statements in 4.11-12, we might be tempted to identify non-believing Jews as the first set of descendants in 4.16 and Gentile believers as the second set. Instead, the second group, 'those who are descendants by participating in Abraham's faith' in 4.16, are the believing Gentiles *and* believing Jews from 4.11-12 (cf. Rom. 9.30; Gal. 3.7). The first set of descendants in 4.16 (τῷ ἐκ τοῦ νόμου) refers to *non-Christian* Jews (cf. Rom. 9.5), but the second part of this verse makes it clear that all of the ἐκ πίστεως descendants, both Jewish and Gentile, participate in the inheritance which was first promised to Abraham's ἐκ τοῦ νόμου biological seed.[22]

However, if we have understood the syntax in these statements correctly, the guarantee in 4.16 of continuity within the divine promise with reference to Abraham's descendents ἐκ τοῦ νόμου seems to be at odds with the assertions in 4.12-15 that insist that faith is the sole determiner of inheritance (cf. Rom. 9.8). In fact, this discussion in Romans 4 contains the same blend of continuity and discontinuity about God's promises and Abraham's descendants as appears in the olive-tree metaphor in Rom. 11.17-26. Those who believe without circumcision in Rom. 4.11 correspond to the wild branches newly grafted into the olive tree. Likewise, the circumcised believers in 4.12 correspond to those natural branches, which are attached to the olive tree by faith. Romans 4.16 refers to the group containing those who are ἐκ τοῦ νόμου, and corresponds to the natural

---

21   Dunn, *Romans*, 1.216, and Hays, *The Conversion of the Imagination*, pp. 76–77, though on different grounds.

22   *Contra* Moo who thinks on the basis of 4.11-12 that 4.16 refers to believing Jews and believing Gentiles, though he concedes that Paul could be referring to unbelieving Jews in 4.16 in a way reminiscent of Rom. 11.11-30 (*Romans*, p. 278).

branches that have been broken from the olive tree (Rom. 11.17, 23). There may also be in 4.16 a prefiguring of 'all Israel' in 11.26a, since 4.16 refers to Abraham as the father of 'all of us' (Ἀβραάμ ὅς ἐστιν πατὴρ πάντων ἡμῶν). If all this is true, then 4.16, which insists that the descendant who is ἐκ τοῦ νόμου is an heir through faith (διὰ τοῦτο ἐκ πίστεως), has implications for one's reading of Rom. 11.25-26.[23] Yet despite these last more controversial matters, it is clear that Rom. 4.11-16 and 11.17-24 both describe *two people-groups that are descended from Abraham but are differentiated by the principle of faith*, Jewish and Gentile believers on the one hand and non-Christian Jews on the other.[24]

The logic in the remainder of 4.16-25 is easy to follow:

- Both sets of Abraham's descendants (non-Christian Jews and all Christians, 4.16) are destined to participate in the promises to Israel through faith.
- Abraham's faith that God's promise was true rested on his confidence in God's ability (1) to bring life to what is dead, and (2) to create the real from the unreal (4.17-21).
- The person who participates in Abraham's faith is someone who fully trusts these divine abilities (4.23-25).

In the final step of this argument, Paul several times returns to the idea that Abraham had faith in God's ability to overcome death, an idea that he sees as an analogue to the believer's faith in the God who raises Jesus from the dead (4.17, 19, 24). However, it is significant that when Paul first deploys this motif in 4.17b he utilizes it in the context of describing Abraham as the 'father of many nations', joining it to the idea that God is able to create *ex nihilo*. Thus, God not only overcomes the dead state of

---

23 The correspondence between the groups in Rom. 4.11-12, 16 and the groups depicted in Rom. 11.17-26 leads me to support several aspects of N.T. Wright's (minority) interpretation of 11.25-26 (*The Climax of the Covenant* [Minneapolis: Fortress, 1993], pp. 246–51; id., 'The Letter to the Romans', in Leander Keck [ed.], *The New Interpreter's Bible* [Nashville: Abingdon, 2000], 10.688–90). With Wright I think that 'all Israel' in 11.26 refers to Gentile and Jewish Christians, and that the Jewish Christians in this group are included in all Israel by faith rather than through a *Sonderweg* (cf. Rom. 4.16a in light of the interpretation of 4.16 offered here). See also Myles M. Bourke, *A Study of the Metaphor of the Olive Tree in Romans XI* (Washington, DC: Paulist Press, 1947), pp. 79–83.

24 *Contra* Hodge, *If Sons then Heirs*, pp. 41, 88–89, who thinks that the two groups in these verses are (non-Christian) Jews and believing Gentiles. Because Hodge rejects the idea that Paul's gospel is addressed to non-Christian Jews, she has to resist the idea that Rom. 4.16 mediates the Abrahamic promise to those ἐκ νόμου on the basis of faith (διὰ τοῦτο ἐκ πίστεως; 4.16a). She posits that the faith spoken of here is the faith of Abraham, rather than the faith of Jesus Christ, despite the fact that the discourse in Rom. 4 stands as an apology for the inclusive nature of πίστις Χριστοῦ (Rom. 3.22, 26, 30). Her exegesis rests upon her understanding of the use of Paul's 'ἐκ language' to represent a generative power that is able to transmit the Abrahamic promises (*If Sons then Heirs*, pp. 79–91), exegesis that seems to put far too much weight on a preposition, especially in view of Paul's notoriously opaque usage.

Abraham's body and the deadness of Sarah's womb, but he also calls into existence a seed, a set of descendants where previously there had been none.[25] For Paul, Abraham's paternity of believing Gentiles is not symbolic, representative, or spiritual. Paul thinks that God creates a kinship between Abraham, uncircumcised Gentile believers, and circumcised Jewish believers that is as real as any claims about kinship κατὰ σάρκα.[26]

2. *1 Corinthians 10.1*

First Corinthians 10.1 lies in a larger discourse in which Paul addresses concerns about the eating of food sacrificed in pagan temples. In chs 9 and 10, Paul develops two examples that instruct the community on the proper use of Christian freedom. First Corinthians 9.24-27 is a pivotal section around which the examples in 1 Cor. 9.1-23 and 10.1-11 are balanced. In 9.1-23 Paul uses his own apostolic practice as a positive example of the way that personal liberty should give way to the interests of the community. The pivotal section in 9.24-27 introduces the idea of self-discipline as a limit to liberty, and in 10.1-11 Paul goes on to describe a negative example from Israel's history that illustrates the dangers of a lack of self-discipline.

Paul's use of ἀδελφός and πατήρ in 1 Cor. 10.1 is noteworthy:

> I do not want you to be unaware, brothers and sisters (ἀδελφοί), that our ancestors (οἱ πατέρες ἡμῶν) were all under the cloud, and all passed through the sea.

The employment of ἀδελφοί in the introduction to a paragraph about the experiences of the Exodus generation reinforces the notion discussed earlier, that the New Testament use of such familial language derives from Jewish usage. We should also note that Paul uses a first-person plural pronoun in this verse and that this usage continues the first-person description of his apostolic ethic in 9.24-27. The first-person plural in 10.1 is all the more conspicuous because an example from Israel's history directly follows. Paul's use of οἱ πατέρες ἡμῶν suggests that in his view the family relationships that exist within the Christian community apply not only to the present and future of the community but to the past as

---

25 Wright, *The Climax of the Covenant*, p. 248.

26 Similarly Buell, 'The Politics of Interpretation', p. 241. Moo and Hays may be cited as examples of readings that threaten to domesticate the power of Paul's appeal to family language in this passage ('spiritual father' in Moo, *Romans*, pp. 269–70; and Hays's references to Paul's 'symbolic' statements about Abraham as a 'representative' figure [' "Have We Found Abraham?" ', pp. 90, 92]). Paul's references to God's ability to create *ex nihilio* (... καλοῦντος τὰ μὴ ὄντα ὡς ὄντα in 4.17b; see also Dunn, *Romans*, 1.216) suggest that Paul is speaking of new kinship relations with Gentiles that are as 'real' as any other kind of ethnic relationship.

well. That Paul would consider himself kin to the Exodus generation is no surprise, but that he would view the all-Gentile or mixed Jewish and Gentile group of Christians at Corinth as kin to that generation is astonishing. In this verse, Paul declares himself kin to the Christians at Corinth through his use of ἀδελφοί, and explicitly refers to his *common ancestry and shared history* with these Christians. If we recall Anthony Smith's observation that shared myths of ancestry are essential to ethnic group formation and that shared history plays a crucial role in ethnic group survival, then we will better appreciate the latent power of the realism with which Paul presupposes a common 'ethnic' origin and history with the Gentile and Jewish Christians at Corinth.[27] This is a potent example of the way that Paul used the great narrative of Israelite redemption to help shape the identity and values of new Christian converts.

In the context of 1 Corinthians 8–10, Paul's appeal from their shared family history functions as a warning to believers against the dangers of idolatry.[28] Paul uses typological language in recounting several details in the story – the ancient Israelites ate 'spiritual bread' and drank a 'spiritual drink' from a 'spiritual rock'. Yet, Paul does not give warrant for understanding his usage of the specific terms ἀδελφός and πατήρ in a spiritualized, typological, or metaphorical manner. Spiritualized under-standings of ἀδελφός and πατήρ appear frequently, however, in second-ary literature, for example in Anthony Thistleton's translation of 10.1: 'I do not want you to fail to recognize, my dear fellow Christians, that our spiritual ancestors were all under a cloud and all passed through the sea.' Thistleton translates ἀδελφοί and πατέρες as 'dear fellow Christians' and 'spiritual ancestors', respectively, maintaining that in this context Paul's meaning has more in common with Hellenistic usage than with Jewish usage. He notes in justification of these translations that 'brother' can describe intimate associations outside of families and that 'father' sometimes referred to similarity of character rather than common ancestry.[29] In protesting Thisleton's translation of 10.1 I do not mean to suggest that Paul never used spiritualized, typological, or metaphorical language. In 1 Cor. 10.1-18 Paul draws a lesson from history to serve as an example for his Gentile Christian kin (τύπος; 10.6), and his references to 'spiritual' food and drink in 1 Cor. 10.3-4 seem to exemplify this usage (see also Gal. 4.21-31; Rom. 5.14; but cf. 1 Cor. 2.15; 3.1; 15.46).

---

27   Leonhard Goppelt makes a similar point about the realism of Paul's language in 'Paulus und die Heilsgeschichte: Schlussfolgerungen aus Röm. IV und 1 Kor. X. 1-13', *NTS* 13 (1966): 31–42 (35–39).

28   R.B. Hays, *First Corinthians* (Louisville: John Knox Press, 1997), p. 159.

29   Thistleton, *The First Epistle to the Corinthians*, p. 724.

Nevertheless, Paul's figurative or typological language in this context does not immediately settle the question of how he uses ἀδελφός and πατήρ in 1 Cor. 10.1 or elsewhere in the corpus. Paul never signals that these words are figurative or fictive. In fact, the only occasion on which he gives a signal that he is using ἀδελφός in an unusual way is when he qualifies the usage at Rom. 9.3 to speak of his 'fleshly' brothers (τῶν ἀδελφῶν μου τῶν συγγενῶν μου κατὰ σάρκα).

Thistleton could be right in thinking that Paul's use of the word derives more from Hellenistic usage than Jewish usage. However, Thistleton's preference for this background may derive from an unstated though common assumption about the biological nature of ethnic and racial relationships. I think it likely that Thistleton and others prefer the Hellenistic background for Paul's use of familial language, and end by 'spiritualizing' the language, because they assume that a Jewish usage applies only in biological relationships, relationships that are generally absent when it comes to Paul and his converts. While Thistleton's translation of 1 Cor. 10.1 communicates his interpretive assumptions more explicitly than other translations, many share the trajectory of his interpretation with reference to Paul's concept of Christian intimacy.[30] Nevertheless, shared history plays an important function in group identity formation, and spiritualized interpretations of Paul's use of family language in this passage can obscure our appreciation for this dynamic.

In Chapter 2, we saw that a shared history is one of the six characteristics by which one may detect *ethnie* in antiquity. According to Anthony Smith, shared history is the intergenerational glue that plays a critical role in ethnic group survival.[31] What in the end defines an ethnic group, according to Smith, is its unique history and its unique response to that history, and from these flow its other cultural marks of individuality and its sense of collective uniqueness.[32] A shared history provides the vehicle by which a group comes to understand its uniqueness, and this becomes translated over time into group self-awareness. Thus, when Paul appeals to examples from Israel's history and frames them as a history shared with Gentile Christians, the telling of history becomes an act of identity formation. Paul's unique interpretations of the story define the group, setting it apart from other groups with a claim on this story. To our appreciation of his typological interpretations of food or drink, we may add a cognizance of the way in which these interpretations create

---

30 Lloyd Lewis approaches Paul's 'metaphorical' use of familial language through anthropology. He describes Paul's language as that of a 'pseudo-family' wherein kinship speech conveys the expectations that group members have for one another ('An African American Appraisal of the Philemon–Paul–Onesimus Triangle', in Felder [ed.], *Stony the Road We Trod*, pp. 232–46 [236]).

31 Smith, *The Ethnic Revival*, pp. 65–66.

32 Smith, *The Ethnic Origins of Nations*, p. 66.

within the group an awareness of itself as unique. Spiritualizing Paul's references to 'fathers' or 'brothers', on the other hand, obscures the fact that as a *history* the story is a purveyance of group survival that fosters a sense of kinship and thereby communicates a sense of ethno-racial belonging. For Paul, biology did not determine kinship.

3. *Philemon 16*

Paul's use of familial language in Philemon is also intriguing, not least because of the tantalizing questions that arise from a close consideration of this brief, very personal letter of mediation.[33] On the surface, at least some of the details surrounding the occasion of the letter are straightforward. Paul writes a personal letter to Philemon, a Phrygian of Colossae, a Christian brother who is among the select group of associates whom Paul addresses as co-workers in the gospel (Phlm. 1, Φιλήμονι τῷ ἀγαπητῷ καὶ συνεργῷ).[34] As in the case of Pliny's letter to Sabinianus in which Pliny intercedes on behalf of a former slave who seeks mediation between him and his patron, Onesimus may have sought out Paul's intercession with Philemon, having been accused of harming his master in some way.[35] Be that as it may, we may be certain that while in Paul's company Onesimus had become both a believer (10) and a close intimate of Paul's (τὰ ἐμὰ σπλάγχνα; 12); Paul had even begun to think of him as an assistant sent by Philemon to aid him in his ministry (13).

There are real questions about the specific kind of favor that Paul wants Philemon to do for him (τὸ ἀγαθόν; 14). Does he want Philemon to return Onesimus to Paul (13), free Onesimus from slavery (16), cancel his debt

---

33 See S.K. Stowers on letters of mediation (*Letter Writing in Greco-Roman Antiquity* [Philadelphia: Westminster, 1986], p. 155).

34 A consideration of passages in which Paul addresses others as co-workers suggests something of the intimacy and affection that he had with and for these kinds of associates: Philemon (Phlm. 1); Prisca and Aquila (Rom. 16.3-4); Timothy (Rom. 16.21; 1 Cor. 4.17); Epaphroditus (Phil. 2.25-27); and Euodia, Syntyche, and Clement (Phil. 4.3). The inference that Philemon is a Phrygian at Colossae depends on the 'near universal' assumption that the Onesimus of Phlm. 10 is also the Colossian Onesimus of Col. 4.9 (J.D.G. Dunn, *The Epistles to the Colossians and to Philemon* [Grand Rapids: Eerdmans, 1996], p. 300).

35 Dunn, *Colossians and Philemon*, pp. 304–305 (Phlm. 18). Indeed, the similarities between the two letters extend beyond their circumstances to their rhetoric. Both writers communicate their positive opinion about the slave's demeanor or character, both appeal to the addressee's nobility of character, and while both are also conscious of their authority vis-à-vis the recipient, they issue appeals rather than commands (Pliny, *Epistle* 9.21.17-18; see translation in Stowers, *Letter Writing*, p. 160). The differences between the two letters, however, are revealing. Dunn thinks that Onesimus may have been accused wrongly; note εἰ in line 18: εἰ δέ τι ἠδίκησέν σε (*Colossians and Philemon*, pp. 338–39). Most importantly, while Pliny seeks a restoration of the past relationship between the unnamed freedman and Sabinianus, Paul seeks a transformed relationship congruent with the new connection as brothers in Christ between Philemon and Onesimus.

(18–21), or deepen the terms of their relationship (16–17)? Despite these questions, there can be little doubt that Paul's affection for both parties saturates the letter.[36] Philemon is beloved by Paul (1), and Paul praises the love that Philemon bestows on other Christians (5). Paul bases his exhortation to Philemon on love (9) and Philemon's history of ministry to the saints (διό; 8). In fact, the whole appeal section of the letter in vv. 8-20 is bracketed and infused by the idea of affection. Paul praises Philemon for refreshing the affections of other Christians (τὰ σπλάγχνα τῶν ἁγίων ἀναπέπαυται; 7), and he closes the appeal by asking for the same favor for himself (ἀνάπαυσόν μου τὰ σπλάγχνα ἐν Χριστῷ; 20). However, by v. 20 we know that Paul has really asked that Philemon refresh Onesimus, since Paul has earlier named Onesimus as the object of his own affections (τουτ᾽ ἔστιν τὰ ἐμὰ σπλάγχνα; 12). Further, in the context of the love language just discussed, the kinship language in this letter becomes even more affective, hailing Philemon as ἀδελφός at three strategic places in the appeal section (7, 16, 20). In addition, Paul calls Onesimus his child and refers to Onesimus' conversion as a birthing (10).

Most intriguing for our purposes is the usage of kinship language in v. 16. There Paul suggests that if Onesimus is a brother who is especially beloved by Paul, then Onesimus will be that much more beloved by Philemon both ἐν σαρκὶ καὶ ἐν κυρίῳ (16). C.F.D. Moule thinks that Paul has ordinary human existence in mind as the meaning of ἐν σαρκὶ similar to the meaning in 2 Cor. 10.3, but admits that this text is not an exact parallel to ours and that it is difficult to find one in Paul.[37] Following somewhat similar reasoning, many see here a reference to Onesimus' earthly social status as a slave (cf. Gal. 3.3; Phil. 3.3-5).[38] It is puzzling, however, that here there is no indication that manner of life is in view as there is in 2 Cor. 10.3 and Gal. 2.20, which contain περιπατοῦντες and ζάω respectively. In addition, in Phlm. 16 the phrases ἐν σαρκί and ἐν κυρίῳ are linked instead of being set in opposition to each other, as happens in Gal. 3.3 and Phil. 3.3-4.[39] Norman Petersen offers a very interesting interpretation of this verse that also focuses on the issue of manumission. For Petersen 'in the flesh' and 'in the Lord' represent two social spheres, and Paul insists that Philemon must now relate to

---

36 Lloyd Lewis, who also approaches Philemon through the prism of its utilization of familial language, has a particularly engaging discussion of the 'love' theme in this letter ('An African American Appraisal').

37 C.F.D. Moule, *The Epistles of Paul the Apostle to the Colossians and to Philemon* (Cambridge: Cambridge University Press, 1957), p. 148.

38 See, for example, Ralph Martin, *Colossians and Philemon* (Frome and London: Butler and Tanner, 1974), p. 167; Eduard Lohse, *Colossians and Philemon* (trans. William Poehlmann; Hermeneia; Philadelphia: Fortress, 1971), p. 203; and Dunn, *Colossians and Philemon*, p. 336; O'Brien, *Colossians, Philemon*, p. 298.

39 Robert Jewett, *Paul's Anthropological Terms* (Leiden: Brill, 1971), p. 134.

Onesimus as an equal in both spheres.⁴⁰ There is much to commend in Petersen's argument, particularly in the way it refuses to conflate 1 Cor. 7.21-24 with what appears in Philemon. However, the interpretation falters on two points. First, it derives the meaning of 'in the flesh' from texts where it is in opposition to 'in the Lord' instead of being linked as in this verse. Second, it focuses on the comparison between slavery and brotherhood in the first half of v. 16 (οὐκέτι ὡς δοῦλον ἀλλ᾽ ὑπὲρ δοῦλον, ἀδελφὸν ἀγαπητόν), instead of the comparison in degrees of brotherly intimacy in the latter half of v. 16 where the 'in the flesh' phrase actually appears (ἀδελφὸν ἀγαπητόν, μάλιστα ἐμοί, πόσῳ δὲ μᾶλλον σοὶ καὶ ἐν σαρκὶ καὶ ἐν κυρίῳ).

Interpreters who connect ἐν σαρκί to Philemon's slave status miss the point of comparison in the latter half of v. 16, either ignoring it or focusing on an implied request for manumission in this verse as in Peterson's understanding. In context, the point of comparison in v. 16 is the intimacy between Onesimus and Paul on the one hand, and the intimacy between Onesimus and Philemon on the other. Paul mentions his attachment to Onesimus several times, calling him 'my child' (10), 'my very heart' (12), and a 'beloved brother' – one who is especially so (16, ἀδελφὸν ἀγαπητόν, μάλιστα ἐμοι). This last indication of intimacy is the most important one for our purposes because Paul uses his intimacy with Onesimus as the basis for imagining the possibilities about a relationship between Onesimus and Philemon. Paul believes that the new relationship between Onesimus and Philemon can go beyond that which Paul shares with Onesimus as a beloved brother in Christ, because Onesimus and Philemon are brothers *both* ἐν κυρίῳ and ἐν σαρκί. Paul probably means that he and Onesimus are brothers ἐν κυρίῳ (cf. Rom. 16.8) but that Onesimus and Philemon can go beyond this brotherhood because they are brothers both in the Lord and in the flesh. In other words, Paul is not here using σάρξ as a general term for physical life, including slave status or economic class; how could that property be greater in the Onesimus–Philemon relationship than in the Onesimus–Paul relationship? Does Paul expect that Philemon and Onesimus can experience *greater* filial feeling than he has for Onesimus because of their prior history as master and fugitive slave? Paul is not using the phrase 'in the flesh' in opposition to 'in the spirit', as in 2 Cor. 4.11, or as a reference to the lower, sinful nature, as he does in Rom. 8.8-9. Instead, Paul mentions brotherhood in the flesh as if it is something that may *enrich* a brotherhood in Christ.

Eduard Schweizer identifies seven categories that describe the way that σάρξ functions in Paul.⁴¹ In this article, Schweizer assigns Phlm. 16 to the category in which σάρξ refers to the OT sense of the interconnection of

---

40 Petersen, *Rediscovering Paul*, pp. 93–99.
41 E. Schweizer, 'σάρξ, σαρκικός, σάρκινος', *TDNT* 8.99–151.

the generations and physical descent within earthly, national Israel. Despite this category assignment, he nonetheless maintains that the word refers to the master–slave social relation rather than to kinship in Philemon, arbitrarily ruling out the idea that blood relationships may be operative in this text. Indeed, most of the texts in this portion of his discussion refer to physical descent (Rom. 4.1; 9.3, 5, 8; 11.14; 1 Cor. 1.26; 10.18; Gal. 4.23, 29; Phil. 3.3), and the two texts in this category cited along with Phlm. 16 that supposedly do not take on the physical descent nuance probably belong in a different category.[42] Schweizer's assumption that σάρξ is a reference to slavery probably hinges on the appearance of δοῦλος in 16a. In v. 16a, however, slavery seems to be specifically minimized as an applicable category, whereas brotherhood, a kinship relation, is affirmed in the same verse. While I do think that Paul hints at Onesimus' manumission by the phrase οὐκέτι ὡς δοῦλον in v. 16a, kinship is the point of comparison at which the relationship between Onesimus and Philemon has greater potential than that between Onesimus and Paul in v. 16c. In speaking about the kinship ἐν σαρκί between Onesimus and Philemon, Paul is probably referring to the general Greco-Roman notion that a common kinship emerges from a common homeland.[43] If so, then Paul suggests that the new Christian kinship between Philemon and Onesimus is even closer than the bonds of affection between Paul and Onesimus because Philemon and Onesimus share two kinds of kinship bonds, one in the flesh and the other in the Lord (cf. τῶν ἀδελφῶν μου ... κατὰ σάρκα; Rom. 9.3). This implies that just as Paul recognized continuing ethnoracial relationships between himself and non-Christian Jews (Rom. 9.1-3) as well as between non-Christian Jews and Abraham (Rom. 4.16; 9.5), he also recognized the influence of ethno-racial relationships among those Christians who 'used to be Gentiles' (1 Cor. 12.2).

This brief consideration of the role of kinship in Rom. 4; 1 Cor. 10.1; and Phlm. 16 illuminate something of the internal dynamics of Christian community according to Paul, and form a backdrop for the portrait of Paul's self-identity and group identity discussed in the next section. In sum:

---

42   1 Cor. 3.3 and 2 Cor. 10.4 seem to refer to human reasoning and probably belong to the category which includes references pertaining to the 'whole of man's physical existence', encompassing health and sickness (Gal. 4.13), physical trials (1 Cor. 7.28), and mental capacity (Rom. 6.19) (Schweizer, 'σάρξ, σαρκικός, σάρκινος', pp. 125–35).

43   On the common homeland of Onesimus and Philemon, see n. 34 above. On the confluence of Greco-Roman ideas of kinship and territory, see Chapter 3 above. The idea that σάρξ possibly refers to a relation between Onesimus and Philemon as that between fellow citizens also appears in Wilhelm Schauf, *Sarx: Der Begriff 'Fleisch' beim Apostel Paulus unter besonderer Berücksichtigung seiner Erlösungslehre* (Münster: Verlag der Aschendorffschen Verlagsbuchhandlung, 1924), pp. 109–10.

1   Paul's claims about Christian kinship have a realism that tells us that he thought of the Christian community in familial terms and that he saw genuine kinship relationships emerging from God's ability to create the real out of the unreal.

2   Abraham is the ancestor of believing Jews and believing Gentiles, and these descendants are the heirs of Abraham's legacy of faith. Along with ἐκ πίστεως descendants, however, Abraham also has a second group of descendants, non-believing Jews or ἐκ τού νόμου descendants, and Paul declares that the latter too will receive the promised inheritance through faith in accordance with grace (cf. ἔλεος in Rom. 11.17-32).

3   When in 1 Cor. 10.1 Paul mentions that the Exodus generation was also the ancestor of the mostly Gentile Christians at Corinth, his interest is not in shared bloodlines but in shared history. In both Rom. 4.23-24 and 1 Cor. 10.11 Paul views the history of Israel as particularly important and instructive for the Christian community, and, more importantly, as forming a shared history among Gentile Christians, Jewish Christians, and pre-Christ Jews.

4   Finally, according to Phlm. 16, birth kinship can strengthen the bonds of Christian kinship.

2. Paul's Self-Identity and Group Affiliation

In *Early Judaism*, Martin Jaffe explores the relationship between religion as a way of life and personal identity. According to Jaffe:

> [Religion] heightens awareness of morally binding connections between the self, the human community, and the most essential structures of reality ... Personal identity in a religious setting ... includes far more than the web of relations containing the individual, the family, friends, or immediate social group of one's personal acquaintance. It normally includes a conception of how all these relationships are connected to generations of the distant past and the far-off future, as well to the forces and powers that are held to account for the world as it is.[44]

Jaffe's description of religion sets the stage for this investigation of Paul's identity by emphasizing the way that religion and personal identity are inextricably linked in the past and present by connections to other individuals and groups. As suggested by Jaffe, inevitably we will find that it is impossible to synthesize Paul's comments about his own identity without learning about his 'web of relations' or relational matrix.

We know Paul primarily through two self-characterizations that were integral to his self-image – he was an apostle to the Gentiles convinced of the truth of the gospel of Jesus Christ, and he was descended from the

---

44   Martin Jaffe, *Early Judaism* (Upper Saddle River, NJ: Prentice-Hall, 1997), p. 7.

people of Israel. The remainder of this chapter pursues an understanding of Paul's self-identity by examining texts that describe Paul through these images. I begin with a shorter section on Paul's apostleship, even though his self-identity as an Israelite is chronologically prior to his apostleship. The section on Paul's apostleship examines two passages in detail, while the second, longer section on Paul as an Israelite synthesizes the passages about Paul's group membership and Israelite identity across a number of texts.

a. *Paul the Apostle to the Gentiles*

Clearly, Paul's commission as apostle to the Gentiles was tremendously important to his self-understanding (Rom. 1.5, 13; 11.13-14; 15.16, 18; Gal. 1.16; 2.2, 7-9; 1 Thess. 2.16), and it is fitting that we examine this aspect of his self-identity, if only briefly. Of these texts, we consider Rom. 11.13-15 and Gal. 1.15-16 below, since these texts not only provide insight into Paul's apostolic identity but also offer clues about his relational matrix.

1. *Romans 11.13-14*

Paul has two rhetorical goals in the passage that contains Rom. 11.13-14. Romans 11.11-24 first describes the way that Jewish rejection of faith in Christ inaugurates a chain of events that paradoxically ends by producing Jewish acceptance of this faith. The chain of events involves Israel and the Gentiles in a symbiotic relationship in God's plan of redemption, in which the actions of each group contribute to the other's salvation. To start, Jewish rejection of faith in Christ somehow enables the extension of salvation to the Gentiles for an unknown period of time (11.11, 25). Next, Gentile 'fullness' in the gospel provokes Israel to jealousy, a jealousy that moves Israel in turn to accept salvation (11.11-15). Having laid out the mutual interdependence of Israelites and Gentiles in redemption, Paul finally warns his Gentile audience against a dangerous arrogance towards Israel. Gentiles should not assume that Israel's rejection is permanent and that Gentiles replace Israelites in the patriarch's family tree (11.19, 23-24).

We are most interested in 11.11-15, a passage in which Paul connects his ministry to the cycle of salvation described in the larger context. In 11.11 Paul repudiates the notion that Israel's misstep has led to a complete rejection by God. Instead, according to God's plan Israel's misstep results in salvation for the Gentiles, a salvation that stimulates Israel to jealousy. Paul elaborates on this idea in 11.12: if Israel's misstep results in riches for the world and for Gentiles, then surely their acceptance of Christ will result in even greater riches. Then, in a parenthetical statement in vv. 13–14, Paul explains that his own ministry to Gentiles is also a ministry to Jews:

And I say to you Gentiles accordingly, as long as (ἐφ' ὅσον) I am apostle to the Gentiles, if I could somehow make my biological kin (μου τὴν σάρκα) jealous and save some of them, then I hold my ministry in honor (δοξάζω). (Rom. 11.13-14, LLS)

The translation above differs from the usual one because most scholars reject the temporal interpretation of ἐφ' ὅσον ('for as long as'). This difference probably results from the fact that most regard Paul's comment in this verse as not truly indicative of how he understood his ministry over time.[45] As will become apparent, however, I maintain the temporal interpretation of this phrase for just that reason. That is, I think there is evidence in the corpus that Paul's sentiment in Rom. 11.13-14 represents his central conviction about his ministry and its contribution to the unfolding drama of the gospel of Christ, and the translation above better communicates this aspect of Paul's logic.[46] Paul expects (παραζηλώσω; future tense, 11.14) that the continuing significance of his own ministry to Gentiles (δοξάζω; present tense, 11.13) remains tied to the possibility that he will be able to provoke Jewish jealousy of Gentile salvation and thus stimulate Jewish salvation. For all practical purposes, therefore, Paul's mission to Gentiles has Jewish salvation as its ultimate goal.

As implied in the discussion of the translation of ἐφ' ὅσον above, there are various opinions about the way in which we should understand Paul's remarks in 11.13-14 about the function of his apostolate. While Brendan Byrne agrees with the assessment that Jewish salvation is the ultimate goal of Paul's ministry, Munck goes beyond what is said here, maintaining that Paul believed that his was a decisive role in the unfolding drama of the gospel.[47] Dunn, on the other hand, recognizes that stimulating Jewish jealousy is a 'crucial factor in the final act of the world drama' for Paul, but rejects the idea that this is the ultimate goal to which Paul's ministry moves. For his part, Moo dismisses the remarks, deciding that Paul here offers only one of the lesser motivations for his work.[48] With a view towards understanding Paul's missionary practice, E.P. Sanders maintains that in Romans Paul considers for the first time the failure of the Jewish mission in light of his own singular success with Gentile evangelism. According to Sanders, Paul revises the traditional scheme to fit the facts; God will save Israel only after the salvation of the Gentiles, and not before as expected. In so doing, he assigns himself only a minor role in the

---

45 Dunn, *Romans*, 2.655. On ἐφ' ὅσον in a temporal sense, cf. especially 2 Pet. 1.13, Mt. 9.15 (BDAG, s.v. ἐπί, 18.b). See also Gal. 4.1: 'For as long a time (ἐφ' ὅσον χρόνον) as the heir is a child, he is no different from a slave.'

46 δοξάζω is at the end of the clause in 11.13 for emphasis.

47 Byrne, *Romans*, p. 339; Johannes Munck, *Paul and the Salvation of Mankind* (trans. Frank Clarke; Richmond, VA: John Knox Press, 1959), pp. 36–68.

48 Dunn, *Romans*, 2.656, 669; Moo, *Romans*, p. 691 n. 45.

mission to Israel.[49] I propose, however, that Rom. 11.13-14 represents an accurate statement of the goals of Paul's commission and that an examination of Gal. 1.15-24 casts doubt on the idea that he assigns himself a role in a mission to Israel only as an afterthought.

2. Galatians 1.15-24

Appendix IV of NA[27] indicates that Gal. 1.15 alludes to Isa. 49.1. According to this index, there are 28 citations or allusions to verses in Isaiah 49 across 12 New Testament works, making these verses among the most-quoted OT passages in the early church.[50] Verses from this chapter appear six times in Paul (Rom. 9.16; 14.11; 2 Cor. 6.2; 7.6; Gal. 1.15; Phil. 2.7), five times in Luke, twice in Acts, and once each in Ephesians and Hebrews.[51] Overall, this text seems to have been a favorite of writers in Paul's orbit.[52] I include a translation of the first six verses here for convenience in following the subsequent discussion:

> [1]'Hear me you islands, and pay attention O nations! In due course, it will be established', says the Lord. He called my name from my mother's womb (ἐκ κοιλίας μητρός μου ἐκάλεσεν τὸ ὄνομά μου), [2]and he appointed my mouth to be like a sharp sword. He hid me under the covering of his hand, he appointed me as a select arrow; thus in his quiver he protected me. [3]He said to me, 'You are my slave (μοι δοῦλός μου εἶ σύ), O Israel – in you I will be glorified (ἐν σοὶ δοξασθήσομαι).'

> [4]Then I said, 'Vainly I have labored, that is, I have given my strength in futility and for nothing. Because of this, the turning point of my life is with the Lord, and my suffering has been in the presence of my God.' [5]Yet now thus says the Lord, the one who created me from the womb as his very own slave (ὁ πλάσας με ἐκ κοιλίας δοῦλον ἑαυτῷ), to gather Jacob and Israel to him – 'I will be gathered and I will be glorified before the Lord (καὶ δοξασθήσομαι ἐναντίον κυρίου), and my God will be my strength!' – [6]He said to me, 'A great thing has been done in you; you have been called to be my servant to establish the tribes of Jacob, and to turn around the dispersed ones of Israel. Behold, I appoint you to be a testament to all of the races of humanity (τέθεικά σε εἰς διαθήκην

49 Sanders, *Paul, the Law and the Jewish People*, pp. 184–85.

50 Other frequently cited OT passages include Deut. 32 (36 times in 12 NT works); Daniel 2 (34 times in eight NT works), Dan. 7 (57 times in seven NT works) and Daniel 12 (28 times in nine NT works); Isaiah 40 and 53 (29 times in 12 NT works and 42 times in 13 NT works respectively).

51 An allusion to Isa. 49.18 at Rom. 14.11, as affirmed by the editors of NA[27], is not convincing. The editors apparently discern an allusion in the expression ζῶ ἐγώ, λέγει κύριος. However, this phrase occurs several times in the LXX outside of Isa. 49.18 (Num. 14.28; Zeph. 2.9; Jer. 22.24; 26.18), including 11 times in Ezekiel.

52 The remaining references appear in the Apocalypse, where there are six allusions and one quotation, and one reference in each of the Synoptic Gospels.

γένους), to be a light to the nations (εἰς φῶς ἐθνῶν τοῦ εἶναί), so that you will stand for salvation unto the ends of the earth (σωτηρίαν ἕως ἐσχάτου τῆς γῆς).' (Isa. 49.1-6, LLS)

Luke especially associates Isaiah 49 with Jesus: there are allusions to this OT passage both at the scene of Simeon's prophecy at the presentation of Jesus at the temple (Lk. 2.25-32), and at the ascension (Acts 1.8):[53]

> [25]Now there was a man in Jerusalem whose name was Simeon; this man was righteous and devout, looking forward to the consolation of Israel (παράκλησιν τοῦ 'Ισραήλ; cf. Isa. 49.13), and the Holy Spirit rested on him. [26]It had been revealed to him by the Holy Spirit that he would not see death before he had seen the Lord's Messiah. [27]Guided by the Spirit, Simeon came into the temple; and when the parents brought in the child Jesus, to do for him what was customary under the law, [28]Simeon took him in his arms and praised God, saying, [29]'Master, now you are dismissing your servant in peace, according to your word; [30]for my eyes have seen your salvation (τὸ σωτήριόν σου), [31]which you have prepared in the presence of all peoples, [32]a light for revelation to the Gentiles (φῶς εἰς ἀποκάλυψιν ἐθνῶν; cf. Isa. 49.6, 9) and for glory to your people Israel'. (Lk. 2.25-32)

> 'But you will receive power when the Holy Spirit has come upon you; and you will be my witnesses in Jerusalem, in all Judea and Samaria, and to the ends of the earth (ἕως ἐσχάτου τῆς γῆς; cf. Isa. 49.6)'. (Acts 1.8)

As a part of Luke's strategy to associate early church leaders with Jesus' authority, he then explicitly quotes Isa. 49.6 and associates it with Paul at Acts 13.46-47:

> Then both Paul and Barnabas spoke out boldly, saying, 'It was necessary that the word of God should be spoken first to you. Since you reject it and judge yourselves to be unworthy of eternal life, we are now turning to the Gentiles [cf. Rom. 11.13-14]. For so the Lord has commanded us, saying, "I have set you to be a light for the Gentiles (εἰς φῶς ἐθνῶν; cf. Isa. 49.6), so that you may bring salvation to the ends of the earth (εἰς σωτηρίαν ἕως ἐσχάτου τῆς γῆς; cf. Isa. 49.6)"'.

Paul also applies the text to himself. He uses it to refer to his call (Gal. 1.15), his preaching (2 Cor. 6.2), and his ministry (2 Cor. 7.6; Phil. 2.16):

> But when he who set me apart from my mother's womb and called me (ἐκ κοιλίας μητρός μου καὶ καλέσας; cf. Isa. 49.1) by his grace was pleased to reveal (ἀποκαλύψαι) his son in me (ἐν ἐμοί), so that I might

---

53 Allusions to Isa. 49.12, 22 in Luke also appear in Jesus' teaching at Lk. 13.29 and 15.5 respectively.

preach him to the Gentiles, I did not then consult with flesh and blood. (Gal. 1.15-16, LLS)[54]

For he says, 'At an acceptable time I have listened to you, and on a day of salvation I have helped you' [Isa. 49.8]. See, now is the acceptable time; see, now is the day of salvation! (2 Cor. 6.2)

But God, who consoles the downcast (ὁ παρακαλῶν τοὺς ταπεινούς; cf. Isa. 49.13), consoled us by the arrival of Titus. (2 Cor. 7.6)[55]

It is by your holding fast to the word of life that I can boast on the day of Christ that I did not run in vain or labor in vain (κενόν ἐκοπίασα; cf. Isa. 49.4). (Phil. 2.16)

From the allusions at Gal. 1.15; 2 Cor. 7.6; and Phil. 2.16, we can see that Paul read himself into the implied story in Isaiah 49 on at least these three occasions. Yet, a closer examination of Gal. 1.15-24 suggests that Isaiah 49 has shaped this passage to a greater degree than that realized by the editors of NA[27]. In addition to the allusion to Isa. 49.1 in Gal. 1.15, there is also an allusion to Isa. 49.3 in Gal. 1.23-24:[56]

They only heard it said, 'The one who formerly was persecuting us is now proclaiming the faith he once tried to destroy'. [24]And they glorified God in me (ἐδόξαζον ἐν ἐμοὶ τὸν θεόν). (LLS)

The phrase ἐδόξαζον ἐν ἐμοὶ τὸν θεόν echoes ἐν σοὶ δοξασθήσομαι from Isa. 49.3.[57] Further, the phrase ἐν σοί from Isa. 49.3 may explain the somewhat unexpected use of ἐν ἐμοί in Gal. 1.16 and 1.24. There is no consensus in the interpretation of these ἐν ἐμοί phrases in Gal. 1.16 and 24, and several modern commentaries completely ignore the prepositional phrase.[58] Here once again Paul reads his own experience in light of the implied narrative of Isa. 49. In fact, given the clear linguistic imprints of Isa. 49.1 and 3 in this opening section of Paul's autobiography, it is not

---

54   With many, I think the words ὁ θεός in Gal. 1.15 are a later gloss. J.B. Lightfoot notes similar additions in Pauline text such as Gal. 1.6; 2.8; 3.5; 5.8; Rom. 8.11; Phil. 1.6; 1 Thess. 5.24 (*Saint Paul's Epistle to the Galatians* [London and New York: Macmillan, 1865], p. 82).

55   There is another possible echo to Isa. 49.13 that is not listed in NA[27] but is similar to the one at 2 Cor. 7.6: the idea of God's comfort at 2 Cor. 1.3-4.

56   So also Lightfoot (*Epistle to the Galatians*, p. 86), and Richard Longenecker, *Galatians* (WBC; Dallas: Word Books, 1990), p. 42.

57   Longenecker, *Galatians*, p. 42.

58   For example, Hans Betz notes that the 'mystical experience' interpretation of ἐν ἐμοί has fallen into disfavor. He himself takes the phrase as equivalent to a simple dative, but ultimately decides that for Paul internal and external visions of Christ may have been all of a piece (cf. Gal. 1.15; 1 Cor. 9.1; 15.8; Acts 9.1-9; *Galatians: A Commentary on Paul's Letter to the Churches in Galatia* [Philadelphia: Fortress, 1979], p. 71). Lightfoot, on the other hand, seems to combine the two alternatives, speaking of a revelation made through Paul to others (*Epistle to the Galatians*, p. 83; see also Richard Hays, 'The Letter to the Galatians', in Keck [ed.], *The New Interpreter's Bible*, 11: 183–348 [215]).

too difficult to see the thematic coherence between Isa. 49.2 and the autobiographical narrative in 1.16-17. In these verses, Paul may be speaking about his hiddenness from other leaders of the church during this period in a manner that echoes Isa. 49.2:[59]

> He hid me under the covering of his hand, he appointed me as a select arrow; thus, in his quiver he protected me. (Isa. 49.2, LLS)

Even after we notice these additional allusions to Isaiah 49, however, we have not exhausted the thematic correspondence between Paul's narrative and the ideas in that prophetic chapter. For example, the correspondences between Galatians 1 and Isaiah 49 draw our attention to Isa. 49.5-6:[60]

> Yet now thus says the Lord, the one who created me from the womb (cf. ἐκ κοιλίας in Gal. 1.15) as his very own slave (cf. δοῦλος in Gal. 1.10), to gather Jacob and Israel to him – 'I will be gathered and I will be glorified (δοξασθήσομαι; cf. ἐδόξαζον ἐν ἐμοὶ τὸν θεόν in Gal. 1.24) before the Lord, and my God will be my strength!' – He said to me, 'A great thing has been done in you, you have been called (κληθῆναί σε; cf. καλέσας in Gal. 1.15) to be my servant to establish the tribes of Jacob, and to turn around the dispersed ones of Israel. Behold, I appoint you to be a testament to all of the races of humanity (διαθήκην γένους), to be a light to the nations (εἰς φῶς ἐθνῶν τοῦ εἶναί σε; cf. ἐν τοῖς ἔθνεσιν in Gal. 1.16), so that you will stand for salvation unto the ends of the earth. (Isa. 49.5-63, LLS)

The many correspondences between Gal. 1.15-24 and Isa. 49.1-5 suggest that Paul sees himself as a light to the Gentiles as described in Isa. 49.6. Yet these numerous correspondences also demand that we consider whether the motif earlier in Isa. 49.6 of the servant as the gatherer of Israel also reverberates in the literary space of Gal. 1.15-16. Paul's statements in Rom. 11.13-14 confirm the idea that Paul understood his mission to extend to both Jews and Gentiles as described in Isaiah 49. He sees himself as having received a prophetic call (Gal. 1.15; Rom. 1.1; cf. Isa. 49.1), as having endured a time of hiddenness (Gal. 1.16-17; cf. Isa. 49.2), and as having experienced the comfort of God throughout his ministry (Phil. 2.16; 2 Cor. 3.4; 7.6; cf. Isa. 49.13). He is a slave of Christ (δοῦλος; Gal.

---

59   Hays makes a similar suggestion about echoes of Isa. 49.4 in 2 Cor. 5.18–6.2: 'If [the] whole depiction of the servant's charge (Isa. 49.1-13) is read in counterpoint with Paul's account of "the ministry of reconciliation" in 2 Cor. 5.18–6.2, as Paul's citation of Isa. 49.8 [in 2 Cor. 6.2] encourages us to do, both texts take on a new resonance. Even Paul's admonition that the Corinthians not accept the grace of God "in vain (*eis kenon*)" echoes the Servant's lament in Isa. 49.4: "I have labored in vain (*kenōs*), and I have given my strength for vanity and for nothing"' (R.B. Hays, *Echoes of Scripture in the Letters of Paul* [New Haven: Yale University Press, 1989], p. 225 n. 48).

60   Dunn (*Romans*, 1.8), Munck (*Paul and the Salvation of Mankind*, p. 26), and Longenecker (*Galatians*, p. 30) all note the similarities with Rom. 1.1, 5.

1.10; cf. Isa. 49.3, 5), but a slave in whose ministry God is glorified (δοξάζω; Gal. 1.24; Rom. 11.14; cf. Isa. 49.3, 5). Above all, he serves not only as a light to the Gentiles but also as a gatherer of the dispersion of Israel (Gal. 1.16; Rom. 11.13-14; cf. Isa. 49.5-6).

These conclusions are consonant with those of Traugott Holtz, who clearly reads Paul against the background of Isaiah and discusses a relationship between Isaiah 49 and Rom. 11.13-14, though without adducing all of the allusions to Isaiah 49 described here.[61] Betz, on the other hand, reasons that though Paul saw his mission as limited to Gentiles, he nevertheless conceived of it in terms of Jewish eschatology and as 'a part of his Jewishness'. Moreover, he warns against importing ideas from Isaiah about Paul's apostleship. Dunn and Bruce associate the 'servant of the Lord' motif with Jesus instead of Paul, viewing Paul as a participant in Jesus' ministry as the Servant of the Lord rather than thinking that Paul saw himself in such terms.[62] However, given that these scholars see several allusions to Isaiah 49, it seems puzzling that they reject the possibility suggested by the allusions to Isaiah 49 that Paul saw himself as involved in 'the gathering of Israel', an idea that is explicitly confirmed in Rom. 11.13-14. Are these scholars influenced by Luke's association of the text with Jesus? Are they perhaps persuaded that Paul's comments in Rom. 11.13-14 are isolated references, and that Paul only hits on this idea of his admittedly indirect ministry to Jews in anticipation of the difficulties he is likely to face in Jerusalem? Since Paul probably wrote Galatians and Romans far enough apart in time to allow Paul to change his arguments, the fact that the allusions to Isaiah 49 in Galatians are made explicit in Romans 11 tells against this scenario for understanding Romans. Romans 11.13-14 is no afterthought or consideration of a problem that had previously gone unrecognized, as maintained by Sanders, but clearly reveals important information about Paul's understanding of his mission, information that lies just below the surface elsewhere in his writings. Although we will now turn to a consideration of a different aspect of Paul's self-identity, in the next chapter we will pursue additional evidence that Paul ultimately saw his apostleship in terms of the gathering of Israel.

b. *Paul the Israelite*

Karl-Wilhelm Niebuhr's analysis of Paul's Jewish identity holds that Paul's appeal to his Jewish background in Gal. 1.13-14; 2 Cor. 11.22-23; and Phil. 3.5-6 demonstrates that his Jewish identity was integral to his

---

61   Betz, *Galatians*, pp. 70, 72; Traugott Holtz, 'Zum Selbstverständnis des Apostels Paulus', *Theologische Literaturzeitung* 91.5 (1966): 321–30.

62   Dunn, *Romans*, 1.8; F.F. Bruce, *The Epistle to the Galatians* (Grand Rapids: Eerdmans, 1982), p. 92.

work as apostle to the Gentiles. Niebuhr holds that far from disregarding his former life as a law-observant Jew, Paul tells of his past as an exemplary Jew as a way of establishing his authority to address the question of the role of the law for Christians.[63] In an article that considers many of the passages reviewed in this section, Dunn concludes that Paul's identity was in flux. Paul thought of himself as a Jew in a qualified sense, but he embraced Israelite identity and sought to promote his understanding of Israelite identity among his converts.[64] On the other hand, John Barclay also examines many of the texts discussed here and concludes that Paul was an apostate Jew.[65] A careful review of these and related texts brings us closer to Barclay than to Dunn or Niebuhr, showing that while Paul makes regular *reference* to his Jewish background, he refrains from *identifying* himself as a Jew.

1. *'Israelites' in Romans 9–11*

We begin our discussion of Paul's self-identity and relational matrix with a discussion of Romans 9–11, in which Paul's use of the word 'Israel' creates no shortage of interpretive difficulties. In this passage, we are particularly interested in noting Paul's group affiliation and in determining the number and nature of the groups in Paul's relational matrix. Beginning with Rom. 9.3, we see that Paul refers to 'brothers' who are his relatives according to the flesh. 'Brother' is a family term that appears no less than 113 times in his letters, more frequently than in any other part of the Bible. What is intriguing is that there are only two cases apart from Rom. 9.3 where ἀδελφός refers to a biological relationship. First Corinthians 9.5 and Gal. 1.19 both use ἀδελφοί in reference to Jesus' brothers, and since the people in question are Christians even in these instances, Rom. 9.3 is the only place in the Pauline corpus in which the word applies to a non-believer. Thus, it seems that for Paul 'brothers' and 'brothers who are kindred according to the flesh' are potentially two separate groups, Christians and non-Christian Jews respectively.

Paul calls these non-Christian Jews 'Israelites' in Rom. 9.4. In view of his own self-description as an 'Israelite' later in Rom. 11.1, this would seem to indicate that he and these non-Christian Jews were members of the same group, despite the fact that Paul is 'in Christ' and they are not. On the other hand, Paul's claim in 9.6 that the word 'Israel' does not include everyone descended from Israel points in a different direction

---

63 Karl-Wilhelm Niebuhr, *Heidenapostel aus Israel: Die jüdische Identität des Paulus nach ihrer Darstellung in seinen Briefen* (Tübingen: J.C.B. Mohr, 1992), e.g., pp. 20–23, 87–103, 110, 158–75.

64 Dunn, 'Who did Paul Think He Was?'.

65 John Barclay, 'Paul among Diaspora Jews: Anomaly or Apostate?' *JSNT* 60 (1995): 89–120.

(Rom. 9.6-13, 25-9; 11.5-6). While Paul concedes common descent with these brothers, the ensuing discussion makes it clear that he does not acknowledge that Jews are ἐξ Ἰσραήλ if they are not in Christ (Rom. 10.1-13; 11.13-14).[66] Thus it seems that there are at least two kinds of Israelites in Paul's relational matrix, Israelites like Paul – that is, 'true' Israelites – and those who are Israelites merely κατὰ σάρκα. Though confusing, in Romans 9–11 the word 'Israel' can refer to either group.[67]

Paul's self-identification as an Israelite in Rom. 11.1 is similar to the expression in 2 Cor. 11.22, where he describes his Jewish Christian opponents in Corinth with the same set of characterizations that he uses of himself: they are Hebrew, Israelite, descendants of Abraham, and servants of Christ:

> I ask, then, has God rejected his people? By no means! I myself am an Israelite (ἐγὼ Ἰσραηλίτης εἰμι), from the seed of Abraham, a member of the tribe of Benjamin (ἐκ σπέρματος Ἀβραάμ, φυλῆς Βενιαμίν). (Rom. 11.1, LLS)

> Are they Hebrews (Ἑβραῖοί εἰσιν)? So am I. Are they Israelites (Ἰσραηλῖταί εἰσιν)? So am I. Are they the seed of Abraham (σπέρμα Ἀβραάμ εἰσιν)? So am I. [23]Are they servants of Christ? ... I am a better one. (2 Cor. 11.22, LLS)

In both texts the word 'Israelite' stands without a qualifying phrase and thus contrasts with references to Israelites in other texts (e.g., 1 Cor. 10.18; 2 Cor. 3.7; Gal. 6.16). For instance, when Paul refers to Ἰσραὴλ κατὰ σάρκα in 1 Cor. 10.18, we gain additional insight into Paul's group affiliation. In 1 Cor. 10.16-18 Paul contrasts Christian and Jewish styles of eating sacrifices and in v. 18 refers to a group that he calls 'Israel according to the flesh', a phrase which is usually taken as a reference to the Israelites of the wilderness generation (cf. 1 Cor. 10.1-5).[68] On the other hand, it is possible that the group in 10.18 is that composed of Paul's non-Christian Jewish contemporaries who offer sacrifices to God in Jerusalem. While tense forms are not always a reliable indicator of the

---

66 Sanders, *Paul, the Law and the Jewish People*, p. 175; Munck, *Paul and the Salvation of Mankind*, p. 279. Niebuhr (*Heidenapostel aus Israel*, p. 161), on the other hand, supposes that Paul refers to these non-Christian Jews as brothers because of his continuing belief that they are members of God's elect people.

67 Similarly Wright, 'The Letter to the Romans', p. 688.

68 Hans Conzelmann, *A Commentary on the First Epistle to the Corinthians* (trans. James W. Leitch; Philadelphia: Fortress Press, 1975), p. 172; F.W. Grosheide, *Commentary on the First Epistle to the Corinthians* (Grand Rapids: Eerdmans, 1953), p. 234; C.K. Barrett, *The First Epistle to the Corinthians* (New York and London: Harper & Row, 1968), p. 235; Gordon Fee, *The First Epistle to the Corinthians* (NICNT; Grand Rapids: Eerdmans, 1987), p. 470. Fee adds that Paul's reference to Ἰσραὴλ κατὰ σάρκα in 1 Cor. 10.18 implies the existence of an Ἰσραὴλ κατὰ πνεῦμα (*First Corinthians*, p. 470 n. 38).

time at which an action takes place, Paul's use of aorist and present indicative verbs in this chapter is suggestive, as may be seen by comparing the aorists used for the group in 10.3-4 (βρῶμα ἔφαγον ... ἔπιον πόμα ... ἔπινον γὰρ ...) with the present indicative used for the group in 10.18 (οἱ ἐσθίοντες τὰς θυσίας κοινωνοὶ τοῦ θυσιαστηρίου εἰσίν).[69] Further, Paul uses a present-tense verb to address the Corinthian congregation in 10.1a (οὐ θέλω γὰρ ὑμᾶς ἀγνοεῖν, ἀδελφοί) but then switches to an exclusive use of aorist indicatives to describe the wilderness generation in 10.1b-11. After 1 Cor. 10.11, there are no other aorist indicatives in the chapter, and present-tense verbs appear in every verse from 10.13 to the end of the chapter in 10.33 with the exception of an aorist imperative in 10.15.[70] In other words, all of the actions of the historical group in 10.1-11 are described by means of aorist indicatives, after which these forms disappear. While this analysis is not conclusive, it at least opens the possibility that Paul refers to his non-Christian Jewish contemporaries when he speaks of 'Israel according to the flesh' in 10.18.

The third-person reference to 'Israel according to the flesh' in v. 18, moreover, contrasts with a Christian 'we' group in vv. 16 and 17 that participates in the Lord's Supper. We can infer from Paul's first-person plural reference to the group in 10.16-18 that Paul includes neither himself nor the Corinthians in the 'Israel κατὰ σάρκα' group, despite his self-identification as an Israelite in Rom. 11.1. In addition, the often negative associations of σάρξ in Paul are completely absent from the only other unambiguous references to pre-Christ Israel in the corpus; 2 Cor. 3.7 and 3.13 refer to Moses-era Israelites as 'sons of Israel'.[71] Furthermore, the idea that 'Israel according to the flesh' refers to Paul's non-Christian Jewish contemporaries seems viable in view of the way that Paul refers to these Jews in Rom. 9.3-4, calling them 'my kindred κατὰ σάρκα' and

---

69 Porter argues that tense forms communicate an author's subjective description of action and do not necessarily describe action as it 'objectively' takes place, even in the indicative mood. He does concede, however, that the nature of the perfective aspect, which is grammaticalized by aorist tense forms, results in a high frequency of this tense form in descriptions of past time action (Stanley E. Porter, *Verbal Aspect in the Greek of the New Testament, with Reference to Tense and Mood* [Studies in Biblical Greek; New York: Peter Lang, 1993], pp. 102–103, 198–99). Given this overlap, it is reasonable to explore whether and in what way this correspondence between past time action and aorist tense forms applies in 1 Cor. 10.

70 Present indicatives predominate except in 10.14, 24-25, 32 where present imperatives exhort the congregation to exhibit specific behaviors. The aorist imperative in 10.15 does not appear in a context that refers to past time action.

71 Paul's reference to Israelites in 2 Cor. 3.4-18 is not so much a negative comment on the deficiencies of the old covenant as it is a comparison between the old covenant and the new. The old covenant is glorious, but its glory is surpassed by the glory of the new (2 Cor. 3.7-9; see Sanders, *Paul, the Law and the Jewish People*, pp. 137–39).

'Israelites' in consecutive clauses (τῶν συγγενῶν μου κατὰ σάρκα, οἵτινές εἰσιν Ἰσραηλῖται).

It is possible that Israel κατὰ σάρκα in 1 Cor. 10.18 refers to pre-Christ Israel, as maintained by those who point to the clear reference to this group from history in 1 Cor. 10.1-5. This conclusion, however, stands in tension with the way Paul speaks of this historical group in 2 Cor. 3.7 and 3.13 and with the way he describes Jewish Christians in 2 Cor. 11.22. On the other hand, the reference in 1 Cor. 10.18 mirrors the way he refers to non-Christian Jews in Rom. 9.3-4.[72] In addition, a reference to ancient Israel in 10.18 becomes more doubtful given that Paul switches from a narrative using aorist verbs to speak about past actions in 10.1-11, to a discussion using present indicatives to speak about contemporary concerns in 10.13-33. All of this suggests that we can name the two groups of Israelites implied in Rom. 9.1-6 'Israel' and 'Israel κατὰ σάρκα'.

Returning to Romans 11, we can see that the olive-tree metaphor that appears in 11.17 subtly modulates the image used in Romans 9 to describe the division in Israel between those in Christ and non-believers. Now the latter become 'some' branches that have been broken from the cultivated olive tree. Since most scholars rightly take the root of the olive tree as a representation of the patriarchs, the tree must represent 'Israel', even though faith is the criterion by which branches become or remain attached to the tree (Rom. 11.20, 23; cf. 4.11-12).[73] The olive-tree metaphor thus brilliantly illustrates the three central groups in Paul's relational matrix: wild branches are those (former) Gentiles that are grafted into the tree based on faith (ἀγριέλαιος; 11.24); cultivated but broken branches are unbelieving Jews (καλλιέλαιος; 11.24); and branches connected to the tree, both wild and cultivated, are Gentile and Jewish Christians (11.20, 23). The metaphor depicts how both sets of branches, those now connected and those now broken, did or do grow out of (i.e., 'descend from') the root of the patriarchs, and it shows that the vital thing is whether or not the branches are attached to the tree.

In the conclusion of the discourse, Paul anticipates an eschatological reunion of Israel and Israel κατὰ σάρκα through Christ (Rom. 11.25-26).[74] The division in Israel between Jewish Christians and non-Christian

---

72 See Nils A. Dahl, 'Der Name Israel: Zur Auslesung von Gal.6,16', *Judaica* 6 (1950): 161–70 (163). According to Dahl, Gal. 4.29 shows that the antithesis between Ἰσραὴλ κατὰ σάρκα and Ἰσραὴλ κατὰ πνεῦμα (i.e., Christians) was close to hand in Paul even if not explicit.

73 See, for example, Moo, *Romans*, p. 705 and Käsemann, *Romans*, p. 310.

74 For a description of the questions and interpretive options at Rom. 11.25-26 (e.g., ethnic vs. spiritual Israel, eschatological vs. historical salvation, salvation through Christ vs. *Sonderweg*) and the scholars who adopt them, see the summary in Joseph A. Fitzmyer, *Romans* (AB; New York: Doubleday, 1993), pp. 618–20. For interpretations that engage the interpretation above pro and con, see Wright, 'Letter to the Romans', pp. 688–90; C.E.B.

Jews is, therefore, in Paul's mind, temporary. Nevertheless, the idea that there are two separate groups of Israelites *prior to the eschaton* still holds, and thus is applicable to the question of Paul's self-identification. With all this in mind, we can see that Paul's relational map contains at least four groups to which the word 'Israel' may be applied:

1   Paul and his Jewish-Christian opponents at Corinth are Israelites in an unqualified sense (Rom. 11.1; cf. 2 Cor. 11.22; Phil. 3.5). Though the point is debated, I maintain that Paul is referring to this group when in Gal. 6.16 he calls Jewish and Gentile Christians the '*Israel of God*'.

2   In Romans 9–11 Paul distinguishes 'elect' Israel (9.4, 6-8; 11.1-5) from hardened, 'broken off' Israelites (9.18; 11.20, 25). Based on the discussion above, I am proposing that this group corresponds to *Israel* κατὰ σάρκα (1 Cor. 10.18; Rom. 9.3-4).

3.   Abraham and the '*sons of Israel*' are the ancestors both of the Israel of God and of Israel κατὰ σάρκα, as discussed above (2 Cor. 3.7, 13; Rom. 4.11-12, 16).

4.   In Paul's view, '*all Israel*' is the unification of the Israel of God and Israel κατὰ σάρκα at the eschaton (Rom. 11.25-26; cf. 11.15).

2. Philippians 3.2-9

Philippians 3.2-9 most clearly shows that Paul's discussions about Christian identity take place within the framework of the Jewish understanding of race described in Chapter 3. Here Paul describes his identity by means of a contrast between his former identity in the flesh (ἐν σαρκί) and his new identity in Christ (ἐν Χριστῷ).

He opens the passage with a pointed remark, declaring in 3.2-3 that worship or serving (λατρεύοντες) in the Spirit represents 'true' circumcision, and portrays physical circumcision as a mutilation, a deformity. By tradition circumcision was the seal of the covenant between God and the progeny of Abraham. After the Maccabean period, circumcision was such an important and time-honored indicium of identity that by Paul's time it had become virtually synonymous with Jewish identity, pointing beyond itself to a Torah-compliant lifestyle (Rom. 3.1).[75] In the language of

---

Cranfield, *Romans, A Shorter Commentary* (Grand Rapids: Eerdmans, 1985), 2.577; Dunn, *Romans*, 2.682–83; Moo, *Romans*, pp. 723–25. The conclusion above, that Paul anticipates a reunion of Israel and Israel κατὰ σάρκα through Christ at the eschaton, emerges from (1) the earlier discussion of the correspondence between Rom. 11.17-24 which assumes faith through Christ, and Rom. 4.11-16 which implies that Christians and non-Christian Jews are separate sets of descendants of Abraham who both ultimately inherit the promises made to Abraham through faith; and (2) the mention of resurrection in Rom. 11.15 which points to eschatological salvation.

75   Hodge, *If Sons then Heirs*, pp. 60–61; Cohen, *The Beginnings of Jewishness*, pp. 39–40; Friedrich Wilhelm Horn, referring to both the Maccabean period and the repression under

identity from Chapter 2, this means that circumcision was an indicium of identity that marked a male as a member of the community and a descendant of Abraham. In fact, Paul himself often uses the word as a synonym for Jewish people, as is apparent in the contrasts between circumcision and uncircumcision in Rom. 3.30; 15.8; and Gal. 2.7.[76]

The two references to circumcision in Phil. 3.3 and 3.5 function similarly. Just as a circumcision/uncircumcision contrast stands by metonymy for Jews and Gentiles in Rom. 3.30; 15.8; and Gal. 2.7 and often signifies their differing lifestyles vis-à-vis the law, so too mutilation (κατατομή) and circumcision (περιτομή) in Phil. 3.2-3 represent two groups characterized by different practices. Although there is doubt about whether this party was actually present in Philippi, the '*mutilation faction*' is probably a polemical reference to Jewish-Christian missionaries who emphasized circumcision and law observance (3.3, 6).[77] The '*[true] circumcision faction*', on the other hand, refers to Christians who instead practice serving 'in the Spirit of God', a characterization that also relates to a certain type of conduct (3.17).

In the context of Phil. 3.5, however, Paul is using circumcision as a sign of Jewish descent, a point that he reinforces in four of the following five clauses.[78] These clauses contain a description of Paul's Jewish heritage and in context put a heavy emphasis on physical kinship ('I also have confidence in the flesh'; cf. 3.3, 3.5).[79] This kinship emphasis appears in

---

Hadrian, points out that attempts to repress circumcision only strengthened its theological significance ('Der Verzicht auf die Beschneidung im Frühen Christentum', *NTS* 42 [1996]: 479–505 [483]; see also Lawrence Schiffman, *Who Was a Jew?* [Hoboken, NJ: Ktab, 1985], pp. 24–25; and Niebuhr, *Heidenapostel aus Israel*, p. 105). In an interesting study Richard Hecht concludes that circumcision is unrelated to the covenant in the Philonic corpus, even though focused on the law. According to Hecht, Philo saw circumcision as a symbol of the mortification of sensual pleasures and therefore as a prerequisite for a life lived in conformance with the law ('The Exegetical Contexts of Philo's Interpretation of Circumcision', in Fredrick E. Greenspahn, Earle Hilgert, and Burton Mack [eds], *Nourished with Peace: Studies in Hellenistic Judaism in Memory of Samuel Sandmel* [Chico, CA: Scholars Press, 1984], pp. 51–79). Romans 3.1-3 may prompt us to think that Paul shared Philo's understanding of circumcision as a sign of a Torah-compliant life. There Paul speaks about faithfulness or unfaithfulness with reference to the 'oracles of God', a statement that is an answer to a question about the value of circumcision.

76 Marcus, 'Circumcision and Uncircumcision', p. 76; Dunn, *Romans*, 1.120, 209; id., 'Who Did Paul Think He Was?', p. 189; Hodge, *If Sons then Heirs*, p. 60.

77 Markus Bockmuehl, *The Epistle to the Philippians* (London: A&C Black and Henrickson, 1998), p. 183; Gordon D. Fee, *Paul's Letter to the Philippians* (NICNT; Grand Rapids: Eerdmans, 1995), pp. 8–10, 293–97; *contra* Gerald F. Hawthorne who thinks these opponents are non-Christian Jews (*Philippians* [WBC; Waco, TX: Word Books, 1983], pp. xlv–xlvii, 125–26).

78 Niebuhr, *Heidenapostel aus Israel*, p. 105.

79 *Contra* Fee, *Paul's Letter to the Philippians*, p. 302, who says that ἐν σαρκί refers 'first to circumcision' and then to life outside of Christ.

the triple use of the phrase ἐν σαρκί (once in 3.3 and twice in 3.4), and the consecutive phrases ἐκ γένους 'Ισραήλ, φυλῆς Βενιαμίν, and ' Εβραῖος ἐξ ' Εβραίων (3.5). Here Paul again characterizes himself as an Israelite, but speaks of his membership ἐκ γένους 'Ισραήλ. This passage is one of only three passages in which Paul uses the word 'race' with respect to a people-group, all of them referring to Jews (2 Cor. 11.26; Gal. 1.14; Phil. 3.5; cf. 1 Cor. 12.10, 28; 14.10). Here, the immediate context suggests that the kinship element of the race dialectic is foregrounded, but it is interesting to note that the other two passages each highlight one of the remaining elements of the dialectic of race: religion in Gal. 1.14 and social group awareness in 2 Cor. 11.26. Although Paul does not explicitly apply the word γένος to believers, we shall see that he nevertheless draws on the elements of the race dialectic in describing Christian identity.

Many scholars take 'Hebrew of Hebrews' as a reference to Paul's ability to speak Hebrew or Aramaic.[80] However, given the context of the consecutive phrases φυλῆς Βενιαμίν and ' Εβραῖος ἐξ ' Εβραίων, he more likely emphasizes the antiquity of his lineage.[81] Both Josephus and the Greek Scriptures mainly use the word 'Hebrew' to refer to pre-exilic Israelites. In Josephus, fully 90 percent of the 313 uses of the word refer to Jews as a group and appear in the first half of *Antiquities*. In the LXX, with only one exception, the word 'Hebrew' appears in contexts in which it is either a reference to Jews by outsiders or a Jewish self-identification in speech to outsiders. A single impulse may link these two uses, in that literate Jews may have preferred to represent themselves to outsiders in terms that communicated the antiquity of their people, since ancient lineages were revered throughout this period. Paul's ability to identify his tribal origins in the φυλῆς Βενιαμίν phrase could serve to enhance his portrait of his lineage.

The next three phrases about law, zeal, and righteousness describe religious behavior as opposed to kinship,[82] and Paul continues to fill out the contrast between ἐν σαρκί and ἐν Χριστῷ in 3.9-11, setting out the

---

80 This inference is probably based on the portrait of Paul in Acts (see Acts 21.40; 22.2; 26.14). Fee calls such interpretations 'strapping Paul in a Lucan straitjacket' (*Paul's Letter to the Philippians*, p. 307 n. 14). Although Niebuhr (*Heidenapostel aus Israel*, pp. 105–7) also sees a reference to language in this clause, he thinks that Paul emphasizes his Jewish descent and origins in this passage, seeing 'Hebrew of Hebrews' as a climactic concluding allusion to people, tribe, family, and home life (p. 107).

81 Harvey notes that 'Hebrew' connotes conservatism or traditionalism and most often invokes an association with Abraham as patriarch (Graham Harvey, *The True Israel: Uses of the Names Jew, Hebrew, and Israel in Ancient Judaism and Early Christian Literature* [Leiden: E.J. Brill, 1996], pp. 9, 116, 124, 129, 146–47, and esp. 132).

82 Niebuhr sees a similar distinction, noting that the ἐκ phrases in 3.5 emphasize origins, while the κατά phrases in 3.5-6 emphasize behavior (Niebuhr, *Heidenapostel aus Israel*, p. 107).

terms of the contrast in vv. 7-8 using the language of gain and loss. In 3.9-11 we learn that being found in Christ first involves a reordering of the relationship with God, that is, δικαιοσύνη no longer comes by means of the law but now through πίστις Χριστοῦ. Finally, in 3.21 we find an appeal to a Christian sense of citizenship involving the kinds of references to state or government normally found in ἔθνος language. According to Paul, Christians are already members of a heavenly πολίτευμα ruled by the Lord Christ, who will presently bring all things into subjection to his rule.[83]

More importantly, we can see that the three elements that operated as synonyms in Romans 4 are also at work in the contrasts in Phil. 3.2-9. In Rom. 3.27–4.22, we saw that terms associated with physical descent, circumcision, and justification from works of law coalesced. Figure 4.2 shows that there are three elements that function as antinomies to these coalesced terms in Phil. 3.3-9: being [found] in Christ (3.3, 9), worship in the Spirit (3.3), and righteousness διὰ πίστεως Χριστοῦ (3.9). An antithesis between circumcision and worship in the Spirit emerges clearly in 3.3a, and an antithesis between righteousness from law and righteousness from πίστις Χριστοῦ emerges just as clearly in 3.9. The last antithesis, between physical descent and being-in-Christ, is admittedly more allusive and thus is more difficult to see, but seems clearest in the latter half of 3.3 (καυχώμενοι ἐν Χριστῷ Ἰησοῦ καὶ οὐκ ἐν σαρκί). In 3.9, Paul may also speak evocatively of this antithesis between physical lineage and being-in-Christ when he talks of being found in Christ. This verse is reminiscent of the lineage discussion in Gal. 3.16, 28, in which Paul says that Christ is the one seed of Abraham and that believers are one in Christ (3.16: καὶ τῷ σπέρματί σου, ὅς ἐστιν Χριστός; 3.28: ὑμεῖς εἷς ἐστε ἐν Χριστῷ Ἰησοῦ).

Furthermore, it is easy to discern the three elements in the Jewish dialectic of racial identity behind the two antithetical triads. First, the antithesis between righteousness or justification by law and righteousness through πίστις Χριστοῦ clearly represents the religious component of racial identity. Second, as we have just seen, in 3.3-5 boasting in Christ seems to be in opposition to boasting in the flesh via indicators of physical descent, a contrast that corresponds to the kinship element in the model of Jewish racial identity. Finally, as we have also seen, Paul uses ἡ κατατομή and ἡ περιτομή as polemical metonymies for distinct people-groups, and the usage corresponds to the social identity element in the model of race. The specific social difference at work in this contrast has to do with identifying practices, since 'mutilation' was a polemical reference to a group that was emphasizing circumcision and law observance, while 'circumcision' was a reference to Christians who 'serve in the Spirit of

83   Ibid., p. 102.

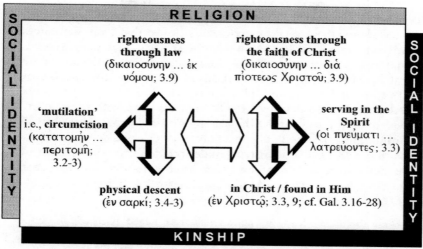

Figure 4.2 – Antitheses in Philippians 3.3-9

God'. Thus, this key Pauline text on the contrast between Jewish and Christian identity proceeds in terms of the elements from the Jewish model of racial identity, elements that are also visible in Paul's arguments about justification in Rom. 3.27–4.22. Further, as we noted earlier when the same elements appear in Rom. 3.27–4.22, justification by works of law, circumcision, and physical descent from Abraham are virtual synonyms, an observation that is congruent with the idea that these elements were already available as a framework for identity within Paul's Jewish matrix.[84] In other words, when Paul reached for language to describe the apocalyptic creation of a new people in Christ, he articulated the contours of this new identity by drawing freely on the construct of race that already existed in his social context, a construct containing an association between kinship, social distinctiveness, and beliefs about God.

3. *Galatians 2.13-15 and Romans 3.5, 9*
Galatians 2.13-15 is important for discerning Paul's views on Christian identity, and I will revisit these verses in Chapter 5. For the purposes of

---

84 In his essay on Paul's treatment of Abraham in Romans 4, Richard Hays makes a similar point: 'Throughout Paul's discussion from 3.27 to 4.22 there is an interweaving – indeed a virtual equation – of three theoretically distinguishable motifs: justification by works of the law, circumcision, and physical descent from Abraham. The connection of these motifs is not a systematic one; they are bound together, in a way characteristic of Paul, by an *associative* logic. All three are components of a particular "profile" of Jewish ethnic/religious self-understanding that Paul is seeking to correct' (*The Conversion of the Imagination*, pp. 78–79; emphasis original). I would add that Paul's 'correction' proceeds in terms of distinctively Christian ethno-racial reasoning.

the present discussion, however, we note one interesting aspect in these two passages – these verses represent the closest that Paul ever comes to identifying himself as Jew. However, we see that Paul actually refrains from doing so when we notice the designations of all of the actors in this narrative and consider the implications of these verses for understanding Paul's relational matrix and self-identity.

Galatians 2.13-15 describes Paul's confrontation with Peter after the arrival of a group sent by James, presumably from Jerusalem. The confrontation concerns Paul's reaction to Peter's withdrawal from table fellowship with Gentile Christians under pressure from this party (2.12). Note that Paul calls Peter a 'Jew' when he censures him, and that Peter is compelling the 'Gentiles' at Antioch to observe Jewish food laws (2.14-15; cf. 2.13):

> And the other Jews (οἱ λοιποὶ Ἰουδαῖοι) joined [Cephas] in this hypocrisy, so that even Barnabas was led astray by their hypocrisy. But when I saw that they were not acting consistently with the truth of the gospel, I said to Cephas before them all, 'If you, though a Jew, live like a Gentile and not like a Jew, how can you compel the Gentiles (τὰ ἔθνη) to live like Jews? We ourselves are Jews by birth (ἡμεῖς φύσει Ἰουδαῖοι) and not Gentile sinners; yet we know that a person is not justified by the works of the law but through faith in Jesus Christ. (Gal. 2.13-16)

Setting aside the matter of Peter's Jewishness for a moment, we should pause at Paul's use of the word 'Gentile' to refer to people who are certainly Christian converts. Paul carefully distinguishes his converts from Gentiles in 1 Thess. 4.3-5, and he speaks in the past tense of converts' Gentile identity in 1 Cor. 12.1-2.[85] With these passages in mind, it is likely that Paul refers strictly to birth circumstances when he speaks about Gentiles and Jews in Gal. 2.14 (cf. 2.7, 9).[86] Galatians 2.15 confirms this point when Paul identifies himself and other Jewish Christians as 'Jews by birth'.[87] In context and against the background of the other texts considered here, this indicates that even though Paul and Peter were Jews

---

85 Barclay notes Paul's apparent desire to avoid placing his Gentile converts in the negative category of 'Gentile sinner' (Barclay, 'Paul among Diaspora Jews', p. 107).

86 See also Longenecker, *Galatians*, p. 78.

87 Given the contrasting reference to Gentiles, φύσις refers to 'origin' rather than 'nature' (i.e., character or temperament acquired through growth). Thus, the word here means 'birth', as it frequently does when associated with persons (LSJ, s.v. φύσις). So also many scholars and English versions: Helmut Merklein, '"Nicht aus Werken des Gesetzes ... ". Eine Auslegung von Gal 2, 15-21', in Helmut Merklein, Karlheinz Müller, and Günter Stemberger (eds), *Bibel in jüdischer und christlicher Tradition* (Bonn: Anton Hain, 1993), pp. 121–36 (123); Betz, *Galatians*, p. 115; Bruce, *Galatians*, pp. 136–37; BDAG, s.v. φύσις; Helmut Koester, 'φύσις', *TDNT* 9.272; Longenecker, *Galatians*, p. 83; NET, NIVB, NIV, NJB, NRSV, RSV; *contra* J.L. Martyn, *Galatians* (AB; New York: Doubleday, 1997), p. 248; NAU.

by birth, Paul considered them to be Jews no longer, a perspective corroborated by Paul's earlier reference to his 'former life in Judaism' (Gal. 1.13).[88]

Some scholars also think that Paul identifies himself as a Jew via the first-person plural verbs in Rom. 3.5, 9. Moo's summary of the two principal approaches to this notoriously difficult passage can help address this possible objection.[89] Moo identifies an older, traditional approach that holds that Paul addresses Jews in 3.1-4 (or 1-3) but that he shifts to address humanity in general in 3.4 or 3.5-9.[90] Moo then identifies a recent and now more popular approach that sees Paul addressing Jews from 3.1 to 3.9a.[91]

> Then what advantage has the Jew? Or what is the value of circumcision? [2]Much, in every way. For in the first place the Jews were entrusted with the oracles of God. [3]What if some were unfaithful? Will their faithlessness nullify the faithfulness of God? [4]By no means! Although everyone (πᾶς ... ἄνθρωπος) is a liar, let God be proved true, as it is written, 'so that you may be justified in your words, and prevail in your judging'. [5]But if our injustice serves to confirm the justice of God, what should we say? That God is unjust to inflict wrath on us? (I speak in a human way [κατὰ ἄνθρωπον λέγω].) [6]By no means! For then how could God judge the world? [7]But if through my falsehood God's truthfulness abounds to his glory, why am I still being condemned as a sinner? [8]And why not say (as some people slander us by saying that we say), 'Let us do evil so that good may come'? Their condemnation is deserved! [9]What then? Are we any better off (προεχόμεθα)? No, not at all; for we have already charged (προῃτιασάμεθα) that all, both Jews and Greeks, are under the power of sin. (Rom. 3.1-9)

---

88 Sanders (*Paul, the Law and the Jewish People*, p. 175) reads Gal. 1.13 in a similar fashion; cf. Barclay, 'Paul among Diaspora Jews', p. 113. On the other hand, Gal. 2.15 is often read as Paul's affirmation of his Jewishness (e.g., Harvey, *The True Israel*, p. 7; R.B. Hays, 'The Letter to the Galatians', in Keck [ed.], *The New Interpreter's Bible*, 11: 183–384 [236]; Hodge, *If Sons then Heirs*, p. 57).

89 In addition to the two approaches described here, a different line of interpretation views this passage as a Pauline dialogue with a hypothetical interlocutor, an approach that puts the statements in 3.9 on the lips of this interlocutor. On this approach see S.K. Stowers, 'Paul's Dialogue with a Fellow Jew in Romans 3.1-9', *CBQ* 46 (1984): 707–22; id., *A Rereading of Romans*. For a critique of Stowers see R.B. Hays, ' "The Gospel Is the Power of God for Gentiles Only"? A Critique of Stanley K. Stowers' *A Rereading of Romans*', *Critical Review of Books in Religion* 9 (1996): 27–44. Compare Stowers' approach with Douglas A. Campbell, 'Determining the Gospel through Rhetorical Analysis in Paul's Letter to the Roman Christians', in L. Ann Jervis and Peter Richardson (eds), *Gospel in Paul: Studies on Corinthians, Galatians and Romans for Richard N. Longenecker* (JSNTSS; Sheffield: Sheffield Academic Press, 1994), pp. 314–36.

90 E.g., Sanday and Headlam, *Romans*, pp. 68–77.

91 Moo, *Romans*, pp. 179–202 and many others.

Notwithstanding the weight of recent scholarly opinion, I follow the first approach described by Moo and maintain that Paul speaks of Jews only in 3.1-4a, and thus does not identify himself as a Jew via the first-person plurals in 3.5, 9. Three textual details support this claim. First, when Paul does clearly speak of Jews in 3.1-4a, he does so in the third person. Second, in 3.4b-6 the phrases 'let ... everyone be a liar', 'I speak in a human way', and 'judge the world' respectively signal a broadening of the topic beyond issues strictly related to Jews. Third, the two first-person plural verbs in 3.9 (προεχόμεθα present middle, 'offer an excuse'[92]; and προῃτιασάμεθα aorist middle, 'charged beforehand') must both refer to the same subject – Paul himself, since only Paul can be the subject of the latter verb. Thus, 3.9 means

> What then? Do I offer excuses [when in 3.7-8 I suggest people should not be judged as sinners when our falsehood abounds to his glory]? No! I have already accused both Jews and Greeks, that they are all under the power of sin. (LLS)

4. *Romans 2.17-29*

Paul does not explicitly identify himself or his group affiliation in Romans 2, but his discussion of circumcision and the law in this chapter is of interest here because of what it reveals about Paul's concept of Jewish identity. While many exegetical difficulties arise in interpreting this passage, the majority opinion understands Paul to be engaged in discussing Jews and Jewish identity in 2.17-29.[93] We have already noted that the first three chapters of Romans argue that both Jews and Gentiles

---

92   BDAG, s.v. 'προέχω', 2.

93   See for example, Dunn, *Romans*, 1.119–28; Sanders, *Paul, the Law and the Jewish People*, pp. 123–32; Byrne, *Romans*, p. 105; Sanday and Headlam, *The Epistle to the Romans*, pp. 67–68; Moo, *Romans*, p. 157; and Käsemann, *Romans*, p. 75; Esler, *Conflict and Identity*, pp. 151–53; *contra* N.T. Wright, against the majority opinion, who argues that Paul refers to Christians in Rom. 2 ('The Law in Romans 2', in James D.G. Dunn [ed.], *Paul and the Mosaic Law* [Tübingen: J.C.B. Mohr, 1996], pp. 131–50). According to Wright, 2.25-29 describes Gentile Christians because of (a) its similarity to Rom. 7.6; 2 Cor. 3.6; and Phil. 3.3 (but all of these contain a reference to Christ within two verses while no such reference appears near Rom. 2.25-29); (b) the apparent allusion to the new covenant passage in Ezek. 36.24-28 (but even Wright concedes that this text refers to Jews among the nations, not Gentiles); (c) use of the (divine) passive verb λογισθήσεται in 2.26 (cf. 4.3-23; but 'righteousness' is explicit in Rom. 4, not circumcision); (d) the assertion that Paul is anticipating his later arguments and here contrasts the Jew who does not keep the law with the Gentile Christian who keeps or fulfills the law. This last step in Wright's argument is interesting but does not conform to the language that Paul uses to describe the difference between 'keeping' and 'fulfilling' the law elsewhere. When Paul speaks of Christians who fulfill the law, he uses a form of the verb πληρόω (Rom. 8.4; 13.8-10; Gal. 5.14; 6.2). In contrast, the verb in 2.26 that describes law observance is φυλάσσω, which is one of many verbs that denote Jewish obedience to the law (e.g., πράσσω, ποιέω, ἐμμένω, τελέω, etc., see Moo, *Romans*, p. 170 n. 21).

are equally accountable to God and under the wrath of God, and most scholars agree that Romans 2, for all its puzzles, is the Jewish counterpart to the indictment of Gentiles in Romans 1. Of interest here are several elements in Paul's criticism of Jewish religion from Romans 2. First, in Rom. 2.17-24 Paul rejects the idea that simple membership in the Jewish race confers privilege. Paul insists that pride in membership must be accompanied by a Jewish lifestyle, and implies that the mere existence of Torah-breaking Jews and the condemnation of such is enough to demonstrate that Jewish birth alone does not confer an advantage over Gentiles when it comes to God's judgement (Rom. 2.13-15).[94]

Paul's point that Jewishness entails obedience to Torah emerges also in 2.17-20. In the context of Paul's critique of a misplaced confidence in membership in the Jewish people, this section contains an extended description of what it means to be identified as 'Jewish'. A diatribe in vv. 21–22 that calls that named identity into question interrupts the description in vv. 17–20.[95] Verses 17–20 primarily depict Jewish identity in terms of how the law functions in relationships between Jews and outsiders, while the questions in vv. 21–22 more briefly focus on an individual Jew's conduct vis-à-vis the law. Although the 'if' statement begun in 2.17-20 is interrupted by the questions in vv. 21–22, the ideas of 'boasting' and 'naming' are resumed in 2.23 and signal the end of the unit by reiterating its major concern – that the one who identifies himself as a Jew stands in a unique relationship to the law and thus to outsiders (2.17, 19, 20, 23-24, 29).[96] In other words, Paul argues that one cannot be a 'true Jew' without a public alignment with the Torah. Further, in 2.25-29 Paul undercuts his interlocutor's pride in circumcision as a sign of the covenant between Jews and the God of Abraham and thus as a distinctive mark of Jewish identity. Instead, Paul insists that the true significance of circumcision emerges in its association with covenant obedience.[97]

94   George P. Carras, 'Romans 2,1–29: A Dialogue on Jewish Ideals', *Biblica* 73.2 (1992): 183–207 (199–200); Dunn, *Romans*, 1.114; see also Käsemann, *Romans*, p. 69.

95   Günther Bornkamm, 'Paulinische Anakoluthe', in id., *Das Ende des Gesetzes* (Munich: Chr. Kaiser Verlag, 1966), pp. 76–78; Käsemann, *Romans*, pp. 69–71.

96   Similarly, Moo, *Romans*, pp. 161–63. In addition, see Moo's discussion of the way that Paul ironically reuses Isa. 52.5, which in context indicts foreign powers for their oppression of God's people: 'Perhaps Paul intends the reader to see the irony in having responsibility for dishonoring God's name transferred from the Gentiles to the people of Israel' (p. 166). Cf. Merklein, ' "Nicht aus Werken des Gesetzes ..." ', p. 123.

97   In particular, Carras' approach accounts for the particularly 'Jewish' tenor of Rom. 2 (e.g., 2.12-15, 26; cf. Sanders, *Paul, the Law and the Jewish People*, pp. 123–35, who maintains that the text is a Jewish synagogue sermon) and the way the passage functions with reference to the rhetorical questions in Rom. 3.1. The questions in Rom. 3.1 ask for an explicit description of the advantages of Jewish vs. Gentile identity, questions that seem urgent after Paul has systematically deconstructed a commonly accepted catalogue of Jewish advantages (cf. n. 17 above on Paul's rhetorical questions). Carras should also be

Within this framework, we can see that this text contains important information about the main elements of Jewish identity. Paul criticizes Jewish practice when there is no consistency between the criterion and indicium of Jewish identity. In 2.17-24, he points out that lack of Torah observance calls one's membership in the Jewish people into question, while 2.25-29 makes the same point about the indicium of circumcision. The visible indicium is meaningless if the sign of the covenant is not accompanied by covenant obedience (cf. Jer. 9.23-25).[98] In making this argument, Paul displays a sophisticated understanding of the proper relationship between indicium and criterion. An indicium is valuable only to the degree that it corresponds to the realities of group membership. When Paul insists that circumcision is meaningful only when it points beyond itself to true membership as gauged by obedience to Torah, he reinforces the point from 2.17-24. Further, his reference to uncircumcised Gentile law keepers who will judge Jews is a dramatic overstatement. When circumcision is not accompanied by the obedience to Torah that is at the heart of Jewish identity, the sign is so worthless that even the uncircumcised will have a higher status at the judgement than Torah-breaking Jews.[99] In all this, Paul describes his understanding of Jewish identity and practice in terms that could have passed muster in many Diaspora synagogues.[100] Below we will see that this portrait of Jewish identity stands in considerable tension with Paul's description of his own behavior, and thus raises questions about his identity and group affiliation.

5. *1 Corinthians 9.19-23, 10.32*

On the issue of Paul's Jewishness, 1 Cor. 9.19-23 is the passage that represents a significant retreat from Jewish identity. In contrast to the

---

commended for his interpretation of 2.17-24, which is superior to interpretations that see in this passage an indictment of all Jews for the failures of a few (cf. Heikki Räisänen, *Paul and the Law* [Tübingen: J.C.B. Mohr, 1983], p. 100; *contra* Käsemann, *Romans*, p. 69) or the implication that the law must be done perfectly (Moo, *Romans*, p. 168).

98   Since Jer. 9.23-25, with its mention of circumcision transformed into uncircumcision, is the background for the latter half of Rom. 2, it is likely that Paul is anticipating the discussion in Rom. 9 in which he makes use of the disjunction between 'the elect' and 'the rest'. In other words, via his deconstruction of circumcision in Rom. 2, Paul opens the first salvo of his later argument in 9.6 that 'not all Israelites are truly from Israel'. See Sanday and Headlam, *The Epistle to the Romans*, p. 67; C.E.B. Cranfield, *The Epistle to the Romans* (Edinburgh: T&T Clark, 1975), 1.176.

99   Carras, 'Romans 2,1–29', p. 158.

100   I do not think that Paul borrowed heavily from homiletical material in the Jewish Greek-speaking Diaspora in composing the chapter as Sanders does, but I agree with his major point that it represents a not uncommon view among Diaspora Jews about the relationship between identity and keeping the law (see Sanders, *Paul, the Law and the Jewish People*, pp. 123–35).

straightforward statements of Israelite identity elsewhere, here Paul describes his ability to be 'like' Jews who are under law and 'like' Gentiles who are without law. This passage occurs in a discourse about the responsibilities of Christian liberty that extends from 1 Corinthians 8 to 11.1, and is especially concerned with the question of eating meat originally sacrificed in pagan temples. We saw earlier that ch. 9 frames this issue as a balance between liberty (ἐξουσία; 1 Cor. 8.9; 9.4, 5, 6, 12, 18) and self-sacrifice for the sake of others in the community. In its nearer context, 9.19-23 concludes Paul's personal illustration of this principle, describing the way that he freely relinquishes his apostolic right to support from the churches in order to remain above reproach in his ministry.

With reference to 9.19-23, some scholars assert that these verses characterize Paul's missionary strategy only, and debate whether Paul intends them for application within the Christian community.[101] A related question more pertinent here concerns whether Paul speaks of non-Christian Jews or Christian Jews in 9.20. On the one hand, Paul's use of 'save' (σώζω) in 9.22 favors a reference to the former, especially since the placement of this verb at the end of the sentence for emphasis explicates his use of 'gain' (κερδαίνω) throughout this section. On the other hand, the reference to the 'weak' in the same verse (9.22) recalls the earlier discussion of weak Christians lacking in knowledge (8.7), and favors the understanding that Paul refers to Christian Jews in 9.20.

I do not think that the argument of ch. 9 is limited to a defense of Paul's apostolic rights or missionary practice; instead, he illustrates the principles that are to apply in interpersonal relationships within the community. Paul chooses to relate the story for the purposes of influencing the behavior of Christians, and both the example in 9.19-23 and the other practice highlighted in ch. 9 (i.e., apostles receiving support from their churches) provide illustrations of the main theological principle developed in this discourse. Thus, it seems likely that when Paul speaks of Jews in 1 Cor. 9.20, he refers to non-Christian Jews rather than Jewish Christians, even if some Jewish Christians constitute the audience for his exposition in ch. 9.

In 9.19-23, Paul speaks about Jews in the third person and speaks with nearly perfect ambivalence about Jewish practices and sensibilities. Just as Paul displays a willingness to assume a temporary yoke of law, he also

---

101 Against Paul's application of these verses to evangelism see G. Bornkamm, 'The Missionary Stance of Paul in Acts and his Letters', in L. Keck and J.L. Martyn (eds), *Studies in Luke-Acts* (Nashville: Abingdon, 1966), pp. 194–207; for other perspectives see Wendell Willis, 'An Apostolic Apologia? The Form and Function of 1 Corinthians 9', *JSNT* 24 (1985): 33–48 (37); Stephen C. Barton, 'All Things to All People: Paul and the Law in the Light of 1 Corinthians 9.19–23' in Dunn (ed.), *Paul and the Mosaic Law*, pp. 271–85 (279); and P. Richardson and P. Gooch, 'Accommodation Ethnics', *Tyndale Bulletin* 29 (1978): 89–142 (97).

displays a willingness to assume a situational antinomianism. I characterize Paul's ambivalence as nearly perfect because he is careful to adopt a certain existential reserve. With respect to those under law, he is not himself under law (μή ὢν αὐτὸς ὑπὸ νόμου) and with respect to those without law, he is not free from law but he is in the law of Christ (μὴ ὢν ἄνομος θεοῦ ἀλλ' ἔννομος Χριστοῦ). The clear implication of this text is that even though Paul feels free to assume these kinds of behaviors in evangelism, neither of these behaviors or labels describe Paul's true socio-religious identity. Paul's ambivalence towards the law in this text is entirely at odds with his description of Jewish identity in Rom 2.17-29, discussed above. Thus, when Paul maintains that he can 'become *like* a Jew', he clearly implies that he does not see himself as a Jew in the first place.[102]

The reserve with reference to Jewish identity at 9.19-23 is especially interesting in view of a statement near the end of the discourse. The discussion about Christian liberty and responsibility in 1 Corinthians 8–10 ends at 10.32, where Paul concludes his teaching in a single sentence: 'Give no offense to Jews or to Greeks or to the Church of God.' Here we see that Paul has three groups in view and that in this case, he sees himself as a member of this third collective. Further, when we recall our earlier discussion of the circumcision/uncircumcision contrast as a metonymy for Jews and Gentiles in Paul, we will be able to see that the tripartite division in 1 Cor. 10.32 is reiterated elsewhere in the corpus in the perspective of Gal. 6.15: 'Neither circumcision . . . nor uncircumcision, but new creation!'

---

102   Although this seems to me to be a rather straightforward conclusion from this text, the idea that Paul has dissociated himself from being Jewish is routinely rejected, either implicitly or explicitly. See for example, Conzelmann, *The First Epistle to the Corinthians*, p. 160; Fee, *First Corinthians*, p. 428; Richardson and Gooch, 'Accommodation Ethics', p. 96; and Hays, *First Corinthians*, p. 153. C.K. Barrett, on the other hand, seems to have changed his mind on this point, maintaining that Paul was a Jew in one commentary (Barrett, *The First Epistle to the Corinthians*, pp. 210–11), but later on holding that he 'could become a Jew only if, having been a Jew, he had ceased to be one and become something else' (*A Commentary on the First Epistle to the Corinthians* [London: A&C Clark, 2nd edn, 1971], p. 211). I think that there is a reluctance to acknowledge that in 1 Cor. 9.19-23 Paul withdraws from Jewish identity due in part to a well-meaning desire to avoid even the appearance of Christian anti-Judaism. Such political reactions from the interpretive community may be useful and even necessary in the wake of the Shoah and beyond. But it seems to me that a retreat from Jewish identity is problematic when 'Jewish' somehow represents a negative or undesirable identity, a stance clearly at odds with Paul's own inclinations (Rom. 9.1-3; 11.15). Perhaps it may be possible to achieve similar political ends by reclaiming both the more likely interpretation of 1 Cor. 9.19-23 described above, along with Paul's own positive construction of Jewish identity. For more on how my interpretation of Paul's identity engages the problem of Christian anti-Judaism see Chapter 6 below, pp. 217–24.

3. A Former Jew

a. Christian Kinship in Paul

Our consideration of passages in the Pauline corpus that provide insight into Paul's self-understanding has also shed light on the way in which Paul understood the relationships between the groups in his social world. We noted that Paul's frequent use of ἀδελφός for non-biological relationships is strikingly distinct from the usage in the LXX, the Gospels, and Acts. A closer consideration of Romans 4 suggested that kinship is the primary category by which Paul conceived of the Christian community, and that he saw this community as composed of both uncircumcised and circumcised 'descendants of Abraham', the founding ancestor of all who demonstrate an Abraham-like faith through Christ (Rom. 4.11-12, 16, 24). From 1 Cor. 10.1, we learned that Israelite history was the real heritage of Gentile Christians as well as Jews. If, as I maintain, Anthony Smith is correct in his judgements about *ethnie* and shared history, Paul's interpretation of Israelite history helps create and sustain group awareness and promote group survival. All of this evidence suggests that Paul was actively engaged in reshaping a narrative about identity, from his frequent and fundamentally subversive deployment of kinship language to the rewriting of genealogical ties to include Gentile Christians in Abraham's family tree.[103]

From our analysis of Phil. 3.2-9 we saw that biological kinship is the operative contrast to being found in Christ. Albert Schweitzer describes being-in-Christ as a collective experience that puts the elect in solidarity with Christ in a way that 'takes on for Paul a quasi-physical character'.[104] Schweitzer thinks that the corporality of existence in Christ (ἐν Χριστῷ) is such that a believer cannot simultaneously exist in Christ and in the flesh (ἐν σαρκί).[105] We saw in our consideration of the letter to Philemon, however, that Paul himself extols the possibility of a new relationship between Philemon and Onesimus both ἐν σαρκί and ἐν Χριστῷ, in a way that joined notions that are elsewhere set in antithesis. Though Schweitzer was on target in his characterization of the being-in-Christ experience as collective, corporal, and 'quasi-physical', the idea of a collective and tangible notion of Christian *kinship* as described here makes best sense of all the data. Following Schweitzer's lead on this matter, however, I would insist that our re-presentations of the being-in-Christ phenomenon communicate the same concreteness and material emphasis that is implicit in Paul's thought, lest we obscure the relationship-shaping power that is

---

103 Hodge, *If Sons then Heirs*, p. 33.
104 Albert Schweitzer, *The Mysticism of Paul the Apostle* (trans. William Montgomery; Baltimore and London: Johns Hopkins University Press, 1998), p. 110.
105 Ibid., p. 129.

latent in his use of kinship language. It is true that Paul uses this language as a metaphor for relations within the church, because biological kinship relationships only approximate the analogous connections within the church. Yet, if we constantly refer to Paul's kinship language as 'mere metaphor', we risk forgetting that there are real relationships to which the metaphors point.[106] We forget, for instance, that for Paul the Christian life is one involving a slavery-like bondage to God and to brothers and sisters in the community (Gal. 1.10; 2 Cor. 4.5). For Paul, the experience of being-in-Christ is a unique kinship relation with the power to shape behavior, create obligations, and alter destiny.

b. *Race and Paul's Relational Map*

With reference to personal characteristics, we found evidence that Paul's individual identity involved choices among several possible subject positions and potentially competing loyalties. On the one hand, Paul unambiguously refers to himself and his Jewish Christian opposition in Corinth as Israelites (Rom. 11.1-2; 2 Cor. 11.22-23), but he effectively acknowledges two kinds of Israel in Romans 9–11 when he points out that not everyone born from the Israelite race is a member of Israel. Even though he continues to affirm the relationship between non-Christian Jews and the patriarchs, and between himself and non-Christian Jews, Paul calls himself a Jew only when speaking about his birth. More importantly, he distances himself from a Jewish self-identification when he speaks of becoming *like* a Jew for the sake of evangelism to Jews (cf. Gal. 1.14; 2.15; 1 Cor. 9.19-20).

Although Paul's use of the word 'Israel' is slippery in Romans 9–11 to say the least, his use of the term 'Jew' is considerably more stable across the corpus. Paul normally refers to non-Christian descendants of Abraham in the third person as 'Jews', and he avoids using this term in self-identifications (cf. Gal. 1.14; 2.15; 1 Cor. 9.19-20), a reserve that coheres with the suggestion that Paul places himself and non-Christian Jews in separate though related groups. Indeed, it seems that Paul has a similar reserve with respect to Jewish and Gentile Christians. He identifies Gentile Christians as children of Abraham (Rom. 4.11; Gal. 3.7; Gal. 3.29), just as he refers to himself in this manner in Rom. 11.1 and 2 Cor. 11.22. He speaks of Gentile Christians as Israelites in Gal. 6.16 and calls them the 'Church of God' in 1 Cor. 10.32, but he never calls such

---

106   Daniel Boyarin's treatment of the 'spiritual' vs. the 'literal' in Rom. 2.28-29 in *A Radical Jew* is the clearest expression of the tendency to conflate 'spiritual' with 'unreal', though Boyarin only makes explicit a tendency that it much more widespread. Boyarin's hermeneutic is discussed in more detail in Chapter 6.

Christians 'Jews'.[107] All of this suggests that Paul combines in himself both ascribed and voluntary elements of identity, as he thinks of himself as someone who was born a Jew but no longer considers himself one. That he privileges the voluntary without dismissing the ascribed is apparent from the way that he divides people into three distinct groups – Gentiles, Jews, and believers – while maintaining that the latter two collectives form separate groups of descendants from Abraham (Rom. 4.11-12, 16). Thus, in one sense Paul was both Jewish and Christian given that he was born Jewish and later chose to identify with Christ; but in another sense he was a former Jew, because he did not hold to both of those identities with equal loyalty when he considered the arc of his personal narrative (Phil. 3.3-11).

Although Paul belongs to the group composed of Jewish and Gentile Christians, we can only make a tentative suggestion about whether his preferred name for that group is 'Israel' or the 'Church of God'. When speaking about his own identity the preferred name for the group is 'Israel' (Rom. 11.1; 2 Cor. 11.22; Phil. 3.3; cf. Gal. 1.14; 2.15). He uses the title 'Israel of God' in Gal. 6.16 for Jewish and Gentile Christians in the context of a highly charged controversy over the identity and characteristics of descendants of Abraham. In contrast, the naming of Christians in 1 Cor. 10.32 occurs in a setting that is not nearly as contentious, and in this context he not only names the group, but also explicitly articulates his tripartite social matrix, speaking of 'Jews, Gentiles, and the Church of God' (cf. Gal. 1.13). Since all of his explicit self-identity statements occur in settings in which his self-identification as an Israelite is a polemical response to various controversies, it could be that the phrase the 'Church of God' represents Paul's basal reflection about the group name, despite the fact that 'Israel' appears more often when Paul's self-identification and group designations are weighed in the balance together.

The previous discussion also illuminates the racial character of Paul's thinking about identity. Earlier, I described a model for the ancient Jewish concept of race as a dialectic involving religion, kinship, and common social characteristics. At first sight, the fact that this model involves kinship as a significant component might raise doubts that Paul conceived of Christian identity as 'racial'. Yet we found that kinship was very much a concern of Paul's, emerging not only in his habitual use of kinship language, but also in his defense of justification by faith in Romans 4. In fact, Paul may represent an ancient example of Smith's observation that groups try to shore up the weakest components of identity early in their

---

107 Sanders, *Paul, the Law and the Jewish People*, p. 174; cf. Peter Tomson, 'The Names Israel and Jew in Ancient Judaism and in the New Testament', *Bijdragen Tijdschrift* 47.3 (1986): 266–89; Harvey, *True Israel*, p. 268.

assembly process.[108] When viewed from the perspective of ethno-racial formation, Paul's vision of the believer's relationship to Abraham not only shores up the missing kinship component of Christian identity vis-à-vis Jewish identity concepts, but also provides a rival version of history for the emergent group. This rival history sharpens the new group's sense of identity in the near term and, more importantly, provides an intergenerational narrative that is critical for the group's long-term survival.[109]

Though, again, I make no claims about ideas that prevailed historically in Paul's churches, we found that the Jewish model of race formed a better background for Paul's thought. The model of ethnicity, which consists of a dialectic involving religion, conflict, territory, and government, does not provide the same heuristic value. Ethnic themes, to be sure, occasionally appear as subtexts in his discourse, for example in the conflict described at 1 Thess. 2.13-16 and in the catalogue in 2 Cor. 11.22-24, as well as the reference to citizenship in Phil. 3.20 (cf. 1.27). Be that as it may, these themes do not form the main lines of Paul's identity discourse. In contrast, we saw that the Jewish elements of racial identity appeared together in Rom. 3.27–4.22 and Phil. 3.2-9, which are key passages about Paul's group- and self-identification.

More importantly, in Phil. 3.2-9, Paul depicts his pre-conversion *and* post-conversion identities in ways that utilize all of the elements in the model of race. Both pre-conversion and post-conversion identities involve a deeply religious focus on righteousness, whether it comes from the law or from faith. There is also a clear social group differentiation of practices in terms of the mechanisms by which the group orders its worship of the God of Abraham, whether by the Spirit or by the practices signified by circumcision. In addition, Paul regularly expresses his identity in terms of kinship, whether in speaking about the physical kinship of his former life in Judaism or in referring to eschatological kinship in the new creation community (Phil. 3.3, 9; Gal. 1.14; 3.15; Phlm. 16; 1 Cor. 10.1). We saw that Paul draws on an association between law, descent from Abraham, and circumcision that is available from his Jewish framework and that he sets these entities in antithesis to Christian elements in Phil. 3.2-9. We will see similar antitheses between Jewish and Christian elements of racial identity in our study of Galatians below. Thus, given this evidence of the racial character of Paul's thought about identity, I am suggesting that his relational schema included three distinct races: Jews, Gentiles, and the Church of God (1 Cor. 10.32).

---

108   Smith, *The Ethnic Origins of Nations*, p. 31.
109   Ibid., p. 26.

c. *Identity, Religion, and Ethnicity Revisited*

In view of the earlier discussion about the elasticity of group loyalties, we may question whether and how Paul's relational matrix allows for multiple identity affiliations. As noted in Chapter 2, while individuals occupy multiple subject locations that can vary by context (e.g., the black male as either oppressor or oppressed), they do not hold these different affiliations with equal strength and devotion. Thus, we ask, How did Paul conceive of the relationship between an individual's prior group affiliation and his or her new identity in Christ?

We start by considering evidence of Paul's continuing sense of physical kinship with non-Christian Jews (Rom. 9.1-3; 11.14). His angst in Romans 9–11 about non-Christian Israelites is so well known that knowledge of this anxiety may have been instrumental in obscuring his remarkable reticence to identify himself explicitly as a Jew. We also noted the distancing language he uses when he speaks about Jews, as if discussing a third party in 1 Cor. 10.32 and 1 Cor. 9.19-23. All the same, if we take him at his word in 1 Cor. 9.19-23, he did participate in Jewish evangelism at some level despite his primary mission to Gentiles (cf. Acts 13.14-41; 14.1; 17.1-3, 10-11; 18.4-8; 19.8). All of this indicates that he had some level of sympathy with those sharing his birth identity, even though his paramount allegiance was to Christ and the church.

We see a similar ambiguity in his attitudes to his Gentile converts, since on the one hand he calls them 'Gentiles' when referring to their birth identity (Gal. 2.14), but on the other when considering their current group allegiances, he insists that they 'used to be Gentiles' (1 Cor. 12.2). We saw that it was possible to imagine that Paul acknowledged continuing physical kinship between non-Christian Gentiles and Gentile Christians just as he did in his own situation, an inference supported by my reading of Phlm. 16. On the other hand, Paul may have believed that the ἐν σαρκί relationship between Philemon and Onesimus was restored only *after* Onesimus' conversion, since the analogy between Paul's relationship with non-Christian Jews and Gentile Christians' relationships to non-Christian Gentiles is not perfect. Paul's passion for unsaved Jewish people and his hopes for their inclusion in the new creation community are inextricably linked to his eschatology, in that the salvation of Israel has a cosmic significance that may not apply with reference to the salvation of Phrygians or others. However, given the symbiotic relationship that Paul describes between Gentile and Jewish salvation in Rom. 11.13-32, I think that Paul's arguments favor seeing a situation among Gentiles that is analogous to Paul's relationships with non-Christian Jews (cf. 1 Cor. 7.12-16).

Yet we have to qualify this picture of harmonious multiple ethno-racial group allegiances. Some might argue that the references to synagogue discipline in 2 Cor. 11.24 suggest that Paul had a stronger attachment to the synagogue than the subordinated sympathy I describe above. This perspective holds that Paul's oft-received synagogue discipline hints at his continuing sense of solidarity with and submission to the Jewish community.[110] On such a reading, Paul could be conceived as having strong allegiances both to the new Christian group and to the synagogue. Nevertheless, this perspective needs to deal with the fact that Paul terms such incidents 'persecution' (e.g., Gal. 4.29; 5.1; 6.12). It is possible to interpret these incidents as indicative of the Jewish community's perceived right to administer discipline, thus admitting the possibility that those administering 39 lashes did not see themselves as punishing an 'outsider'. However, it is inappropriate to silence Paul's own voice, as we do when we suggest that his experience of persecution implies his 'submission' to the authorities administering the penalty. The idea of 'submission' must be read into the texts in question (2 Cor. 11.22-24; Gal. 4.29; 5.11) and clashes with Paul's description of them as 'persecution'. In view of the fact that Paul felt victimized by non-Christian Jews and the distance he assumed from Jewish identity at 1 Cor. 9.19-23 and Gal. 1.13, I think that it goes much too far to suggest that his allegiance to Jewish identity was equal to his loyalty to Christ. On the other hand, our discussion of his apostolic identity revealed that he thought of himself as both a light to the Gentiles and a gatherer of Israel, thus his zeal and concern for non-Christian Jews went bone deep. The fact that Paul was repeatedly repudiated by synagogues indicates not so much his continuing identification with them, but his abiding commitment to Jewish evangelism. Recalling that when identity is even partially selected and situational then it becomes a political statement, we should understand Paul's explicit alignment of himself with the Church of God as a statement of his most important loyalties (1 Cor. 10.32).

I end this chapter with an observation about the frequent references in current Pauline scholarship to Paul's 'Jewishness' or 'Jewish ethnicity'. When moderns consider the question of Paul's identity, they often maintain that Paul continued to be a Jew, because for them the word 'Jew' describes an ethnic identity that is permanent. For example, in an article already mentioned in the section on Paul's Israelite identity, Dunn thoughtfully struggles with the limitations imposed by popular ideas about ethnicity:

---

110 See the discussion in John M.G. Barclay, *Jews in the Mediterranean Diaspora* (Berkeley, Los Angeles, and London: University of California Press, 1996), pp. 394–95; Sanders, *Paul, the Law and the Jewish People*, pp. 190–92. Sanders maintains that the opposite is true as well: the authorities administering the punishments felt that they had jurisdiction over Paul.

> When Paul first believed in Jesus, did he cease to be a Jew? Put like that, the question invites the answer, No! Of course Paul did not cease to be a Jew – how could he? . . . Complications emerge, however, as soon as we realize the ambiguity and unclarity of the terms involved. Does 'Jew' denote an ethnic identity (which of course Paul retained) or a religious identity?[111]

Notwithstanding the unfortunate parenthetical remark in the last line, this promising start at a new perspective on Paul's identity stumbles into a preoccupation with geography a few lines later:

> It is difficult to avoid an ethnic sense for the term 'Jew'. The term itself derives from the region/country 'Judea'. A Jew was firstly a Judean, identified by Judean origin and native land.[112]

Dunn then ends by retreating totally into Greco-Roman ethnic reasoning when he cites Barclay's summary of Jewish identity in the Diaspora as being built on the core of ancestry and custom.[113] Together, these scholars cite territory, kinship, and custom as the core of Jewish ethnicity, ignoring the component of religion that we found to be significant in ancient Jewish models for both race and ethnicity in the period. They have imposed a modern notion of ethnicity onto an ancient Jewish context. This imposition might not have been so serious if the analysis had concerned a Greco-Roman culture, since we saw that there were many similarities between ancient Greco-Roman models and modern popular concepts, but it is much more serious when applied to ancient Jewish constructions of identity. In particular, Dunn is at fault for treating ethnicity and religion as two separate identity categories.

However, if we accept that religion is the criterion of ancient Jewish constructions of race and ethnicity, we will see that Paul's conversion – or better, his transformation – entailed a change in racial identity. He no longer identified himself as a Jew, because for him the word 'Jew' referred to a race determined principally via a specific and ordered relationship to God. Note, however, that Paul's explicit self-identification as an 'Israelite' in contrast to his references to himself as a 'Jew' only in contexts that highlight his non-Christian past are not tantamount to what is today called anti-Semitism or anti-Judaism. Paul does not denigrate the Jewish heritage or people and, as I argued above, his devotion to his 'kinsmen according to the flesh' emerges in numerous ways and places in his epistles (Rom. 9.1-3; 1 Cor. 9.19-20; Phil. 3.4-6; 2 Cor. 3.7, 9). My interest in highlighting Paul's self-identity as a formerly Jewish Israelite focuses on a desire to understand his relational matrix and the key role that religious

---

111   Dunn, 'Who Did Paul Think He Was?', p. 179.
112   Ibid., p. 179.
113   Ibid., p. 181, citing Barclay, *Jews in the Mediterranean Diaspora*, p. 404.

faith played in his choices about ethno-racial identity; it does not emerge from a reluctance to associate him with the word 'Jew' and whatever negative images have accrued to that term in racist discourse.[114]

In fact, there are several modern tendencies in discussions about race and ethnicity that obscure our ability to understand Paul's ethno-racial identity and its implications for Christian identity. First, there is a modern tendency to see 'race' as negative and alien, a trend that will cause many to resist this discussion of Jewish and Christian identity. Further, moderns see ethnicity and race as permanent, and ethnicity and religion as separate, views that obscure the recognition that Paul's retreat from Torah entails a similar withdrawal from Jewish ethno-racial identity. Contrary to scholars who use an anachronistic definition of race or ethnicity and take it for granted that Paul continued to think of himself as Jew,[115] Pauline self-identity texts interpreted against the framework of ancient Jewish constructions of race suggest that Paul identified himself as an Israelite who was born a Jew but no longer was one. Paul's perspective on and response to the Christ event apocalyptically altered his relationship with God, his relationship to his kinsmen, and his interactions with the radically Other. That is to say, Paul and his Jewish-born and Gentile-born Christian family had become members of a new racial entity.

---

114   Cf. Harvey's concern that 'the word "Jew" has been seriously affected by negative overtones given to it by Christians' (*True Israel*, p. 7). See also Daniels, *White Lies, passim*.

115   E.g., Betz, *Galatians*, p. 70: e.g., '[Paul] took his appointment [as an apostle] to be part of his Jewishness'; Dunn, *Romans*, 1.232, cf. 1.216; id., 'Who Did Paul Think He Was?'; Hays, 'Galatians', p. 236; id., *Echoes*, pp. ix–x; Hodge, *If Sons then Heirs, passim*; Munck, *Paul and the Salvation of Mankind*, p. 279; Niebuhr, *Heidenapostel aus Israel*, see pp. 131, 142–48, *et passim*; Räisänen, *Paul and the Law*, p. 200. Sanders represents an interesting case in that *Paul, the Law and the Jewish People*, pp. 171–99, describes Paul's relational map similarly to the portrayal here and even speaks of a 'third race' (pp. 173, 207), yet without a sustained discussion of Paul's ethnicity per se (cf. pp. 175, 199). John Barclay's nuanced discussion in 'Paul among Diaspora Jews' is difficult to categorize on this point (cf. pp. 89–90, 116–19). The essay begins by identifying Paul as a Diaspora Jew for the purposes of comparing him to other such Jews in terms of assimilation, acculturation, and accommo-dation to Greek culture. But even though Barclay refers to ethnicity, race, and Paul's 'Jewishness' in ways that are anachronistic along with the scholars cited above, Barclay concludes that Paul was an 'apostate' whose 'Jewishness' was repudiated by 'the vast majority of his contemporaries' (pp. 110, 118–19). Barclay reaches this conclusion by contrasting Paul's own continuing self-identification as a Jew with his repudiation by other Diaspora Jews (pp. 89–120).

Chapter 5

THE DIALECTICS OF RACE RELATIONS IN CHRIST

If, as we argued above, Paul experienced a change in racial identity, what is the character of his new race and how does it engage the other groups in Paul's social matrix? This chapter explores the nature of Christian identity in Galatians in terms of the key identity parameters introduced in Chapter 2, *membership criteria* and *membership indicia*, as well as the intergroup dynamics among the three races in Paul's social world. We will see that the defining criterion of membership in the new race is faith in Christ and that the Spirit is the key indicium marking a member's participation in the Christian community. In addition, having found evidence in the last chapter that Paul saw the gathering of Israel as part of his mission and self-identity, this chapter will explore other evidence in Galatians of Paul's interest in the eschatological gathering of Israel, an interest that clarifies Paul's vision of the relationships between Jews, Gentiles, and the Church of God.

1. *Membership Criteria*

In Galatians more than any other work in the Pauline corpus, Paul's polemic against Jewish-Christian missionaries articulates a Christian identity that is apocalyptically differentiated from its Jewish counterpart. In this epistle, Paul argues against a conflation of Jewish and Christian identity that has been successfully propounded by missionaries among the Galatians who are persuading these Gentile Christians of the importance of circumcision and other Jewish religious customs (Gal. 1.6; 4.10; 5.2, 7). By close attention to Paul's counterclaims, we can reconstruct the main lines of the arguments offered by these missionaries. What emerges most clearly is that he and his opponents operated from vastly different visions of Christian community. While the missionaries apparently saw lack of Torah observance as a barrier for Gentile inclusion, Paul was adamant that circumcision and full obedience to Torah constituted an abandonment of the new creation community that had grave eschatological consequences. The controversies that divide Paul and the Jewish-Christian missionaries strike at the heart of what it means to belong to the community of those in Christ.

In the latter half of the autobiographical opening sections of Galatians, Paul develops his ideas about membership criteria for this new community, and we begin our investigation of this criteria by focusing on the phrases 'the truth'/'the truth of the gospel'. The narrative and comments in Galatians 2 establish what Paul means by the phrase 'the truth of the gospel' and provide the terms under which he discusses faith in Christ as the criterion of Christian identity (2.16). The first part of Paul's narrative in Galatians 1 emphasizes his independence from human authority, but in the second part of his story in Galatians 2, the narrative peaks in the description of the confrontation at Antioch (2.11-14). In 2.15-21, Paul comments on the Antioch episode in a way that presents the key message of the argument, while gathering the early support of the audience.[1] Here, Paul employs rhetoric in a way that not only attempts to capture Peter's good will, but also includes in the implied audience Paul's Jewish-Christian opponents in Galatia, who thus 'overhear' his speech to Peter.[2] It is in this context that Paul's use of the phrases 'the truth'/'the truth of the gospel' in 2.5, 14, and 5.7 points to the core of the gospel and thus the central criterion of membership.

In effect, Martyn argues that the phrase describes the criterion of Christian identity when he suggests that Paul's linkage of the nouns 'truth' and 'gospel' implies that the 'truth *is* the gospel' and that *that* is what is eschatologically at stake in Galatia (1.8-9; cf. 5.7-10).[3] The noun 'truth' appears three times in Galatians: twice in the phrase ἡ ἀλήθεια τοῦ εὐαγγελίου (2.5, 14) and once independently (5.7). In context, the phrase in Gal. 2.5 refers to Paul's conviction that Christians have freedom vis-à-vis circumcision and the law in Christ (Gal. 2.3-4). In 2.14 'the truth of the gospel' could be narrowly confined to the nullification of food laws in Christ (cf. 2.12), or more broadly, it could refer to the renunciation of a Torah-compliant lifestyle (2.14) as seen in his rejection of works of law (2.16) and righteousness through the law (2.21). If 2.5 and 2.14 leave us with a choice between a narrow and broader understanding of what Paul means by 'the truth of the gospel', 5.7 seems to favor the broader idea ('Who prevented you from obeying the truth?') Coming on the heels of Paul's statement that 'neither circumcision nor uncircumcision counts for

---

1   Martyn identifies this section as the *captatio benevolentiae* where an author 'captures his audience by means of a friendly reference to something he shares with them' (*Galatians*, pp. 20–21, 246–47).

2   Ibid., p. 248.

3   Ibid., p. 198; Longenecker, *Galatians*, p. 53; Ernest De Witt Burton, *The Epistle to the Galatians* (ICC; Edinburgh: T&T Clark, 1921), p. 86. On the other hand, Betz thinks that the phrase refers to 'the doctrine of grace', but notes that there are other possibilities (e.g., 'the true gospel' [cf. 1.6-9] and 'the real consequences of the gospel'; Betz, *Galatians*, p. 92).

anything; the only thing that counts is faith working through love' (5.6) it seems clear that the word 'love' alludes to the discussion of behavior in Galatians 5 and represents Paul's core expression of the gospel. 'Faith working through love' encapsulates the whole message of the epistle and functions as Paul's statement of the criterion of Christian identity.[4]

If the 'truth of the gospel' refers to the central idea of 'faith working in love' (5.6-7), then we must additionally understand the meaning of 'faith'. Though the meaning of 'faith' in 5.6 is not explicit, 'faith' and 'truth' also figure prominently in 2.14, and there 'faith' refers to 'faith in Christ'.[5] In Galatians 2–3 Paul presents the gospel in terms of a contrast between 'faith in Christ' (πίστις Χριστοῦ) and 'works of law' (ἔργα νόμου). Beginning with Galatians 5, Paul uses abbreviated forms of these phrases, πίστις for πίστις Χριστοῦ and νόμος for ἔργα νόμου, a shorthand that uses one of the words for the larger idea.[6] Thus the core message of the gospel, 'faith working in love', refers to the outworking or practical demonstration of πίστις Χριστοῦ in the actions and behavior of the community. The criterion for membership in the new community is πίστις Χριστοῦ actualized in deeds of love.

Earlier, I suggested that because circumcision signified a Torah-observant life and since it was such an ancient and reliable indicium of identity, it thereby practically functioned as the criterion of Jewish identity. We found confirmation that Paul shared this understanding in Rom. 3.1-2 where he states that the foremost value of circumcision is exhibited by the fact that the Jews were entrusted with the oracles of God

4   The summary of the gospel in 5.6-7 is a statement of the criterion of Christian identity, though Gal. 2.14, to be sure, occurs in a vital part of the letter. Nevertheless, the question of sin in the life of a believer brackets the statement of the criterion of identity in 2.14 and lends importance to the question of sin in a way that is better captured in 5.6. The interpreter who overlooks the discussion of the spirit in Gal. 5 has missed an important element of Paul's gospel. See J.M.G. Barclay's monograph, which makes the point that questions of identity and behavior are the central issues in Galatians, and thus Gal. 5–6 is of central importance in interpreting Galatians (*Obeying the Truth: A Study of Paul's Ethics in Galatians* [Edinburgh: T&T Clark, 1988], pp. 56–83); *contra* Martyn (*Galatians*, p. 245), who focuses on 2.16 as the 'core' of Paul's message.

5   For the interpretation of πίστις Χριστοῦ as a subjective genitive, see M. Barth, 'The Faith of the Messiah'; Johnson, 'Romans 3.21-26 and the Faith of Jesus'; Hays, *Faith of Jesus Christ*. Though I use the objective genitive in this translation, certainty on this issue is difficult since not all of the evidence from the Pauline corpus points in the same direction (cf. Gal. 3.22; Gal. 2.16; see Hays, *Faith of Jesus Christ*, pp. 161–62). I will tend to favor construing the phrase as an objective genitive because of the importance of Gal. 2.16 to the analysis here and later in ch. 5, and because the objective genitive is almost certainly in view in that passage. Yet given the ambiguity in the Greek elsewhere in Galatians and Romans, when I am not referring to Gal. 2.16 or its context I will either leave the Greek phrase untranslated or use the English phrase 'faith of Christ' as the most literal translation of the Greek.

6   Betz, *Galatians*, p. 262.

in the law. With this in mind, we can see that 2.16; 2.21; and 5.6 all stand as statements of the criterion of Christian identity. According to Paul, the in-Christ community membership criterion is antithetical to the necessity of living a Jewish lifestyle and all indications that point to it, and it affirms the exclusive centrality of faith in Christ as expressed in love for others and especially for other believers (Gal. 5.6; 6.10). The idea that 'the faith [of Christ] working through love' expresses the heart of Paul's gospel parallels the way that 'righteousness through [works] of law' (Gal. 2.21) encapsulates the central criterion of Jewish identity expressed in terms of covenantal nomism. Obedience to the law is the response to God's election of Israel demonstrated in the lives of the Jewish people.

The fact that circumcision was an indicium that functioned as a criterion and signifier of the Torah-observant lifestyle also helps explain Paul's otherwise puzzling insistence that the mark of circumcision severs one's relationship with Christ. As an accurate and long-used signifier of the Torah-observant lifestyle that thus functions as the defining criterion of membership in the Jewish people, circumcision from Paul's perspective identifies *Jewishness*. In other words, circumcision was not merely a mark of identity; it had become equated with Jewish identity. Gentile Christians became Jews when they received circumcision, and the transaction represented a deliberate change in ethno-racial identity, an act that had serious consequences when the criterion of identity in both races concerned the character of the relationship with God.

A closer consideration of 2.16 confirms that in Paul's mind Jewishness was separate from 'in-Christness'. Figure 5.1 shows that Gal. 2.16 contains a chiasm which revolves around the central claim of the verse in segment D: 'Even we have trusted in Christ Jesus in order that we might be righteoused by faith in Christ'.[7] The clauses B and B' and C and C' are balanced pairs, with the latter clause in each pair restating the earlier clause of the pair. For example, clause C 'except through the faith of Christ' is restated and elaborated by clause C' 'not by works of law'.[8] More importantly, πᾶσα σάρξ ('all flesh') in clause B' restates ἄνθρωπος, which is normally translated 'man' or 'person' in clause B.[9] The law no longer restricts access to justification from God, but now *all* flesh, not just

---

7   See the similar chiastic structure in Martyn, *Galatians*, p. 250. Ian Thomson points out that ideas developed in the center of a chiasm receive special prominence (*Chiasmus in the Pauline Letters* [Sheffield: Sheffield Academic Press, 1995], p. 43).

8   Thomson notes that the ideas that are symmetrically balanced in chiasms 'have the effect of making the combined impact of element X with its chiastic partner X' more than the impact of X and X' taken in isolation' (*Chiasmus*, pp. 39, 43).

9   Gaston's suggestion, that Paul uses ἄνθρωπος to refer to Gentiles (*Paul and the Torah*, pp. 65–66) utterly fails in light of the chiastic balance between ἄνθρωπος and πᾶσα σάρξ described here (cf. Gager, *The Origins of Anti-Semitism*, p. 233, and Hodge, *If Sons then Heirs*, p. 176 n. 72 who agrees with Gaston, though on different terms).

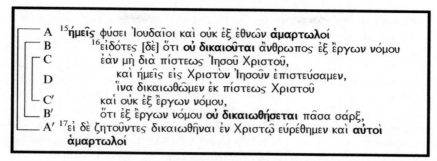

Figure 5.1 – Chiasmus in Galatians 2.15-17

Jewish flesh, receives justification through faith in Christ.[10] All this suggests that we should translate 2.16 as follows:

> Knowing that humanity is not made righteous by works of law but only through faith in Jesus Christ, even we [Jews] have trusted in Christ Jesus, so that we might be made righteous by faith in Christ and not by works of law; because works of law do not righteous all [kinds of] flesh. (LLS)

The missionaries who insisted that Gentiles must become Jews and thereafter adhere to the Torah-observant lifestyle had missed the fact that the gospel requires a shift among Jews as well. The gospel demands that both Gentile flesh *and* Jewish flesh adopt a new criterion of identity, effectively becoming members in a new racial group.[11]

However, the chiasm in 2.16 actually extends from 2.15 to 2.17a as shown in Figure 5.1. As indicated by the word 'sinners' (ἁμαρτωλοί) at the end of 2.15 and 17a, the outer structure introduces the topic of sin into the discussion for the first time in Galatians. The abrupt introduction of a new topic possibly indicates that Paul turns to the issue of sin to rebut the arguments of the Jewish-Christian missionaries. Given Martyn's description of 2.15 as the *captatio benevolentiae*, Paul, Peter, and Paul's Jewish-Christian opponents in Galatia are all included in the first-person plural address: 'We are Jews by birth and not Gentile sinners' (ἡμεῖς φύσει Ἰουδαῖοι καὶ οὐκ ἐξ ἐθνῶν ἁμαρτωλοί). Here Paul uses common Jewish insider language that distinguishes Jews from those outside, those who by definition are not only Gentiles but who are also sinners by default, since those outside the Jewish community do not have the Torah.[12] Therefore,

---

10 Martyn, *Galatians*, p. 249.

11 Similarly, E.P. Sanders, *Paul, the Law and the Jewish People*, pp. 172–76; *contra* Hodge and Gaston (see n. 9 above).

12 This kind of language is common in the OT and Jewish literature; see for example, Ps. 9.17 ('Let *sinners* be driven away into Hades, [that is,] all the nations that forget God'); 1 Macc. 2.42-44 ('Then there united with them a company of Hasideans, mighty warriors of

even though Paul and his Jewish-Christian opponents at Galatia were born Jewish, they too have entered the realm of πίστις Χριστοῦ (2.15-16).[13]

Galatians 2.17b-18 goes further, asking about the status of a person who sins after having been justified in Christ: 'But if, in our effort to be justified in Christ, we ourselves have been found to be sinners, is Christ then a servant of sin?' (NRSV).[14] While we cannot be certain about the nature of the dispute about sin between Paul and his opponents, the relationship of 2.15 to 2.17a seems to ask whether the gospel is responsible for making the person revert to the status of 'Gentile sinner' (ἆρα Χριστὸς ἁμαρτίας διάκονος; 2.17c), perhaps a charge made by the Jewish-Christian missionaries.[15] Alternately, these missionaries may have argued that obedience to Torah offers a means of dealing with sin, a provision lacking in Paul's Torah-free gospel. Paul couches his answer in terms of 'status', stating that someone becomes a sinner only when he or she re-establishes the influence of Torah, and this seems to favor the first possibility as the Jewish-Christian argument, though not to the exclusion of the latter, as we will see shortly.[16] His bottom line is to reject the idea that the *gospel* is at fault: '*Christ* is not a servant of sin in this situation; I prove *myself* a transgressor (παραβάτην) in this case' (cf. 2.18b).

However, there is even more at stake in the question raised and answered in 2.17-18, two issues related to the term 'found' (εὑρέθημεν) in the latter part of 2.17. The first concerns the implication of the lexeme εὑρίσκω, while the second concerns the referent of the plural subject in the term εὑρέθημεν and the emphatic 'we ourselves' in 2.17. With regard to the word εὑρίσκω, Richard Hays notes in a discussion of Rom. 4.1 that Paul often uses a construction containing (a) the verb εὑρίσκω with an unexpressed εἶναι and (b) a predicate nominative or adjective that together means 'to find *someone* to be *something*'. Listing Gal. 2.17 among the verses exhibiting this pattern, Hays suggests that Paul uses this construction as an 'exegetical-dialogical' term that refers to the results of some kind of investigation or inquiry. Hays sees Paul's use of this

---

Israel, all who offered themselves willingly for the law... They organized an army, and struck down *sinners* in their anger and renegades in their wrath; the survivors fled to the Gentiles for safety'); see also Ps. 1.1-2 (LXX); Sir. 12.1-18; *Pss. Sol.* 17.5.

13   Merklein, '"Nicht aus Werken des Gesetzes..."', p. 123: 'The negative assessment [implicit in the word 'sinner'] serves only as a background in order to bring to expression the salvation-historical advantage of Jewish Christians. They are "Jews by nature" and therefore – originally – *not* sinners like the Gentiles' (emphasis original); cf. Martyn, *Galatians*, p. 248.

14   See Martyn, *Galatians*, pp. 253–55; and especially Longenecker, *Galatians*, pp. 89–90.

15   Similarly, Martyn, *Galatians*, pp. 253–55; Burton, *The Epistle to the Galatians*, p. 125.

16   See also J.B. Lightfoot, *Saint Paul's Epistle to the Galatians* (London and New York: MacMillan, 10th edn, 1890), pp. 116–17. Lightfoot prefers the first interpretation because it preserves the same understanding of ἁμαρτολός in 2.15 and 2.17.

construction as a parallel to the rabbinic use of the phrase מה מצינו ב,
which means, 'What do we find (in Scripture) concerning ... ?', where
'found' refers to the result of an exegetical investigation of Scripture.[17] If
Hays is right about the meaning of Paul's use of 'found', then the phrase
in 2.17 'we are found to be sinners' refers to a status emerging from an
investigation of Scripture, since the mention of the law in 2.19-21 is
connected to 2.17-18 by an explanatory γάρ.

The idea that Paul is most concerned with what sin and Torah
communicate about status also receives support from the use of the word
παραβάτης ('one who transgresses') in 2.18b. Paul's only other use of
παραβάτης occurs in conjunction with the cognate noun παράβασις (an
overstepping or transgression) in Rom. 2.23-27, where he discusses the
fact that violations of law can result in excommunication. The use of the
word παράβασις in other contexts in the canon also conveys the idea of
excommunication. While in English the word 'transgression' is often
taken as a synonym for 'sin', the LXX does not reflect this kind of
synonymous usage, given that other Greek words are used to translate the
common Hebrew words for sin (e.g., άμαρτία, άμάρτημα). At least one of
the three LXX occurrences of παράβασις appears in an apparent reference
to apostasy in Ps. 100.3 (MT 101.3) where it translates a Hebrew verb for
'falling away': 'I have not set before my eyes any unlawful thing; I have
hated the ones practicing transgressions' (Heb: סטים; 'those falling away'
NRSV).[18] At 2 Macc. 15.10 the same verb refers to the breaking of oaths by
the unrighteous, and in Wis. 14.31 it seems to represent the sin of the
unrighteous in contrast to the righteousness of covenant members. The
sense of apostasy as found in Ps. 100 (LXX) also seems implicit in many of
the New Testament usages. Παράβασις and παραβάτης are used 12
times in the New Testament (Rom. 2.23, 25, 27; 4.15; 5.14; Gal. 2.18; 3.19;
1 Tim. 2.14; Heb. 2.2; 9.15; Jas 2.9, 11), in many of which it is possible to
translate the word with 'apostasy' or 'apostate'.[19]

I propose that παράβασις ('transgressor') in Gal. 2.18 means 'apostate', and that the word may be read in contrast to έθνῶν άμαρτωλοί
('Gentile sinners') in 2.15 and 2.17. Paul deliberately chooses a word that
often conveys the sense of excommunication or apostasy, comparing the
one who has fallen away from Christ (2.18b) with those who under the old
social matrix 'by nature' or 'by origin' (φύσει, 2.15) have been outside the
covenant all along. Thus, if εύρίσκω refers to an investigation of

---

17   Hays, '"Have We Found Abraham?"', pp. 82–83. Outside of Rom. 4.1 and Gal. 2.17,
the other Pauline passages that Hays cites are 1 Cor. 4.2; 15.15; 2 Cor. 5.3; 9.4; 12.20.

18   Also see BDB, s.v. שׂט, cf. שָׂטָה.

19   There are similar usages in Josephus, *J.A.* 18.81, and Philo, *Spec. Laws* 2.242. In this
analysis, 'apostasy' refers to a pattern of behavior that demonstrates an intention to abandon
God's covenant and that results in being cut off from the covenant community (Sanders,
Paul and Palestinian Judaism, pp. 147, 157, 237–38).

Scripture, and παραβάτης refers to one who is an apostate, the question in 2.17a-b asks, Is it the fault of the gospel when we who are justified in Christ are found to be sinners according to Scripture? Galatians 2.17c-18 answers by rejecting the idea that Christ is at fault – indeed, the only one at fault in this situation is one who demonstrates that he is an apostate who rebuilds devotion to the law.[20] That is, the law's power as an authoritative arbiter of an individual's status vis-à-vis the criterion of Jewish identity has been 'brought down' or nullified via co-crucifixion with Christ (2.18-19). According to Paul, circumcision and the Torah-observant lifestyle associated with it represent a 'rebuilding' of the law that has been canceled by Christ and that has the effect of nullifying the grace of God (2.21).[21] Later we will see that in 3.10-14, Paul elaborates on the results achieved through Christ's tearing down of the law, results that initiate a key eschatological dialectic in the relationships between Jews and those in Christ.

All of this suggests that the missionaries have not only spoken about obedience to law but have also raised the issue of sin in their arguments in favor of circumcision. Paul begins to respond to this issue by insisting that obedience to the law while justified in Christ is, literally, a dead issue. For Paul, circumcision and law are intimately connected as indicia and criteria of Jewish identity, as are the ethno-racial identifiers Ἰουδαῖοι, ἐθνῶν, ἁμαρτωλοί, and ἐν Χριστῷ. Together these terms are the central foils for his articulation of Christian identity. If the missionaries believe subsequent sin makes the person who is justified in Christ revert to the status of Gentile sinner, Paul's answer implicitly rejects that dualistic schema, inserting a boundary between παραβάτης and ἐν Χριστῷ that is analogous to that between Ἰουδαῖοι and ἐθνῶν ἁμαρτωλοί. Religious issues such as sin, circumcision, and faith, then, are the key terms that alter ethno-racial status.

2. Membership Indicia

What does Galatians tell us about the distinctive identity markers of the community in Christ? We have already seen that πίστις Χριστοῦ operating through love articulates Paul's version of the central criterion of Christian identity, and that this criterion is analogous to the Jewish

---

20   Merklein, ' "Nicht aus Werken des Gesetzes …" ', pp. 128–29.

21   In his study of chiasmus in Paul, Thomson discusses how Gal. 6.3-10 operates as a 'framing' passage that comments on the preceding chiasm in 5.13–6.2 (*Chiasmus*, pp. 145–49, 223). Though Thomson's study prevents broad generalizations, it may be that 2.17b-21 functions similarly in relation to the chiasm in 2.15-17a.

criterion of righteousness via a Torah-ordered life.[22] If there is a Christian analogue for circumcision, does it too exhibit a dual function in that the analogue is an indicium that also functions as the criterion of identity? In the last chapter, we saw that analysis of other Pauline epistles reveals an antithesis between circumcision and worship in the Spirit, and in Galatians 3–5 we find confirmation of this dialectic. For Paul, the Spirit is the ultra-reliable indicium of Christian identity as well as the means by which life is ordered in the eschatological community, and this is analogous to the way in which circumcision is both the behavioral sign of the Torah-ordered life and the premier marker of identity.

a. *A New Sign (Galatians 3.2-5)*

Paul's case against the law as a requirement for community life in Christ appears in the series of arguments in 3.1–5.12, in which he demonstrates the validity of his claims through appeals to Scripture and tradition (3.6–4.11; 4.21-31) that are interwoven with appeals based on the experience of the community (3.1-5; 4.12-20; 5.1-12). Given these two types of arguments, it is fitting that we find the first description of the new indicium of Christian identity in an argument that appeals to experience (3.1-5). Since indicia typically include behavioral signifiers as well as material or physical signs, it is no surprise that Paul appeals to members' real-life experiences with indicia in developing an argument about the group's identity. For Paul, the indicium of Christian identity par excellence is the Spirit, and in keeping with this view, he moves from a discussion about his central conviction about Christian identity and membership criteria in 2.15-21 to a series of questions that recall the community's experience with the Spirit. He begins the discussion about core convictions by stating the one aspect of the gospel that all Christians, Jewish and Gentile alike, would accept independently of their stance on the law – 'even we [Jews] have trusted in Christ Jesus' (2.16). Similarly, in 3.1 he begins a direct address to the Galatians with an appeal to what was for Paul a universally acknowledged and distinctively Christian mark of identity, an appeal to the community's experience with the Spirit.

Galatians 3.1-5 begins abruptly and proceeds with staccato questions that are all phrased to make the community realize that their experience of the Spirit constitutes a powerful statement about the validity of Paul's gospel. Because the direct address to the Galatians in 3.1 and the asyndeton and rapid-fire rhetorical questions in 3.1-5 unmistakably signal the start of a new section, the logical relationship between 2.15-21 and the

---

22 I do not insist that righteousness with God through Torah is the single membership criterion for all Jews of the period in all places. Rather, as the investigations in Chapters 3 and 4 demonstrate, this criterion did operate for many Jews, among whom Paul can be numbered.

21; 3.17, 23-24; 5.18).[26] Indeed, the phrase 'works of law' itself seems to be intentionally general and comports with other general references in Galatians and the usage of a similar phrase at Qumran (2.17-19; 3.19; 4.21a; possibly 6.1).[27] Finally, Galatians gives several indications that Paul understood that the law had to be taken as a whole, perhaps in opposition to what his opponents were advocating (3.10; 5.3, 14).[28]

Dunn tries to strike a balance between the idea of works of law as a subset and viewing the phrase as a general reference to the whole law. He recognizes that the phrase 'works of law denotes all that the law requires of the devoted Jew' but suggests that Paul focuses on the 'social function' of the law: 'Works of law refer not exclusively but particularly to those requirements which bring to sharp focus the distinctiveness of Israel's identity'.[29] Although Dunn does not use the terms, his analysis appeals to the ideas of indicia and criteria of identity as described herein. He sees the law as defining the essence of Jewish identity – a criterion – and circumcision and food laws as 'focusing the distinctiveness of Israel's identity', that is, as indicia. While one can dispute whether a given indicium usefully and accurately assesses identity – compare for example Philo's dispute with allegorists who substitute symbolic regard for literal observance of certain laws (*Migration* 89–93) – rejection of the criterion of identity entails a comprehensive rejection of the identity. Dunn's exegesis attempts to exploit this distinction, holding that Paul rejected the indicia works of circumcision and food laws without totally rejecting the law as the essence of Jewish identity. What Dunn misses is the idea that reliable and long-used indicia begin to act as criteria of identity, a reality exemplified by the case of Jewish circumcision. By failing to understand this dynamic, Dunn misses the idea that Paul's rejection of circumcision essentially entailed a rejection of the central criterion of Jewish identity, given that for him, circumcision acted as a proxy for observance of the law as a whole. In other words, Paul did not nuance Jewish identity as an ethnic Jew by tinkering with a law or laws on the margins, he struck at the practice that pointed to the heart of his understanding of Jewishness and

---

26 Exceptions to the general rule that Paul refers to the law in its entirety in Galatians are 3.13; 5.23, and possibly 4.21b; 6.2, 13.

27 1QS 5.7-9, 20-21, 23; cf. James D.G. Dunn, 'Works of Law and the Curse of the Law (Galatians 3.10-14)', *NTS* 31 (1985): 523–42 (528). This 1QS passage contrasts with the usage in 4Q398 frag. 14–17ii.3, where the subset of laws under discussion is plainly indicated. Yet even in this latter passage the subset is discussed and set in the context of the whole law. See Geza Vermes (ed.), *The Complete Dead Sea Scrolls in English* (New York: Penguin, 1997).

28 Betz discusses several possibilities as to what Paul's opponents advocate. They may have been libertines, practitioners of circumcision as a magical rite, or exponents of a 'partial' or 'special' Torah (Betz, *Galatians*, pp. 316–17). Decisions between these alternatives would require more evidence than we have.

29 Dunn, 'Works of the Law', p. 531.

articulated a separate identity centered on the new criterion of faith in
Christ.[30]

For Paul, the law as a whole was the central criterion of Jewish identity
and thus determined the Jewish lifestyle, even as circumcision was the
proxy for that lifestyle as well as the preferred indicium for making
judgements about who was in or out of the Jewish race. Just as
circumcision in Judaism could patrol the boundary between God-fearers
and Jews, for Paul in 3.1-5 the Spirit is the sentinel on the border between
Christian and non-Christian identity. To wit, Gal. 3.1-5 represents a
transition from the discussion in 2.1-14 about the indicia of Jewish
identity to a discussion about the indicia of Christian identity. Paul
implicitly sets up a contrast between circumcision and *kashrut* on the one
hand and the Spirit on the other by juxtaposing 3.1-5 with 2.1-21. His
opening gambit in these verses is striking in that his use of rhetorical
questions expresses his confidence that the Galatians' experience of the
Spirit was real, concrete, and adequate as the basis of a contrast between
observable works of law and faith in Christ. In other words, 'Paul does
not seek to convince the Galatians that they really have received the
Spirit; the argument works the other way around. He argues from the
indisputable empirical fact that they have received the Spirit in order to
convince them that no further validating action is required.'[31]

We can learn a great deal about the Spirit as indicium from 3.1-5.
Structurally, the argument about the community's experience of the Spirit
begins via contrasts in a set of paired questions in 3.2-3:

> Did you receive the Spirit from a report of faith or from works of law?
> Having begun in the Spirit, why do you now continue to maturity via
> circumcision? (LLS)

The questions recall the contrast between law and faith from 2.16 and
clearly imply several things about Paul's understanding of the Spirit (cf.
3.4-5). First, the Spirit is distinctively associated with faith and presumably πίστις Χριστοῦ (2.16), and by implication, it is *not* associated with
obedience to the law. The opening clause in the question in 3.3, 'having
begun in the Spirit ...', leaves no room for the possibility that the
Galatians received the Spirit through obedience to law, and the implication is that the Spirit marks membership in the πίστις Χριστοῦ group.
Second, by recognizing the implied answer to the question in 3.2 – that is,
the Spirit came by faith – Paul sets the antithesis between faith and law in

---

30   *Contra* Dunn, 'Who did Paul Think He Was?', pp. 174–93.

31   Hays, 'Galatians', 11.251. Udo Borse suggests that Paul may have been speaking of
glossolalia (1 Cor. 12.30; 13.1; Acts 2.4; 10.46) or prophetic speech (1 Cor. 14.1-39; Acts 19.6)
when he refers to divine manifestations of power in 3.5 (*Der Brief an die Galater* [Regensburg:
Friedrich Pustet, 1955], p. 123).

3.2 parallel to the antithesis between Spirit and flesh in 3.3. The analogy implied in these verses, that faith is to Spirit just as the law is to flesh, suggests that in this context Paul uses σάρξ as a synonym for circumcision.[32] Hence, the Spirit is the sign of faith among Christians just as circumcision is the sign of obedience to the law among Jews (cf. Rom. 1.5; 16.26).

Third, Gal. 3.3 also introduces a contrast between ἐναρξάμενοι and ἐπιτελεῖσθε (cf. Phil. 1.6). The word ἐνάρχομαι generally conveys the idea of beginning; thus, we understand Paul to refer to the fact that the Galatians experienced the Spirit as they entered the new community. Fourth, it is possible to understand ἐπιτελέω in similar temporal terms as ending, but ἐπιτελέω also conveys the sense of 'completing' or 'bringing to completion or perfection' (cf. 2 Cor. 7.1).[33] Thus, Spirit and circumcision are not only alternate ways by which a person may enter a community but also alternate means of gaining maturity. Indeed, the idea of progress towards perfection recalls Paul's earlier questions about the nature of the relationship between sin and justification in the gospel (2.17-18). There Paul insisted that Christ does not make a person a sinner; a person reveals herself as a transgressor when she rebuilds works of Torah. While that earlier answer addressed the question of sin from the perspective of the person's status and membership in the community, here Paul addresses sin in terms of progress in the faith (cf. προκόπτω in 1.14) or maturity. The rhetorical question in 3.3 implicitly identifies the Spirit as the true agent or means of maturity, a theme Paul develops in detail in Gal. 5.5, 16-25.

b. *A New Lifestyle (Galatians 3–5)*

While considerations of space preclude a thorough examination of the role of the Spirit in Galatians, we need to survey the principal lines of the

---

32   Martyn (*Galatians*, p. 294) also sees in σάρξ a literal reference to circumcision because it has been set in opposition to πνεῦμα in this passage, referring to it in context as 'a severed piece of flesh'. On the other hand Schweizer ('σάρξ, οαρκικός, οάρκινος', p. 133) sees in this occurrence of σάρξ a description of legalism. The emphasis on circumcision earlier in the letter also provides support for the σάρξ as circumcision interpretation (Gal. 2.3, 7-9, 12), though it may be argued that Paul's use of the word to refer to his own (circumcised) bodily existence in a nearby text may point in another direction (2.20). In my judgement, the explicit association in 6.12-13 between σάρξ on the one hand and circumcision and law on the other tips the balance towards seeing σάρξ as a reference to circumcision. For an extensive discussion of Paul's use of σάρξ see Robert Jewett, *Paul's Anthropological Terms: A Study of Their Use in Conflict Settings* (Arbeiten zur Geschichte des antiken Judentum und Urchristentums, 10; Leiden: Brill, 1971), pp. 49–166.

33   See Martyn, *Galatians*, pp. 284, 289, 292–94.

idea as Paul develops it in chs 3–5.[34] The main lines of the argument in Galatians 3–4 are well known. According to Paul, those with faith in Christ follow in the tradition of Abraham's own faith. These people share in the blessing to the seed of Abraham inasmuch as they are in Christ, who is himself *the* seed of Abraham. In Gal. 3.14 we see that Paul equates Spirit with the terms 'blessing' and 'promise' from the Abrahamic narrative, seeing in the receipt of the Spirit among Gentile and Jewish Christians the eschatological fulfillment of God's promise to Abraham. The identification of 'promise' with Spirit becomes so strong in 3.14 that we would be remiss if we did not consider Paul's discussion of 'promise' in Galatians as a possible source of information about the Spirit. Thus, we learn that the Spirit is given to all who believe (3.22; cf. Rom. 8.9, 14; 1 Cor. 12.13), inaugurates the believer's participation in Christ (3.29; cf. 1 Cor. 6.19 with 6.14), and is the agent that puts humans 'into' Christ (4.23, 29; cf. Rom. 8.9; 1 Cor. 6.17).

Intriguingly, πνεῦμα also contributes to the construction of race in the allegory of Hagar and Sarah in 4.21-31. Paul allegorizes the women as covenants (4.24) and then as geographic entities (4.25-26) and depicts each woman as giving birth to children who correspond to these covenants and territories. In 4.29, the Spirit appears in conjunction with birth language as Paul contrasts the means by which these women give birth to their children; Hagar gives birth κατὰ σάρκα, and Jerusalem-above (i.e., Sarah) gives birth κατὰ πνεῦμα. In other words, just as the old covenant produces members via flesh or biological kinship, the Spirit produces members for the new community.[35] Indeed, Paul may have drawn upon a not-uncommon motif in ancient literature which figured πνεῦμα as a physical and crucial procreative element in developing this aspect of Spirit.[36]

This language prompts us to consider whether the terms of the allegory signal racial divisions of the kind observed in the last chapter in Paul's thinking. In the allegory, the matriarch of the Ishmaelites, Hagar, represents all three of the elements of racial identity in ancient Judaism as described in Chapter 3: a means of reckoning kinship (4.23, 29), a particular religious orientation with embedded membership criteria (4.24-25), and a social boundary (4.30, 5.2). As for the matriarch of Paul's

34 See Charles Cosgrove, *The Cross and the Spirit: A Study in the Argument and Theology of Galatians* (Macon: Mercer University Press, 1988); David Lull, ' "Pneuma" in Paul's Letter to the Churches of Galatia: An Interpretation of the Spirit in Light of Early Christian Experience in Galatia, Paul's Message to the Galatians, and Theology Today' (unpublished doctoral dissertation, Claremont Graduate University, 1978).

35 Flesh and Spirit are contrasting means of generating the seed of Abraham (Martyn, *Galatians*, pp. 431–66); *contra* G. Schrenk ('Was bedeutet "Israel Gottes"?' *Judaica* 5 [1949]: 81–94 [90]), who sees a contrast between earth and spirit.

36 Hodge, *If Sons then Heirs*, pp. 74–76.

group, we see that Sarah too represents a means of calculating descent (4.23, 29) and socially occupies the 'insider' space of the boundary drawn in 4.24-25. The allegory does imply a religious orientation or distinction for Sarah's children, but Paul does not discuss religious conduct for the κατὰ πνεῦμα group in the allegory proper, though this becomes a major emphasis later in Galatians 5. In the OT, Hagar's offspring, that is, the descendants of Ishmael, were considered a lineage and ethnic entity separate from Israel, even though both groups were descendants of Abraham (Gen. 17.20; 36.2-3; Ps. 83.4, 6); similarly, Paul assigns the offspring of these women to different lineages and ethno-racial entities. Indeed, the very terms of the allegory reveal Paul's dependency on kinship logic and the emphasis he places on a religious principle as a differentiator of people-groups.[37]

Without question, the Spirit is the primary vehicle for religious conduct in Paul's eyes, and Galatians 5 spells out the function of the Spirit in the Christian life. Having already 'begun' in the Spirit (3.3), believers await eschatological fulfillment in it (5.5). Christians are also led by the Spirit (5.18), meaning that they walk by it and live lives that are ordered by it (5.17, 25; cf. Rom. 8.2). Finally, the Spirit produces 'fruit' in the life of the believer, that is, the Spirit acts as an agent of moral transformation (5.22-23; cf. 2 Cor. 3.18). In Galatians 5, we see that Paul again uses contrasts in his discussion of the Spirit, but they differ from the kind of spirit–flesh antithesis introduced in 3.3. He again sets Spirit over against flesh, but instead of flesh as circumcision, here flesh is a manner of conduct or mode of life (5.16-17, 19-23). Galatians 5 also introduces a direct contrast between Spirit and law, which are mutually exclusive mediators that order life (5.18).

In Galatians, Paul draws on the same contrasting identity elements from Phil. 3.3-6. In Phil. 3, we saw that Paul placed the old identity triad of law/circumcision/physical descent in opposition to the new triad of faith/Spirit/being-in-Christ, but in Galatians the contrasts are not nearly as terse as the antitheses in Philippians. For example, in Phil. 3.9 law stands in antithesis to faith, but in Galatians Paul contrasts law with faith (2.16; 3.2), Christ (5.4), and Spirit (5.18). In Phil. 3.2-9, circumcision is in antithesis to Spirit, but in Galatians circumcision contrasts with faith (5.6), Christ (5.2-3), and Spirit (3.3; cf. 6.12-13). In Philippians 3 kinship is in antithesis to being-in-Christ (cf. 3.3-4; 3.3, 9), but in Galatians kinship contrasts with faith (3.7), being-in-Christ (3.28-29), and Spirit (4.23, 29).

---

37 We should also mark the fact that the allegory involves a territorial dimension (i.e., Sinai, Jerusalem, Jerusalem-above), which was a prominent feature of identity discourse – although more associated with ethnic than with racial constructs of identity. In Chapter 3, we identified the constituent features of ancient Jewish understandings of ethnicity as including religion, conflict, government, and territory.

Taken together, each element of Christian identity is in antithesis to every Jewish element of identity. Thus, the elements of Christian identity coalesce as opposites of Jewish identity in Galatians, in much the same way that the Jewish identity elements of circumcision, physical descent, and justification by law operate as synonyms for one another in Romans 3–4.

Nevertheless, Paul does show preferences when it comes to deploying specific identity elements in certain kinds of discourse. 'Law' often appears in contexts having to do with justification and appears to be the element most implicated in calculating boundaries vis-à-vis group membership (2.16; 3.2; 5.4).[38] Paul expresses the idea of physical descent in two ways: through an implied contrast between faith-sonship and natural-sonship in 3.7, and through birth imagery in the allegory of 4.23 and 4.29. Thus, physical descent imagery is mainly deployed in Paul's efforts to establish believing Gentiles as members of the lineage of the patriarchs.[39] Finally, 'circumcision' and 'spirit' are used in two kinds of discourse, that which describes lifestyle issues in the community and that which describes entering the community. Thus, much as in Philippians 3, 'spirit' and 'circumcision' act as indicia of membership for those who enter the community but also as signs that point beyond the simple fact of membership to represent a mode or manner of life. On the other hand, Paul's use of the terms 'Christ/in Christ' and 'faith' seems more diffuse, since these terms appear in each of the discourse areas mentioned, consistent with our earlier claim that the criterion of Christian identity is faith in Christ as expressed in love for others. More importantly, discourse about life in the community is the most common topic connected to Christian identity elements in Galatians, and this discourse is saturated with Spirit-talk, revealing Paul's deep concern for Spirit as a mediating agent of religious behavior in the community.

Thus, Paul leans heavily on a Jewish matrix in explicating the role of the Spirit in Christian identity, for he describes it not only as an identity marker, but also in association with behavior. If righteousness according to the law normally attends the mark of circumcision in a Jewish frame of

---

38   Cf. Sanders' discussion of Paul's language on the topic of 'getting in' vs. 'staying in' the Christian community (*Paul, the Law and the Jewish People*, pp. 5–10).

39   Indeed, the language of kinship in Galatians is very rich. Here Paul uses ἀδελφός and πατήρ, terms that are familiar from our study of kinship language in Rom. 2, 4, 9; 1 Cor. 10; and Phlm. 1.16, but now mixed with the images of heir (κληρονόμος: 3.29; 4.1, 7), son (υἱός: 1.16; 2.20; 3.7, 26; 4.4, 6, 7, 22, 30), child (τέκνον: 4.19, 25, 27, 28, 31), and mother (μήτηρ: 4.26; and figuratively in 4.21–5.1). There are also references to labor and delivery metaphors (ὠδίνω: 4.19). In Galatians this mixture also includes more complicated family language, including direct references to adoption (υἱοθεσία: 4.5), inheritance customs (κληρονομέω: 4.30; 5.21; cf. 3.15-17), and the conflict between legitimate and illegitimate offspring (4.29-30).

reference (Phil. 3.6), so too does the Spirit produce its own fruit in terms of behavior (Gal. 5.22-23). Our discussion about the Spirit in Galatians 3–5 depicts the *Spirit* as the analogue of circumcision and not baptism as is sometimes suggested, and is thus the true indicium of membership that points beyond itself to a way of life and an ordered worship of God.[40] Just as circumcision signals physical descent as a means of entrance into the community and as such signifies membership in terms of both kinship and religious behavior, so too the Spirit functions as a means of incorporation (4.29), a premier indicium (3.1-5), and an ordering power of conduct and life.

c. *New Name (Galatians 6.16)*

The conclusion of Galatians also yields information about the group name as an indicium of the new race. In the last chapter, we learned that there is some ambiguity in Paul's thought when it comes to the question of the name of the group we now know as 'Christians'. There we saw that Paul referred to himself and his Jewish-Christian opponents as 'Israelites' but never associated himself with those whom he calls Ἰουδαῖοι. Further, we saw several instances in which Paul refers to Gentile Christians using terminology normally associated with Israelites, calling them seed of Abraham, heirs, descendants of the patriarchs, and so on. But, despite this application of insider Jewish terminology to Gentiles, we could point to one only passage in which Gentile Christians may have been addressed explicitly as Israelites, in the concluding blessing of Galatians, which includes the phrase Ἰσραὴλ τοῦ θεοῦ (Gal. 6.16).

Turning our attention to this verse at the conclusion of Galatians, we can identify three questions that must be answered in order to determine whether Paul's application of the phrase Ἰσραὴλ τοῦ θεοῦ includes the Gentiles in the Christian community. First, given that the exact phrase appears nowhere else in Christian or Jewish literature, does Paul ever implicitly associate the word 'Israel' with Gentile Christians? This last question requires an assessment of 1 Cor. 10.18 and Rom. 11.26, texts that frequently figure in studies of Gal. 6.16. Second, do the contents of the letter provide a clue about the group or groups addressed in this final blessing? Third and most importantly, how should we understand the second καί in the phrase εἰρήνη ἐπ' αὐτοὺς καὶ ἔλεος καὶ ἐπὶ τὸν Ἰσραὴλ τοῦ θεοῦ – as an epexegetical καί or a conjunction?

The view that Gal. 6.16 refers to the church seems to have been

---

40 *Contra* Horn ('Der Verzicht auf die Beschneidung', pp. 486, 504–5) who makes the analogy between baptism and circumcision as initiation rites in Christianity and Judaism respectively. Instead, I would suggest that baptism is best seen as an analogy to birth, paradoxically as the moment of the Christian's identification with the death of Jesus (Merklein, '"Nicht aus Werken des Gesetzes ..."', p. 129).

seriously challenged only in the post-World War II era. While most
scholars still seem to hold that Gal. 6.16 refers to only one group and that
the καί is epexegetical, D. Gottlob Schrenk initiated fresh debate with his
1949 article 'Was bedeutet "Israel Gottes"?' In a much-cited dialogue
between 1949 and 1950, he and Nils Dahl debated whether 'the Israel of
God' referred to the church.[41] Schrenk claims that the phrase refers to
Jewish Christians in Galatia who faithfully follow the canon of Gal. 6.15
that circumcision and uncircumcision are adiaphora in Christ. Dahl, on
the other hand, holds that the Israel of God consists of the church of
believing Jews and believing Gentiles.

In his first article, Schrenk is primarily concerned to dismiss the idea
that Gal. 6.16 can be used to interpret 'Israel' in Romans 9–11. The article
quickly disposes of the possibility that Paul implies or refers to the church
as Israel in Rom. 11.26. Schrenk states that Paul uses Ἰσραὴλ κατὰ σάρκα
in 1 Cor. 10.18 only to communicate that Israel's service to God at the
altar belongs to the past, and he notes that Paul never explicitly uses the
phrase Ἰσραὴλ κατὰ πνεῦμα. Romans 9.4-6, 27-29, and 11.1-8 show that
'Israel' refers to the Jewish people of God. With reference to Rom. 11.26,
which is often mentioned as support for an inclusive interpretation of Gal.
6.16, Schrenk asserts that it is improbable that Paul associates 'Israel' with
non-Christian Jews in 11.25 but includes both Jews and Gentiles in 11.26
without any indication that the definition has changed.[42] On the question
of Gal. 6.16 itself, Schrenk analyzes epexegetical statements elsewhere in
Paul and finds that all of them share a feature that is exactly reversed in
Gal. 6.16: normally, the narrower group appears second and is added to
larger, general group which appears first (see 1 Cor. 3.5; 8.12; 12.27; 14.27;
15.38; 2 Cor. 5.15).[43] Reasoning that Ἰσραὴλ τοῦ θεοῦ cannot refer to

---

41   Schrenk, 'Israel Gottes?'; id., 'Der Segenwunsch nach der Kampfepistel', *Judaica* 6
(1950): 170–90; Nils A. Dahl, 'Der Name Israel: Zur Auslesung von Gal.6,16', *Judaica* 6
(1950): 161–70. For interpretations in line with Schrenk, see Burton, *The Epistle to the
Galatians*, pp. 357–58; Franz Mussner, *Der Galaterbrief* (Freiburg, Basel and Vienna: Herder,
1974), p. 417; Bruce, *Galatians*, p. 275; W.D. Davies, 'Paul and the People of Israel', *NTS*
24.10 [1977]: 4–39). Following Dahl, see Lüdemann (*Paulus und das Judentum*, pp. 27–30);
Sanders, *Paul, the Law and the Jewish People*, pp. 173–76; Betz, *Commentary*, pp. 322–23;
Hays, 'Galatians', 11.346; Longenecker, *Galatians*, pp. 298–99.

42   Schrenk, 'Israel Gottes?' pp. 81–83, 89–90. W.D. Davies adds that if Paul were
speaking of Gentile Christians as the Israel of God in Gal. 6.16, one would expect this idea to
be reiterated in Rom. 11, where Paul explicitly addressed the status of Israel ('Paul and the
People of Israel', pp. 10–11 n. 2). On the other hand, Ulrich Luz points out that Rom. 11 is
not so concerned with the salvation of Jews as with countering Gentile arrogance (*Das
Geschichtsverständnis des Paulus* [München: C. Kaiser, 1968], pp. 292–94), which suggests to
him that it would have been counterproductive to apply the name 'Israel' to Gentile
Christians, since this action might increase their arrogance. In my opinion, both Davies'
argument and this rebuttal are arguments from silence and thus inherently inconclusive.

43   Schrenk, 'Israel Gottes?', pp. 84–86.

non-Christian Jews given the context of Galatians, Schrenk concludes that the only group that fits the context, Paul's previous style, and Paul's broader use of the word 'Israel' is believing Jews who walk according to the rule outlined in 6.15.[44]

For his part, Dahl agrees that 'Israel' does not refer to Jewish and Gentile Christians in Rom. 11.26; rather, Jewish Christians are called 'the remnant' or 'the elect' in Romans 9–11.[45] On the other hand, Dahl asserts that Paul did use language that shows that he transferred the title of Israel to the church: 'children of Abraham', 'the circumcision', 'people of God' (2 Cor. 6.16; Rom. 9.25). Although Schrenk is right that Paul never uses the phrase Ἰσραὴλ κατὰ πνεῦμα in 1 Cor. 10.18; Gal. 4.29 indicates that this terminology was not far from mind.[46] In addition, the Scripture citations in Rom. 4.23-24; 15.4; 1 Cor. 9.10; and 10.11 show that the concept of the 'people of God' had been transferred to the church.[47]

According to Dahl, moreover, it is impossible that 'Israel' refers solely to Christian Jews in Gal. 6.16. Dahl disputes Schrenk's idea that the ἐπὶ ... καὶ ἐπί pattern in 6.16 breaks Paul's habit elsewhere. Instead, Dahl maintains that the pattern is a Hebraism, pointing to Acts 5.11 where the whole is specified last and added to the part, as in Gal. 6.16. More importantly, the whole content of the epistle argues against interpreting the 'Israel of God' as Christian Jews.[48] Galatians 3.7 says that those who believe are sons of Abraham, while Gal. 3.16-27, 29 says that those in Christ are the promised seed of Abraham.[49] Galatians 4.21-31 says that

---

44 Ibid., pp. 84–86.

45 According to Dahl, Rom. 9.6 does not mean that Jews have ceased to be Israel but that there is a 'difference between physical descendants of Israel and bearers of the promise'. Further, Rom. 11.25-31 does not suggest that every individual Israelite will be saved, 'but that Israel as the bearer of the promise cannot simply be identified with Jewish Christians' ('Der Name Israel', p. 162). See also Martyn (*Galatians*, p. 577), who says that Romans 11 reverses Paul's identification of the church as Israel in Gal. 6.16 (p. 577).

46 Dahl, 'Der Name Israel', p. 163.

47 Sanders also contributes to this line of thought, amassing evidence that Paul frequently uses dualistic terminology that associates Christians with 'true Israel': descendant/not descendant of Abraham (Rom. 4, Gal. 3), my people/not my people (Rom. 9.25; cf. Hos. 2.1, 25), the changed ones/the perishing ones (2 Cor. 3.18–4.3; Phil. 3.18-20). In addition, Gal. 3 and Rom. 4 say that believers, not Jews, can claim Abraham's inheritance, a stance that is reiterated in Rom. 9.6, where Paul invokes the principle that 'not all Israel are Israel' and cites Isaac and Jacob as examples (9.7-13). Sanders adds that 'true Israel' is not a third race in Paul's thought (even if it was a third race in terms of a 'social reality'), because all Israel will ultimately be included in 'true Israel' (*Paul, the Law and the Jewish People*, pp. 174–78).

48 See also Harvey, *True Israel*, pp. 225–26. Even though Harvey argues against seeing the 'True Israel' idea in Paul, he concedes that this passage more than any other 'lends itself to this interpretation'. He dismisses the idea to the margins of Paul's thought, however, because of the polemical context in Galatians.

49 Also, see Sanders, *Paul, the Law and the Jewish People*, p. 174 and Lüdemann, *Paulus und das Judentum*, pp. 28–29.

Christians, like Isaac, are children of promise, while Ishmael is a type of
Ἰσραὴλ κατὰ σάρκα. Finally, in Gal. 6.11-18 Paul mounts a final rejection
of the Jewish Christian missionaries and tries to persuade the Galatians to
be loyal to his apostolic instructions (6.12-14, 15, 17). Dahl concludes: 'It
is unthinkable that in 6.16 [Paul] wants to introduce an entirely new
thought and has added a prayer for peace on behalf of Jewish Christians
as a reconciling final word ... It is more probable that in this context Paul
transfers the ... name of Israel to the Christians'.[50]

In disagreement with Dahl, however, Peter Richardson sets out to
demonstrate that Gal. 6.16 defines two groups and has benedictions
corresponding to both groups, which are indicated by the two instances of
ἐπί in the verse.[51] Richardson admits the possibility that an early version
of the Birkat ha-Shalom, the Nineteenth Benediction of the *Shemoneh
Esreh* in the Babylonian Talmud, is a plausible background for Paul's
final blessing in Gal. 6.16, but he notes that there are key differences
between the two blessings.[52] Literally translated, the Talmudic blessing
reads: 'mercy upon us and upon all Israel your people'. Whereas the
Shemoneh Esreh contains two groups, in which a smaller group is
expanded into a larger, in Gal. 6.16 there is one larger group of Christians
who walk according to the rule of 6.15, but this collective contracts into a
smaller group of Jewish Christians (Ἰσραὴλ τοῦ θεοῦ).[53] Richardson
achieves this understanding by repunctuating 6.16 and construing εἰρήνη
ἐπ' αὐτούς with καὶ ὅσοι τῷ κανόνι τούτῳ στοιχήσουσιν and ἔλεος καὶ
ἐπὶ τὸν Ἰσραὴλ τοῦ θεοῦ as a separate unit. He arrives at the following
translation: 'May God give peace to all who will walk according to this
criterion and mercy also to his faithful people Israel.' Agreeing with those
who believe that Paul would never bless his opponents in this way in this
letter, Richardson adds that 'mercy' which connotes 'salvation' in Paul,

50   Dahl, 'Der Name Israel', pp. 167–68. Sanders adds that Gal. 6.16 is part of the letter
summary, so that 6.12-13 recalls 2.14 and 6.14 recalls 2.20. The 'rule' in 6.16 is a summary of
the argument that circumcision is not required in Christ. Those who press for circumcision
are anathema to Paul (1.8-9), and he hardly puts these opponents under the same blessing as
those who say that circumcision does not matter (*Paul, the Law and the Jewish People*, p. 174;
cf. Lüdemann, *Paulus und das Judentum*, pp. 28–29).

51   Richardson, *Israel*, pp. 74–84.

52   The benediction is first attested in the Babylonian Talmud, which is generally dated to
the fifth or sixth century CE. Richardson's idea rests on the hypothesis that early versions of
the material later codified in the Talmud may have been available in Paul's time.

53   Richardson, *Israel*, pp. 76–79. Betz agrees that the *Shemoneh Esreh* is remarkably like
Gal. 6.16 and that Paul is likely dependent on it. However, according to Betz, the 'upon us' in
Shemoneh Esreh is transformed into 'upon them' in Gal. 6.16, and the remaining parts of the
Shemoneh Esreh and Gal. 6.16 are equivalent in that they extend to all members beyond those
in the present location (*Galatians*, p. 322).

'ironically' refers to future believing Jews rather than to Paul's opponents in Galatia.[54]

In terms of the three questions that have driven our inquiry into Gal. 6.16, there is some agreement on two of the issues among those who have participated in the debate. Scholars agree that the contents of the letter make it impossible for Paul to apply the phrase to non-Christian Jews. In addition, there is agreement that outside of Galatians Paul never explicitly applies the term 'Israel' to the church, though there is debate about whether he says something that amounts to the same thing in 1 Cor. 10.1, 18; Gal. 4.21-31; or Rom. 11.26.[55] In my opinion, however, none of the scholars considered here has offered a convincing parallel for the phrase καὶ ἐπὶ τὸν Ἰσραὴλ τοῦ θεοῦ in Gal. 6.16. Some of the parallels that Schrenk offers can barely stand as examples of the epexegetical καί, much less as parallels for Gal. 6.16 (e.g., 1 Cor. 14.27; 2 Cor. 5.15); Dahl's appeal to Acts 5.11 is only marginally better. The closest use of an epexegetical structure is in Rom. 5.14, where the same καὶ ἐπί combination appears: ἐβασίλευσεν ὁ θάνατος ἀπὸ Ἀδὰμ μέχρι Μωϋσέως καὶ ἐπὶ τοὺς μὴ ἁμαρτήσαντας ἐπὶ τῷ ὁμοιώματι τῆς παραβάσεως Ἀδάμ ('Death exercised dominion from Adam to Moses, *even over* those whose sins were not like the transgression of Adam', NRSV; emphasis added). The two clauses joined by this epexegetical καί define a single group that is further defined in the second clause, a relationship that holds as well in Gal. 6.16. This, in combination with observations about the arguments in Galatians and the way that Paul transfers people-of-God language to the church, means that the 'Israel of God' refers to both Jewish and Gentile Christians in 6.16.

In Chapter 2, we found that among the six characteristics in Anthony Smith's framework for the identification of ethnic groups in history, a

---

54 Richardson, *Israel*, p. 82; cf. Betz, *Galatians*, p. 322, who rightly notes that there is no signal in the text to alert the reader to an ironic use of 'mercy'.

55 Ulrich Luz defends the idea that 'all Israel' in Rom. 11.26 refers to Jews and Gentiles (*Das Geschichtsverständnis*, pp. 268–300). I might add that there is some evidence that this reading finds favor with at least two church fathers. Theodoret of Cyrene: 'And all Israel names those who believe, whether from the Jews, quite so, having a native/natural relationship with reference to Israel, or whether from the Gentiles, according to the relationship of faith joined together with it' ('Interpretation of the Letter to the Romans', in J.-P. Migne [ed.], *Patrologia graeca*, vol. 82, col. 180, LLS). See also Augustine of Hippo, who reads Rom. 11.26 in conjunction with 1 Cor. 10.1, 18 and Gal. 6.16 (*Letters* 149, translated by Sister Wilfrid Parsons in R.J. Deferrari [ed.], *Fathers of the Church: A New Translation* [New York: Fathers of the Church, 1953], 20.253; Latin text in J.-P. Migne [ed.], *Patrologia latina*, vol. 33, cols. 637–38). Schrenk makes a good point when he says that it is unlikely that 'Israel' refers to non-Christian Jews in 11.25 but includes Gentile Christians in 11.26. As discussed in Chapter 4, however, the discourse that reaches its conclusion in 11.25-32 began in Rom. 9.1-6, where Paul was willing to shift the meaning of Israel within the space of a few verses (Wright, *The Climax of the Covenant*, pp. 246–51).

collective name focuses group awareness, summarizes the distinctive history of the group, and communicates something about group charac- teristics and achievements. According to Smith, groups that were unnamed in antiquity may have been in the process of ethnic formation. Our own study of Jewish and Greco-Roman identity in antiquity found that a different mix of characteristics was important among different groups; in fact, names were not a significant element of identity in either the Greco-Roman or the Jewish models.[56] Indeed, Paul's ambivalence about naming his new group becomes a nearly perfect illustration of this finding. Not only is there no single name for the new group in his writings, but Paul's language in naming the groups now called 'Jewish' and 'Christian' is messy. In various contexts he qualifies the word 'Israel' so that it applies to almost every one of the groups in his social world: Gal. 6.16 – Israel of God; 1 Cor. 10.18 – Israel according to the flesh; 2 Cor. 3.7, 13 – sons of Israel; Rom. 11.26 – all Israel.[57] As opposed to the relative dearth of names for the new group, there is almost no end to the ways that he describes these groups in other terms (e.g., the circumcision, new creation, those from faith, those from law, saints, the called, etc.).

Thus, it could be that the rarity with which Paul applies the names the 'Israel of God' or the 'Church of God' (1 Cor. 10.32) to the Christian group simply reflects the fact that 'naming' was not an important aspect of group identity for Paul and other ancient Jews. Alternately, it could be that the rarity of naming reflects the fact that the Christian group was early in the process of ethno-racial formation. Anthony Smith's opinion about the importance of group self-naming and debates in New Testament scholarship about the significance of Paul's use of the name 'Israel' may be nothing more than additional evidence of the gap between ancient Jews and modern scholars about what is important in establishing group identity. Nevertheless, there is merit in Smith's observations about how group names function. Notwithstanding the rarity with which Paul explicitly names his group, Gal. 6.16 at least represents a case in which use of the name communicated something important about the origin and destiny of the group. Those who form the Israel of God are the descendants of the patriarchs κατὰ πνεῦμα. They are heirs of the promised blessing to Abraham's seed, a blessing which has been revealed as the Spirit of Christ. They are the sons of God κατὰ πνεῦμα, whose life in the flesh has been transformed in Christ. They are a new creation of God.

---

56 Names were associated with ethnicity in 3% and 1% of the non-Jewish and Jewish identity texts, respectively. The idea of naming was less than 1% in the corresponding models of race.

57 As I pointed out in Chapter 4, however, we should note that he used Ἰουδαῖος in a far more restricted sense.

3. *Intergroup Relationships*

As we have seen, circumcision identifies those who are Jewish and represents Torah in its function of separating Jews from all others. We have also seen that the boundary between Jews and Christians concerns faith in Christ as the central and exclusive criterion of identity, with the Spirit as the premier indicium and ordering power in the new community. Yet the relationship between Jews and Christians in Paul's social matrix is more complicated than that implied by the mere existence of a boundary. Investigation of Gal. 3.10-14 shows that the separation of Jews from Christians is far from simple. As opposed to a Jewish-Christian boundary that mimics the traditional separation of Jews from Gentiles, in Paul's view a unique eschatological interdependence between Jews and Gentile Christians has sprung into existence. We saw in the previous chapter that Paul linked his self-identity to the symbiotic relationship between Jews and Gentiles in the new community (Rom. 11.13-14). In this section, we will find additional support for the idea that the eschatological interrelationship of Jews and Gentile Christians lies at the heart of Paul's self-identity and his gospel.

a. *Galatians 3.10-14; 4.4-6*

Christopher Stanley succinctly describes the apparent contradiction between Paul's assertion in 3.10a that everyone who does works of law is under a curse on the one hand, and on the other hand, the actual content of the Deuteronomy quotation in 3.10b that supports his assertion, namely, that everyone who does *not* do works of law is accursed.[58] The traditional solution to this problem maintains that Paul's unstated premise is that the 'curse of the law' is the impossibility of successfully doing all points of the law. E.P. Sanders, however, maintains that this premise cannot be read into the text at this location and is unsupported elsewhere in Galatians.[59] Sanders suggests that Paul used Deut. 27.26 only because the collocation of the words 'curse' (ἐπικατάρατος) and 'law' (νόμος) in the verse provides an excellent counterpoint to the words 'blessing' and 'faith' in the preceding discussion (Gal. 3.6-9).[60] While I agree that 3.10 does not say that the law brings a

---

58 Both Martyn and Stanley survey the interpretive options in the scholarship for handling this apparent contradiction: Martyn, *Galatians*, pp. 309–11; Christopher Stanley, 'Under a Curse: A Fresh Reading of Galatians 3.10-14', *NTS* 36 (1990): 481–511 (482–86).

59 Sanders, *Paul, the Law and the Jewish People*, pp. 23–24. This traditional view also fails to account for Paul's own testimony about his blamelessness with reference to the law in Phil. 3.6. A good description of the traditional reading is available in Mussner, *Der Galaterbrief*, pp. 223–26; cf. Stanley, 'Under a Curse', p. 482; and especially Bruce, *Galatians*, pp. 158–61.

60 Sanders, *Paul, the Law and the Jewish People*, pp. 23–24.

new section beginning in 3.1-5 must be investigated. The two sections share several common elements, including references to Christ (2.16-17, 19-21; 3.1), crucifixion (συνεσταύρωμαι in 2.19 and ἐσταυρωμένος in 3.1), and flesh (σάρξ in 2.16, 20; 3.3). Even more important, both sections contain the antithesis between works of law and faith, in that in the 11 verses between 2.16 and 3.5 the noun πίστις and the phrase ἐξ ἔργων νόμου each appear five times.

'Works of law' both identify and characterize the Jewish community that worships the God of Abraham. As discussed above, law is the ordering medium through which the community worships God (Deut. 30.9-10; *3 Macc.* 3.3-4; *4 Esd.* 7.89; Josephus, *Ag. Ap.* 2.152-156, 165; Philo, *Abraham* 60–61, 114, *Migration* 130; *Embassy* 210). Because the Jewish legal code addressed the specifics of so many aspects of life, Jewish performance of the law was widely noted in antiquity, and the literature of the day took particular note of Jewish dietary practices and Sabbath observance.[23] Thus, from one perspective, reference to the Jewish law is essentially a reference to Jewish culture. Nonetheless, there is debate about whether the phrase 'works of law' in Galatians is a categorical heading that refers to the law in its totality, or whether in context Paul refers only to a particular subset of laws that function as indicia because of their strong association with Jewish culture. This subset would include laws related to circumcision, and might include commandments about Sabbath observance and dietary practices.[24]

On the one hand, the fact that Paul mentions circumcision 13 times, more often than any other particular 'work of law' in Galatians, favors a narrow construal of the phrase. In addition, he mentions or alludes to the other indicia laws in the epistle (e.g., Sabbath observance at 4.10), and the topics of circumcision and food laws appear in close proximity to the first mention of ἔργα νόμου (2.3-12).[25] On the other hand, Paul also mentions concern for the poor in 2.10 (cf. Deut. 24.19), something mandatory in Jewish law but not normally considered particularly distinctive of Jewish identity. Moreover, reference to the law in its totality is implicit in his mention of 'Judaism' (1.13-14), 'the traditions of my fathers' (1.14), and 'living like a Jew' (2.14). Most of the 32 occurrences of νόμος in Galatians are properly construed as references to the law in its entirety (e.g., 2.19,

---

23 Sabbath: Persius, *Satirae*, 5.176-184: 'When the day of Herod comes round, when the lamps ... spat forth their thick clouds of smoke ... at the sabbath of the circumcised' (Stern, 1.436). See also Plutarch, *De superstitione* 8 (Stern, 1.549) and Seneca, *Epistulae morales* 95.47 (Stern, 1.432). Food: Plutarch, *Quaestiones convivialum libri IX* 4.4.5 (Stern, 1.550–55); Arrian, *Epicteti dissertationes* 1.22.4 (Stern, 1.542).

24 Norman H. Young prefers the former alternative in 'Who's Cursed – and Why? (Galatians 3.10-14)', *JBL* 117.1 (1998): 79–92 (80) along with most other exegetes.

25 The noun and verb for circumcision appear in the following verses in Galatians: 2.3, 7-9, 12; 5.2-3, 6, 11; 6.12-13, 15.

curse because it is impossible to do *all* the law, I do think that Paul's interest in the quotation is concerned with the twice-used 'all' (πᾶς), a term that reappears in a significant context later in Galatians (5.3). Martyn's view is that Paul responds to Deut. 27.26 because the missionaries used this text to try to persuade the Galatians to obey the law.[61] However, whether Paul selected the text himself or whether he counters a text and arguments offered by his opponents, the important point is that we interpret the claims in 3.11-13 against the ideas in 3.10 and not against some inferred premise, as in the traditional reading of this passage.

We can evaluate the phrase 'the curse of the law' by examining Paul's words in introducing the OT citation, since throughout this section the introductory remarks interpret the subsequent citations.[62] Paul preserves the Septuagint's ἐπικατάρατος in 3.10b, but he emends the Septuagint's participle κεκατηραμένος (pf. ptc. from the verb καταράομαι, 'to curse') to ἐπικατάρατος (adj., 'under a curse') in v. 13b. Yet when in 3.10b and 3.13a he uses his own words in the interpretive introduction to the citation in 3.10a, he utilizes the phrase ὑπὸ κατάραν instead of the adjective. The basic force of ὑπο with the accusative ('under the authority of') comports well with Paul's characterization of the law elsewhere (3.23), so that we could paraphrase 3.10 as follows:

> As many as there are whose identity is derived from the works of law[63] are *under the authority* of a curse, because it is written, 'Everyone who does not abide in everything written in the book of the law so as to do it, *has actually incurred a curse.*' (LLS)

This translation presses the difference between being under the *authority* of a curse, that is, being threatened by a curse as a penalty for wrongdoing, and being in the state of actually suffering the *effects* of a curse. In the narrative context of Deuteronomy 27 where the citation originates, the difference between a threatened curse-penalty and the penalty itself is perfectly reasonable, since there the people give their 'Amen' to the idea that curses legitimately fall on those who fail to keep all the laws just recited. In other words, in the story of Deuteronomy, the people do not with their 'Amen' acknowledge receipt of the effects of curse-penalties, but only give their oath to live under the authority that wields these penalties.[64]

---

61 Martyn, *Galatians*, pp. 117–26, 302–306.

62 Sanders, *Paul, the Law and the Jewish People*, p. 22.

63 On the translation of ἐξ ἔργων νόμου in 3.10 as those 'whose identity is derived from the works of the law', see Mussner, *Galaterbrief*, p. 223; Hays, 'Galatians', 11.257.

64 With a similar conclusion, but on different grounds, see Stanley, 'Under a Curse', pp. 500, 509; Norman Bonneau, 'The Logic of Paul's Argument on the Curse of the Law in Galatians 3.10-14', *NovT* 39 (1997): 60–80 (73), N.H. Young, 'Pronomial Shifts in Paul's

The matter of the groups addressed by Paul's first- and second-person pronouns is critical to the interpretation of Gal. 3.13-14. Specifically, 3.10-14 begins Paul's clarification of the way that the Christ event affects the bonds of law and the requirements for obedience to the law in the new creation community. But what group does Paul address in these verses? Does he speak to the entire community marked by the indicium of the Spirit, or do his remarks specifically apply to his Jewish Christian opponents? Is it possible that his remarks concern non-Christian Jews? Answers to these questions have to account for the opening phrase in 3.10 (ὅσοι ... ἐξ ἔργων νόμου εἰσίν) and the first-person plurals in 3.13-14.

In view of Paul's emphatic insistence in 3.1-5 that the Galatian Christians are ἐξ ἀκοῆς πίστεως and *not* ἐξ ἔργων νόμου, the use of the phrase ἐξ ἔργων νόμου in 3.10 would seem to rule out the possibility that the sentences address their situation. Thus, it seems that 3.10-14 discusses the situation of Jews, describing them as being subject to the curses of Deuteronomy in the event that they do not do 'all the things written in the book of the law', a view reinforced by the original context of the quotation from Deuteronomy. There is more debate, however, about the composition of the persons or groups addressed in the first-person plurals in 3.13-14 ('Christ redeemed us from the curse of the law ... so that we might receive the promise of the Spirit.') For example, Bonneau and Donaldson interpret the 'we' as inclusive of the whole community, while Wright thinks that the pronouns refer to Jewish Christians.[65] Before 3.13-14, the previous use of the first-person plural is in 2.15 ('We are Jews by birth'), where there is no ambiguity about the reference, and it applies to Paul and other native Jews like Peter and Barnabas. Because the key phrase ἐξ ἔργων νόμου appears for the first time in Galatians in 2.16 and makes a final appearance in 3.10, it is even more likely that the first-person plurals address the same groups.

Martyn suggests that the epistolary audience for this first-person reference in 2.15 includes Paul's Jewish-Christian opponents in Galatia as well.[66] Where most interpreters content themselves with describing the

---

Argument to the Galatians', in T.W. Hillard, R.A. Kearsley, C.E.V. Nixon, and A.M. Nobbs (eds), *Ancient History in a Modern University*, vol. 2: *Early Christianity, Late Antiquity and Beyond* (Grand Rapids: Eerdmans, 1998), pp. 81–88.

65 Bonneau, 'The Logic of Paul's Argument', p. 79; T.L. Donaldson, 'The "Curse of the Law" and the Inclusion of the Gentiles: Galatians 3.13-14', *NTS* 32 (1986): 94–112 (95–99); Wright, *The Climax of the Covenant*, pp. 143, 154. See especially the summary on this topic in Stanley, 'Under a Curse', p. 506 n. 68. In light of the discussion below, we should note especially Longenecker's comment that Paul signals his identification with his Gentile converts in Galatia not via first-person pronouns, but by addressing them as ἀδελφοί (Longenecker, *Galatians*, p. 229; see Gal. 1.11 and 4.31).

66 Martyn, *Galatians*, p. 248. Charles B. Cousar admits the possibility adopted here that the plural refers to Jews in 3.13-14 as in 2.15, but he finally decides against it on the grounds

Galatian congregation as all Gentile,[67] Martyn notices many details in the text of Galatians that suggests that Paul addresses his Torah-observant Jewish Christian missionary opponents as if they are still among the Galatians (1.6-9; 3.1-2, 5; 4.17; 5.10-12; 6.12-14).[68] Thus, when we read 3.13 as referring to Jews only, we understand that the verse states that Christ's substitutionary death frees Paul, Torah-observant Jewish Christian missionaries, and all such 'Jews by birth' from the obligation to observe all the details of the law. Paul uses the first-person plural to acknowledge that both he and his opponents are among those now freed from the obligation of full observance, acknowledging that such Jewish Christians formerly lived under the authority of the law and were subject to its penalty of excommunication.

The idea of release from a previous governing authority lies behind the choice of the word ἐξαγοράζω ('set free') in 3.13. The redemption wrought by Christ is not a wholesale freedom from any rule of law (cf. 1 Cor. 9.21), but rather is a deliverance that frees those under the authority of the law from the need to do *everything* in the law, a conclusion that follows directly from the way in which the curse is described in 3.10b.[69] This fact is often ignored, largely because interpreters broaden the scope of 3.10-14, approaching the text as if the paragraph presented a summary of the entire role of the law with respect to the new community founded by Christ. Instead, we shall see that in the context of 2.16–3.14, 3.10-14 is a discourse about how Christ's death liberates Jews from the obligation to

---

that unlike Romans 'Galatians offers little or no concern for the salvation of the Jews qua Jews' (*A Theology of the Cross* [Minneapolis: Fortress, 1990], pp. 115–16). However, Cousar's solution fails to deal adequately with the problem of how Gentiles can be said to be under the curse of the law. Cousar's suggestion that the law is a curse to Gentiles because it excludes them does not seem consistent with 3.10, where Paul associates the curse with those who are already ἐξ ἔργων νόμου.

67   E.g., Mussner, *Galaterbrief*, p. 8.

68   Martyn, *Galatians*, p. 118; see also pp. 28, 117–18, and the notes in the commentary on the verses listed above. Martyn argues that the audience of 2.15-21 includes the Jewish-Christian missionaries even as it also describes Paul's thoughts about the incident at Antioch. Martyn notes (1) that Paul changes from a direct reference to Peter in 2.14 to the first-person plural in 2.15 in a way that deliberately broadens the reference, and (2) that Paul's shift to the first-person singular in 2.20 within this same paragraph signals that he is directly refuting his opponents' arguments. Martyn also makes a case for direct reference to the missionaries in 1.6-9. Here he notes that the present tense of εἰμί in 1.7 indicates that the missionaries are, to Paul's mind, still present (see also Mussner, *Galaterbrief*, p. 57; cf. 5.10-12); we should also take note of ἄρτι as a deictic indicator for this section in 1.9. In 5.10, Martyn sees a reference to the leader of the group of missionaries, whom Paul avoids naming as an indication of disdain (p. 425).

69   Alternately, Jan Lambrecht understands the curse as the curse of sin in 'Abraham and His Offspring: A Comparison of Galatians 5,1 with 3,13', *Biblica* 80.4 (1999): 525–36 (527), and similarly Bonneau, 'The Curse of the Law', p. 69. Both readings seem to be unduly influenced by Paul's discussion of the law in Romans.

observe Torah in every detail.[70] Galatians 3.13 maintains that Deut. 21.23 pronounces a curse on Jesus, but given the distinction discussed above between ἐπικατάρατος and ὑπὸ κατάραν in 3.10, we would say that Jesus became a curse in the sense of being a *recipient* of the curse. In other words, the law testifies that the manner of Jesus' death is a fitting application of the penalty of excommunication that falls upon those who are not steadfast in performing all the works of the law. Thus Jesus received the penalty of excommunication on behalf of all those Jews who are ἐξ ἔργων νόμου and who fail to comply with all of the details of the law. Therefore the realm of life of participation in the law (ἐν νόμῳ) is bounded by an oath of full observance and is opposed to the realm of life based on the faith of Christ (ἐκ πίστεως); it is exchanged for participation in the life of Christ (ἐν Χριστῷ Ἰησοῦ; 3.11-14). Redemption from the curse results in the freedom to live under a new authority, under the ordering of the Spirit, the law of Christ, and the rule of new creation ethics (5.25; 6.2, 15-16).

The double ἵνα clauses in 3.14 are theologically dense and laden with possibilities that interpreters debate in the literature on Galatians. Figure 5.2 is a diagram from R.B. Hays's *The Faith of Jesus Christ* that depicts the actors in the implied narrative in 3.13-14 and in 4.3-6. It is not necessary to review the conventions and narrative theory associated with these diagrams since we can simplify them as follows:[71] each diagram shows God as an agent who sends three gifts to three recipients by means of Christ. Thus, in 3.13-14 the implied narrative in the text shows God sending (1) freedom to 'us', (2) the blessing of Abraham to Gentiles, and (3) the Spirit to 'us'. Although scholars debate the identity of the groups corresponding to the pronouns in the text, the diagram shows a common set of assignments in parentheses.[72] While many interpreters make assignments that are similar in most details to the ones shown in Figure

---

70 Many interpreters see Paul's comments in 3.13 as applying specifically to Jews: Burton, *The Epistle to the Galatians*, p. 169; Nils A. Dahl, *Studies in Paul: Theology for Early Christian Mission* (Minneapolis: Augsburg, 1977), p. 132; Gaston, 'Israel's Enemies', pp. 405–7; against Martyn, *Galatians*, p. 335, who thinks that the various schemes of assigning ethnic groups based on Paul's use of pronouns largely rests on detecting highly speculative pre-Pauline traditions in 3.13-14 and 4.4-6. Martyn's exegesis, which treats both first- and second-person pronouns as if they were all first person, is especially unsatisfying with respect to 4.6. As shall become evident, my own exegesis uses Paul's pronouns to identify different groups, but it depends only on Paul's similar use of language in other epistles, without any recourse to pre-Pauline traditions.

71 In *The Faith of Jesus Christ*, Hays uses these structures to identify the 'actants' (agents and objects) and common narrative sequences in these verses (*Faith of Jesus Christ*, pp. 84–106). I use the diagrams here simply for the clarity they provide in showing a mapping of pronouns to groups of Jews and/or Gentiles.

72 E.g., Lightfoot, *Notes on the Epistles of St. Paul*, pp. 138–39, Burton, *The Epistle to the Galatians*, pp. 169, 176; possibly Longenecker, *Galatians*, pp. 121–24. Betz (*Galatians*,

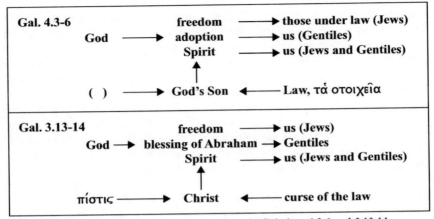

Figure 5.2 Actors, Agents, and Recipients in Galatians 4.3-6 and 3.13-14
Source: R.B. Hays, *The Faith of Jesus Christ*, Fig. 18: Topical sequence octantial structures in
Gal. 4.3-6 and 3.13-14 (p. 107)

5.2, most of them suffer from the same liability. In one point or another, these schemes normally involve different referents for the same pronoun within the space of a sentence or two. For example, the first-person plural 'us/we' refers to 'Jews' in 3.13 but 'Jews and Gentiles' in 3.14; it refers to 'Gentiles' in 4.3 but 'Jews and Gentiles' in 4.5-6. What would normally strain credulity is accepted in the case of these passages and excused as Paul's awkward incorporation of pre-Pauline traditions. Yet we will find that a consistent mapping of the pronouns in these difficult passages is possible if we first examine similar ἵνα constructions in Paul.

For the purposes of this discussion, we will examine two other passages in which consecutive ἵνα clauses appear – one in 2 Cor. 9.3 and the other in 2 Cor. 12.7:

> But I am sending the brothers in order that (ἵνα) our boasting about you may not prove to have been empty in this case, so that (ἵνα) you may be ready, as I said you would be. (2 Cor. 9.3)

> Therefore, to keep me from being too elated, a thorn was given me in the flesh, a messenger of Satan to (ἵνα) torment me, to (ἵνα) keep me from being too elated. (2 Cor. 12.7)

Along with Gal. 3.14, these two verses reveal a pattern that holds in six of the seven other occurrences of consecutive ἵνα clauses in Paul, in that the

---

pp. 148, 153) agrees that Paul speaks of Jews in 3.13, but only Gentile Christians in 3.14 (λάβωμεν), while Gaston thinks Gentile Christians are in view in both 3.13 (despite the reference to 'us') and 3.14 (*Paul and the Torah*, p. 74).

two clauses represent a short-range purpose and a longer-range result with respect to the action described in the preceding main clause.[73] Both 2 Cor. 9.3 and 12.7 demonstrate the basic pattern of the action-purpose-result relationship: the first ἵνα clause identifies the immediate short-range purpose of the action specified in the preceding main clause, while the second ἵνα clause identifies the long-range result of that action. In the case of 2 Cor. 9.3, the main action is Paul's commissioning of the brothers, which Paul intends for the benefit of two parties (see 2 Cor. 9.4). He sends these brothers first with a view to ensuring that his own prior boast about the Corinthians remains credible, and so that the brothers can ensure that Corinthians will be ready when Paul later comes to call upon them to make a donation. Grammatically, the two clauses are not related to each other; both are dependent on the action in the main clause. Practically, however, the second ἵνα clause describes the result of the action–purpose pair defined by the main clause and the first ἵνα clause. Second Corinthians 12.7 also exhibits the double ἵνα pattern, but while Paul has intentions for two different parties in 2 Cor. 9.3, the purpose and result clauses affect the same party in 2 Cor. 12.7, in this case Paul himself. The fact that the final ἵνα clause specifies the ultimate result is even clearer in 2 Cor. 12.7, where the result is stated at both the start and the end of the verse for emphasis.

We find a similar situation in Gal. 3.13-14, and we note that these verses also describe an action that appears to have different groups in view with respect to the short-range purpose and ultimate result specified in double ἵνα clauses:

> Christ redeemed us from the curse of the law by becoming a curse for us – for it is written, 'Cursed is everyone who hangs on a tree' – in order that (ἵνα) in Christ Jesus the blessing of Abraham might come to the Gentiles, so that (ἵνα) we might receive the promise of the Spirit through faith. (Gal. 3.13-14)

We have already determined that the first-person plural pronoun in 3.13 refers to Jews, so that 3.13 describes the particular benefits of redemption for Jews as it frees them from the obligation of full Torah obedience.[74]

---

73   This kind of consecutive ἵνα construction occurs in Rom. 7.13; 1 Cor. 4.6; 2 Cor. 9.3; 11.12; 12.7; and Gal. 3.14 and 4.5. Second Corinthians 11.12 represents the exception to the pattern described herein, since in that verse the second ἵνα clause is dependent on the first ἵνα clause instead of both being dependent on the main verb.

74   Burton agrees that Jews are in view in the first-person pronoun in 3.13, but disagrees that the first-person plural in 3.14 applies only to Jews, maintaining that we should expect an explicit ἡμεῖς in the second ἵνα clause if that were the case. Granted, an explicit ἡμεῖς would add emphasis to the structure, but it is not required grammatically. Perhaps Burton's real objection emerges later when he goes on to state that 'it is difficult to see how the reception of the Spirit by the Jews could be conditioned upon the Gentiles obtaining the blessing of

Contrary to Hays and others, however, there is no textual signal that hints at a change in referent for the plural pronoun one verse later, in 3.14. This preference is especially attractive given our interpretive strategy of reading 3.10-14 in light of 2.15 where Paul uses the first-person plural for the first time in the letter and thus, as it were, defines the 'we' in these chapters in Galatians: ἡμεῖς φύσει Ἰουδαῖοι καὶ οὐκ ἐξ ἐθνῶν ἁμαρτωλοί. If we have decoded these pronouns correctly, and if 3.13-14 is then considered against the pattern of the double ἵνα construction discussed above, we see that Paul articulates a critical precondition in the plan to redeem 'all flesh' that was first outlined in 2.16. The purpose of Christ's death is to enable the Gentiles to participate in Abraham's blessing (3.14a), but the mechanism of that participation is Christ's work in freeing Jews from the obligation to observe all parts of the law (3.13a).[75]

Given that 3.13-14 are in asyndeton with respect to the previous statements in this passage, there is no explicit identification of the way that Jewish redemption from the curse relates to Gentile inclusion; interpreters must try to infer the connection from information gleaned elsewhere in Paul. Betz connects freedom from the 'curse of the law' with freedom from slavery to the 'elements of the cosmos' described later in Galatians (4.3, ὑπὸ τὰ στοιχεῖα τοῦ κόσμου ἤμεθα δεδουλωμένοι), an association that is helpful but not illuminating.[76] Hays, on the other hand, thinks that allusions to Isaiah's description of Israel's restoration from exile in Romans (e.g., Isa. 2.2-4; 60.1-22) have shaped Paul's understanding of the eschatological inclusion of Gentiles. In this scenario, Christ's death frees Israel from exile and allows the ingathering of the Gentiles to take place.[77] Nevertheless, the asyndeton that obscures the logical relationship between 3.10-12 and 3.13-14 also suggests that we may infer the connection from the immediate context.

The relationship between Jewish redemption from the curse-penalty of excommunication and Gentile inclusion probably lies within the context of Paul's discussion of 'works of the law', a phrase that was first

---

Abraham'. To borrow from text-critical methods, however, we should prefer the more difficult reading especially when it conforms with the author's literary style rather than adopting a solution that requires an appeal to hypothetical sources (i.e., pre-Pauline baptismal traditions).

75 Hays, *Faith of Jesus Christ*, p. 79 ('widespread agreement'); Betz, *Galatians*, p. 151; Dahl, *Studies in Paul*, p. 171.

76 Betz, *Galatians*, pp. 148–49.

77 Hays, 'Galatians', 11.261. Hays does not give details about Paul's use of Isaianic texts but cites Ross Wagner's development of this idea in *Heralds of the Good News: Paul and Isaiah 'In Concert' in the Letter to the Romans* (NovTSup; Leiden: Brill, 2001). According to Wagner, Paul uses Isaianic texts that herald the inclusion of Gentiles in Israel's restoration as prophecies with respect to his own gospel and mission to Gentiles. Wagner highlights Paul's references to Isa. 28.16 (Rom. 9.33; 10.11); 52.7 (Rom. 10.15); and 65.1-2 (Rom. 10.20) as particularly important in developing this theme (Wagner, *Heralds*, p. 353).

introduced in 2.16 and last mentioned in 3.10. First, we should note that 3.11-12 revisits the subject of 'status' vis-à-vis the law (i.e., 'the one who is righteous'), an issue that first appeared in 2.15-18 where Paul spoke of statuses: 'Jews by birth', 'Gentile sinners', and 'transgressors'. In addition, 2.15-21 is a commentary on the incident at Antioch where Peter and others were forcing 'Gentiles to live like Jews' (2.14). Indeed, the Jewish obligation to obey everything in the law is what helped produce the fracture in the community at Antioch initially. Thus, reading 3.13-14 in view of the issue of status vis-à-vis the law and the Antioch narrative, we could infer that Christ's redemption of Jews from the curse-penalty of excommunication prevents them from being 'found sinners' (cf. 2.17) for any infraction of law, and thus eliminates pressure on them to 'force the Gentiles to live like Jews' (cf. 2.14). Christ's work tears down the barriers between 'Jews by birth' and 'Gentile sinners', freeing Jews from having to force Gentiles to adopt the law, and providing a way for both to participate in life in Christ (2.18-21; 3.28-29). Thus, we could paraphrase 3.10-14a as follows:

> [10]All who receive their identity from the works of law are threatened by a curse, because it is written, 'Everyone who does not abide in everything written in the book of the law in order to do it, will be cursed by excommunication' [Deut. 27.26; 29.18-20, 26]. [11]Yet no one receives the status of 'righteous' by observing the law because [Hab. 2.4 says] 'those who are righteous will live by faith' [cf. Gal. 2.16]. [12]In addition, we know that the righteous person does not achieve that status by law observance, because the law is not about faith but about doing. Indeed, it [Lev. 18.5] says, 'the one doing the law lives by the law'. [13]Christ has redeemed us Jews from the penalty of excommunication, tearing down its ability to find us to be 'sinners' and 'transgressors' [2.17-18]. [14]This redemption happens so that in Christ Jesus the blessing of Abraham might come to the Gentiles in a way that does not hinder our life together in Christ [cf. 2.15-21]. (LLS)

However, there is *interdependence* that emerges from the last part of the double ἵνα in 3.14b that was omitted above: '. . . so that (ἵνα) we [Jews] might receive the promise of the Spirit through faith'. In this last ἵνα clause, the reception of the Spirit among Jews appears to be dependent on the participation of the Gentiles in the new community (3.14a), and represents the ultimate goal of Christ's redeeming action among the Jews in 3.13. While this dependence between Gentile inclusion and the coming of the Spirit to Jews is surprising, the double ἵνα in 4.4-5 expresses a similar sentiment. As with the ἵνα clauses in 2 Cor. 12.7, however, there is only one group that is the beneficiary of the action in the double ἵνα clause in 4.4-5. 'Those under law' in 4.5a are Jews, and are the same group as the 'we' who receive adoption in the second ἵνα clause in 4.5b:[78]

> [4]But when the fullness of time had come, God sent his son, born from a woman, born under the law, [5]to (ἵνα) redeem those who were also under the law, that is to redeem us Jews, so that (ἵνα) we might finally receive the adoption as heirs. [6]Indeed, we Jews have received the spirit in our hearts and have cried out 'Abba, Father', because you Gentiles have also become children. (Gal. 4.4-6, LLS)

Read this way, 4.4-5 expresses the same sentiment as that expressed in 3.13, 14b, that is, Christ's death redeems Jews from the penalties of the law, and 4.6 describes the same dependency as that described in 3.14, that is, Jews receive the Spirit because Gentiles have become sons of Abraham.[79] In effect, Paul states that the curse of the law that mandates full observance of Torah cannot rule over the new community in Christ because this obligation separates Jews and Gentiles in Christ, a separation that in turn impedes symbiotic interdependence in the gospel. Full observance of the law prevents Gentile inclusion in the community, and, given the logic of 3.13-14 and 4.4-6, it therefore impedes the ultimate manifestation of God's eschatological victory – that is, the Spirit among the Jews.[80]

b. *Galatians 3.22-29*

Paul's use of the first-person pronouns to refer to the situation of Jews continues in 3.22-25, but it breaks off abruptly in 3.26-29, where he again

---

78   Hays interprets τοὺς ὑπὸ νόμον in 4.5a and the 'we' in 4.5b as belonging to different groups (Hays, *Faith of Jesus Christ*, p. 78). However, given that first-person references bracket 4.5a, appearing three times in 4.3 and again in 4.5b, it is better to see Paul as using the third-person phrase τοὺς ὑπὸ νόμον to emphasize the correspondence between Jesus' birth under the law and the state of those who are redeemed from the law. This repetition of ὑπὸ νόμον also reinforces the characterization from 4.2-3 of the law as an 'elementary spirit' (ὑπὸ τὰ στοιχεῖα), guardian, and steward (ὑπὸ ἐπιτρόπους ... οἰκονόμους).

79   The textual tradition that substitutes 'your' (ὑμῶν) for the much better attested 'our' (ἡμῶν) in 4.6 when speaking of those hearts that received the spirit as a result of Gentile sonship shows that ancient interpreters objected to Paul's meaning in the same way that modern interpreters continue to balk at these pronouns. For example, see Hodge, who inserts the easier reading ὑμῶν without justification, presumably because it suits her interpretation that Paul speaks only to Gentiles in this passage. Her insistence that 'those under law' in 4.5 refers to Gentiles is similarly asserted without warrant (*If Sons then Heirs*, pp. 68–71).

80   In Rom. 11.12, 15 and 15.8-9 this same sort of theological interdependence appears to be at work in Paul's thought. Donaldson's analysis ('The "Curse of the Law"', p. 98) has many similarities with that offered here but fails to notice the prevailing pattern in the double ἵνα construction in Paul. He therefore reaches a conclusion opposite to ours, namely, that the Jews have been redeemed for the ultimate benefit of Gentiles.

uses the second-person pronouns to address the situation of Gentiles.[81] At first glance, this switch from the first-person plural to the second-person plural in 3.26 would seem to argue against our hypothesis that different groups are addressed via first- and second-person pronouns, for many would argue that Gal. 3.26-29 addresses the whole community of Jews and Gentiles in Christ. It is true that the sentiments in 3.26-29 apply to Jewish Christians as well as to Gentile Christians, but this emerges from Paul's first-person paradigmatic speech in Gal. 2.19-21 and not from Gal. 3.26-29:

1　Paul's co-crucifixion with Christ (2.19c) anticipates the imagery of Gentile baptism into Christ (3.27a).

2　The cryptic statement 'It is no longer I who live, but it is Christ who lives in me' (2.20a) anticipates the idea that Gentiles have been 'clothed with Christ' (3.27b).

3　Tellingly, 2.20b ('the life I now live in the flesh') parallels Gal. 3.28 and indicates that when Paul tells Gentiles that in Christ they are 'no longer Jew or Greek' and so on, he is chiefly making a claim about the quality of 'life in the flesh' in Christ, regardless of whether one was originally born Jewish or Gentile.

Returning to Galatians 3.22-29 then, we see that Paul uses much the same logic as that which we saw earlier in 3.10-14, beginning by addressing the situation of Jews in 3.22-25 and Gentiles in 3.26-29. In 3.22-24, Paul describes the Jewish situation under the law prior to the coming of Christ, but here he uses the image of the pedagogue as disciplinarian instead of the motif of the threatened curse from Deuteronomy 27. In this new context, 3.25, with its explicit statement that the law ceased to function as a pedagogue for the Jews after the coming of Christ, is analogous to the way that 3.13, with its statement that Christ's death frees the Jews from the penalties of noncompliance with the law, functions in its paragraph.

More importantly, 3.25 has a relationship to 3.26 that is analogous to the relationship of 3.13 to 3.14. The inferential γάρ at the beginning of 3.26 indicates that what follows specifies the ground or basis for the preceding verse. With an eye on this inferential particle, we are able to discern the reason for the otherwise puzzling shift from the use of first-person to second-person pronouns:[82] The basis upon which Jews are

---

81　Longenecker (*Galatians*, p. 149) agrees that Jews are addressed in 3.23, but he thinks that all Christians addressed are addressed in 3.26-29 because Paul is quoting an early tradition.

82　Most scholars assign the shift in pronouns to the fact that Paul appeals to a traditional baptism formula in 3.26-29 (e.g., Longenecker, *Galatians*, p. 152). This is similar to the hypothesis that pre-Pauline traditions in 3.13-14 and 4.4-6 explain the grammatical awkwardness in those passages. While I do not in principle oppose the idea that Paul incorporates early Christian hymns or other set pieces into his epistles (e.g., Phil. 2.6-11), I

released from the custody of a pedagogue after the coming of Christ is the fact that the Gentiles have become 'sons of God' and have 'put on' Christ in baptism in a way that eclipses any prior ethno-racial, gender, or social status differences (3.26; cf. 4.5-6).[83] In light of our earlier consideration of 3.10-14 and 4.4-6, we can now see that, with 3.22-29, all three passages describe interdependence between Gentiles and Jews, each passage focusing on a different aspect of the dialectic. Galatians 3.10-14 concentrates on Jews and the way that law observance is an obstacle to Gentile inclusion and receipt of the Spirit. Galatians 3.22-29 adds that in Christ the power of sin is broken for both Jews and Gentiles; as Gentiles are adopted and transformed in Christ, Jews no longer need the protection and guardianship of the law. Finally, Gal. 4.4-6 reflects on the way that the Spirit marks a coming-of-age for Jews who are adopted into the lineage of Christ. This last passage occurs in a context that implicitly exhorts Gentiles to appropriate the same imagery as they think about their own release from prior governing στοιχεῖα (cf. 4.1-5, 7-11).[84]

Paul, then, consistently speaks in these three passages of the mutual dependence between Gentiles and Jews by alternating his use of first- and second-person pronouns. It is true, however, that Paul has not given us explicit information about the reasons for this dialectic. Earlier, we discussed the fact that interpreters are forced to speculate about the more generally accepted idea that Gentile inclusion is dependent on Jewish freedom from the 'curse' of the law. The interpretation offered here suggests that Jewish freedom from the law smoothes the way for the incorporation of Gentiles into the Christian community, avoiding conflicts like the one in Antioch. More difficult is the other side of the interdependence, in that Paul does not tell us *why* Jewish receipt of the Spirit is dependent on Gentile inclusion in the community. Yet by

---

think that the logical similarities between 3.10-14; 3.22-29; and 4.4-6 suggest that what is normally thought to be part of non-Pauline traditional material was actually composed by Paul himself. See, for example, Longenecker, who while finally coming down in favor of a 'traditional saying', admits that the language in these verses is very like Paul's own (*Galatians*, p. 152).

83   Many interpretations of Gal. 3.28 rely on the idea of a pre-Pauline baptismal formula because of the sudden intrusion of gender and social status into a discussion of ethnic or religious descriptions. Note, however, that the three pairs in Gal. 3.28 are three ways of reckoning status, and thus represent a fitting conclusion to the discussion of status vis-à-vis righteousness and sin that was begun in 2.15-18; also see Brigitte Kahl's study of the gender language in Galatians in 'No Longer Male: Masculinity Struggles Behind Galatians 3.28?', *JSNT* 79 (2000): 37–49.

84   Paul uses στοιχεῖα as an umbrella term for governing authorities. For Jews, the law is the στοιχεῖα or elemental principles under which they have been ordered as if they were no better than slaves (4.1, 3-4), while the 'not-gods' worshipped by Gentiles are the principles to which they had been enslaved prior to their baptism (4.8-9). Neither Jews nor Gentiles in Christ need to submit to ruling principles after attaining their majority as heirs.

reintroducing the issue of sin from 2.17-18, the first verse in Gal. 3.22-29 suggests that sin forges the connection between the elimination of the law as the pedagogue for Jews and Gentile transformation in Christ. Prior to Gentile inclusion, Scripture imprisons everything under sin to await the coming of faith (3.22), but Jews are released from the guardianship of Torah only after Gentiles become clothed in Christ (3.25-26). Though we can only guess in the absence of an unequivocal statement, the relationship of Jewish freedom from the law and Gentile adoption as children here could be predicated on the idea that Jews no longer require the protection of the law (ἐφρουρούμεθα; 3.23) after Gentiles are transformed from sinners to sons (3.27-29). Once Gentile outsiders become insiders and all of the heirs walk in step with the Spirit, the law no longer needs to operate in its function of identifying and separating (συγκλειόμενοι; 3.23) transgressors from the people of God (cf. 2.17-18; 5.18).

Still, this conjecture says nothing about the mechanics of the interdependence between these events. Thus, while these passages in Galatians 3–4 describe the *existence* of the interdependence between Jews and Gentiles in Christ, we learn little about the *nature* of this dialectic until Rom. 11.11-32. There we see that it is temporally quantitative, in that Jewish salvation is dependent on the attainment of the 'fullness' of Gentile inclusion (Rom. 11.25), and that it operates via jealousy (11.11, 13-14). On the other hand, Galatians does give additional information about the Gentile dependence on Jews. While Romans suggests that the *offer* of salvation to Gentiles depends on Jewish rejection of the gospel (11.11), in Galatians we learn that Gentile *acceptance* of the gospel is dependent on Jewish redemption from the curse-penalty of the law that requires the observance of Torah. In addition, the treatment of Gal. 1.15-24 in Chapter 4 suggested that the symbiotic redemption of Jews and Gentiles in Christ in Galatians 3–4 is also commensurate with Paul's self-identity as the light to the nations and the gatherer of Israel. In other words, Galatians 3–4 is a less mature exposition of the symbiotic relationship between Jewish and Gentile salvation that becomes explicit in Romans 11.

Thus, even though I have introduced different readings of 3.13-14; 3.22-29; and 4.4-6, I have not offered ideas that are alien to Paul's thought, since the themes in these passages also appear in Gal. 1.15-24; Rom. 11.13-14; and 11.25-32. I imagine, however, that this comparison will prove to be both an asset and a liability, since the principal objection to this interpretation will likely be its similarity to a motif that is at home in Romans 9–11 but 'alien' to Galatians 3–4. That is to say, why would Paul include information about interdependence in the redemption of Jews and Gentiles in Christ in Galatians, an epistle to a Gentile-Christian community? It seems to me that an answer to that question could proceed in one of several different directions. I list three possibilities below, described in increasing order of likelihood:

1   Paul unintentionally includes a description about his understanding of the interdependence between Jewish and Gentile salvation in Christ; the information simply 'leaks out'. Paul explicitly teaches about the dependence between Gentile inclusion in the community and Jewish freedom from the law because he does not want the Galatians to abandon God in a reckless adoption of law that nullifies the grace of God in Christ (1.6-9; 2.21). Teaching about the dependence between Gentile inclusion and the coming of the Spirit among the Jews, however, is not deliberate but trickles out because both sides of the dialectic form an organic unity in his mind – he cannot describe the aspect pertinent to Gentiles without inadvertently revealing aspects that are more relevant to Jews. This dynamic may be analogous to the mechanism by which we learn about Paul's self-understanding as a gatherer of Israel and light to the Gentiles through intertextual echoes of Isaiah 49, when he describes his call as an apostle to Gentiles in Gal. 1.15-24.

2   Paul discusses both the Jewish and the Gentile sides of the interdependence because he writes with two audiences in mind. Although the Galatian churches were all-Gentile congregations, Paul tells the Galatians that the coming of the Spirit to the Jews is dependent on Gentile inclusion because he does not know how far some of the members may have gone in adopting the mindset of the Jewish-Christian missionaries. In other words, Paul does not directly address the Jewish-Christian missionaries when he reveals this information, but he does address the arguments raised by these Jewish-Christians.[85]

3   Most likely of all, Paul gives information about factors operating on both Jews and Gentiles because he was addressing the Galatians *and the Jewish-Christian missionaries who were still with them*. Paul's Jewish-Christian opponents were persuading the Galatians to receive circumcision and become law-observant Jews, and they were themselves in danger of being cut off from Christ. Further, if the missionaries persuade Gentiles to abandon the gospel, these Gentiles cannot become 'sons of God' and thereby hasten the coming of the Spirit to the Jewish people as a whole. The discussion in Galatians about the dialectic of interdependence is not prompted by contemplation of God's faithfulness to Israel, as in Romans. Rather, Paul has internalized the idea of God's faithfulness to Israel in his self-identity as a gatherer of Israel as well as a light to the nations (Gal. 1.15-24). It takes nothing more than the possibility that Gentile Christians would abandon God's gospel and thus

---

85   Betz, *Galatians*, p. 4; Longenecker, *Galatians*, p. lxxxix.

interrupt the operation of the symbiotic dialectic to stimulate his discussion about Jewish and Gentile interdependence in the gospel.

Taking this third possibility as our position, we see that Paul wanted the Galatians and the Jewish-Christian missionaries to know that Gentile adoption of the law would be no service to the Jewish community. A true concern for the Jewish community would recognize that barriers to Gentile inclusion would result in barriers to Jewish salvation. Persons who promote the re-erection of Torah are, therefore, anathema, cut-off, and separated from the mercy of God because they thereby endanger Jewish salvation (1.8-9; 2.18; 4.30; 5.4; 6.16). Jewish freedom from the law is like the freedom of attaining one's majority after being little better than a slave as a minor, and should serve as a model for Gentiles who have been released from slavery to not-gods and adopted into the family of faith. On the other hand, Paul exhorts everyone in Christ to live in freedom under the ordering power of the Spirit as a means of dealing with sin (4.31–5.1; 5.13, 16, 18).

The lack of Jewish Christians in the Galatian churches will not stand in tension with my reading if we recognize that the ethno-racial makeup of the Galatian congregations is separate from the question of whether there were Jewish Christians in the audience of the letter.[86] Ideas about the ethnic composition of these churches, and the associated assumption about the absence of Jewish Christians in the audience of the letter, may be bound up with interpretive choices about the location of the Galatian churches. The South Galatia theory, which locates these churches near the Mediterranean in the Roman province of Galatia, may more easily account for the presence of Jews or Jewish Christians in the congregations proper.[87] The now favored North Galatia theory, however, which places these churches among the historic Celts in Ankyra and Pessinus closer to the Black Sea, seems inconsistent with a Jewish presence in Galatia, and proponents reject the idea of Jewish Christians in these congregations. Nevertheless, Martyn, who favors the North Galatian theory and the Celtic origins of the Gentile Christians there, also maintains, as mentioned earlier, that Paul assumed that the Jewish-Christian missionaries were still present in Galatia as he wrote his epistle. The fact that Martyn's arguments for the presence of the missionaries focus on exegetical details

---

86   According to Betz, Gal. 3.2-3, 13-14, 23-29; 4.2, 5; and 5.1 do not imply that Jewish Christians were among the Galatians (*Galatians*, p. 4).

87   Longenecker denies this rather common association. Following Burton, Longenecker favors the South Galatian theory, and when listing a number of specious arguments on both sides of the issue includes the following: 'That Jews would have been present in the churches of the south, but were not living in the north ... is patently false' (*Galatians*, p. lxviii).

in the letter and do not rely on the location of the Galatian churches demonstrates that these positions are not mutually exclusive.[88]

Notwithstanding the reasons for denying a Jewish-Christian presence at Galatia, this kind of an objection moves in the wrong direction. We should not simply rule out the idea that there were Jewish Christians in the audience based on the 'ethnicity' of the Galatians. Instead, we should note the way in which Paul's arguments address Jewish Christians, and add these observations to our assessment about the ethnoracial composition of the Galatian congregations, revising our understanding about the occasion of the epistle and the presence of the Jewish-Christian missionaries in Galatia as necessary. Just as most scholars infer the presence of Jewish Christians in the congregation at Rome because of the contents of the letter despite the fact that it is formally addressed to Gentiles there (cf. Rom. 1.6, 13; chs 9–11), so too should we revise our opinion about a Jewish-Christian presence in Galatia. The discussion of the symbiotic dialectic of Gentile and Jewish salvation in 3.13-14, 22-29, and 4.4-6, as well as the contents of 1.6-9; 2.15-21; and 5.1, suggest that Paul is aware of the Jewish-Christian missionaries in Galatia, either present, expected, or so recently departed that the Jewish Christians and his letter have 'crossed in the mail', so to speak. I would suggest, in the final analysis, that it is easier to account for the text as it stands if we infer the continuing presence of the Jewish-Christian missionaries in Galatia than it is to believe that the text reflects pre-Pauline traditions written in a Pauline style, which have been awkwardly incorporated into a letter that otherwise exhibits some rhetorical sophistication.

Thus, Galatians gives a bit more detail about the dialectic between Gentile and Jewish entrance into the eschatological community that is discussed in Rom. 11.11-32. It is true that the argument changes from Galatians to Romans. Galatians describes the interdependence between Gentile inclusion and Jewish freedom from law, while Romans 9–11 primarily examines Jewish salvation after a period of 'hardness'. Romans mentions jealousy as an instrument that pushes Jews toward acceptance of the gospel, while Galatians focuses on the coming of the Spirit as the

---

88   Martyn, *Galatians*, pp. 15–16, 28; Mussner, *Galaterbrief*, p. 57, who nevertheless specifically rejects the idea that 3.13-14, 23-29, and 4.2-5 apply to Jewish Christians. On the North Galatians theory see also Betz (*Galatians*, pp. 1–5), who rejects the idea that there were Jewish Christians in the audience of the letter. Bruce (*Galatians*, pp. 3–18), who argues for the South Galatian theory, assumes that 'Jews, Greeks, and perhaps Romans' would have been among the letter's audience. Bruce also notes that the interpretive choices about the location of the churches is also highly correlated with the interpreter's assessment of the historical reliability of Acts (i.e., South Galatian theory correlates to high reliability of Acts), but that this correlation is not a necessary one (*Galatians*, p. 17; see also Longenecker, *Galatians*, p. lxvii; Burton, *The Epistle to the Galatians*, pp. xxi–xliv; Thomas Witulski, *Die Addressaten des Galaterbriefes* [Göttingen: Vandenhoeck & Ruprecht, 2000]).

product of the interdependence between Gentile and Jewish salvation. Still, just as it is possible to discern the correspondence between Romans 4 and Galatians 3 despite their differences, so too it is possible to see the correspondence between the implied narrative in Gal. 3.13-14/23-29/4.4-6 and that in Rom. 11.13-14, 25-32. In both works, the ultimate manifestation of God's eschatological victory is the salvation of the Jewish people.

4. *A Narrative of Interdependence*

Cornell's proposal, that narrative lies at the heart of identity discourse, illuminates our consideration of Christian identity in Galatians. This discussion of Galatians exposes the narrative about the connection between Jewish and Christian identity that grounds Paul's arguments against his Jewish-Christian opponents. Recalling that Cornell maintains that identity takes a narrative form particularly during periods of rupture when events shatter often-unarticulated assumptions, we see that Paul's narrative responds to a perceived rupture in Jewish identity that emerges in the aftermath of the resurrection of Jesus. This rupture prompts him to reconcile his convictions about his birthright with his emerging understanding of the role of the Spirit as an ordering power and identity marker. In Galatians, Paul re-narrates the central myth of Jewish identity so that the traditional kinship story about law and the promise of land now describes kinship in terms of faith and the promise of the Spirit.

While we recognize that the episodes in Paul's narrative emerge from traditional versions of Israel's story described in the LXX, there is little doubt that he selects events and plots narrative turns not with an eye on fidelity to these familiar stories, but with a view towards reassessing them in light of new developments. The juxtaposition of 'law' and 'curse' was probably as easily misunderstood then as now, and the relegation of a law-observant wing of the new movement to the subordinated status of Hagar's lineage could only have inflamed. Yet even as these narrative events provoke, Paul's rhetorical object is clear: he wants to inculcate the sufficiency of faith and Spirit as central values for life in the new community. As Cornell observed, the plotting of events in an identity narrative can help reveal how a narrator understands the relationships between her group and key constituencies, and in this respect, Paul's purpose clearly emerges from the plotline described above. He is concerned to produce a story about the new group that not only narrates the meaning of membership, but also bridges a potential schism among the descendants of Abraham. Paul's narrative tells how those in Christ and those from the law will both participate in salvation in the aftermath of the Christ event.

Thus, if identity emerges as a narrative that captures the group's understanding of its experiences and central beliefs, then Paul's narrative, at its heart, encapsulates the *value of interdependence*. In Chapter 4, we learned that the symbiotic relationship between Jewish and Gentile salvation that is described in Rom. 11.13-15 and 25-32 is consistent with Paul's self-identity as one who saw himself as a light to the nations and a gatherer of Israel in the mold of the Servant of the Lord. In Galatians, we see that this dialectic of interdependence between Jews and Gentiles with reference to freedom from the law and participation in Christ forms the very heart of Paul's gospel. Paul depicts the giving of the Spirit to Jews who are redeemed by the death of Christ as the final object of the actions initiated by the coming of God's Son (Gal. 4.4-6), a result that is dependent on the adoption of Gentiles into the family of God (4.6a).

However, by using the language of mutual dependence in his arguments to both Gentile Christians and Jewish-Christian missionaries in Galatia and by appealing to this dialectic, Paul underscores the fact that the re-erection of Torah obligations among Gentile believers obstructs God's eschatological victory among the Jews. When Paul speaks of Jewish adoption in Christ, he indicates that Jews participate in the same dual in-the-flesh and in-the-Spirit kinship that he associates with Christ (cf. Gal. 4.4-6; Rom. 1.3-4).[89] Further, he wants to ensure that Gentiles do not see Jews as enemies, and that Jews know that they have nothing to fear from the transformations of identity wrought in the new age. Thus Paul's narrative is a narrative of multiplicity that emphasizes hybridity and the integration of Jews and Gentiles with reference to redemption in Christ. Narratives of multiplicity focus on connection rather than separation, and Paul's narrative of the new race blurs the boundaries between Jews and Greeks in Christ and describes an interlocking history, destiny, identity, and value set.

We have seen that there are four key groups and intergroup connections in Paul's relational matrix, and these connections temporally span the pre-Christian era, the Christian period, and the eschaton and beyond. Prior to the revelation of Christ in history Paul thinks that there is only one people of God and group of descendants from Abraham; he names them the 'sons of Israel' (2 Cor. 3.13). Next, in Paul's time, that is, the period subsequent to Christ, two people-groups are descendants of the sons of Israel: Israel according to the flesh and the Israel of God. These groups correspond to the two sets of branches in Rom. 11.17-24, and the two groups in Rom. 4.16 as discussed in Chapter 4. Finally, at the eschaton, the coming of the Redeemer reunites these two groups into a single

---

89   Hodge points out that adoption was a common way of creating kinship among once disparate groups in antiquity, but balks at the application of this terminology to Jews in Gal. 4.5 (*If Sons then Heirs*, p. 70; cf. her discussion of Christ's dual kinship in Rom. 1.3-4 on pp. 30, 115).

community when 'all Israel' will be saved (Rom. 11.26). Thus, after Christ and before the eschaton, the Jewish people are split wherein some are in Israel κατὰ σάρκα and some are in the Church of God (i.e., the Israel of God), and Paul resists any amalgamation of these separate identities. At the eschaton, Paul's relational map again exhibits continuity as all Israel is redeemed, both Israel κατὰ σάρκα and the Israel of God. Whether one sees in Romans 11 a universalism by which everyone is saved, or whether one thinks instead that parts of each group will receive salvation, the important point is that after the eschaton there is only one group visible in this glimpse of Paul's eschatological hope.[90]

Our consideration of Paul's relational map and group identification against the backdrop of narrative identity constructs helps illuminate the framework within which the blend of continuity and discontinuity in Paul's thought takes place. Given that the criterion of identity for Christians and Jews was formed around religion and contained ideas about God at their center, group identity, both racial and ethnic, is more fluid than modern ethno-racial constructs, and it is this fluidity and impermanence that brings coherence to what appear to be contradictory impulses in Paul's thought. The rigidity in our thinking about ethnic and racial identity normally confounds attempts at synthesizing the shifts in Paul's depictions of the people(s) of God and their relationships to Abraham and Christ respectively. We assume that if Gentiles are 'grafted' into the lineage of the patriarchs they must become 'Jews' in some sense because, for moderns, 'Jewishness', after all, is calculated via descent from Abraham, either spiritually or biologically. Coherence vanishes when the boundaries between these groups are calculated using this modern tendency to privilege physical descent as determinative of identity. If, on the other hand, we think about the relationships between these groups in terms of the more flexible element of religion as the defining criterion of identity, we will be able to see the coherence among the different portrayals of the people of God. We will understand that Paul's relational map included one people of God in the past, two groups of people who can make that claim before the coming of the Redeemer, but only one people in the eschatological future.

Finally, the consideration of Christian identity in Galatians reinforces our conclusion that Paul's concept of community in Christ is indebted to the Jewish understanding of ethno-racial identity. Although Paul resists the fusion of Jewish and Christian identity advocated by his opponents in Galatia, his clarification of the key elements of Christian identity nevertheless mimics the way the Jewish criterion and indicium converged in the practice of circumcision. The Spirit functions in a way roughly

---

90 Wright, 'Letter to the Romans', 10.688–89, for a concise description of the main interpretive options.

parallel to that of circumcision in that both indicia simultaneously demarcate group membership and characterize a way of life. Circumcision signals physical descent as a means of entrance into the community and as such signifies membership in terms both of kinship and of religious behavior. In the same way, Spirit functions both as a means of incorporation into the lineage of the patriarchs (Gal. 4.29) and as an indicium that signals membership and acts as an agent of moral behavior (Gal. 3.1-5; 5.22-23).

In addition, Paul continues the Jewish preference for talking about believers as family members, and he has the same heightened sensitivity to socio-religious boundaries and border crossings, continuing an uncompromising devotion to a religious principle as the defining criterion of the group's identity, organized here around the principle of faith in Christ. Less emphatic, but still discernible, was a territorial dimension in Paul's thought, as he associates 'Jerusalem-above' with those who are descendents of Abraham and Sarah κατὰ πνεῦμα, thus incorporating an ethnic feature into a predominantly racial model of identity. Moreover, throughout Galatians we have seen the triad of Jewish racial identity elements that we first encountered in Rom. 3.27–4.22 – justification by law, descent from Abraham, and circumcision. Throughout Galatians these elements were set in opposition to the triad of Christian identity elements that we encountered in Phil. 3.2-9: justification by faith, being-in-Christ, and Spirit. The relatively simple, two-dimensional set of oppositions in Phil. 3.2-9 became in Galatians a three-dimensional relationship in which the elements in the Jewish construct were each opposed to every element in the Christian construct. In Chapter 4, we surmised that the Jewish triad was already available to Paul from his Jewish social background; but his manipulation of the Christian elements in Galatians suggests that he is using these associations with a great deal more freedom, an observation that implies that the new construct is either original to him or of a recent vintage. Thus, the portrayal of Christian racial identity developed here is that of an *emergent, newly formed, Jewish-like racial group.*

CONCLUSION

Chapter 6

RACIAL CHRISTIANITY AND IDENTITY POLITICS

J.K. Rowling gives us racism, though with a different spin on 'race', in the rich and textured Wizarding world of the vastly popular *Harry Potter* series. In the Wizarding world, races are defined by whether or not a wizard has non-magical parents. 'Muggles' are the race of non-magical people who are normally unaware of the parallel world of wizards and witches and magical creatures. 'Purebloods' have only wizards and witches in their lineage, and many go to great lengths to keep their bloodlines and society in general untainted by Muggle influences. 'Half-bloods', those wizards with at least one Muggle parent or Muggles in their lineage, like Harry Potter himself, occupy a somewhat uncomfortable in-between status, but at least escape being called 'mudbloods', a racially charged epithet akin to 'nigger' in the United States, but reserved for wizards who have two non-magical parents. Wizarding world pureblood fanaticism comes complete with its own evil arch-villain, Lord Voldemort, whom Harry is destined to meet in a final battle. A half-blood himself, Voldemort and his pureblood followers perpetrate violence against Muggles and Muggle-born members of the Wizarding community. 'Blood traitor', however, is the epithet Voldemort and company reserve for pureblood wizards who have the unspeakably bad judgement not only to embrace mudbloods and half-breeds, but also to promote Muggle welfare outright.

It seems to me that Paul might have earned the label 'blood traitor' through his embrace of uncircumcised Gentiles, his adamant refusal to countenance their obedience to Torah as the central institution in Jewish life, and his bold claim of kinship with these Gentile Christians. Because Jewish concepts of race and ethnicity placed religion at the center of identity instead of place of origin or kinship, Jewish identity had an elasticity not found in the other constructions of identity considered here. In spite of this elasticity, however, it is still true that Jews participated in the general cultural ethnocentrism of antiquity.[1] Jews may not have

---

1 Hirschman, 'Rise and Fall of the Concept of Race', pp. 4–9; Smith (*The Ethnic Origins of Nations*, p. 47) defines ethnocentrism as exclusive attitudes towards outsiders and outside influences, and disdain or fear of external lifestyles. Ethnocentrism includes a sense of group centrality, cultural uniqueness, and superiority towards others.

participated in a deterministic Greco-Roman racism that stigmatized peoples based on place of origin, but with their in-group sense of cultural superiority and disdain for 'Gentile sinners', Paul's contemporaries would have been quick to castigate his 'kinship' with these Gentile sinners.

In recent years, Daniel Boyarin, an orthodox Jew himself, has tried to reclaim some of Paul's cultural heritage by reading him as a Hellenistic Diaspora Jew in the mold of Philo. According to Boyarin, Paul like Philo tries to resolve the tension between Judaism's claims about a universalistic creator and its particularistic culture centered on genealogy and concrete practices. According to Boyarin, Paul is a Jewish cultural critic, and even though this description is not as unkind as the label 'blood traitor', both depict a person at odds with his culture. Boyarin ultimately sees Paul as the locus of a Christian tendency to flatten difference and normalize Western male identity. On the other hand, Brad Braxton reads Galatians with an eye towards bringing Paul's words to bear on issues of race and ethnicity as they relate to African Americans, and he sees in Paul a careful concern for preserving ethnic identity within a religious context. Caroline Johnson Hodge offers yet a third alternative, viewing Paul as a loyal member of the Jewish people, one who is devoted to seeing Gentiles grafted into the Jewish family tree, albeit as a subordinate bough.[2] My reading of Paul associates him with the creation of a completely new ethno-racial particularity and thus contrasts with Boyarin, Braxton, and Hodge. This concluding chapter will engage these three interpretations, comparing each of their portraits with the reading of Paul developed here, along with an examination of the way that each rendering of Paul engages contemporary identity concepts.

1. *Suppression of Difference in Christ: Daniel Boyarin's* A Radical Jew

Boyarin's *A Radical Jew: Paul and the Politics of Identity* is a provocative reading of Paul that sees Gal. 3.28 as the centerpiece of Pauline thought. This portrait of Paul begins by identifying areas in which Paul was influenced by his culture. Boyarin understands Paul to have been profoundly influenced by the Hellenistic 'desire for the One', which is apparent in much philosophy and religion. According to Boyarin, the Hellenistic pursuit of unity – which often becomes a 'fear of diversity' – produced among the ancients a desire for univocity in interpretation and a need to find meaning in texts that no longer reflected their concerns. Thus, the Jewish Diaspora's confrontation with Greek culture gave rise to an allegorized Judaism through symbolic readings of the Hebrew Scriptures

---

2   Hodge, *If Sons then Heirs*, p. 143, marvelously develops the family tree image.

that allowed these ancient texts to address the concerns of Jews living in the Diaspora. Diaspora Jewish authors pursued the spiritual meaning of texts, producing an allegorical mode of interpretation that is especially visible in the works of Philo of Alexandria. Boyarin stops just short of claiming Philo as a background for Paul, but believes that Philo makes explicit what is implicit in Paul regarding the use of an allegorical hermeneutic. Boyarin develops the idea that both Philo and Paul use allegorical interpretation that is based on Platonic dualism, which sets a higher realm of spirit against a lower realm of matter.

According to Boyarin, Paul's dissatisfaction with Jewish particularism lies at the heart of his mission. Paul's overriding theological problem with Judaism was the tension between the universalistic content of the Torah's claims about God and the particularism of Torah's forms.[3] Paul is profoundly interested in the oneness of humanity and the elimination of human hierarchies, and he sees as a moral and religious necessity the eradication of all distinctions between peoples in Christ's spiritual body. While Philo's allegorical approach emphatically rejects a corresponding allegorization of Jewish practice, Paul's allegorizing hermeneutic replaces 'embodied signs with spiritual signifiers', ultimately resulting in a suppression of all physical difference, particularly gender and ethnic Jewish distinctions (Gal. 3.28).[4] In terms of Jewish practice, Paul's spiritual signifiers effectively obliterate Jewish ethnicity since, according to Boyarin, ethnicity in the ancient world was essentially constituted via kinship networks. Paul substitutes an allegorical genealogy for a physical one, and via baptism he offers a solidarity 'in the Spirit' that transcends ethnicity and gender. The literal participation in the Abrahamic promise that takes place via Jewish kinship is replaced by an allegorical participation in the promise via the notion of being 'in Christ' (Gal. 4.22-31). Paul, therefore, is inherently supersessionist, since he defines identity for the people of God in a way that denies Israel's self-understanding as a community constituted by genealogy and concrete observances. Paul's call to Oneness brings equality but also constitutes a threat to Jewish difference or any other sort of distinction.

As mentioned above, Boyarin reads Paul through the lens of dualistic Platonism, in which the phenomenal world represents the higher 'inner' spiritual realm that is opposed to the lower 'outer' material plane.[5] Taking

---

3 One reviewer was puzzled by Boyarin's derivation of Paul's universalism from Hellenistic culture, rather than from the universalistic elements of Israel's own tradition. See Jay M. Harris, 'The Circumcised Heart', *Commentary* 99.6 (1995): 57–60 (59).

4 Boyarin, *A Radical Jew*, p. 25, compares Paul's approach to 'works of law' with Philo's approach to the practice of law in *Migration* 89–93.

5 Boyarin's discussion of Rom. 2.28-29 is similar to Bultmann's interpretation of this verse in his discussion of σάρξ (Rudolf Bultmann, *Theology of the New Testament* [trans. Kendrick Grobel; New York: Charles Scribner's Sons, 1951], 1.234–35).

Rom. 2.28-29 as a key text, Boyarin detects throughout Paul allegorical binaries that pit the literal and fleshly against the figurative and spiritual. The key phrases κατὰ σάρκα and κατὰ πνεῦμα are taken to mean 'literal' and 'spiritual', and these phrases provide the hermeneutical nexus of Paul's understanding of identity, respectively figuring the particularistic and the universal. Boyarin detects in Rom. 2.28-29 three sets of oppositions that mutually interpret one another, and together define Paul's hermeneutic which pits the literal against the spiritual: outer (ὁ ἐν τῷ φανερῷ) versus inner (ὁ ἐν τῷ κρυπτῷ), in the flesh (σαρκὶ περιτομή) versus in the heart (περιτομὴ καρδίας), and in the letter (γράμματι) versus in the spirit (ἐν πνεύματι). For Boyarin, the terms on the left sides of the oppositions are equivalent, so that 'outer' = 'in the flesh' = 'literal'. The terms on the right sides of the oppositions are likewise equivalent: 'inner' = 'in the heart' = 'spiritual'.

Boyarin's analysis of Rom. 2.28-29 is worth quoting at length, as this passage embodies his understanding of Paul's 'allegorical' construction of identity:

> But, now we come to the climax and crux of [Rom. 2], for here Paul thoroughly redefines precisely those theological terms to which we can expect that his Jewish interlocutor would have been assenting until now. The Jew has agreed that being Jewish is not sufficient for salvation, and one needs works as well. However, he does not mean keeping ... all of the commandments, whether ritual or moral in nature, both those that divide the Jews from other peoples and those that bind them to others. The first category – synechdochized here by circumcision but certainly including food rules and Sabbaths – means nothing in the work of salvation. Such rules are only outer practices ... In other words, in this coda to the chapter which seems until now to be calling Jews to repent and keep the Law as they have understood it – a keeping that maintains ethnic identity and specificity, Paul introduces his major concern ... producing a new, single human essence, one of 'true Jews' whose 'circumcision' does not mark off their bodies as ethnically distinct from any other human bodies ... 'True Jewishness' ends up having nothing to do with family connection (descent from Abraham according to the flesh), history (having the Law), or maintaining the cultural/religious practices of the historical Jewish community (circumcision), but paradoxically consists of participating in a universalism, an allegory that dissolves those essences and meanings entirely.[6]

Later in the work, Boyarin's description of the political results of Paul's religious program is compelling reading for anyone who has considered the tensions between Christian identity and the modern politics of ethnic particularism. For Boyarin, Paul's universalism in Gal. 3.28 and the olive-

6 Boyarin, *A Radical Jew*, pp. 93–95.

tree metaphor in Romans 11 represent two critical moments in which Paul allegorizes Jewish ethnic identity out of existence. Like many other interpreters of Paul, Boyarin has reduced the idea of 'oneness' in Gal. 3.28 to the idea of 'sameness'; for Boyarin the text obliterates ethnic and gender difference in Christ. Boyarin's analysis of the olive-tree metaphor in Rom. 11.17-24 holds that ethnic Israel, distinguished by a particular genealogy, history, and set of material practices, no longer constitutes the root into which other peoples have been grafted. Instead, it is Jewish Christianity, devoid of 'works of law' and characterized by trust in Christ, that is now the root sustaining all branches. For Boyarin, Paul thus allegorizes out of existence both Jewish ethnic difference and the essence of traditional Jewish self-identity.

Boyarin sees Paul's thought as inherently supersessionist, because the community of grace replaces the community of flesh, even if there are some ethnic Jews included in the new community. He absolves Paul of any overt anti-Judaism, recognizing that he actually writes to invalidate the notion of ethnic supersessionism among Gentile Christians, but along the way, Paul has redefined the idea of 'remnant' so that it excludes the idea of faithfulness to Jewish practices. If Paul has obliterated the legitimacy of ethnic and gender difference, as Boyarin maintains, then it becomes easier to discern the edge of Boyarin's critique, since there is no lack of interpreters who use Paul's treatment of Jewish and Gentile differences as a model for Christian 'oneness' with respect to racial and gender difference today.

Specifically, Boyarin believes that Pauline theology involves the possibly unintended suppression of all ethno-racial and gender difference, and especially the obliteration of Jewish identity. When combined with power, suppression results in arrogance and the politics of hate, and is tragically observable in the Western tradition of confrontation with Jewish difference. In an evenhanded way, Boyarin also castigates rabbinic ideology as unnecessarily insulated and thereby indifferent to 'Others'. Boyarin proposes a 'Diaspora identity' that offers a way forward. Diaspora identity is a construct that is divorced from power and exists apart from homeland, institutions, and other constructions of auto-chthony. It is an identity that preserves community and inclusiveness while simultaneously maintaining the particular distinctiveness of identity.[7]

Boyarin's work raises four issues of interpretation, and I briefly address each of these below:

1. *Boyarin claims that Paul's dissatisfaction with Jewish particularism lies at the heart of Paul's mission.* While scholars who have reviewed

7   Ibid., pp. 258–59.

Boyarin's work are impressed with his careful interaction with a broad range of New Testament scholarship, the claim cited above prompts the major criticism of his work. Boyarin's own interests in cultural criticism and ethnic and gender politics are seen as unduly influencing his reading of Paul and his choice of Gal. 3.28 as the center of Paul's thought. By this choice, Boyarin has undervalued the Christ event as determinative of Paul's theology. In the words of one reviewer, 'Boyarin studiously avoids dealing with the back half of his theme verse in Paul: "... for you are all one in Christ Jesus".'[8]

2. *Boyarin describes Paul and Philo as indebted to the same allegorizing impulse and reads Rom. 2.28-29 through this allegorizing lens, using it as the centerpiece for his understanding of Paul's hermeneutic.* John Barclay skillfully and systematically addresses Boyarin's interpretation of Paul as a representative of a Hellenistic Judaism in the same mold of Philo.[9] Barclay shows that Philo and Paul represent different modes of engagement with Jewish culture. Barclay analyzes Philo's position on circumcision, showing that he is a fundamentally conservative figure, insisting on literal observance of circumcision because, among other things, he is concerned to maintain a favorable opinion with the masses.[10] On the other hand, Paul has a revolutionary approach to this traditional Jewish rite, effectively rendering it superfluous (Rom. 2.25-26). Rather than currying favor with the masses, Paul insists that 'true Jews' win praise from God [only] when they prioritize circumcision of the heart over that of the flesh.[11]

If Gal. 3.28 is the text from which Boyarin draws his conclusions about the cultural politics of Pauline theology, Rom. 2.28-29 is the lens through which he interprets his theme verse. The key step in Boyarin's interpretation of this passage occurs in his reading of the contrast between 'outer' = 'in the flesh' = 'literal' on the one hand and 'inner' = 'in the heart' = 'spiritual' on the other. '*Spiritual*' thus contrasts with 'literal' and is equated with 'figurative' or '*allegorical*'. Barclay shows, however, that in this text 'spirit' does not invoke a Hellenistic inner/outer dualism, but refers to God's

---

8   Beverly Gaventa, Review of *A Radical Jew: Paul and the Politics of Identity* by Daniel Boyarin, *Theology Today* 52.2 (1995): 290. See also Stephen Fowl, Review of *A Radical Jew: Paul and the Politics of Identity* by Daniel Boyarin, *Modern Theology* 12 (1996): 131–33.

9   John Barclay, 'Paul and Philo on Circumcision: Romans 2.25-29 in Social and Cultural Context', *NTS* 44 (1998): 536–56.

10   Ibid., pp. 540–43.

11   Ibid., pp. 543–46. We may insert the idea of 'only' into the translation of Rom. 2.29 even though it does not appear in the text, because the rhetorical question in 3.1 asking about the value of circumcision shows that Paul was fully aware that his thinking in 2.25-29 was far from the Jewish norm (ibid., p. 546). Barclay's interpretation clearly agrees with our assessment of Paul as a 'blood traitor'.

spirit.[12] He goes on to note, 'In truth, Boyarin uses the term "allegorical" in an extremely wide sense, covering any interpretation which tends towards the "spiritual", "ahistorical", "universal", or "non-material", even referring to baptism and the Christian community as "spiritual" and therefore "allegorical".'[13]

3. *Boyarin assumes that Jewish identity in antiquity was based on kinship networks.* Boyarin criticizes Paul's 'spiritualized' brand of Jewish religion because even if it includes ethnic Israel, it first redefines Jewish national identity. My interpretation, however, suggests that this criticism relies on two faulty assumptions – that Paul saw himself as Jewish, and that the 'essence' of ancient Jewish identity was physical descent. While Chapters 3, 4, and 5 address these assumptions in detail, we can briefly summarize the conclusions here. Chapter 3 demonstrated that even though kinship networks were important in Jewish thought, religious values were at the center of Jewish identity for many. Among these Jews, identity was constructed around worship of the God of Abraham, Isaac, and Jacob, a worship ordered by Torah. In Chapter 4, we saw that Paul drew on these ideas of racial and ethnic identity to articulate a vision of Christian identity. Paul saw himself as one who had been born Jewish but who now participated in a Jewish-like race that was an apocalyptic new creation through the Christ event, which among other things resulted in the creation of a new kind of kinship in Christ. In Chapter 5, we saw that the center of Christian identity is the worship of the God of Abraham διὰ πίστεως Ἰησοῦ Χριστοῦ, a worship ordered via the Spirit.

4. *Boyarin claims that Paul's construction of identity is at the heart of a Christian tendency to flatten difference and normalize Western male identity.*[14] In Chapter 2, we did find evidence that supports Boyarin's claim that Christianity is implicated in the normalization of white identity. European race discourse in the sixteenth through eighteenth centuries narrated encounters with Africans during the so-called Age of Discovery as encounters with peoples of inferior society and religion. Questions about the origins of different races during this period were answered by appeals to the biblical narrative, and Europeans' inability to find African peoples in the

---

12   Ibid., pp. 550–53.

13   Ibid., p. 555.

14   Addressing this claim requires an assessment and diagnosis of the modern scene far beyond the purview of this investigation, but I will present some evidence that addresses Boyarin's claims with reference to modern identity constructs. Another caveat that applies to my ability to assess Boyarin's claim is that I did not consider gender when examining constructions of identity, instead focusing on race and ethnicity. Because of this, while I am not able to cite social-science research that either proves or disproves his claim about 'Western males', I will be able to comment with respect to the normalization of 'whiteness' in Western society.

Bible (apart from the so-called 'curse of Ham') affirmed their early assessments of the inferiority of black peoples.[15] In the latter part of the eighteenth and early part of the nineteenth centuries, when European and early US society needed rationalizations for the institution of slavery, the Christian worldview articulated the 'white man's burden', a view that meant that Christians would assume the responsibility to civilize and proselytize Blacks, Native Americans, and other peoples of color. In the latter nineteenth and twentieth centuries, negative images originally associated with blacks were provisionally extended to new groups of European and non-European immigrants. These negative images of immigrants and non-whites as 'savage', 'uncivilized', or 'cursed' all derived from 'minus-one ethnicity', that is, the relegation of all deviations from the white Anglo-Saxon Protestant norm to lesser categories of being.[16] In other words, all peoples outside of the group of white Anglo-Saxon Protestants were considered 'abnormal' by virtue of the fact that the WASPs were doing the naming.

Thus, we agree with the claim that there is a tendency in 'Christianity' whereby differences are marginalized. Too often, white European Christian power-holders have assumed that the normalization of Christian identity means the normalization of white identity. Moving now to a consideration of the second part of Boyarin's claim, we must ask, however, whether this marginalization of difference is really a feature of Pauline theology or is instead a property of 'Christian culture'. On this aspect of Boyarin's analysis, I disagree that Pauline Christianity is inherently hostile to difference. Rather than understanding Paul to have eliminated difference, I maintain that Paul espoused a completely new particular identity alongside of the Jewish identity that already existed in his period. Paul is not responsible for the flattening of difference that takes place in Western 'Christian' culture, although I do not at all dispute Boyarin's assessment that such a flattening has taken place in cultures that are nominally 'Christian'.[17] After all, Paul himself lived in a world in

---

15   Jordan, *The White Man's Burden*, pp. 9–10; Goldenberg, *Curse of Ham*.

16   Jacobson, *Whiteness*, pp. 274–80. Michael Banton describes 'minus one ethnicity' as a 1950s phenomenon (*Racial and Ethnic Competition*, p. 65), but Tonkin, McDonald and Chapman point out that the concept of 'ethnicity' has had this 'us' vs. 'them' duality throughout much of recorded history (*History and Ethnicity*, pp. 15–16).

17   Musa Dube presents a sophisticated analysis of the way that the biblical narrative is implicated in the imperialism of 'Christian' nations that 'authorizes' the taking of lands belonging to non-Christians:

> [Even though] the text [has] its own historical world and environment ... the text also travels in the world and participates in history, continuing to write its story far beyond its original context and readers. The text continues to live and to inscribe its authority through its Western readers and their institutions that uphold it. In

which the Jewish community was severely marginalized, and he went on to found new 'Israelite' communities that were marginalized to an even greater extent (Gal. 6.16; 2 Cor. 11.24). In short, Paul's movement was one *without substantial coercive power* and thus literally incapable of 'erasing difference' in the way that Boyarin alleges. However, since Paul does call all believers regardless of birth to participate in a new identity in Christ, one may still ask whether or not he unwittingly articulated religious ideals that went on to marginalize and suppress ethnic, racial, and gender difference once the movement gained power. Paul could not have foreseen the possibility of Christian hegemony, and clearly, a power politics that marginalizes every departure from a Christian European white male ideal is possible only after Constantine.

2. *Fighting Anti-Judaism in Pauline Scholarship: Caroline Johnson Hodge's* If Sons Then Heirs

Caroline Johnson Hodge's work is mainly an investigation of ethnicity and kinship themes in Paul, taking aim at those who view Christianity as a religion that transcends ethnicity and represents a neutral, inclusive identity that goes beyond the markers of culture and normal human practices.[18] Hodge argues that for Paul, kinship and ethnicity are not metaphorical; lineage, paternity, and peoplehood are the pre-eminent categories for understanding status before God, and are all central to his arguments. Ethnic and religious categories cannot be disentangled in Paul; he uses ethnic discourse to construct a myth of origins for Gentile Christians that relies on the logic of patrilineal descent. According to

---

addition, the text has maintained a recognizable impact through its various readers and their different institutions, *regardless of whether this was the intention of the author or not.*

Insofar as the centrality of geography and the ideology that authorize the entering and taking of the lands of foreign people is traced to the Exodus-Canaan mythological story, the postcolonial historical experience strongly suggests that at the heart of biblical belief is an imperialist ideology ... which operates under the claims of chosenness. (Dube, *Postcolonial*, p. 17; emphasis added)

Dube makes a powerful argument about the way that the Conquest story shaped the colonial imagination and validated Western imperialism, but her arguments about the influence of the Conquest narrative in shaping the Gospel of Matthew is less successful. Even though the Israelite Conquest narrative is troubling, Dube illegitimately reads the Conquest and thus imperialism in every intertextual echo of Exodus imagery in Matthew (Dube, *Postcolonial*, pp. 127–56). Further, Dube emphasizes geography in her deconstructions of imperialism in the biblical narrative, but this emphasis conflicts with the finding in Chapters 3–5 here, that territory had only peripheral significance in Second Temple Jewish and Christian constructions of identity.

18 Hodge, *If Sons then Heirs*, p. 4.

Hodge, patrilineal descent is an ideology used in the construction of identities and group membership that also mediates the power relationships between groups. This ideology is based on a concept of descent emerging from biological processes, which are viewed as 'natural' and thus perceived as removed from human manipulation, but additionally incorporating hierarchies of power embedded in the kinship relationship.[19] According to Hodge, this mechanism describes how Paul manipulates descent by plugging Gentiles into the Israelite family tree. For Hodge, Paul is a Ἰουδαῖος who believes that Jesus is the Messiah; though Paul insists that Jews and Gentiles in Christ share a common ancestor, he does not collapse them into a new group of Christians, but maintains that they are separate, hierarchically ordered lineages descended from Abraham.

Hodge maintains that while Paul never suggests that Jews-in-Christ ever have to give up their ethnic and religious identity, he repeatedly stresses that Gentiles do; thus, Jews are marked by continuity, but Gentiles marked by discontinuity.[20] Paul's gospel is the insight that in Christ, the Gentiles are a people of God, while Jews in Christ are those who accept this good news without demanding that Gentiles take on the Jewish yoke of the law. In other words, for Hodge Christ is the solution for Gentiles but not Jews, and Christ and Torah are exclusive of each other; Christ is for Gentiles, but Torah continues as the means for righteousness for Jews.[21] Hodge's reading capitalizes on Gal. 3.8 which defines the gospel as the Abrahamic promise that God would bless the Gentiles in him. Nevertheless, her construction does not engage Paul's comments about his identity in Christ in Phil. 3.9, where he plainly includes himself among those whose righteousness comes from Christ *instead of Torah*. Her general argument that Paul is simply identifying with his Gentile converts in passages where he seems to include himself among those who are saved in Christ cannot survive the specifics of Paul's personal testimony in this verse. Moreover, when Phil. 3.3-9 is interpreted in light of the notion that Paul's concept of ethno-racial identity focused on religious and social elements as much as kinship, as discussed in Chapter 4, we see that the text also challenges Hodge's assertion that Paul never makes exhortations that imply that Jews should relinquish elements of their ethnic identity.

Hodge's book is most valuable in its work in undermining the idea that Christianity is universalizing and non-ethnic:

19   Ibid., pp. 19–21.

20   Ibid., p. 141. The big departures between my reading of Pauline theology and Hodge's concern the trajectory in Pauline scholarship that each of us follows: while my work pursues a new perspective, third-race reading, Hodge's work follows the Gaston/Gager two-covenant theory.

21   Also see Gager, *The Origins of Anti-Semitism*, pp. 200–201, and Gaston, *Paul and the Torah*, p. 21 *et passim*.

> Those who claim such a de-ethnicized Christianity fail to recognize that certain aspects of Jewish culture are normative for Christians. ... Christians tend to view their religion as one that transcends ethnicity; they have translated these particular markers of identity into an ethnically neutral, all-inclusive tradition which is somehow beyond normal human characteristics of culture, its discourses and practices. ... In this study, I argue for a new way to read kinship and ethnic language in Paul that dismantles the contrast between a universal, 'non-ethnic' Christianity and an ethnic, particular Judaism.[22]

Her exploration of kinship as an identity theme thus augments many of the observations made here. For example, Hodge asserts that the common phrase in identity literature 'fictive kinship' is terminology that suggests that such kinship is 'less real' than other kinds of kinship. In fact, while many often formulate kinship in terms of biological relationship, it is frequently established by other criteria such as common practices, language, and religion.[23] According to Hodge, there are both fixed and mutable elements of ethnicity, despite the fact that ethnicity is regularly predicated on kinship. For example, Paul's use of baptism in Christ to create a new lineage appeals to both fluid and fixed factors. His use of a religious ritual that authorizes the creation of kinship for Gentiles is an inherently fluid, ad hoc notion. On the other hand, his deployment of a fixed notion such as 'seed' appeals to birth as an ascribed, natural, and thus unquestioned concept, and establishes a social ordering based on the logic of patrilineal descent.[24] Along these lines, her description of Gal. 3.28 is well worth reading.[25] According to Hodge, the hierarchical ordering of identity that emerges from the logic of patrilineal descent affords believers the opportunity to situationally select and emphasize their in-Christness over ethnic, gender, or other components of identity.

When Hodge maintains that Paul's self-descriptions incorporate situational ethnicity, she means that Paul's different identity layers are nested within his larger identity of being Jewish, each layer emphasized or de-emphasized depending on the situation. Here she notes that the 'in-Christ' element added to Paul's identity does not represent another ethnicity, but 'falls within *Jewish* boundaries'.[26] In other words, Hodge maintains that for Gentiles, 'in-Christness' is not its own ethnic identity but something that allows them to participate in Jewish ethnicity. Yet when Hodge's Paul 'encourages gentiles in Galatia to rank their "in-Christness" higher than their other available identities, as he himself has

---

22 Hodge, *If Sons then Heirs*, p. 4.
23 Ibid., p. 16.
24 Ibid., p. 16, citing Buell, *Why This New Race?*, pp. 7–13, 37–41.
25 Hodge, *If Sons then Heirs*, pp. 126–31.
26 Ibid., p. 120 (emphasis original).

done' in Gal. 3.28,[27] her argument comes close to participating in the
same universalizing discourse in Christianity that she works to undermine.
If Christianity is not an ethno-racial entity, how does Paul's emphasis on
his in-Christness over his Jewish identity differ from traditional interpretations that teach that believers should lay aside their ethnic identity to
achieve an ethnic neutrality in Christ?

Hodge's work has not seriously engaged a 'third race' interpretation,
and her adoption of the Gaston/Gager two-covenant reading represents a
minority opinion that does not seem to have engendered robust
engagement in Pauline scholarship.[28] Scholars that do interact with this
interpretive trajectory confine themselves to basic disagreements about
whether Paul ever used the phrase 'works of law' to refer to Jewish
obedience to the law, a position held by an early proponent of this thesis.
The discovery of a very similar phrase at Qumran greatly undermined that
argument, and there seems to be little interest in addressing other
components of this interpretive trajectory.[29] For example, Hodge and
other proponents of the Gaston/Gager thesis energetically claim that Paul
never claims to be speaking to Jews or connects his own teaching to
Jews.[30] Yet there are indications in the Pauline epistles that Paul did
indeed have a teaching ministry to Jews, among which the evidence at 1
Cor. 9.19-23 is the strongest. Further, it is impossible to overlook the
numerous direct addresses to Jews in the epistle to the Romans (2.17-29;
4.1, 16; 7.1, 4; 9.24; 11.5; cf. Gal. 2.19), not to mention the evidence of
addresses to a Jewish audience in Galatians as discussed in Chapter 5.[31]
Hodge focuses on Paul's use of the word ἄνθρωπος in Gal. 2.16 and

27   Ibid., p. 129.
28   David Aune, 'Recent Readings of Paul Relating to Justification by Faith', in David E.
Aune (ed.), *Rereading Paul Together: Protestant and Catholic Perspectives on Justification*
(Grand Rapids: Baker Academic, 2006), p. 220; Jeffrey Peterson, 'Review of Stanley Stowers'
A Rereading of Romans', *Restoration Quarterly* 39.1 (1997): 50–53. Frank Thielman's
appendix in *From Plight to Solution* is a notable exception, containing a sustained
engagement of Gaston and Gager, who are two early and major proponents of the thesis that
Hodge takes up (*From Plight to Solution: A Jewish Framework for Understanding Paul's View
of the Law in Galatians and Romans* [Leiden; New York: E.J. Brill, 1989; reprint, Eugene,
OR: Wipf and Stock, 2007], pp. 123–32 [page citations are to the reprint edition]).
29   See Boyarin, *A Radical Jew*, p. 272 n. 9. Hodge is not persuaded that the evidence
from Qumran means that the phrase 'works of law' or its Hebrew equivalent truly described
Jewish practices, but does not give reasons for her continuing skepticism. Further, she
maintains with Gaston that Paul addresses Gentiles only in Gal. 2.16, though her case in this
instance seems predicated on arguments about the ethnic makeup of the audience of
Galatians, rather than Gaston's focus on the interpretation of ἄνθρωπος (*If Sons then Heirs*,
p. 176 n. 74; cf. Gaston, *Paul and the Torah*, pp. 64–70).
30   Hodge, *If Sons then Heirs*, p. 9; also see the more complete defense of this idea in
Stowers, *A Rereading of Romans*.
31   Richard Hays's critique of the idea that Romans does not address Jews is particularly
trenchant ('The Gospel is the Power of God').

insists that the faith versus works of law righteousness described in this verse applies only to Gentiles, a view that seems incomprehensible in view of the way that he specifically addresses Jews in the preceding verse.[32] She tries to sustain the idea that righteousness through faith applies only to Gentiles by narrowly defining 'gospel' in terms of Gal. 3.8, yet it seems clear that in Romans 'gospel' is defined as 'the righteousness of God to all who believe', which righteousness comes 'through faith in Jesus Christ for all who believe' (1.16; 3.22).[33]

Hodge's interpretation clearly challenges Christian anti-Judaism, particularly in her insistence that Paul's thought hierarchically orders Jewish and Gentile attachments to Abraham's family tree. Appealing once again to the logic of patriarchal descent, her reasoning effectively normalizes hierarchy as a theological principle of human organization, applying it to Jews and Gentiles in Christ even as it reorders present-day Christian assumptions about hierarchy, substituting Jews for Christians at the top. Her exegesis focuses on the olive-tree metaphor in Rom. 11.17-24, finding hierarchical logic that privileges Jewish attachments to the olive tree in several images: cultivated versus wild fruit, natural versus unnatural branches, and Jewish roots versus grafted Gentile branches. She further notes that Christ is only the 'point at which the wild branches are grafted', though I would maintain that Christ is the means by which any branch is, or remains, attached to the tree.[34] According to Hodge, Gentiles and Jews are separate but hierarchically related peoples, and not a single unified group of Christ-followers who do not have an ethnic association. She writes that the resulting ethnic identity for Gentiles is established via aggregative linking to a Jewish network, a process used to advantage the Jews as the privileged pedigree in the new genealogical system.[35] Thus, while Jews and Gentiles-in-Christ each have their own separate ethnic identities and lineages and are both loyal to the God of Abraham, Jews are ranked higher as natural descendants of the patriarch.

Despite the fact that Hodge has developed a nuanced portrait of Paul's appeal to ethno-racial reasoning, this work, like the others engaged here, defines 'ethnic' in modern terms. Nowhere has Hodge considered the nature of ethnicity or race as a construct in antiquity particularly with respect to Jewish ethno-racial identity; she assumes throughout that

32   *If Sons then Heirs*, p. 58; see also p. 176 n. 72. For more on the interpretation of Gal. 2.15-16 ('We [ἡμεῖς] are Jews by birth and not sinners from among the Gentiles. But, knowing that a person [ἄνθρωπος] is not justified by the works of the Law but through faith in Christ Jesus, even we [καὶ ἡμεῖς] have believed in Christ Jesus'), see the discussion on pp. 168–72 above.

33   See Thielman, *From Plight to Solution*, pp. 127–29, for an additional critique of Gaston and Gager's interpretations of Rom. 1.16 and 3.22.

34   Hodge, *If Sons then Heirs*, p. 145.

35   Ibid., p. 146.

physical descent is the central component of ethnicity. More dangerous from my perspective, however, is her insistence that *hierarchy* is the governing principle in Paul's relational matrix, depicting Jews as the honored and superior subgroup within the people of God. There is little doubt that this reading of Paul goes a long way towards assuaging Christian anti-Judaism, but it does so by merely inverting the old scourge of theological imperialism, rather than rooting it out. In addition, her reading fails to account sufficiently for Pauline texts that challenge this view of Jewish privilege and hierarchy. For example, traditional accounts of Christian hierarchy are not without textual warrant, given that Gal. 3.28; Phil. 3.8; and 2 Cor. 3.7-11 all suggest that Paul would have put 'in-Christness' at the apex of his schema, regardless of birth ethnicity. In my judgement, Hodge's interpretation has also underestimated the impact of Paul's apocalypticism with respect to intergroup relations; Paul had no interest in establishing hierarchical relationships among peoples in his social matrix, because, as shown in Chapter 5, his social matrix was temporary as he looked forward to the eschatological reunification of Ἰσραὴλ κατὰ σάρκα and Ἰσραὴλ κατὰ πνεῦμα.

It is true, as Hodge notes, that given the history of Christian anti-Judaism, interpreters must be aware of the context in which their interpretations appear. Yet, with her, I would maintain that this awareness must nuance the appropriation or significance of the interpretation, and not the interpretation itself. No matter how uncomfortable it may be for twenty-first-century readers, I think that Paul did preach the apocalyptic creation of a new community in Christ, modeled on but separate from the people of his birth, a new race centered on a new faith principle. If his differentiation between the church and Jews later became fodder for anti-Jewish sentiment in the years and centuries since Paul, this was caused no doubt by the erosion among his followers of his own love for the Jewish people and his convictions about God's never-ending faithfulness to them.

Nevertheless, interpreters should be aware of their times and the contexts into which their work emerges. Thus, cognizant of this present post-Shoah, postcolonial moment, we can appeal to Howard Winant's racial formation theory as a useful heuristic for evaluating interpretations of Paul as racial projects. In Chapter 2, we learned that for a given context Winant identifies a racial project as racist if it creates or perpetuates existing hierarchies among racial groups.[36] Hodge's interpretation endeavors to undermine the existing power imbalance between modern Jews and Christians by reversing it. Attempting to gainsay the common

---

36 Hodge's and my readings of Paul are both essentialist; Hodge's essentialism focuses on descent, whether natural or adopted, and mine focuses as single-mindedly on religious perspectives.

notion that Christianity's non-ethnic universalistic appeal is superior to Judaism's narrow, particularistic culture, Hodge's reading insists that Christianity is not only every bit as particularistic as Judaism, it actually participates in Judaism. Even though this reading challenges the existing ethno-racial imbalances between Christians and Jews, it does so by creating a potentially new power imbalance. While we cannot predict the outcome of such a project, if race relations in the United States are any gauge, her project would only promote a different and equally dysfunctional racial hierarchy based on physical descent.

The narrative basis of my third-race reading of Paul, however, deconstructs the balance of power between Christians and Jews, not by instituting a different hierarchy, but by emphasizing racial mixedness, both in terms of what we mean by 'race' and how we think of 'purity' or 'sameness'. Hybrid identities offer resistance through implicit and explicit boundary crossings that transgress sacrosanct borders; they bring a theoretical destabilization of essentialism that is powerfully disruptive of the status quo. The conception of Christianity as an ethno-racial construct that blends religion, common descent, and social practice effectively challenges the old narrative of Christianity as a neutral, universalistic, race-and-ethnicity-transcendent entity. This reading does not suggest that Christianity transcends race; instead, when it describes Christianity as the third race and Paul as a former Jew, it transgresses by articulating a *trans-racial identity* – not a post-racial identity – by characterizing every Christian as racially blended in terms of their own personal identity and history. In Christ, Paul and other Christians have been transformed from one racial identity to another, and this trans-racial identity construct at once destabilizes modern essentialist constructions of identity and contemporary racial hierarchies.

Moreover, this reading confronts the post-colonial, post-Shoah reader with the idea that hierarchy is not the prevailing relationship between the lineages in Pauline theology; instead, interdependence is the linchpin of Paul's gospel. Indeed, it is my hope that emphasis on this relational dynamic in Paul's thought would not only relieve fears that this third-race reading participates in Christian anti-Judaism, but that this emphasis could help to improve the tenor of the dialogue between Christians and Jews. It would be better for Jewish–Christian dialogue if the conversation could focus on how as separate peoples each group brings unique and necessary insights about God, instead of fixating on competing claims about being God's most favored people.[37] Specifically and with an eye on

---

37 Notice how the tone of this study differs from Frank Thielman's characterization of the typical third-race interpretation: 'These scholars, taking the "traditional" view of Paul's attitude toward the law, have seen Paul as an apostate from Judaism who looked back on his "former manner of life" with scorn and who encouraged other Jews to imitate him in leaving

the power dynamics in modern history, I propose that Jewish–Christian dialogue might improve if the Christian participants in such conversations entered them to recover attitudes about God, faith, life, and practice that have been preserved in the Jewish community, beyond attempting to persuade Jews about the truth of Christian beliefs. Such a tone might recover some of the spirit of mutuality once imagined by the former Jew who never lost his zeal for his birth race, nor ever compromised his fierce and unswerving commitment that he should preach to all, to the Jew first and then also to the Gentiles.

3. *Ethnic Particularity in Christ: Paul and Brad Braxton's* No Longer Slaves

We can develop our understanding of the opportunities in Paul's gospel by interacting with a third reading of Paul, this time one emerging from an African American matrix. In *No Longer Slaves: Galatians and African American Experience*, Brad Braxton describes the contours of African American biblical hermeneutics and pursues a reading of Galatians through this lens as a demonstration of the kinds of interpretive possibilities opened up by this hermeneutic. According to Braxton, African American biblical hermeneutics seeks liberative readings that empower African Americans individually and uplifts them socio-politic-ally, as members of a community bound together by the common experience of being 'dark-skinned in a country that worships whiteness'.[38] Braxton describes this hermeneutic as one that employs reader-response strategies and (1) begins with social experience and the importance of community; (2) reads Scripture as a commentary on the experiences of the African American community; and (3) rejects ruling-class ideologies such as racism. This hermeneutic does not seek to establish itself as 'the proper interpretation of the text'; instead, it offers these readings as valid interpretive possibilities alongside other interpretive models. Such read-ings are especially targeted at people who are 'uninspired by or not helped by traditional white or Eurocentric interpretations'.[39] Braxton maintains

---

the life of Torah for allegiance to Christ. Because Paul's attitude was so bitter toward Judaism, and because Paul felt that Jews had been replaced as the people of God by Christians, these scholars argue, Paul's attitudes planted the seeds of anti-Semitism' (*From Plight to Solution*, p. 123). My study emphasizes (1) Paul's imitation of the function of the law, not denigration of it; (2) Paul's continuing affection for Judaism and the Jewish people; and (3) Paul's understanding of the interdependence of Christians and Jews in God's plan of redemption.

38   Braxton, *No Longer Slaves*, pp. 11, 13. This quoted phrase operates as Braxton's description of the criterion of African American racial identity.

39   Ibid., pp. 17–18.

that the essence of an African American hermeneutic is biblical exposition that has ramifications for present social experience, unlike historical methods that are 'often unwilling to reckon fully with contemporary issues such as racism'.[40]

Braxton also disagrees with Boyarin's interpretation of Paul. Indeed, he offers a reading that arrives at diametrically opposed results. If Boyarin thinks that Pauline theology flattens difference, Braxton insists that Paul's argument in Galatians preserves ethnic particularities among Christians. Braxton's reading primarily depends on his understanding of the key phrase 'works of the law'. In Chapter 5, I argued against the perspective that this phrase applies to a subset of laws and practices. Instead, Paul's arguments against works of the law amount to a wholesale rejection of law as central to identity. By embracing the idea that Paul objects only to specific works of law that inhibit fellowship between Jews and Gentiles, however, Braxton is able to maintain that Paul's opposition to 'Jewish culture' only extends to specific boundary-making Jewish practices. Beyond the issue of these boundary practices, Paul affirms Jewish culture and does not require that Jewish Christians abandon their 'cultural distinctions':[41]

> As long as the works of the law are understood in the context of the Christ event ... then such works are not inherently antithetical to the Christ event. No Jew would have thought that works of the law impugned God's grace. Thus, it was possible for Jewish Christians to continue doing works of the law without nullifying the grace of God manifest in the Christ event.[42]

In Paul's rejection of circumcision as a requirement for Gentile Christians, Braxton sees an affirmation of Gentile Christians' right to exist as Gentiles. Braxton is explicit on this point: 'In other words, Paul preached a law-free gospel among Gentiles in order to insure ethnic diversity in the Church', not obliterating difference but obliterating *dominance*.[43]

---

40   Ibid., p. 29. Braxton's own deft wielding of historical-critical methods throughout his discussion of Galatians underlines the point that historical methods in the hands of Eurocentric interpreters may be *unwilling* rather than *unable* to account for contemporary issues of racism in encounters with the biblical text. Although nothing but historical and literary methods are employed in this book, contemporary issues of racism shape my posture in the exegetical task just as they have shaped the stance of every white male conducting historical-critical analyses, if only by virtue of the kinds of questions asked of the text. My own experience as an African American female who has had her existence labeled, named, and circumscribed by powerful outside Others, prompted the *historical* question that drove this investigation: 'What if "race" or "ethnicity" meant something different to ancient Jews than white-male-dominated modern scholarship has appreciated?'

41   Ibid., pp. 72–76.

42   Ibid., p. 81.

43   Ibid., pp. 90, 94 (emphasis original).

Braxton frequently cites J.D.G. Dunn's work on the phrase 'works of law', in which the focus is on how the 'social function' of the law highlights the distinctiveness of Israel's identity.[44] In Chapter 5 I noted that this interpretation misses the potential conflation of the ideas of identity indicia and criteria, when the law is seen as defining the essence of Jewish identity (criterion), while circumcision and food laws function to 'focus the distinctiveness of Israel's identity' (indicia). If circumcision becomes so identified with Jewish identity, it can stand as a synonym for the law that defines what it means to be Jewish. Thus, Paul's rejection of circumcision as one of a few distinctive 'works of the law' becomes a rejection of the central criterion of Jewish identity and entails a full rejection of Jewish culture. Contrary to Braxton, Paul does not affirm Jewish culture aside from the 'social function of the law', because for Jews like Paul in the period, there *is* no Jewish culture aside from the society-defining function of law.

Further, while I agree with Braxton that Paul rejects the idea that Gentiles have to become Jews, it is by no means clear that this stance is a Pauline endorsement of Gentile identity, as Braxton himself recognizes.[45] Paul goes beyond simply refusing to turn Gentiles into Jews; in Paul's thought, rather, Gentile-born Christians are really no longer Gentiles (1 Cor. 12.2). But it is also true that Paul assumes a greater emotional attachment between Christians who share a biological or geographic origin than between Christians with different origins (Phlm. 16; Rom. 9.2-3). Both his own mission to the uncircumcised and his acknowledgement of Peter's mission to the circumcised recognize that evangelists may be called to preach to different ethnic or racial groups (Gal. 2.7-9). None of this, however, indicates that Paul perceives diverse ethnic identity *within* the new creation identity in Christ (Gal. 3.28). Braxton not only underestimates the radical nature of the transformation of identity through Christ in Pauline thought, but more importantly, with Boyarin, Hodge, and other scholars cited at the end of Chapter 4, he fails to consider that Paul was operating with a different understanding of the nature of ethnic and racial identity than they do. These scholars all assume a modern notion of ethnic and racial identity that is permanent and determined at birth, in contrast to the elastic ancient Jewish understanding of race and ethnicity, which emphasized religion and formed the background for Paul's thought. Even though Paul recognized the persistence of what moderns identify as ethnic differences on the other side of Christian conversion, these differences vanish in importance compared to what constituted racial difference in his eyes – the worship of God διὰ πίστεως Ἰησοῦ Χριστοῦ (Gal. 2.15-21; 3.28).

---

44   Dunn, 'Works of the Law', p. 531.
45   Braxton, *No Longer Slaves*, pp. 70–71.

Braxton's conclusion that Paul worked to establish the legitimacy of ethnic difference in Christ is as faulty as Boyarin's conclusion that Paul obliterated ethnic difference in Christ. Both conclusions assume that the pre-eminence of territorial and genealogical particularity in modern thought is also true of Jews like Paul in the ancient world. This modern emphasis is consistent with and possibly derived from the ancient Greco-Roman models of race and ethnicity discussed in Chapter 3, but not with the ancient Jewish constructs of identity described there. Paul worked to create a unity and common identity in local Christian congregations based on a conviction about how to worship God after the coming of Christ. Indeed, Braxton's vision of separate ethnic Christian enclaves does nothing but baptize post-slavery Christian conditions with respect to the separation of black-born and white-born Gentile Christian communities. Different communities may have different reasons for wanting to maintain the status quo of ethnically and racially separate congregations, but later interpreters cannot blame Paul for this vision, any more than they can blame him when arrogant, armed, and imperialistic powers read themselves into Paul's narrative and take up his gospel.

4. *Race Relations and Paul's Gospel*

As with Hodge's hierarchically ordered Jewish and Gentile lineages, Braxton's ethnically and racially separate Christian communities overlook the importance of the interdependence that is at the heart of Paul's gospel. A major finding of this study is that symbiotic interdependence between peoples is the new creation dialectic at the heart of Paul's conception of Christian identity. According to Paul, God uses and implicates Jews and Gentiles each in the plan of salvation for the other. For ancient Jews and Gentiles, this dialectic operated between peoples who stood on opposite sides of a deep social and religious boundary. According to Paul, God uses this dialectic to fulfill the ancient promises to Israel.

The question remains, however, as to whether there can be a modern appropriation of Paul's understanding of the ethno-racial character of Christian identity. If our earlier consideration of modern conceptions of race suggests that power dynamics and oppression constitute the quintessence of racism in contemporary race relations, then Hodge's inversion of modern Jewish–Christian intergroup power dynamics offers nothing more than a tragically familiar reprise of the status quo. Yet my own observation that Paul routinely subordinates his birth identity to his new racial identity in Christ could prove equally dangerous with reference to personal situationally selected identity if uncritically adopted by already oppressed contemporary ethno-racial groups. Would it be meaningful for white-born Christians to subordinate their whiteness to their in-Christ identity when the construct of whiteness and its privileges remain invisible for the vast majority? On the other hand, while it might be easier for someone who is already oppressed to submit his or her birth identity to a 'better' or 'higher' identity in Christ, would it be healthy or wise to do so? It seems to me that neither of these outcomes significantly challenges the current state of affairs.

Yet the scandal of Paul's gospel is that it preaches a transformed identity, unapologetically demanding that Christians give preference to the Christian race over the birth race. Yet it may be true that Paul's scandalous gospel nevertheless presents an opportunity to reimagine race relations within Christian communities inasmuch as this new race emerges out of a symbiotic interdependence between Jews and Gentiles, a dynamic that might be fruitfully appropriated in the context of modern race relations. The dialectic of interdependence is even better known via the body-of-Christ metaphor in 1 Corinthians 12. Paul's description of the 'body' in this text exhibits the same symbiotic interdependence that we have seen in the dialectic between Jewish and Gentile salvation in Galatians 3–4 and Romans 11. In 1 Corinthians 12, this mutual interdependence is integral to life in Christ and is not restricted to the subject of entrance into the community. Further, the dialectic of interdependence is also a first cousin to the mutual submission of the Pauline ethic in the Christ hymn in Phil. 2.5-11 that sets the framework for the discussion of identity in Phil. 3.3-9. According to Brian Blount, such an ethic does not require that Christians empty themselves of a divinity that they do not have, but that they empty themselves of what they hold most dear.[46]

Current race relations within the Christian confession in the United States manifest a failure to grasp either the racial character of Christian identity or the symbiotic and redemptive nature of the race relations at the theological center of Christian identity. Interdependence and mutuality requires that whites live in a way that eschews an 'unmarked' status and visibly adopt a lifestyle that marks them as members of a distinctive race. As Braxton puts it, it requires that they 'act black':

> 'Black' here is understood metaphorically to mean a thoroughgoing and imaginative attempt on the part of whites to view the world from another vantage point than their current position of privilege and power. Such efforts on the part of white persons, especially those who are Christians, are more than exercises in sympathetic understanding. Such efforts begin to usher in the subversion of traditional power

---

46   Brian K. Blount, *Then the Whisper Put on Flesh: New Testament Ethics in an African American Context* (Nashville: Abingdon, 2001), p. 131.

dynamics that, I believe, typifies an allegiance with the inbreaking kingdom of God.[47]

Even as whites empty themselves of their privilege as an expression of interdependence and mutuality in Christ, the scandal of Paul's gospel would require that, for the sake of Christ, blacks embrace an identity that eschews a group-centered focus on social, economic, and political righteousness to a body-of-Christ-centered focus on these and other issues. Specifically, it means that Christian blacks would foreswear 'nation building' in the church as a substitute for kingdom building in the world, nation building that exchanges the gospel for the American dream.[48] In other words, living life as if race were a matter of theology instead of skin color means that both whites and blacks would have to live life as blood traitors, who each consider the needs of the other over their own, and the needs of Christian kinfolk above all others – no matter what their skin color. White-born and black-born Gentile Christians could only manage such selfless feats of imagination through humble acceptance of the facts of identity mentioned above. Christians no longer favor bonds of allegiance to their birth identity (Phil. 3.3-9; 1 Cor. 12.2); they are ever-conscious that they all are Gentiles who have adopted an alien history and have been transformed into an alien race (Gal. 3.26-29); and they know and live in the transformed reality that is created by God's grace and mercy (Rom. 11.17-24).

As a community, Christians in the United States must recognize how deeply the history of the idea of race is intertwined with the development of the American church. In the United States, the church is an institution that normalizes the effects of slavery. Further, racially separate churches violate the interdependence that would characterize authentic Pauline Christian communities and would allow both black- and white-born Christians a fuller grasp of the nature of redemption. We cannot here fully consider these matters; let it suffice to say that the formation of the white church derived in no small measure from white Christians' failure to

47 Braxton, *No Longer Slaves*, p. 42.

48 I am indebted to Willie Jennings for this idea and for other insights, discussed below, about the effects of race on the formation of the American church. Braxton's comment below provides an illustration of what is meant by African American 'nation building':

> Throughout Galatians 3–4 Paul has labored persistently to demonstrate to the Galatians that they are children of Abraham and rightful heirs of the promises of the covenant blessings.
>
> Galatians 4.1-11 offers crucial insights for the African American liberation movement. Life in twenty-first century America . . . could very well be considered a 'present evil age'. . .
>
> As in the ancient case, so too in the modern, 'the elements of the world' are beings, forces, and *ideologies that would prohibit the promises of America from being disseminated broadly*. (Braxton, *No Longer Slaves*, p. 99; emphasis added)

recognize the quasi-physical transformation involved in new creation identity. Because the gospel changes the nature and status of flesh, a slave's conversion changed the nature of his or her status *and* flesh. Many white theologians and leaders continue to lead their churches happily segregated because they fail to grasp that their own status and flesh are affected by the gospel as well. Forgetting that they are alien Gentiles who have lost their birthright and access to white privilege, these leaders preach a gospel that is disembodied, too often 'spiritual' or symbolic à la Boyarin, and abstracted from a concern for righteousness according to the flesh.

On the other hand, inasmuch as the experience of blackness forced slaves to view their identity as inextricably bound up with their flesh, the experience of slavery and racism helped slaves recognize the fact that the gospel changes the status of flesh.[49] Nevertheless, although the best of the black church tradition preserves a full-bodied worship that acknowledges the radical transformation that occurs in Christ, many leaders of the black church have lost sight of one aspect of the transcendent nature of the gospel message. Racism not only created deep social, economic, and political disparities between blacks and whites, but it also subverted black access to the intellectual tradition and history of the church. The combination of socio-economic hardship and fractured moorings in the intellectual tradition of the church can produce an overemphasis on material matters, such as is exhibited in an isolationist black Christian nationalism or in preaching the perversion that the good news is that Christ gives economic prosperity to the faithful. Again, this subject demands thorough treatment on its own, but at a minimum it can be said that the body of Christ in this country is impoverished because aspects of the transformative effects of the gospel have been preserved in separate segments of the church, each handicapped by the lack of the other.

Paul's gospel renounces every attempt to normalize community relations around a set of social conventions, practices, behaviors, or appearances that belong to the powerful. In fact, Boyarin makes an attractive proposal when he advocates a 'Diaspora identity' that eschews power, homeland, and other manifestations of autochthony while preserving community and a distinctive ethnic (or racial) identity. A racial construction of Christian identity that embraces powerlessness and exile along with the transformation of racial and ethnic birth identity that occurs in Christ would not only preserve the best of Jewish being-in-the-world as Boyarin maintains, but also the best of pre-Constantinian Pauline Christianity. When Christians suspend the bonds of allegiance to

---

49   For more information on the formation and deformation of a slave's bodily identity see Anthony Pinn, *Terror and Triumph: The Nature of Black Religion* (Minneapolis: Fortress, 2003).

their birth identity even as they preserve the memory of having been born Gentiles who were 'aliens from the commonwealth of Israel and strangers to the covenants of promise' (Eph. 2.12), they manifest a Christianity that offers hope to a society desperate for racial reconciliation. These Christians demonstrate that they are Paul's intellectual heirs and blood traitors on behalf of the blood of Christ.

APPENDIX

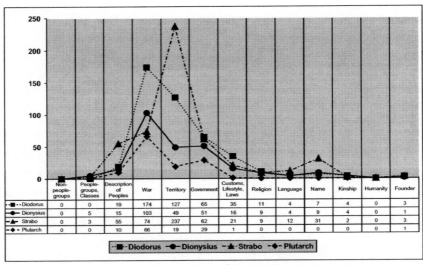

Figure A.1 – Ideas Associated with Ἔθνος in Non-Jewish Authors

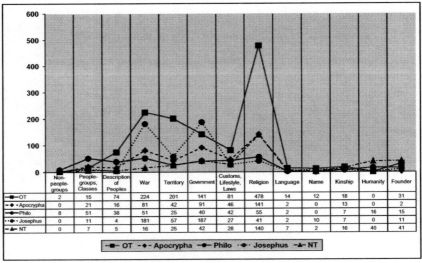

Figure A.2 – Ideas Associated with Ἔθνος in Jewish and Christian Authors

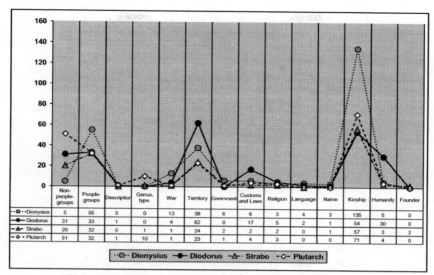

	Non-people-groups	People-groups	Description	Genus, type	War	Territory	Government	Customs and Laws	Religion	Language	Name	Kinship	Humanity	Founder
··O·· Dionysius	5	55	0	0	13	38	6	6	3	4	3	135	5	0
●Diodorus	31	33	1	0	4	62	0	17	5	2	1	54	30	0
△Strabo	20	32	0	1	1	24	2	2	2	0	1	57	3	2
◇Plutarch	51	32	1	10	1	23	1	4	3	0	0	71	4	0

··O·· Dionysius ●Diodorus △Strabo ◇Plutarch

Figure A.3 – Ideas Associated with Γένος in Non-Jewish Authors

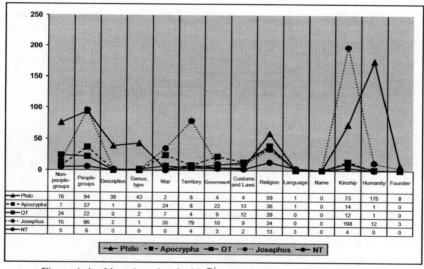

	Non-people-groups	People-groups	Description	Genus, type	War	Territory	Government	Customs and Laws	Religion	Language	Name	Kinship	Humanity	Founder
▲Philo	76	94	39	43	2	8	4	4	59	1	0	73	175	8
■Apocrypha	7	37	1	0	24	8	22	13	36	1	0	14	1	0
■OT	24	22	0	2	7	4	9	12	39	0	0	12	1	0
●Josephus	15	96	2	1	35	79	10	9	34	0	0	198	12	3
●NT	5	6	0	0	0	4	3	2	13	3	0	4	0	0

▲Philo ■Apocrypha ■OT ●Josephus ●NT

Figure A.4 – Ideas Associated with Γένος in Jewish and Christian Authors

Bibliography

Alexander, Clare, 'Beyond Black: Rethinking the Colour/Culture Divide', *Ethnic and Racial Studies* 25.4 (2002): 552–71.

Alston, Richard, 'Changing Ethnicities: From the Egyptian to the Roman City', in Tim Cornell and Kathryn Lomas (eds), *Gender and Ethnicity in Ancient Italy* (London: Accordia Research Institute, University of London, 1997), pp. 85–86.

Aristotle, *Politics* (trans. H. Rackham; LCL; Cambridge, MA: Harvard University Press, 1972).

Arrian, *Epicteti dissertationes*, 1.22.4, trans. Menahem Stern, in *Greek and Latin Authors on Jews and Judaism with Introductions, Translations and Commentary* (2 vols; Jerusalem: The Israel Academy of Sciences and Humanities, 1974–1980), 1.542.

Augustine, *The Letters*, in J.-P. Migne (ed.), *Patrologia latina* (162 vols; Paris: 1857–1886), vol. 33, cols 637–38.

——*The Letters*, in R.J. Deferrari (ed.), *Fathers of the Church: A New Translation* (trans. Sister Wilfrid Parsons; New York: Fathers of the Church, 1953).

Aune, David E., 'Recent Readings of Paul Relating to Justification by Faith', in David E. Aune (ed.), *Rereading Paul Together: Protestant and Catholic Perspectives on Justification* (Grand Rapids: Baker Academic, 2006), pp. 188–245.

Azoulay, Katya Gibel, *Black, Jewish and Interracial: It's Not the Color of Your Skin, But The Race of Your Kin, and Other Myths of Identity* (Durham: Duke University Press, 1997).

Bailey, Randall (ed.), *Yet with a Steady Beat: Contemporary U.S. Afrocentric Biblical Interpretation* (Atlanta: Society of Biblical Literature, 2003).

Baker, Lee D., *From Savage to Negro: Anthropology and the Construction of Race, 1896–1954* (Berkeley and Los Angeles: University of California Press, 1998).

——'The Color Blind Bind', in Ida Susser and Thomas C. Patterson (eds), *Cultural Diversity in the United States* (Malden, MA: Blackwell, 2001), pp. 103–19.

Balsdon, J.P.V.D., *Romans and Aliens* (Chapel Hill: University of North Carolina Press, 1979).

Banton, Michael, *Racial and Ethnic Competition* (Cambridge: Cambridge University Press, 1983).

——*Racial Theories* (Cambridge: Cambridge University Press, 1987).

Barclay, John M.G., *Obeying the Truth: A Study of Paul's Ethics in Galatians* (Edinburgh: T&T Clark, 1988).

——'Paul among Diaspora Jews: Anomaly or Apostate?' *JSNT* 60 (1995): 89–120.

——*Jews in the Mediterranean Diaspora* (Berkeley, Los Angeles, and London: University of California Press, 1996).

——'Paul and Philo on Circumcision: Romans 2.25–29 in Social and Cultural Context', *NTS* 44 (1998): 536–56.

Barker, M., *The New Racism* (London: Junction Books, 1981).

Barrett, C.K., *A Commentary on the First Epistle to the Corinthians* (London: A&C Clark, 2nd edn, 1971).

——*The First Epistle to the Corinthians* (New York and London: Harper & Row, 2nd edn, 1971).

Barth, Fredrik, 'Introduction', in Fredrik Barth (ed.), *Ethnic Groups and Boundaries: The Social Organization of Culture Difference* (London: Allen and Unwin, 1969), pp. 9–38.

Barth, M., 'The Faith of the Messiah', *HeyJ* 10 (1969): 363–70.

Barton, Stephen, 'All Things to All People: Paul and the Law in the Light of 1 Corinthians 9.19-23', in James D.G. Dunn (ed.), *Paul and the Mosaic Law* (Tübingen: J.C.B. Mohr [Paul Siebeck], 1996), pp. 271–85.

Baumann, Gerd, *The Multicultural Riddle: Rethinking National, Ethnic, and Religious Identities* (New York and London: Routledge, 1999).

Betz, Hans Dieter, *Galatians: A Commentary on Paul's Letter to the Churches in Galatia* (Philadelphia: Fortress, 1979).

Bhabha, Homi, *The Location of Culture* (New York: Routledge, 1994).

Bhatt, Chetan, 'Contemporary Geopolitics and "Alterity" Research', in Martim Bulmer and John Solomos (eds), *Researching Race and Racism* (London and New York: Routledge, 2004), pp. 16–36.

Blount, Brian K., *Then the Whisper Put on Flesh: New Testament Ethics in an African American Context* (Nashville: Abingdon, 2001).

Bockmuehl, Markus, *The Epistle to the Philippians* (London: A&C Black and Henrickson, 1998).

Bonneau, Norman, 'The Logic of Paul's Argument on the Curse of the Law in Galatians 3.10-14', *NovT* 39 (1997): 60–80.

Bornkamm, G., 'The Missionary Stance of Paul in Acts and his Letters', in L. Keck and J.L. Martyn (eds), *Studies in Luke-Acts* (Nashville: Abingdon, 1966), pp. 194–207.

——*Das Ende des Gesetzes* (Munich: Chr. Kaiser Verlag, 1966).

Borse, Udo, *Der Brief an die Galater* (Regensburg: Friedrich Pustet, 1955).

Bourke, Myles M., *A Study of the Metaphor of the Olive Tree in Romans XI* (Washington, DC: Paulist Press, 1947).

Boyarin, Daniel, *A Radical Jew: Paul and the Politics of Identity* (Berkeley: University of California Press, 1994).

——*Border Lines: The Partition of Judaeo-Christianity* (Philadelphia: University of Pennsylvania Press, 2004).

Braxton, Brad, *No Longer Slaves: Galatians and African American Experience* (Collegeville, MN: Liturgical Press, 2002).

Brodkin, Karen, *How Jews Became White Folks and What That Says about Race in America* (New Brunswick: Rutgers University Press, 2000).

Brown, Michael Joseph, *Blackening of the Bible: The Aims of African American Biblical Scholarship* (Harrisburgh, PA, London, and New York: Trinity Press International, 2004).

Bruce, F.F., *The Epistle to the Galatians* (Grand Rapids: Eerdmans, 1982).

Brunsma, David L., 'Mixed Messages: Doing Race in the Color-Blind Era', in David L. Brunsma (ed.), *Mixed Messages: Multiracial Identities in the 'Color Blind' Era* (Boulder, CO: Lynne Rienner Publishers, 2006), pp. 1–11.

Buell, Denise Kimber, 'Rethinking the Relevance of Race for Early Christian Self-Definition', *HTR* 94.4 (2001): 449–76.

——*Why This New Race? Ethnic Reasoning in Early Christianity* (New York: Columbia University Press, 2005).

Buell, Denise Kimber and Caroline Johnson Hodge, 'The Politics of Interpretation: The Rhetoric of Race and Ethnicity in Paul', *JBL* 123.2 (2004): 235–51.

Bulmer, Martin, and John Solomos, 'Introduction: Rethinking Ethnic and Racial Studies', *Ethnic and Racial Studies* 21.5 (1998): 822–25.

Bultmann, Rudolf, *Theology of the New Testament* (trans. Kendrick Grobel; 2 vols; New York: Charles Scribner's Sons, 1951–1955).

Burton, Ernest De Witt, *The Epistle to the Galatians* (ICC; Edinburgh: T&T Clark, 1921).

Byrne, Brendan, *Romans* (Sacra Pagina, 6; Collegeville, MN: Liturgical Press, 1996).

Byron, Gay, *Symbolic Blackness and Ethnic Difference in Early Christian Literature* (London: Routledge, 2002).

Campbell, Douglas A., 'Determining the Gospel through Rhetorical Analysis in Paul's Letter to the Roman Christians', in L. Ann Jervis and Peter Richardson (eds), *Gospel in Paul: Studies on Corinthians, Galatians and Romans for Richard N. Longenecker* (JSNTSS; Sheffield: Sheffield Academic Press, 1994), pp. 314–36.

Carras, George P., 'Romans 2,1–29: A Dialogue on Jewish Ideals', *Biblica* 73.2 (1992): 183–207.

Carson, D.A., Peter T. O'Brien, and Mark A. Seifrid (eds), *Justification and Variegated Nomism: A Fresh Appraisal of Paul and Second Temple Judaism* (Tübingen: Mohr Siebeck; Grand Rapids: Baker Academic, 2001).

Charlesworth, James (ed.), *The Old Testament Pseudepigrapha* (2 vols; New York: Doubleday, 1983).

Cohen, Shaye, *Josephus in Galilee and Rome: His Vitae and Development as a Historian* (Columbia Studies in the Classical Tradition, 8; Leiden: Brill, 1979).

——'Respect for Judaism by Gentiles According to Josephus', *HTR* 80 (1987): 409–30.

——'"Ἰουδαῖος τὸ γένος" and Related Expressions in Josephus', in Fausto Parente and Joseph Sievers (eds), *Josephus and the History of the Greco-Roman Period: Essays in Memory of Morton Smith* (Leiden and New York: E.J. Brill, 1994), pp. 23–38.

——*The Beginnings of Jewishness* (Berkeley: University of California Press, 1999).

Collins, John J., *Between Athens and Jerusalem: Jewish Identity in the Hellenistic Diaspora* (Grand Rapids: Eerdmans, 2nd edn, 2000).

Connor, W., *Ethnonationalism: The Quest for Understanding* (Princeton: Princeton University Press, 2004).

Conzelmann, Hans, *A Commentary on the First Epistle to the Corinthians* (trans. James W. Leitch; Philadelphia: Fortress Press, 1975).

Cornell, Stephan, 'That's the Story of Our Life', in Paul Spickard and W. Jeffrey Burroughs (eds), *We Are a People: Narrative and Multiplicity in Constructing Ethnic Identity* (Philadelphia: Temple University Press, 2000), pp. 41–53.

Cornell, Tim, 'Ethnicity as a Factor in Early Roman History', in Tim Cornell and Kathryn Lomas (eds), *Gender and Ethnicity in Ancient Italy* (London: Accordia Research Institute, University of London, 1997), pp. 9–22.

Cornell, Tim, and Kathryn Lomas (eds), *Gender and Ethnicity in Ancient Italy* (London: Accordia Research Institute, University of London, 1997).

Cosgrove, Charles, *The Cross and the Spirit: A Study in the Argument and Theology of Galatians* (Macon: Mercer University Press, 1988).

——'Did Paul Value Ethnicity?' *CBQ* 68 (2006), pp. 268–90.

Cousar, Charles B., *A Theology of the Cross* (Minneapolis: Fortress, 1990).

Cranfield, C.E.B., *The Epistle to the Romans* (2 vols; Edinburgh: T&T Clark, 1975).

——*Romans, A Shorter Commentary* (Grand Rapids: Eerdmans, 1985).

Dahl, Nils A., 'Der Name Israel: Zur Auslegung von Gal.6,16', *Judaica* 6 (1950): 161–70.

——*Studies in Paul: Theology for Early Christian Mission* (Minneapolis: Augsburg, 1977).

Daniels, Jessie, *White Lies: Race, Class, Gender, and Sexuality in White Supremacist Discourse* (New York: Routledge, 1997).

Davies, W.D., 'Paul and the People of Israel', *NTS* 24.10 (1977): 4–39.

——*Paul and Rabbinic Judaism: Some Rabbinic Elements in Pauline Theology*, with a Foreword by E.P. Sanders and a Biographical Overview by Dale C. Allison Jr. (Mifflintown, PA: Sigler Press, 1998).

Davis, F. James, 'Defining Race: Comparative Perspectives', in David L. Brunsma (ed.), *Mixed Messages: Multiracial Identities in the 'Color-Blind' Era* (Boulder, CO, and London: Lynn Rienner, 2006), pp. 15–31.

De Silva, David A., *Introducing the Apocrypha: Message, Context, and Significance* (Grand Rapids: Baker Academic, 2002).

Diodorus Siculus (trans. C.H. Oldfather; 12 vols; LCL; Cambridge, MA: Harvard University Press; London: W. Heinemann, 1933–1967).

Dionysius Halicarnassus (trans. Earnest Cary; 7 vols; LCL; London: W. Heinemann; Cambridge, MA: Harvard University Press, 1937–1950).

Dodd, Brian J., 'Christ's Slave, People Pleasers and Galatians 10', *NTS* 42 (1996): 90–104.

Dominguez, Virginia R., 'Invoking Culture: The Messy Side of Cultural Politics', in Marianna Torgovnick (ed.), *Eloquent Obsessions: Writing Cultural Difference* (Durham: Duke University Press, 1994), pp. 237–57.

Donaldson, T.L., 'The "Curse of the Law" and the Inclusion of the Gentiles: Galatians 3.13–14', *NTS* 32 (1986): 94–112.

Dube, Musa, *Postcolonial Feminist Biblical Interpretation* (St. Louis, MO: Chalice Press, 2000).

Dunn, James D.G., 'The New Perspective on Paul', *Bulletin of the John Rylands University Library of Manchester* 65.2 (1983): 95–122.

——'Works of the Law and the Curse of the Law (Galatians 3.10-14)', *NTS* 31 (1985): 523–42.

——*Romans* (2 vols; WBC; Dallas: Word Books, 1988).

——*Jesus, Paul and the Law: Studies in Mark and Galatians* (Louisville: Westminster John Knox, 1990).

——*The Epistles to the Colossians and Philemon* (Grand Rapids: Eerdmans, 1996).

——'Who Did Paul Think He Was? A Study of Jewish–Christian Identity', *NTS* 45 (1999): 174–93.

Ehrman, Bart (ed.), *Apostolic Fathers* (2 vols; LCL; Cambridge, MA, and London: Harvard University Press, 2003).

Elliott, Neil, *The Rhetoric of Romans* (JSNTSS, 45; Sheffield: JSOT Press, 1990).

Ellis, E.E., *Prophecy and Hermeneutic* (Tübingen: J.C.B. Mohr [Paul Siebeck], 1978).

Esler, Philip, *Conflict and Identity in Romans: The Social Setting of Paul's Letter* (Minneapolis: Augsburg Fortress, 2003).

Fee, Gordon, *The First Epistle to the Corinthians* (NICNT; Grand Rapids: Eerdmans, 1987).

——*Paul's Letter to the Philippians* (NICNT; Grand Rapids: Eerdmans, 1995).

Felder, Cain Hope, *Troubling Biblical Waters: Race, Class and Family* (Maryknoll, NY: Orbis Books, 1989).

Felder, Cain Hope (ed.), *Stony the Road We Trod: African American Biblical Interpretation* (Minneapolis: Fortress, 1991).

Finley, M.I., *The Use and Abuse of History* (New York, Harmondsworth, England, and Victoria, Australia: Penguin, rev. edn, 1975, 1987).

Fitzmyer, Joseph A., *Romans* (AB; New York: Doubleday, 1993).

Fowl, Stephen, Review of *A Radical Jew: Paul and the Politics of Identity* by Daniel Boyarin, *Modern Theology* 12 (1996): 131–33.

Gager, John G., *The Origins of Anti-Semitism: Attitudes toward Judaism in Pagan and Christian Antiquity* (New York: Oxford University Press, 1983).

Gans, Herbert, 'Symbolic Ethnicity: The Future of Ethnic Groups and Cultures in America', *Ethnic and Racial Studies* 2 (1979): 1–20.

——'Symbolic Ethnicity and Symbolic Religiosity: Towards a Comparison of Ethnic and Religious Acculturation', *Ethnic and Racial Studies* 17.4 (1994): 577–92.

Gaston, Lloyd, 'Israel's Enemies in Pauline Theology', *NTS* 28 (1982): 400–23.

——*Paul and the Torah* (Vancouver: University of British Columbia Press, 1987).

Gaventa, Beverly, Review of *A Radical Jew: Paul and the Politics of Identity* by Daniel Boyarin, *Theology Today* 52.2 (1995): 290.

Geertz, Clifford, *The Interpretation of Cultures* (New York: Basic Books, 1973).

Gilroy, Paul, *Against Race: Imagining Political Culture beyond the Color Line* (Cambridge, MA: Harvard University Press, 2000).

Glancey, Jennifer, *Slavery in Early Christianity* (Minneapolis: Fortress, 2006).

Goldenberg, David M., *The Curse of Ham: Race and Slavery in Early Judaism, Christianity, and Islam* (Princeton: Princeton University Press, 2003).

Goodenough, Erwin Ramsdell, *An Introduction to Philo Judaeus* (Oxford: Blackwell, 2nd edn, 1962).

Goppelt, Leonhard, 'Paulus und die Heilsgeschichte: Schlussfolgerungen aus Röm. IV und 1 Kor. X. 1–13', *NTS* 13 (1966): 31–42.

Grosby, Steven, 'Religion and Nationality in Antiquity', *European Journal of Sociology* 32 (1991): 229–65.

Grosheide, F.W., *Commentary on the First Epistle to the Corinthians* (Grand Rapids: Eerdmans, 1953).

Hall, Jonathon, *Ethnic Identity in Greek Antiquity* (Cambridge: Cambridge University Press, 1997).

——*Hellenicity* (Cambridge: Cambridge University Press, 2002).

——'New Ethnicities', in Linda Martin Alcoff and Eduardo Mendieta (eds), *Identities: Race, Class, Gender, and Nationality* (Malden, Oxford, and Melbourne: Blackwell, 2003).

Harmon, Amy, 'Love Ya K2a2a, Whoever You Are', *New York Times*, 22 January 2006.

Harnack, Adolph, *The Mission and Expansion of Christianity in the First Three Centuries* (trans. and ed. James Moffat; New York: G.P. Putnam's Sons; London: Williams and Norgate, 1908).

Harvey, Graham, *The True Israel: Uses of the Names Jew, Hebrew, and Israel in Ancient Judaism and Early Christian Literature* (Leiden: E.J. Brill, 1996).

Hawthorne, Gerald F., *Philippians* (WBC; Waco, TX: Word Books, 1983).

Hays, R.B., ' "Have We Found Abraham to Be Our Forefather According to the Flesh?" A Reconsideration of Rom. 4.1', *NTS* 27 (1985): 76–98.

——*Echoes of Scripture in the Letters of Paul* (New Haven: Yale University Press, 1989).

——' "The Gospel Is the Power of God for Gentiles Only"? A Critique of Stanley K. Stowers' *A Rereading of Romans*', *Critical Review of Books in Religion* 9 (1996), pp. 27–44.

——*First Corinthians* (Louisville: John Knox Press, 1997).

——'The Letter to the Galatians', in Leander Keck (ed.), *The New Interpreter's Bible* (Nashville: Abingdon, 2000), 11.183–348.

——*The Conversion of the Imagination: Paul as an Interpreter of Scripture* (Grand Rapids and Cambridge: Eerdmans, 2002).

——*The Faith of Jesus Christ: An Investigation of the Narrative Substructure of Gal. 3.1–4.11* (Grand Rapids and Cambridge: Eerdmans, 2nd edn, 2002).

Hecht, Richard, 'The Exegetical Contexts of Philo's Interpretation of Circumcision', in Fredrick E. Greenspahn, Earle Hilgert, and Burton Mack (eds), *Nourished with Peace: Studies in Hellenistic Judaism in Memory of Samuel Sandmel* (Chico, CA: Scholars Press, 1984), pp. 51–79.

Herodotus, *History* (trans. A.D. Godley; 4 vols; LCL; Cambridge, MA: Harvard University Press; London: W. Heinemann, 1926–1938).

Hinnells, John R. (ed.), *The New Dictionary of Religions* (Oxford: Blackwell, rev. edn, 1995).

Hirschman, Charles, 'The Rise and Fall of the Concept of Race' (unpublished paper, 26 August 2003).

Hoberman, John, *Darwin's Athletes: How Sports Has Damaged Black America and Preserved the Myth of Race* (Boston: Houghton Mifflin, 1997).

Hodge, Caroline Johnson, *If Sons then Heirs: A Study of Kinship and Ethnicity in the Letters of Paul* (New York: Oxford University Press, 2007).

Holtz, Traugott, 'Zum Selbstverständnis des Apostels Paulus', *Theologische Literaturzeitung* 91.5 (1966): 321–30.

hooks, bell, *Outlaw Culture: Resisting Representation* (New York and London: Routledge, 1994).

Horn, Friedrich Wilhelm, 'Der Verzicht auf die Beschneidung im Frühen Christentum', *NTS* 42 (1996): 479–505.

Hornblower, Simon, and Antony Spawforth (eds), *Oxford Classical Dictionary* (Oxford: Oxford University Press, 3rd rev. edn, 2003).

Horowitz, Donald, 'Ethnic Identity', in N. Glazer and D. Moynihan (eds), *Ethnicity: Theory and Experience* (Cambridge: Cambridge University Press, 1975), pp. 111–40.

——*Ethnic Groups and Conflict* (Berkeley: University of California Press, 1985).

——*The Deadly Ethnic Riot* (Los Angeles: University of California Press, 2001).

Horsley, G.H.R., *New Documents Illustrating Early Christianity* (Ancient History Documentary Research Centre, Macquarie University; Alexandria, Australia: J. Bell and Co., 1982).

Isaac, Benjamin, *The Invention of Racism in Classical Antiquity* (Princeton and Oxford: Princeton University Press, 2004).

Jacobson, Jessica, 'Religion and Ethnicity: Dual and Alternative Sources of Identity among Young British Pakistanis', *Ethnic and Racial Studies* 20.2 (April 1997): 238–56.

Jacobson, Matthew Frye, *Whiteness of a Different Color: European Immigrants and the Alchemy of Race* (Cambridge, MA: Harvard University Press, 1998).

Jaffe, Martin, *Early Judaism* (Upper Saddle River, NJ: Prentice-Hall, 1997).

Jenkins, Richard, 'Social Anthropological Models of Inter-Ethnic Relations', in John Rex and David Mason (eds), *Theories of Race and Ethnic Relations* (Cambridge: Cambridge University Press, 1986), pp. 170–86.

——*Rethinking Ethnicity: Arguments and Explorations* (London: Sage Publications, 1997).

Jewett, Robert, *Paul's Anthropological Terms: A Study of Their Use in Conflict Settings* (Arbeiten zur Geschichte des antiken Judentum und Urchristentums, 10; Leiden: Brill, 1971).

Johnson, L.T., 'Romans 3.21–26 and the Faith of Jesus', *CBQ* 44 (1982): 77–90.

Jordan, Winthrop D., *The White Man's Burden: The Historical Origins of Racism in the United States* (New York: Oxford University Press, 1974).

Josephus (trans. H.St.J. Thackeray; 10 vols; LCL; Cambridge, MA: Harvard University Press, 1926–1965).

Kahl, Birgitt, 'No Longer Male: Masculinity Struggles behind Galatians 3.28?' *JSNT* 79 (2000): 37–49.

Käsemann, Ernst, *Commentary on Romans* (trans. Geoffrey Bromiley; Grand Rapids: Eerdmans, 1980).

Kidd, Colin, *The Forging of Races: Race and Scripture in the Protestant Atlantic World, 1600–2000* (Cambridge: Cambridge University Press, 2006).

Kim, Seyoon, *Paul and the New Perspective: Second Thoughts on the Origin of Paul's Gospel* (Tübingen: Mohr Siebeck, 2002).

Koester, Helmut, 'φψσιϛ', *TDNT* 9.272.

Lambrecht, Jan, 'Abraham and His Offspring: A Comparison of Galatians 5,1 with 3,13', *Biblica* 80.4 (1999): 525–36.

Laurence, Ray, 'Territory, Ethnonyms, and Geography: The Construction of Identity in Roman Italy', in Ray Laurence and Joanne Berry (eds), *Cultural Identity in the Roman Empire* (New York: Routledge, 1998), pp. 95–110.

Laurence, Ray, and Joanne Berry (eds), *Cultural Identity in the Roman Empire* (New York: Routledge, 1998).

Leroi, Armand Marie, 'A Family Tree in Every Gene', *New York Times*, 14 March 2005.

Lewis, Lloyd, 'An African American Appraisal of the Philemon – Paul – Onesiumus Triangle', in Cain Hope Felder (ed.), *Stony the Road We Trod: African American Biblical Interpretation* (Minneapolis: Fortress Press, 1991), pp. 232–46.

Lightfoot, J.B., *Saint Paul's Epistle to the Galatians* (London and New York: MacMillan, 10th edn, 1890).

——*Notes on the Epistles of St. Paul* (London: MacMillan, 1895).

Lohse, Eduard, *Colossians and Philemon* (trans. William Poehlmann; Hermeneia; Philadelphia: Fortress, 1971).

Lomas, Kathryn, 'Constructing "The Greek": Ethnic Identity in Magna Graecia', in Tim Cornell and Kathryn Lomas (eds), *Gender and Ethnicity in Ancient Italy* (London: Accordia Research Institute, University of London, 1997), pp. 31–42.

——'Introduction', in Tim Cornell and Kathryn Lomas (eds), *Gender and*

Ethnicity in Ancient Italy (London: Accordia Research Institute, University of London, 1997), pp. 1–8.

Longenecker, Richard, *Galatians* (WBC; Dallas: Word Books, 1990).

Loomba, Ania, *Colonialism and Postcolonialism* (New York: Routledge, 2nd edn, 2005).

Lüdemann, Gerd, *Paulus und das Judentum* (Munich: Chr. Kaiser Verlag, 1983).

Lull, David, ' "Pneuma" in Paul's Letter to the Churches of Galatia: An Interpretation of the Spirit in Light of Early Christian Experience in Galatia, Paul's Message to the Galatians, and Theology Today' (unpublished doctoral dissertation, Claremont Graduate University, 1978).

Luz, Ulrich, *Das Geschichtsverständnis des Paulus* (Munich: Chr. Kaiser, 1968).

Malik, Kenan, *The Meaning of Race* (New York: New York University Press, 1996).

Malkin, Irad (ed.), *Ancient Perceptions of Greek Ethnicity* (Cambridge, MA: Harvard University Press, 2001).

Marcus, Joel, 'The Circumcision and the Uncircumcision in Rome', *NTS* 35 (1989): 67–81.

Mason, David, 'Introduction: Controversies and Continuities in Race and Ethnic Relations Theory', in John Rex and David Mason (eds), *Theories of Race and Ethnic Relations* (Cambridge: Cambridge University Press, 1986), pp. 1–19.

Mason, Steve, *Understanding Josephus* (Journal for the Study of the Pseudepigrapha Supplement Series, 32; Sheffield: Sheffield Academic Press, 1998).

Martin, Dale B., *Slavery as Salvation: The Metaphor of Slavery in Pauline Christianity* (New Haven and London: Yale University Press, 1990).

Martin, Ralph, *Colossians and Philemon* (Frome and London: Butler and Tanner, 1974).

Martyn, J.L., *Galatians* (AB; New York: Doubleday, 1997).

——*Theological Issues in the Letters of Paul* (Nashville: Abingdon, 1997).

McKnight, Scott, *A Light among the Gentiles: Jewish Missionary Activity in the Second Temple Period* (Minneapolis: Fortress, 1991).

Meeks, Wayne, *The First Urban Christians* (New Haven and London: Yale University Press, 1983).

Merklein, Helmut, ' "Nicht aus Werken des Gesetzes . . .", Eine Auslegung von Gal 2,15–21', in Helmut Merklein, Karlheinz Müller, and Günter Stemberger (eds), *Bibel in jüdischer und christlicher Tradition* (Bonn: Anton Hain, 1993), pp. 121–36.

Miles, Richard, *Constructing Identities in Late Antiquity* (London: Routledge, 1999).

Millar, Fergus, *The Roman Near East: 31 BC – AD 337* (Cambridge, MA, and London: Harvard University Press, 1993).

Mitchell, Margaret M., *Paul and the Rhetoric of Reconciliation: An Exegetical Investigation of the Language and Composition of 1 Corinthians* (Louisville: Westminster John Knox, 1993).

Moo, Douglas, *The Epistle to the Romans* (NICNT; Grand Rapids and Cambridge: Eerdmans, 1996).

Moule, C.F.D., *The Epistles of Paul the Apostle to the Colossians and to Philemon* (Cambridge: Cambridge University Press, 1957).

Munck, Johannes, *Paul and the Salvation of Mankind* (trans. Frank Clarke; Richmond, VA: John Knox Press, 1959).

Murray, John, *The Epistle to the Romans: The English Text with Introduction, Exposition and Notes* (Grand Rapids: Eerdmans, 1985).

Mussner, Franz, *Der Galaterbrief* (Freiburg, Basel, and Vienna: Herder, 1974).

Niebuhr, Karl-Wilhelm, *Heidenapostel aus Israel: Die jüdische Identität des Paulus nach ihrer Darstellung in seinen Briefen* (Tübingen: J.C.B. Mohr, 1992).

Norval, Aletta, 'Thinking Identities: Against a Theory of Ethnicity', in Edwin N. Wilmsen and Patrick McAllister (eds), *The Politics of Difference* (Chicago and London: University of Chicago, 1996), pp. 59–70.

O'Brien, Peter, *Colossians, Philemon* (WBC; Waco, TX: Word Books, 1982).

Omi, Michael, and Howard Winant, *Racial Formation in the United States: From the 1960s to the 1990s* (New York and London: Routledge, 2nd edn, 1994).

Oommen, T.K., 'Race, Ethnicity and Class: An Analysis of Interrelationships', *International Social Sciences Journal* 46.1 (1994): 83–93.

Özkirimli, Umut, *Theories of Nationalism* (New York: St. Martin's Press, 2000).

Paget, James Charles, 'Jewish Proselytism at the Time of Christian Origins: Chimera or Reality?' *JSNT* 62 (1996): 65–103.

Parsons, Talcott, 'Some Theoretical Considerations on the Nature and Trends of Change of Ethnicity', in N. Glazer and D. Moynihan (eds), *Ethnicity: Theory and Experience* (Cambridge: Cambridge University Press, 1975), pp. 53–83.

Persius, *Satirae*, trans. Menahem Stern, in *Greek and Latin Authors on Jews and Judaism with Introductions, Translations and Commentary* (2 vols; Jerusalem: The Israel Academy of Sciences and Humanities, 1974–1980), 1.436-37.

Peterson, Jeffrey, 'Review of Stanley Stower's *A Rereading of Romans*', *Restoration Quarterly* 39.1 (1997): 50–53.

Petersen, Norman R., *Rediscovering Paul: Philemon and the Sociology of Paul's Narrative World* (Philadelphia: Fortress, 1975).

Philo of Alexandria (trans. F.H. Colson and G.H. Whitaker; 10 vols; LCL; Cambridge, MA: Harvard University Press, 1929–1962).

Phoenix, Ann, 'Dealing with Difference: The Recursive and the New', *Ethnic and Racial Studies* 21.5 (1998): 859–80.

Pinn, Anthony, *Terror and Triumph: The Nature of Black Religion* (Minneapolis: Fortress, 2003).

Platvoet, Jan, 'The Definers Defined', *Method and Theory in the Study of Religion* 2 (Fall, 1990): 180–212.

Plutarch, *Lives* (trans. Bernadotte Perrin; 11 vols; LCL; London: W. Heinemann; New York: G.P. Putnam, 1917–1951).

——*Moralia* (trans. Frank Cole Babbitt; 14 vols; LCL; London: W. Heinemann; New York: G.P. Putnam, 1927).

——*De superstitione* 8, trans. Menahem Stern, in *Greek and Latin Authors on Jews and Judaism with Introductions, Translations and Commentary* (2 vols; Jerusalem: The Israel Academy of Sciences and Humanities, 1974–1980), 1.549-50.

——*Quaestionum convivialum librum IX* 4.4.5, trans. Menahem Stern, in *Greek and Latin Authors on Jews and Judaism with Introductions, Translations and Commentary* (2 vols; Jerusalem: The Israel Academy of Sciences and Humanities, 1974–1980), 1.550-62.

Porter, Stanley E., *Verbal Aspect in the Greek of the New Testament, with Reference to Tense and Mood* (Studies in Biblical Greek; New York: Peter Lang, 1993).

——*Idioms of the Greek New Testament* (Sheffield: JSOT Press, 2nd edn, 1994).

Pye, Michael (ed.), *Continuum Dictionary of Religion* (New York: Continuum, 1994).

Räisänen, Heikki, *Paul and the Law* (Tübingen: J.C.B. Mohr, 1983).

Rappaport, Roy A., *Ritual and Religion in the Making of Humanity* (Cambridge: Cambridge University Press, 1999).

Rattansi, Ali, 'Just Framing: Ethnicities and Racisms in a "Postmodern" Framework', in Linda Nicholson and Steven Seidman (eds), *Social Postmodernism: Beyond Identity Politics* (Cambridge: Cambridge University Press, 1995), pp. 250–86.

——'Western Racisms, Ethnicities, and Identities in a "Postmodern" Frame', in A. Rattansi and S. Westwood Rattansi (eds), *Racism, Modernity, and Identity* (Cambridge: Polity Press, 1994), pp. 15–86.

Rex, John, 'The Role of Class Analysis in the Study of Race Relations – A Weberian Perspective', in John Rex and David Mason (eds), *Theories of Race and Ethnic Relations* (Cambridge: Cambridge University Press, 1986), pp. 64–83.

Richardson, Peter, *Israel in the Apostolic Church* (Cambridge: Cambridge University Press, 1969).

Richardson, P., and P. Gooch, 'Accommodation Ethnics', *Tyndale Bulletin* 29 (1978): 89–142.

Rockquemore, Kerry Ann, 'Deconstructing Tiger Woods: The Promise and Pitfalls of Multiracial Identity', in Heather M. Dalmage (ed.), *The Politics of Multiracialism* (Albany: State University of New York Press, 2004), pp. 125–41.

Root, Maria P.P., 'Rethinking Racial Identity Development', in Paul Spickard and W. Jeffrey Burroughs (eds), *We Are a People: Narrative and Multiplicity in Construction Ethnic Identity* (Philadelphia: Temple University Press, 2000), pp. 205–20.

Sanday, W., and A.C. Headlam, *The Epistle to the Romans* (ICC; New York: Charles Scribner, 1911).

Sanders, E.P., *Paul and Palestinian Judaism: A Comparison of Patterns of Religion* (Minneapolis: Fortress, 1977).

——*Paul, the Law and the Jewish People* (Minneapolis: Fortress, 1983).

——*Judaism: Practice and Belief, 63 BCE–66 CE* (Philadelphia: Trinity Press International, 1992).

Schauf, Wilhelm, *Sarx: Der Begriff 'Fleisch' beim Apostel Paulus unter besonderer Berück sichtigung seiner Erlösungslehre* (Münster: Verlag der Aschendorffschen Verlagsbuchhandlung, 1924).

Schelkle, K.H., *Reallexikon für Antike und Christentum* (ed. Theodor Klauser; Stuttgart: Hiersemann Verlag, 1954).

Schiffman, Lawrence, *Who Was a Jew?* (Hoboken, NJ: Ktab, 1985).

Schrenk, G., 'Was bedeutet "Israel Gottes"?' *Judaica* 5 (1949), pp. 81–94.

——'Der Segenwunsch nach der Kampfepistel', *Judaica* 6 (1950): 170–90.

Schürer, Emil, *The History of the Jewish People in the Age of Jesus Christ* (ed. Geza Vermes and Fergus Millar; trans. T.A. Burkill; 3 vols; Edinburgh: T&T Clark, 1973).

Schweitzer, Albert, *The Mysticism of Paul the Apostle* (trans. William Montgomery; Baltimore and London: Johns Hopkins University Press, 1998).

Schweitzer, E., 'σάρξ, σαρκικός, σάρκινος', *TDNT* 8.99-151.

Seneca, *Epistulae morales* 95.47, trans. Menahem Stern, in *Greek and Latin Authors on Jews and Judaism with Introductions, Translations and Commentary* (2 vols; Jerusalem: The Israel Academy of Sciences and Humanities, 1974–1980), 1.432-33.

Smallwood, E. Mary, *The Jews under Roman Rule: From Pompey to Diocletian* (Leiden: Brill, 1981).

Smedley, Audrey, *Race in North America: Origin and Evolution of a Worldview* (Boulder, CO: Westview, 1993).

Smith, Abraham, ' "I Saw the Book Talk": A Cultural Studies Approach to the Ethics of an African American Biblical Hermeneutics', *Semeia* 77 (1997): 115–38.

Smith, Anthony, *The Ethnic Revival* (Cambridge: Cambridge University Press, 1981).

——*The Ethnic Origins of Nations* (Oxford: Blackwell, 1986).

——'The Origins of Nations', *Ethnic and Racial Studies* 12.3 (July 1989): 340–67.

——'The Problem of National Identity: Ancient, Medieval, and Modern?' *Ethnic and Racial Studies* 17.3 (1994): 375–99.

——*Nationalism and Modernity* (London and New York: Routledge, 1998).

Smith, Jonathon Z. (ed.), *HarperCollins Dictionary of Religion* (New York: HarperCollins, 1995).

Smith, Jonathon Z., 'Religion, Religions, Religious', in Mark C. Taylor (ed.), *Critical Terms for Religious Studies* (Chicago and London: University of Chicago Press, 1998), pp. 268–84.

Smith, Wilfred Cantwell, *The Meaning and End of Religion* (Minneapolis: Fortress, 1991).

Snodgrass, Klyne, 'Galatians 3.28: Conundrum or Solution?', in Alvera Mickelsen (ed.), *Women, Authority, and the Bible* (Downers Grove, IL: InterVarsity Press, 1986), pp. 161–81.

Snowden, Frank M., *Before Color Prejudice: The Ancient View of Blacks* (Cambridge, MA: Harvard University Press, 1983).

Solomos, John, 'Varieties of Marxist Conceptions of "Race", Class and the State: A Critical Analysis', in John Rex and David Mason (eds), *Theories of Race and Ethnic Relations* (Cambridge: Cambridge University Press, 1986), pp. 84–109.

Spencer, Rainier, 'New Racial Identities, Old Arguments: Continuing Biological Reification', in David L. Brunsma (ed.), *Mixed Messages: Multiracial Identities in the 'Color-Blind' Era* (Boulder and London: Lynn Rienner, 2006), pp. 83–102.

Spickard, Paul, and W. Jeffrey Burroughs, 'We Are a People', in Paul Spickard and W. Jeffrey Burroughs (eds), *We Are a People: Narrative and Multiplicity in Constructing Ethnic Identity* (Philadelphia: Temple University Press, 2000), pp. 1–19.

Stanley, Christopher, 'Under a Curse: A Fresh Reading of Galatians 3.10-14', *NTS* 36 (1990): 481–511.

——'Neither Jew nor Greek: Ethnic Conflict in Graeco-Roman Society', *JSNT* 64 (1996): 101–24.

Stendhal, Krister, 'The Apostle Paul and the Introspective Conscience of the West', *HTR* 56.3 (1963): 199–215.

——*Paul among Jews and Gentiles* (Philadelphia: Fortress, 1976).

Stern, Menahem (ed.), *Greek and Latin Authors on Jews and Judaism with*

Introductions, Translations and Commentary (2 vols; Jerusalem: The Israel Academy of Sciences and Humanities, 1974–1980).

Stowers, Stanley, 'Paul's Dialogue with a Fellow Jew in Romans 3.1–9', *CBQ* 46 (1984): 707–22.

——*Letter Writing in Greco-Roman Antiquity* (Philadelphia: Westminster, 1986).

——*A Rereading of Romans: Justice, Jews, and Gentiles* (New Haven: Yale University Press, 1994).

Strabo, *The Geography of Strabo* (trans. Horace Leonard Jones; 8 vols; LCL; London: W. Heinemann; Cambridge, MA: Harvard University Press, 1960–1970).

Sunderland, P.J., '"You May Not Know It But I'm Black": White Women's Self-Identification as Black', *Ethnos* 62.1–2 (1997): 32–58.

Swarns, Rachel L., 'African American Becomes a Term for Debate', *New York Times*, 29 August 2004.

Takaki, Ronald, 'Reflections on Racial Patterns in America', in Ronald Takaki (ed.), *From Different Shores: Perspectives on Race and Ethnicity in America* (New York and Oxford: Oxford University Press, 3rd edn, 2002), pp. 23–36.

Tcherikover, Victor (ed.), *Corpus Papyrorum Judaicarum*, in collaboration with Alexander Fuks and Menahem Stern (3 vols; published for the Magnes Press, Hebrew University; Cambridge, MA: Harvard University Press, 1957–1964).

Theodoret of Cyrene, 'Interpretation of the Letter to the Romans', in J.-P. Migne (ed.), *Patrologia graeca* (162 vols; Paris: 1857–1886), vol. 82, col. 180.

Thielman, Frank, *From Plight to Solution: A Jewish Framework for Understanding Paul's View of the Law in Galatians and Romans* (Leiden; New York: E.J. Brill, 1989; reprint, Eugene, OR: Wipf and Stock, 2007).

Thistleton, Anthony C., *The First Epistle to the Corinthians* (Grand Rapids and Cambridge: Eerdmans, 2000).

Thompson, Marianne Meye, *The Promise of the Father: Jesus and God in the New Testament* (Louisville: Westminster John Knox, 2000).

Thomson, Ian, *Chiasmus in the Pauline Letters* (Sheffield: Sheffield Academic Press, 1995).

Thrower, James, *Religion: The Classical Theories* (Washington, DC: Georgetown University Press, 1999).

Tomson, Peter, 'The Names Israel and Jew in Ancient Judaism and in the New Testament', *Bijdragen Tijdschrift* 47.3 (1986): 266–89.

Tonkin, Elizabeth, Mary McDonald, and Malcolm Chapman, *History and Ethnicity* (ASA Monographs, 27; London and New York: Routledge, 1989).

Van den Berghe, Pierre, 'Ethnicity and the Sociobiology Debate', in John

Rex and David Mason (eds), *Theories of Race and Ethnic Relations* (Cambridge: Cambridge University Press, 1986), pp. 246–63.

——*Ethnic Phenomenon* (New York: Praeger, 1987).

Vermes, Geza, *The Complete Dead Sea Scrolls in English* (New York: Penguin, 1997).

Wagner, Ross, *Heralds of the Good News: Paul and Isaiah 'In Concert' in the Letter to the Romans* (NovTSup; Leiden: Brill, 2001).

Wallman, Sandra, 'Ethnicity and the Boundary Process in Context', in John Rex and David Mason (eds), *Theories of Race and Ethnic Relations* (Cambridge: Cambridge University Press, 1986), pp. 226–45.

Webber, Jonathon, 'Jews and Judaism in Contemporary Europe: Religion or Ethnic Group?', *Ethnic and Racial Studies* 20.2 (April 1997): 257–79.

Werbner, Pnina, 'Essentialising Essentialism, Essentialising Silence: Ambivalence and Multiplicity in the Construction of Racism and Ethnicity', in Pnina Werbner and Tariq Modood (eds), *Debating Cultural Hybridity: Multi-cultural Identities and the Politics of Anti-Racism* (Los Angeles and London: University of California Press, 1985), pp. 228–35.

Werbner, Pnina, and Tariq Modood (eds), *Debating Cultural Hybridity: Multi-Cultural Identities and the Politics of Anti-Racism* (Los Angeles and London: University of California Press, 1985).

Westerholm, Stephen, *Perspectives Old and New on Paul: The 'Lutheran' Paul and His Critics* (Grand Rapids: Eerdmans, 2004).

Williams, Kim M., 'Linking the Civil Rights and Multiracial Movements', in Heather M. Dalmage (ed.), *The Politics of Multiracialism: Challenging Racial Thinking* (Albany: State University of New York, 2004), pp. 77–97.

Willis, Wendell, 'An Apostolic Apologia? The Form and Function of 1 Corinthians 9', *JSNT* 24 (1985): 33–48.

Wimbush, Vincent L., 'Historical/Cultural Criticism as Liberation: A Proposal for an African American Biblical Hermeneutic', *Semeia* 47 (1989): 43–55.

Wimbush, Vincent L. (ed.), *African Americans and the Bible: Sacred Texts and Social Textures* (New York and London: Continuum, 2000).

Winant, Howard, *The New Politics of Race: Globalism, Difference, Justice* (Minneapolis: University of Minnesota Press, 2004).

Witulski, Thomas, *Die Addressaten des Galaterbriefes: Untersuchungen sur Gemeinde von Antiochia ad Pisidiam* (Göttingen: Vandenhoeck & Ruprecht, 2000).

Woolf, Greg, 'Becoming Roman, Staying Greek: Culture, Identity and the Civilizing Process in the Roman East', *Proceedings of the Cambridge Philological Society* 40 (1994): 116–43.

Wright, David F., 'A Race Apart? Jews, Gentiles, Christians', *Bibliotheca Sacra* 160 (April–June 2003): 131–41.

Wright, N.T., *The Climax of the Covenant* (Minneapolis: Fortress, 1993).

——'The Law in Romans 2', in James D.G. Dunn (ed.), *Paul and the Mosaic Law* (Tübingen: J.C.B. Mohr, 1996), pp. 131–50.

——'The Letter to the Romans', in Leander Keck (ed.), *The New Interpreter's Bible* (Nashville: Abingdon, 2000), 10.393–770.

Young, Norman H., 'Pronomial Shifts in Paul's Argument to the Galatians', in T.W. Hillard, R.A. Kearsley, C.E.V. Nixon, and A. M. Nobbs (eds), *Ancient History in a Modern University*, vol. 2: *Early Christianity, Late Antiquity and Beyond* (Grand Rapids: Eerdmans, 1998), pp. 81–88.

——'Who's Cursed – and Why? (Galatians 3.10-14)', *JBL* 117.1 (1998): 79–92.

Yuval-Davis, Nira, 'Ethnicity, Gender Relations and Multi-culturalism', in Pnina Werbner and Tariq Modood (eds), *Debating Cultural Hybridity: Multicultural Identities and the Politics of Anti-Racism* (Los Angeles; London: University of California Press, 1985), pp. 193–208.

INDEX OF BIBLICAL CITATIONS

Index of Modern Authors